VITAL ENEMIES

VITAL ENEMIES

Slavery, Predation, and the Amerindian Political Economy of Life

FERNANDO SANTOS-GRANERO

University of Texas Press ⟡ Austin

Requests for permission to reproduce material from this work should be sent to:

Permissions

University of Texas Press

P.O. Box 7819

Austin, TX 78713-7819

www.utexas.edu/utpress/about/bpermission.html

⊗The paper used in this book meets the minimum requirements of ANSI/NISO Z39.48-1992 (R1997) (Permanence of Paper).

Library of Congress Cataloging-in-Publication Data

Santos-Granero, Fernando, 1955–

  Vital enemies : slavery, predation, and the Amerindian political economy of life / Fernando Santos-Granero. — 1st ed.

    p. cm.

  Includes bibliographical references and index.

  ISBN 978-0-292-71888-3 (cloth : alk. paper) — ISBN 978-0-292-71913-2 (pbk. : alk. paper)

  1. Indian slaves—America. 2. Slavery—America. 3. Indian captivities—America. 4. Prisoners of War—America. 5. Ethnic conflict—America. 6. America—Ethnic relations—Economic aspects. 7. America—History—To 1810. I. Title.

  E59.S63S26 2009

  970.01—dc22

2008018454

*In memory of my father, Fernando Santos Veiga,
my most faithful reader*

Contents

Illustrations follow page 102.

Acknowledgments

There are several persons without whose encouragement and intellectual support I could not have written this book. Mariella Villasante-de Beauvais, who has done extensive ethnographic research among the Ashaninka of Peruvian Amazonia and the Bidân of Mauritania, urged me to address the question of whether indigenous forms of slavery existed in pre-Columbian tropical America. Our e-mail exchanges while she was editing a book on forms of extreme dependence in Africa (entitled *Groupes serviles au Sahara: Approche comparative à partir du cas des arabophones de Mauritanie* and published by CNRS-Éditions in 2000) were extremely enlightening, for they inspired me to formulate the outline of what would later become a full-blown research project. George Mentore, an Amazonianist colleague and friend, helped me sharpen the focus of the investigation. His skepticism in regard to the highly charged Western notion of "slavery"—expressed in long conversations in his Virginia house—was an incentive to attempt a more phenomenological approach to Amerindian forms of slavery. Joanna Overing, mentor, friend, and former supervisor, read the synopsis of the book and the first draft of the introduction. Her observations and incisive comments, then and later on in her house in St. Andrews, Scotland, helped me place the phenomenon of Amerindian slavery in a broader perspective. Ira Rubinoff, director of the Smithsonian Tropical Research Institute (STRI), generously provided me with the necessary institutional support to carry out research at the Library of Congress during my sabbatical year. He graciously approved an extension of my stay in Washington, D.C., when it became apparent that one year was not enough to gather the extensive data required for the completion of the project. Thanks are also due to the Smithsonian Institution's Scholarly Studies Program, which supported my research at the Library of Congress. Olga F. Linares, STRI colleague and dearest friend, was always available to discuss different aspects of the project. In addition, she undertook the revision of the entire manuscript to ensure that my English was correct. My father, Fernando Santos Veiga, encouraged me to undertake this research project from the very beginning. And he was there to support and encourage me whenever I felt that the task was too vast for me. My deep regret is that he did not live long enough to see this book published. Clara de Souza, my wife for twenty-five years and a sociologist, was my interlocutor and critic throughout the entire research period. She listened to my discoveries, doubts, and ideas and, with her incisive, down-to-earth questions, always helped me to detect weak points and sharpen my arguments. Her unfailing love and companionship, and the affection of our two daughters, have been a constant source of strength during all these years. To all these persons and institutions, my profound gratitude.

VITAL ENEMIES

Introduction

On the very first day Columbus landed in America, he registered in his *Diario* (1991: 67) the first allusion ever made to the existence of captive slavery in native tropical American societies: "I saw some who had marks of wounds on their bodies and I made signs to them asking what they were; and they showed me how people from other islands nearby came there and tried to take them, and how they defended themselves." And he speculated: "I believed and [still] believe that they come here from *tierra firme* to take them captive." Since that fateful twelfth day of October 1492, wherever European conquistadores set foot in the American tropics, they found evidence of indigenous warfare, war captives, and captive slaves.

As early as 1509, to the north, Núñez de Balboa reported that native lords living in coastal Darien, Panama, were carried on the shoulders of slaves (López de Gómara 1946[1552]: 199). In 1515 another conquistador observed that the peoples to the east of Darien kept slaves—identified by the red and black designs that their masters tattooed on their faces—whose main duties were to extract gold, to perform agricultural tasks, and to do other menial services (López de Gómara 1946[1552]: 278). In the early sixteenth-century expeditions undertaken along the Paraguay River, to the south, the Spaniards found a great deal of interethnic warfare associated with the taking of enemy heads as war trophies, the cannibalistic consumption of war prisoners, the trading of captives for gold and silver objects, and the classification of entire populations as "enemy/slaves" (Schmidl 1749[1539]: 19; Martínez de Irala 1912[1542]: 347, 349, 352; Núñez Cabeza de Vaca 1585[1555]: 125v).

On the eastern slopes of the Bolivian Andes, to the west, highland informants told Garcilaso de la Vega (1963[1609]: 322) that since the reign of Tupac Inca Yupanqui, several decades before the Spanish conquest of Peru in 1532, the lowland Chiriguaná groups had been raiding the frontiers of the Inka empire to take captives. Spanish conquistadores told the Court historian Pietro Martire d'Anghiera (1966[1516]: 38v–39r), as early as 1516, that the Caribs of the Lower Orinoco River, to the east, undertook large maritime war expeditions to the Gulf of Paria to procure slaves for themselves from among the Arawak. Conversely, Martín López (1964[1550]: 45–46), one of the first Spaniards to explore the Orinoco River, wrote that the Arawak of the Orinoco delta carried out annual expeditions against the southern Caribs, killing everyone except children, whom they took as captives.

The few references mentioned above allude to the salient characteristics underlying native tropical American slavery: regular raiding of weaker peoples by powerful neighbors; classification of entire populations as enemy/slaves; taking of captives, particularly women and children; inscription of slave status through body marks; assignment of captives to household units; performance of menial services; and trading of war captives in exchange for luxury goods. Early chronicles also flag the existence of other forms of servitude—namely, servant groups and tributary populations. It is therefore puzzling that the topic of native forms of slavery in tropical America has never been directly addressed, despite the existence of an extensive and rich literature on the causes of warfare in the region (Chagnon 1968; Carneiro 1970, 1990, 1994; Lathrap 1970; Meggers 1971; Harris 1974, 1979, 1984; Gross 1975; Harner 1977; Ferguson 1990, 1995, 2000; Whitehead 1992; Kelekna 1998; Valentine and Julien 2003; Chacon and Mendoza 2007).

Reasons for this neglect may be multiple. The most important, and at the same time the most banal, has to do with the historical conditions of tropical American indigenous societies in the late 1930s, at the time when modern anthropologists (e.g., Claude Lévi-Strauss, Irving Goldman, Charles Wagley, and Allan Holmberg, to name but a few) began doing fieldwork in the American tropics. By then, native tropical American peoples had withstood centuries of foreign diseases, encroachment, displacement, genocidal policies, enslavement, and marginalization. They were thus but the stubborn remnants of their former selves. Even isolated peoples who were thought to have escaped the horrors inflicted by European agents were subsequently discovered to be regressive survivors of such process, experienced in a more or less remote past (see Holmberg 1969; Stearman 1989; Balée 1992).

The extant social organization of these peoples—reduced, scattered, culturally impoverished, and having endured forced acculturation, transfiguration, regression, and ethnogenesis—was only a shadow of earlier times. However, even anthropologists such as Lévi-Strauss in his *Tristes Tropiques* ([1955] 1974), who described the terrible consequences of the clash between Amerindian and European peoples, were unaware of the extent to which native tropical American peoples had undergone a fundamental transformation. Only much later would Lévi-Strauss acknowledge: "There, where we believed to have found the last evidence of archaic lifeways and modes of thought, we now recognize the survivors of complex and powerful societies, engaged in a historical process for millennia, and which have become disintegrated in the lapse of two or three centuries, a tragic accident, itself historical, which the discovery of the New World was for them" (1993: 9).

Powerful paramount chiefs, regional confederations, large political centers, elaborate temple ceremonies, extensive public earthworks, and native forms of servitude had ceased to exist by the time these scholars were writing. Consequently, features that had been corroborated by abundant archaeological and historical evidence were ignored or were simply disregarded as exaggerations made by zealous European adventurers eager to impress their royal patrons. This tendency was further reinforced by the structural-functionalist paradigm in vogue at the time, which stressed structure, homeostasis, and synchronicity over process, change, and history. The fundamentally altered lifeways of twentieth-century native tropical American peoples were thus essentialized, envisioned to be "typical" of these societies since times immemorial. This image has become so entrenched that, as Heckenberger (2003: 29) has rightly argued, "many feel that the very notion of native cities, regional bureaucracies, kings, priests, slaves, and the like, is untenable."

In the last decade, a few anthropologists and archaeologists (e.g., Dreyfus 1983–1984; Descola 1988; Whitehead 1993, 2003a; Roosevelt 1993, 1994; Heckenberger 2003, 2005) have insisted on the need to introduce the historical perspective of *longue durée*, providing a richer understanding of tropical American indigenous societies. This has slowly led to a "temporal revolution," by which it has become increasingly accepted that native tropical American societies have changed significantly since the beginning of the Christian era and particularly in the past five centuries (Fausto and Heckenberger 2007: 1; also Hill 1993: 10, 1996: 4). Even those authors who accept that these societies have experienced radical changes in the past five centuries, however, are reluctant to accept the existence of native forms of slavery. They argue, not without reason, that the terms "slave" and "slavery," as used by early European chroniclers, belong to a different semantic universe and thus distort Amerindian social practices (Whitehead 1988, 1990, 1999; Langebaek 1992; A. C. Taylor 1999; Wright 2002). Whereas they may accept that raiding, the taking of war captives, and the incorporation of captives in a more or less subordinate position were widespread practices in precolonial times, they deny that these can in any way be compared to slavery as it is understood in the Western tradition (Steward and Faron 1959: 187; Whitehead 1988: 181; Langebaek 1992: 145). In their view, Amerindian slavery became such only when the demand for slaves in the colonial market forced indigenous peoples to intensify raiding, turning war captives into commodities to be traded for European goods. Native slavery in the American tropics, they conclude, is not an indigenous pre-Columbian pattern but rather a colonial product.

The dismissal of native forms of slavery seems to stem from a certain moral reluctance to discuss an institution of which few traces remain, one that does not fit with the highly egalitarian ideologies and practices of present-day native tropical American societies, and that projects an image of "savagery" that could be (mis)used to deny Amerindians their rights as autonomous peoples. This bias, I would suggest, is also linked to a generalized and persistent perception of slavery as the institution developed in the plantations of the southern United States (Meillasoux 1975: 12), a sort of "ideal type" against which to measure other forms of what Condominas (1998) has called "relations of extreme dependence."

Following this line of argument, scholars have identified five elements that, because they are absent from preconquest native tropical American peoples, prevent us from characterizing war captives as slaves. First, captives were eventually incorporated through marriage or adoption into the families of their captors. Second, captive labor did not free their masters from their productive obligations and was not crucial to the reproduction of their economic system. Third, slaves were not subjected to systematic exploitation and were generally well treated. Fourth, they were not considered to be property, and thus could not be bought, sold, or traded as chattel. Lastly, their status was not hereditary and, hence, they did not constitute a permanent social class. Indeed, some authors suggest that because certain native terminologies liken the status of so-called slaves to that of potential affines, the Amerindian institution of war captives had a kinship dimension that was alien to slavery as it was practiced by contemporary Europeans.

Whereas I agree that the use of the highly charged term "slave" in the context of native tropical American societies might be misleading, I firmly believe that we cannot content ourselves with negative characterizations, explanations of what Amerindian "slaves" were not, rather than explanations of what they were. This, in short, is the main objective of this book: to describe a widespread native institution, and to discuss its importance from a native point of view.

Slavery is only one among various native forms of servitude, often combined in diverse permutations. The focus of this book will therefore be on what I have called native regimes of capture and servitude: the set of patterned relations of extreme dependence that are found within a particular regional system of interethnic power relations at any given juncture. Native regimes of servitude are regional and interethnic because they always involve more than one settlement and more than one people. And they are inscribed in a system of power relationships, for the settlements and peoples involved are engaged in a variety of power struggles, alliances, and associations. These do not respond to random forces—as in a Hobbesian kind of war of "every man against every man"—but are framed by preexisting interethnic hierarchies, balance of forces, and trajectories of interaction. Native regimes of servitude are an ongoing historical product and are thus in permanent flux. This quality of dynamic transformation will become apparent when I analyze the changes experienced by these regimes as the result of the colonial encounter.

Following in the steps of recent scholars of slavery in the Old World (Condominas 1998; Villasante-de Beauvais 2000), I have tried to avoid the use of terms that correspond to other historical realities when discussing Amerindian forms of servitude, favoring instead more historically neutral terms—thus, "tributaries" instead of "vassals" or "serfs"; "commoners" instead of "plebs"; "servant groups" instead of "helots." In other cases, however, such as with the use of the term "slavery," its replacement by other, more general terms, such as "extreme dependence," would have been more confusing than clarifying. To use native terms, as advocated by some scholars, would have been extremely useful if this were a study of a single society. But since it is a comparative work dealing with six different Amerindian peoples, this option would have been more cumbersome than helpful. For these reasons, I have opted to use the term "captive slavery" instead of "slavery," a solution that has the advantage of emphasizing that slavery in tropical America was always the result of warfare and piracy. Likewise, instead of "slave," I have opted to use the terms "captive" and "captive slave," which, as we shall see, are more faithful to the meaning of the native terms used to refer to this kind of dependent.

The present book focuses on the different forms and regimes of servitude existing in tropical America before the arrival of Europeans. Emphasis is thus placed on tropical American indigenous societies at the time of contact. Two problems for those studying the history of Amerindian societies ensue from this perspective: first, what should we consider to be the time of contact? and, second, what should we understand by "contact"? When considering America as a whole, the time of contact is taken to be the time at which Columbus first landed in America. At a more regional level, however, the time of actual contact between Amerindian populations and Europeans varied widely throughout the Americas, depending on the whims of European adventurers and the vagaries of colonial history. Thus, the time of contact is not a precise point in time; rather, it is a long period characterized by multiple, intermittent, and temporally variable phases of contact, culminating in the conquest of the contacted native peoples and the settlement of their lands. In this book, I use the notion of "time of contact" precisely in this way, to signify the period in which a given indigenous society came in contact with Europeans but still retained its political autonomy.

This brings me to the second caveat. It has long been accepted that Amerindian populations experienced the effects of European presence even prior to actually meeting any Europeans. If European agents had an impact even when they were not physically present, how can we be sure that what was observed at the time of contact was indeed how things were in pre-Columbian times? Many scholars would simply assume that we can never be sure, and by so doing, they dismiss all possibilities of knowing how these societies operated in pre-Columbian times. Such a stance is misleading insofar as it supposes a radical break between an essentialized, authentic past and a present reality contaminated by European influence. The impact of Europeans was neither instantaneous nor absolute. It often involved long periods of struggle, accommodation, and negotiation. Changes were not always as rapid and radical as to render impossible the task of identifying native forms of organization and cultural patterns. In fact, from the perspective of the *longue durée*, certain "structures"—environmental conditions, productive strategies, sets of social relations, cultural practices—persisted for long periods of time, changing only very slowly (Braudel 1958). To assume that the European conquest of America changed the history of Amerindian peoples forever, dividing it into an authentic past and a somewhat spurious present, is to project our own Eurocentric biases. Without in any way underrating the dire consequences of the European conquest, one could legitimately argue that for many Amerindian peoples the expansion of the Huari,

Aztec, and Inka empires was equally cataclysmic. Such dramatic events are in the nature of historical processes, but they are in no way more "historical" than other, less radical changes.

If we accept that history is an ongoing process rather than an intermittent succession of dramatic events interspersed by periods of historical paucity, then the statement that it is not possible to know how Amerindian societies were organized in pre-Columbian times is spurious. As Sahlins (2005: 5) has aptly put it: "Whatever the compulsions of the global forces, whatever may be inherent in foreign things or propagated with them, the people are not simply determined by them, since they also bring their own understandings to bear upon the encounter." At most, it could be said that native relations of extreme dependence were analogous to those brought in by the European invaders. Analogies between the cultural baggage of the conquered and the conquerors were not uncommon at the symbolic and discursive levels, as Whitehead (2003b: x) has suggested. Analogous perceptions such as these led to a mutual recognition of resemblances between their respective forms of servitude and facilitated the passage from one to the other. As Myers (1990: 121) observed: "To the degree that change had taken place, it was an aboriginal accommodation to changing conditions rather than change based upon a European model." In other words, it was an indigenization of European practices rather than the Europeanization of Amerindian practices (Sahlins 2005: 6).

Furthermore, as Lovejoy (2000[1983]: 21) has noted for Africa, Europeans were able to integrate Amerindian peoples into the colonial slave trade only "because indigenous forms of dependency allowed the transfer of people from one social group to the other." Given that native forms of extreme dependency coexisted for long periods with slave raiding that was oriented to supply the colonial markets, the contact situation provides an unrivaled opportunity to test the extent to which native models of capture and servitude differed from European imports (see Whitehead, forthcoming: 3–4, for a similar argument). The modifications that native and foreign forms of servitude underwent when adopted by the Other, including the conflicts that arose from such (mis)appropriations, do not represent a "contamination" of pristine pre-Columbian institutions. Rather, they are the best indicators of what specific forms indigenous practices of servitude assumed. ·

Thus, this book is an exercise in reconstructive history, a first attempt to identify the constitutive elements of relations of extreme dependency in the American tropics, by which I understand not only the hot lowlands between the Tropics of Cancer and Capricorn but also those areas outside the tropics yet close enough to them to have tropical climates. This vast region stretches from southern Florida in the north, to the Grand Chaco in the south, and from the piedmont of the Andes and the Central American mountain ranges in the east, to the Antilles and the coasts of Guiana and Brazil in the west. The bulk of the study is constituted by the analysis of six indigenous societies dispersed throughout this region, to wit: the Calusa of southern Florida, the Kalinago of Lesser Antilles, the Tukano of northwest Amazonia, the Conibo of eastern Peru, the Chiriguaná of eastern Bolivia, and the Guaicurú of the Grand Chaco (Map I.o). These societies were all composed by a variety of regional groups that shared a similar cultural matrix, and were sometimes, though not always, linked by common linguistic affiliation. They had blurred boundaries and were far from being culturally homogenous. None of these polities had the kinds of institutions that underpinned state formations such as those of the Maya, Aztec, and Inka. But neither were they egalitarian societies, adamant on questions of personal autonomy and averse to vertical forms of authority like those characteristic of present-day tropical America. More importantly, they all had developed, or were in the process of developing, supralocal forms of authority, often under the guise of hereditary paramount or regional chiefs. The degree of power and authority wielded by these supralocal leaders varied widely, however.

Subsistence patterns and other forms of livelihood also varied. The sea-oriented Kalinago and the river-oriented Tukano and Conibo were conspicuous horticulturalists who complemented gardening with fishing and, to a lesser extent, hunting. In contrast, the Calusa and Guaicurú did not practice agriculture; their livelihood depended largely on fishing and hunting, and on the agricultural produce they exacted from tributary populations. The Chiriguaná stand as an intermediate case: horticulturalists with a strong emphasis on hunting, gathering, and, to a much lesser extent, fishing.

Two common denominators distinguish this set of societies—namely, being adapted to tropical environments, and having slaveholding institutions. It should be emphasized that this sample is *not* representative of the indigenous societies of the American tropics in general. Kept out are those indigenous peoples—similar to the present-day Txicão, Matis, and Parakanã (Menget 1988; Erikson 1986; Fausto 2001)—who took captives from their enemies, incorporating them as full "citizens" through marriage and adoption instead of holding them as slaves. It also excludes

1.0. Locations of the six capturing societies of the sample.

Amerindian societies like the ancient Tupinambá of the Brazilian littoral, who practiced intratribal raiding and the taking of captives for ritual purposes rather than to obtain wives or slaves (Carneiro da Cunha and Viveiros de Castro 1985). And, obviously, it also excludes those societies that did not practice any form of slave raiding. It is essential for the reader to keep these facts in mind. Nothing is more alien to my intention than to contend that all indigenous tropical American societies were engaged in slaveholding, or in other forms of servitude, at the time of contact.

For my purposes in this analysis, and in the interest of making tighter comparisons, I have excluded Amerindian slaveholding societies from other geographical regions of America, such as those from the northwest Pacific coast, greater Lower Columbia, Great Plains, southwest borderlands, and southeast Atlantic coast of North America. I am persuaded, however, that the forms of servitude observed in these societies were very similar to those found in the American tropics (see, for instance, MacLeod 1928; Mitchell 1984; Perdue 1993; Ruby and Brown 1993; Donald 1997; Brooks 2002; Minges 2003; Hajda 2005). And I am convinced that most of the conclusions I arrived at in this study could just as well apply to these similar nonstate societies.

When selecting the societies to include in this study, I took into consideration four criteria. I favored societies that were contacted in the fifteenth and sixteenth centuries over those contacted in later times, to avoid the risk of including societies possibly altered in fundamental ways by the indirect influence of the colonial experience playing itself out over long periods of time. I chose societies for which there was abundant historical documentation so as to be able to gauge the reliability of the historical evidence, using multiple independent sources. I also favored societies that have been the object of modern ethnographic studies, over those that have not, to guarantee access to cultural information that could throw light on little-documented ancient practices. Lastly, I made an effort to include societies from as broad a range of tropical areas as possible, to ensure greater representativity. Not all the societies in the sample comply with the aforementioned four prerequisites, however; they nevertheless all comply with at least three of them. Although subject to improvement, the resulting sample, I believe, represents faithfully the diverse patterns of servility found in native tropical America. However, some aspects of the sample can profit from further clarification.

If one looks at Map I.o, it becomes apparent that societies from Central America and the central regions of tropical South America are excluded from the sample. Indeed, the societies that were included are all located in what could be considered the borderlands of the American tropics. There are solid reasons for this choice. The Amerindian societies located along the Pacific coast of Central America and along the Amazon River and its larger tributaries were among the first to disappear or radically change as a consequence of the spread of European epidemics through long-distance native trading networks and, later on, of the ravages of European slaving expeditions. Coupled with the fact that information from earlier ages was too scant to permit an in-depth analysis, their altered status excluded them as good candidates to incorporate in the sample. In contrast, societies for which there is more abundant historical information were located in what has been dubbed the "tribal zone"—that is, "the area affected by the proximity of a state, but not under state administration" (Ferguson and Whitehead 1992: 3). The Calusa and Kalinago, who were fought over by Spaniards, Frenchmen, Englishmen, and Dutchmen; the Tukano and Guaicurú, who were disputed by Spaniards and Portuguese; and the Conibo and Chiriguaná, who were engaged in a constant struggle against the Spanish colonial empire, were all in this kind of situation.

Location in the interstices or peripheries of the colonial space allowed these societies to resist European domination, retaining their political autonomy for longer periods of time. Taking advantage of the rivalry between European powers, they negotiated better conditions for themselves by pitting one colonial state against the other, changing sides whenever it suited their interests. More importantly, because of their long-term resistance, these societies became of great interest to colonial authorities, who wrote many more reports and other works about them than they did about societies that rapidly succumbed to colonial rule. It has been argued that these societies are a creation of the states against which they were pitted and, thus, that such features as supralocal forms of authority, intensive warfare, and nascent forms of servitude were the result of colonial relations (Ferguson and Whitehead 1992). As we shall see, however, these features were already present in these societies at the time of contact and cannot be attributed to European presence, however indirect. If captive slavery appears as a salient social feature in these societies, it is not because they were tribal creations—which they were—but rather because, having resisted European domination for longer periods, we know more about them than we do about societies that were exterminated in the years immediately after contact. In short, if there is a bias in the sample, it is not due to methodological oversight. Rather, it is the result of a historical situation stemming from unique geopolitical conditions.

Honoring my definition of the notion of time of contact, the sources consulted not only were the earliest available in each case but also were written throughout the period in which the societies of the sample still retained their autonomy. This meant that in some cases the sources to be consulted covered a period of two or even three centuries. To make the amount of literature I surveyed more manageable, I confined the documentary research to published documents. The major task of collecting historical information was carried out at the Library of Congress—especially in the Rare Book and Special Collections Reading Room—during a period of two years (August 2001–July 2003). I reviewed a wide range of documentary sources by all sorts of Spanish, French, Portuguese, Italian, and English writers. Among this mass of records, I conferred priority to documents produced by persons who actually witnessed the events they recounted—conquistadores, missionaries, and explorers reporting about their own experiences—or by lay and religious historians who relied on oral or written accounts obtained directly from eyewitnesses. I excluded most secondary sources—for example, the works of nineteenth- and twentieth-century historians—except when their accounts were based on materials no longer available to present-day scholars. To help readers keep track of the period to which these old sources correspond, I have included in the references that appear in the text not only the year of publication of the edition consulted but also (in square brackets) the date in which the author witnessed or reported the events described. All translations of quotes in languages other than English are mine.

That European sources are prejudiced and biased, and thus totally unreliable concerning knowledge about the history of Amerindian societies, is a frequently voiced remark. Such statements ignore the fact that, as Whitehead (2003b: ix) has pointed out, there is no such thing as an "unprejudiced" or "unbiased" historical source. Historical sources are always "situated"; that is, they are firmly anchored in the place and time they were written and, above all, reflect the personal trajectories and agendas of their authors. Denying the possibility of learning about the history of Amerindian societies using European sources would be tantamount to denying the possibility of knowing the history of any people through any kind of source. This is not to say that we should accept at face value all the information provided by these accounts or that we should espouse the notion that there is only one history. Being aware of the historical juncture in which a document was written, and of the political inclinations or personal agenda of its author, is crucial to the detection of potential biases or downright fabrications. To avoid using unconfirmed or dubious data, I have discarded data that are not verified by at least two independent sources. Whenever I make use of unconfirmed but otherwise suggestive data, I indicate it in the text. Additionally, in the Appendix, I discuss the reliability of thirty-eight of the most frequently cited authors. These methodological procedures have contributed to a better evaluation of the sources and, I hope, to a better depiction and interpretation of Amerindian servile institutions.

Key to the central agenda of historical anthropology is the incorporation of indigenous understandings, ontologies, cosmologies, and historicities to capture native perspectives on historical events and social practices. Insofar as possible, I have strived to incorporate indigenous viewpoints in order to overcome the apparent resemblances between analogous Amerindian and European forms of servitude and identify the unique features of indigenous institutions; a task easier said than done. The ethnocentricity of European colonial agents left little mental room to appreciate, let alone take into consideration, indigenous perceptions. Native points of view have nevertheless been preserved in four types of information that caught the attention of Europeans, because of either their exotic appeal or their pragmatic value: myths, shamanic beliefs, political discourses, and language. I have made use of all these types of data whenever possible, especially of early colonial dictionaries, which proved to be an invaluable source of information on how Amerindians conceptualized what chroniclers labeled as "slaves" and "servants." More importantly, I have avoided "etic" explanations of Amerindian warfare and slavery, in favor of an "emic" approach that relies heavily on Amerindian notions and conceptions (see below).

Following Rivière's call (1993) for the "amerindianization" of key anthropological concepts as a means of achieving a better understanding of Amerindian socialities, I have opted not to begin this book with a definition of slavery as a means to assess whether Amerindian servile practices and institutions conform to it—a top-down kind of strategy. Instead, I have adopted a bottom-up approach by first presenting a brief account of the histories of domination of the capturing societies selected for discussion, emphasizing the regional systems of interethnic power relations of which they were part (Chapter 1). This is followed by a critical examination of the three different regimes of capture and servitude that I have identified as having existed in the region. Captive slavery was practiced by all the societies considered in this study. But whereas among the Kalinago and Conibo it was the main and only form of extreme dependency (Chapter 2), among the Tukano and Chiriguaná it was combined with the subjugation and attachment of servant groups (Chapter 3). And among the Calusa and Guaicurú it coexisted with the subjection of neighboring peoples as tributary populations (Chapter 4). I then explore the sociologies of submission that were characteristic of these societies, focusing on the five aspects that have been singled out in objections to the existence of slavery in native tropical America to see whether they are supported by the historical data (Chapters 5–7). Once the degree to which these objections may be valid has been determined, I explore the ideologies of capture on which Amerindian regimes of servitude are based. These ideologies, equating war captives to prey and captive slaves to pets, facilitated the integration and, later on, assimilation of captive slaves (Chapter 8). Such ideologies are sustained by Amerindian eco-cosmologies that posit that the vital cosmic force that energizes all living beings in the world is finite and scarce, a notion that has given rise to what I call the Amerindian *political economy of life*. I argue that Amerindian warfare in general, and captive slavery in particular, can be understood only within this ideological framework (Chapter 9). Only then do I discuss—in the light of extant theories of slavery and other relations of extreme dependence—whether native tropical American forms of servitude conform to those practices that in other times and places have been labeled "slavery" (Conclusions).

Here, however, I would like to begin from the end. The outright conclusion of this study is that native slavery in tropical America was not a colonial product. Rather, it predated the European presence even though its character differed in several respects from slavery as it was practiced in other historical periods and geographical areas. The uniqueness of native tropical American forms of slavery and servitude resides in their being an extreme expression of the Amerindian political economy of life, a political economy based on the widespread notion that vital energy is finite, generally fixed, scarce, unequally distributed, and in constant circulation. In such an economy, humans, animals, and other beings are conceived of as competing among themselves to accumulate as many potentialities of life as possible through mutual predation and capture. Potentialities of life wrested from enemy Others can assume various forms. In the context of interhuman competition, they adopt the shape of actual persons—generally young women and children of both sexes—or of life forces contained in bodily trophies, magical objects, ritual paraphernalia, and sacred effigies. The logic of Amerindian warfare, I would suggest, lies in this complex of ideas. However, it should be noted that even though all native tropical American societies can be characterized as "capturing societies" engaged in a ruthless competition for potentialities of life, not all capturing societies can be characterized as slaveholding societies. This book seeks to understand Amerindian forms of extreme dependence in societies that practiced captive slavery.

PART I

Histories of Domination

CHAPTER 1

Capturing Societies

All slave-holding societies required victims, only a small number of whom ever came from within. What they needed were victim societies, groups who consisted not of subjects but of outsiders who could be dominated by force.

—JACK GOODY, "Slavery in Time and Space"

Scholars have increasingly become aware that slavery cannot be studied as an isolated phenomenon, detached from its broader social and political context (Villasante-de Beauvais 2000; Klein 1998). They insist on the need to situate slavery and other forms of servitude within the framework provided by internal forms of social stratification. Above all, they recognize the importance of placing these institutions within the regional power systems that allow them to be reproduced. Ignoring the larger context would run the risk of transforming native forms of slavery into epiphenomena—curious and exotic customs without any grounding on the configurations of power and meaning that generate them.

A properly contextualized perspective requires a regional and inter-ethnic approach to the history and prehistory of Amerindian peoples if one is to avoid the pitfalls of ethnically bounded histories and isolated political systems (Dreyfus 1983–1984; Whitehead 1988; Hill 1988, 1996; Santos-Granero 1995, 2002a; Hill and Santos-Granero 2002; Rival 2002; Hornborg 2005). It also requires the analysis of a vast storehouse of information in the form of primary sources and secondary, thematic or case studies. Unfortunately, the existing information about slavery in tropical America is scant. Only the most important manuscript works have been published, and, with some notable exceptions (Renard-Casevitz et al. 1986; Carneiro da Cunha 2002; Whitehead 1988, 1995; Santos-Granero 1992; Salomon and Schwartz 1999; Hill and Santos-Granero 2002), little has been advanced in the field of local or regional ethnohistorical studies. This in no way impedes us from attempting to situate native forms of servitude within the constellation of internal and regional sociopolitical settings in which they originated and developed. Inevitably, however, at the present stage in our knowledge about the history of native tropical American peoples, such efforts must, of necessity, have a preliminary character.

In this chapter, I present a general picture of each of the six capturing societies in the sample and discuss the regional interethnic power systems to which they belonged. I also dwell on the relationships each of these societies entertained with its neighbors, both native and European, and emphasize how the nature of these relationships changed throughout time. I put particular stock on the fact that these peoples were involved in what Menget (1985: 136–137) has called "heterogeneous social systems"—that is, power systems comprising various societies with different sizes, complexity, and military abilities. Because the notion of heterogeneous social systems could be misleading, in that it could be taken to mean societies with internal social stratification, I prefer to call them heterogeneous (or homogenous) regional systems, which is closer to Menget's meaning.

An analysis of each of these societies, and of the regional power systems to which they belonged, must begin with a history of first contacts and a summary of the major events that shaped the relations of these societies with the colonial and national states in which they were eventually inserted. I conclude by discussing the present situation of these indigenous groups, emphasizing the types of relations that members of capturing societies nowadays enjoy with their former subordinates. It is against the backdrop of these interethnic histories of domination that we should consider the principal characteristics of Amerindian regimes of capture and servitude.

KALINAGO OF THE LESSER ANTILLES

The Spaniards first heard about the Kalinago—also known as Island Caribs, Caribbees, or Caraïbes—almost as soon as they landed in America in 1492. The Lucayos of the Bahamas called them Caniba, whereas the Taino of Hispaniola, Cuba, and Puerto Rico knew them as Caribe (C. Columbus 1991[1493]: 331). The Island Caribs called themselves Kallinago (Kalinago) in the men's language and Kalliponam (Karipuna) in the women's language (Breton 1978[1647]: 52; Rochefort 1666[1658]: 205). Here I will refer to them as Kalinago.

Europeans reported early on that Kalinago had different male and female "languages" (Anon. 1988[1620]: 97). Linguists have since determined that these were in fact registers, or variants of the same language. In addition, they possessed a secret military language that was known only to the eldest and bravest warriors (Rochefort 1666[1658]: 179). The substratum of the male and female registers was an Arawakan language, but both exhibited important influences—albeit to different extents—from a Cariban language (Hoff 1995: 38–39). It is not clear whether this linguistic dimorphism was the result of the subjugation of the Arawakan inhabitants of the islands by Carib-speaking invaders, as some local myths suggest (Du Tertre 1667: 361), or the result of intense trading, marriages, and political alliances, as other authors suggest (Whitehead 1995: 9–10; Sued-Badillo 1995). Be that as it may, what we know for sure is that by the time of contact the Kalinago had undergone a process of transethnic change; that is, they had retained their Arawak-based language but had adopted Cariban words and cultural practices (Santos-Granero 2002a,: 39–40).

In the late 1400s, Kalinago territory extended throughout the Lesser Antilles from Grenada to the south, to St. Kitts to the north, including St. Vincent, St. Lucia, Martinique, Dominica, Marie Galante, Guadeloupe, St. Martin, Montserrat, and Antigua (Map 1.1). The Virgin Islands and some of the Leeward Islands, located between St. Kitts and Puerto Rico, were uninhabited and acted as a kind of buffer zone between the Arawakan Taino and the Caribanized Kalinago (Alvarez Chanca 1978[1494]: 37).

When Columbus met the Kalinago in 1493, during his second voyage to America, the Lesser Antilles seem to have been densely populated (Alvarez Chanca 1978[1493]: 28, 33). In Guadeloupe, members of the expedition saw numerous villages made up of thirty family houses, frequently distributed around a circular plaza in the middle of which stood a large communal house (Martire d'Anghiera 1966[1533]: 5r–5v; Breton 1978[1647]: 68). Kalinago subsistence depended predominantly on slash-and-burn cultivation of bitter manioc, from which the people produced cassava flour and bread, and on fishing and the gathering of marine resources. Hunting seems to have been of secondary importance.

Villages were composed of a group of interrelated families under the leadership of a grandfather or great-grandfather, who acted both as village and war leader (Breton 1978[1647]: 134). In some islands, village leaders recognized one or two individuals among them as regional chiefs

1.1. Areas occupied by the Kalinago of the Lesser Antilles and their neighbors, 1500s. K = Kalinago.

with authority over several villages or over the entire island (de las Casas 1986[1560]: I, 454; Rochefort 1666[1658]: 313–314). Village leaders convoked their followers to undertake large enterprises such as the building of a war canoe or large-scale raiding. Kalinago organized annual war expeditions against their traditional enemies, the Taino Arawak of Puerto Rico and the Lokono Arawak of the coasts of Venezuela and Guiana, in order to take captives (Anon. 1988[1620]: 185). Female and children captives were turned into concubines and slaves, whereas adult males were killed and partly eaten in cannibalistic rituals that brought together members of different villages and sometimes the population of entire islands.

The rugged topography of the islands, combined with the warring abilities of its inhabitants, hindered European occupation for more than a century. In the early 1600s, however, the English and the French entered into a race to colonize the Caribbean. The British colonized St. Kitts in 1623, Nevis in 1628, and Antigua and Montserrat in 1632, expelling the Kalinago population. After defeating and expelling its Kalinago population, the French and Dutch occupied St. Martin in 1631. In 1635, French settlers occupied Guadeloupe and Martinique despite the active resistance of the local Kalinago; a decade later, the newcomers definitively expelled the Kalinago from their lands. In 1650, France purchased Grenada from the Kalinago in exchange for European goods and liquor. When the local Kalinago revolted against the French colonists the following year, they were trounced. French expansion often met Kalinago resistance. In 1654 the inhabitants of Dominica killed the Jesuit missionaries who had settled on their island, and they attacked the French settlers of St. Lucia (Pelleprat 1655: 82–85). But by 1655 most of the Kalinago expelled by the British and the French from their islands had taken refuge in St. Vincent and Dominica. As a result, the population of St. Vincent increased to around ten thousand Kalinago, distributed in numerous villages (Pelleprat 1655: 70). A Franco-British treaty signed in 1660 ensured the neutrality of these two islands, which became the stronghold of the Kalinago people.

During this period, Dominica and St. Vincent experienced an accelerated process of Africanization that had begun in the early sixteenth century with the capture of African slaves from wrecked slaving ships, the abduction of African slaves from European plantations, and the seizure of African slaves who had escaped from their European masters (Rochefort 1666[1658]: 293, 324). At first, captured African slaves were resold to Europeans, but later on many began to be incorporated as captive slaves, much as Amerindian war captives. Whereas Kalinago were not opposed to marrying their Arawakan captives, they seldom married African captives (Labat 1724: I, Part 2, 26). Nevertheless, since the latter rapidly adopted Kalinago language and mores, their descendants were allowed to lead independent lives. By the year 1700, however, the "Black Carib" population of St. Vincent had amply surpassed that of the so-called Red or Yellow Carib, forcing the latter to cede the former part of the island for their exclusive use (Labat 1724: II, Part 4, 148). From there, the Black Kalinago constantly raided their former masters to steal goods and women. A similar process took place in Dominica (Anon. 1769: I, 82).

Internal conflicts favored the Europeans; the Red Kalinago sought their support to oust their Black Kalinago enemies. Thus, with the acquiescence of Red Kalinago, the French settled in St. Vincent in 1719 and in Dominica in 1727. Their presence, however, was constantly disputed by the British. In 1763, France ceded both islands to Great Britain, which signed peace treaties with both the Red and the Black Kalinago, assigning them lands to live in. In St. Vincent, disputes between British planters and Kalinago people increased gradually until 1796, when the British Army crushed a large revolt involving both Black and Red Kalinago. Close to 5,000 black Kalinago were deported to the coasts of Honduras. Their descendants, the present-day Garifuna—a term derived from "Kalliponam" or "Karipuna"—live along the coasts of Honduras, Belize, Guatemala, Nicaragua, and Mexico and total approximately 500,000 people. A smaller number of Red Kalinago withdrew into the nearly inaccessible northern region of St. Vincent, where their 3,500 or so descendants still live today. Another 3,400 Kalinago inhabit various settlements in reserved lands on the northeast coast of Dominica.

CONIBO OF THE UCAYALI RIVER

The Conibo—the largest and most powerful of the Panoan-speaking societies of eastern Peru—occupied both margins of the Ucayali River, from the mouth of the Tamaya in the north to that of the Mashansha in the south, as well as the lower portion of the Pachitea River (Map 1.2). Known as Lords of the Ucayali (Girbal y Barceló 1924b [1790]: 308), they were first contacted in 1557, when Spanish conquistador Juan Salinas de Loyola navigated upriver along the Ucayali and Urubamba rivers (Alès 1981). Salinas found four different groups living along these rivers, their territories separated by large tracts of no-man's-land, suggesting that they were hostile to each other. But he also found abundant evidence indicating the existence of long-distance trading networks that connected all these groups. In his report, Conibo people are mentioned by the name "Pariaches." It was only much later, in the 1680s, that the ethnonym "Conibo" appeared in the literature, being probably a Spanish distortion of "Húnibo" (húni = "people"; bo = plural marker), which is the term that Conibo use to refer to themselves.

While traversing the territory of the Pariaches/Conibo, Salinas found numerous villages composed of two hundred to four hundred houses (Alès 1981: 88). If each house contained a single, five-member family,

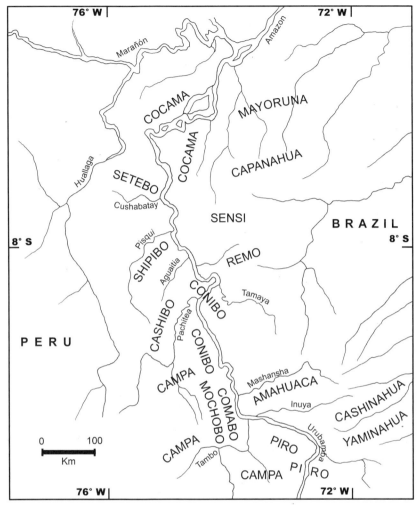

1.2. Areas occupied by the Conibo of the Ucayali River basin and their neighbors, 1600s.

this would yield a population of around 1,000 to 2,000; but given that most Amerindian households are composed of extended families, the population of these large riverine settlements might have been much larger. Each village had its own leader, and, according to Salinas (in Alès 1981: 90), such leaders were "great lords," obeyed and respected much more than those he had found along the Marañón River.

The territory inhabited by Conibo has been described as the "Ucayali lake region" (Stahl 1928: 139–142). It is a basically flat landscape, a large proportion of which is covered by bodies of water. Conibo subsistence pursuits are based on a combination of horticulture, fishing, and, to a lesser extent, hunting. At the time of contact, Conibo horticulture was largely based on the cultivation of maize and sweet manioc. Then as now, sweet manioc was often processed into farinha, or manioc meal, a product that can be stored for up to two years and was the main fare of Conibo men engaged in long-distance trading or war expeditions. By the 1700s, plantains, introduced by the Spanish, had become the main source of carbohydrates in the Conibo diet. These were complemented with fishing and the gathering of riverine and riparian resources and, to a lesser extent, by hunting. Because of its rich resources, and the scarcity of places apt for permanent settlement, the Ucayali *várzea* region was the object of much interethnic competition (Lathrap 1970: 128).

From the mid-sixteenth century to the late seventeenth century, Conibo people had no direct contact with Europeans. In 1685, however, Franciscan missionaries founded a first mission, which they called San Miguel, in a Conibo village that had a population of around 800 people distributed in forty-one houses (Beraún 1981b[1686]: 181). By then, however, their settlement pattern was more dispersed and their population seems to have decreased substantially from Salinas's days, due mainly to epidemics of influenza, measles, and smallpox (Myers 1990: 10). For a period, however, foreign epidemics benefited the Conibo by removing one of their major enemies, the Cocama of the Lower Ucayali (Myers 1988: 66). With the Cocama no longer blocking their passage to the Marañón River, Conibo people were able to begin trading with the Jesuit missions of the Marañón and Huallaga rivers. By the early 1680s, Conibo tradesmen were making annual trips to Laguna, the Jesuit headquarters, to exchange captives and booty, taken from their hinterland neighbors, against metal tools and salt (DeBoer 1984: 33). The 2,300-kilometer round-trip took seventy-five days and involved dozens of large trading canoes.

Raids against interfluvial peoples were not, however, a colonial development. As both Jesuit and Franciscan missionaries were soon to find out, Conibo were renowned pirates and slave raiders. The Ucayali interethnic power system entailed relationships between three types of societies (Santos-Granero and Barclay 1998: xxviii–xxix). The riverine Conibo, Cocama, and Piro fought against each other as equals and periodically raided their weaker semi-riverine neighbors living along the larger tributaries of the Ucayali, namely, the Pano-speaking Shipibo,

Setebo, Cashibo, Amahuaca, Sensi, Remo, Capanahua, Mochobo, and Comabo and the Arawak-speaking Campa (Asháninka, Ashéninka, Machiguenga, and Nomatsiguenga). In turn, the semi-riverine peoples raided the even weaker interfluvial groups living in the headwaters of the tributaries of the Ucayali, such as the Pano-speaking Mayoruna, Cashibo, Cashinahua, and Yaminahua. Conibo warriors took women and children as captive slaves. Since Conibo practiced head elongation and female circumcision—something most of their neighbors did not—and saw them as signs of beauty and moral superiority, slaves were generally identified as being ugly, uncircumcised "round-heads" (Stahl 1928[1895]: 164). Captive men were generally killed; their heads and hearts were cut off and kept as war trophies (Biedma 1981: 95). In addition, Conibo warriors stole everything that had trade value, particularly spun cotton, cotton textiles, feather ornaments, and salt. To enhance their defensive capacity against their numerous enemies, often two or three local groups gathered to live together in a single village, each under the leadership of their own headman (Amich 1975: 93). This explains, in part, why Conibo settlements were so large.

Raiding and pillaging intensified after contact with the Spanish. Each group vied to have access to—and, if possible, to monopolize trade in—iron tools and other European manufactures (DeBoer 1984: 35; Frank 1994: 148). But the Spanish presence also generated unexpected alliances between traditionally hostile groups. When, in 1695, the Jesuits attempted to convert the semi-riverine and interfluvial peoples, thus bypassing the Conibo and Piro who until then had acted as intermediaries, the latter established an alliance to expel the missionaries from the region (Morin 1998: 307). This alliance lasted until 1698, when Conibo and Piro achieved their objective. During the eighteenth and nineteenth centuries, Franciscan missionaries renewed their efforts to convert the native peoples of the Ucayali River basin. Their endeavors, however, were constantly thwarted by indigenous uprisings, the most important of which took place in 1766 (Santos-Granero 1992: 227–232).

By the mid-1800s, Conibo people were in decline, their hegemonic position in the Ucayali River basin having been gravely eroded (Marcoy 1869: I, 674). In the 1870s, they and other Panoan-speaking peoples were finally subjugated, this time not by missionaries but by greedy entrepreneurs scrambling to extract rubber. In the beginning, Conibo and Shipibo were hired by rubber bosses to raid their weaker neighbors, as they had always done. With the passage of time, however, they themselves became engaged in the gathering of rubber through debt peonage. This situation persisted throughout the twentieth century until the 1970s, when Conibo and their former enemies, the Shipibo, united to claim back their rights (Morin 1998: 395–403). Today, thanks to high fertility and lower mortality rates (Hern 1992), the joint Shipibo-Conibo population numbers around 35,000 (Tournon 2002: 143), distributed in 118 titled "native communities" and covering 216,000 hectares (Morin 1998: 408).

TUKANO OF THE VAUPÉS RIVER BASIN

"Tukano" is the name of a language family, of two clusters of Tukano-speaking peoples, and of a language group belonging to one of these clusters. Here I use the term in the second sense, to refer to the eastern Tukano, that is, to the Tukano-speaking peoples inhabiting the Vaupés River basin (Map 1.3). This cluster is composed of about fifteen different Tukano language groups—the best-known, and the ones that I will refer to here being the Tukano proper, Cubeo, Desana, Barasana, Makuna, Wanano, Tariana, Pirá-Tapuya, and Tuyuka. Most Tukano groups practice linguistic exogamy—they marry only people from a Tukano language group different from their own. Most are organized into patrilineal sibs, clans and phratries, have akin myths of origin, and share similar initiation and fertility rituals revolving around the playing of Jurupari sacred flutes. Eastern Tukano refer to themselves as Mahsá—also Mahsa or Makcé—which can be translated as "true people" (Chernela 1993: 47). Here I will refer to the Eastern Tukano in general as Tukano, and to Tukano language groups by their own individual names.

At the time of contact, Tukano people lived in the interfluvial areas along the right bank of the Negro River, then controlled by Manao and Baré, two powerful Arawak-speaking peoples organized in a multiethnic, plurilingual, and hierarchical macropolity (Vidal and Zucchi 1996: 116). During the 1500s, Tukano and other weaker interfluvial groups were regularly raided by Manao and Baré. These attacks increased in the 1600s when the Manao and Baré started providing slaves to both Spaniards and Portuguese (Vidal and Zucchi 1996: 117). In 1727 the Portuguese defeated the Manao, replacing them as the main slave raiders of the Upper Negro and Upper Orinoco. In the following decades, the peoples of the Negro River basin were exterminated through enslavement, nucleation in mission posts, and epidemics, and the area became largely depopulated. All along this period, many Tukano and Arawak-speaking groups

1.3. Areas occupied by the Tukano of the Vaupés River
basin and their neighbors, 1700s.

moved to the tributaries of the Upper Negro and, particularly, into the
Vaupés River basin. The collapse of the Portuguese colonial government
of Manaos at the end of the eighteenth century, and the incapacity of
the Spanish to settle permanently in the region, provided these groups
with some respite, allowing them to recover demographically (Hill
1993: 46). In short, Tukano are a conglomerate of peoples who, having
experienced—albeit indirectly—the colonial impact, managed to escape
to a refuge zone where they were able to reorganize their societies and to
live for about a century without much external interference.

The Vaupés and its larger tributaries are occupied by Tukano- and
Arawak-speaking peoples who live in sedentary villages composed
of large malocas, or multifamily longhouses (Moser and Tayler 1963:
443–444). Each maloca is under the leadership of its founder, who is
known as the "owner of the house." Tukano people combine slash-and-
burn horticulture with fishing, their most important source of proteins.
Although a highly prestigious male activity, hunting is of secondary
importance. Their main crop staple is bitter manioc, from which they
make manioc flour and cassava bread. In contrast, the interfluves are

inhabited by five—others say six—extremely mobile groups, collectively known as Makú (Mondragón 1999; Reid 1979). Makú are organized in small groups or bands. They derive their subsistence largely from hunting and gathering and, at least in colonial times, did not practice agriculture (Sampaio 1985b[1775]: 86).

Tukano social organization is highly hierarchical. Patrilineal sibs within each language group are ranked hierarchically according to the place of disembarkation of their mythical ancestors, with downriver groups ranking higher than upriver groups (Jackson 1983: 152). These status differences were strengthened through rank marriages and expressed in rank paraphernalia (Noronha 1862[1768]: 74). Relations among Tukano language groups have oscillated between exchange and warfare. Because of the rules of linguistic exogamy and patrilocal postmarital residence, language groups constantly exchange women. They also exchange prestige goods that are the specialized product of different language groups (Giacone 1949: 14). In addition, they visit each other to perform collective ceremonies (Jackson 1983: 97).

In the past, warfare between Tukano language groups was common, especially over agricultural lands and fishing grounds (Giacone 1949: 14). Other common causes for warfare were the taking of women and revenge for past killings (Goldman 1963: 162). Warfare was waged between language groups standing in an in-law relationship, between language groups in a fraternal relation, and even between sibs belonging to the same language group (Chernela 2001: 189). In none of these cases, however, did warfare entail the taking of captives to be kept as servants or slaves—although some Tukano groups, like the Cubeo, took captives to consume in cannibalistic rituals (Goldman 1963: 164). In contrast, the relationship between the riverine Tukano and the forest-dwelling Makú involved a variety of forms of servitude that through time ranged from predatory to symbiotic.

It has been argued that Makú lived in the Vaupés River basin long before the arrival of Tukano- and Arawak-speaking peoples (Stradelli 1890[1882]: 445; Nimuendajú 1950[1927]: 163). The invaders—being much more numerous—displaced Makú people from their lands or subjugated them (Coudreau 1887: II, 163–164). The notion that Makú were the original inhabitants of the Vaupés is supported by both Makú and Tukano oral traditions (Giacone 1949: 88; Knobloch 1972: 102). Because of their disparate cultural practices, Tukano have considered Makú as inferior, subhuman people, halfway between humans and animals (Stradelli 1890[1882]: 433). Thus, Tukano did not and still do not intermarry with them. Makú groups displaced by Tukano and Arawak invaders continued to roam freely in the interior areas. Occasionally, however, they were raided by their Tukano neighbors, who captured their children to keep them as slaves or, later on, to sell them to the whites (Coudreau 1887: II, 179; Koch-Grünberg 1995 [1909]: I, 56–57). In contrast, Makú bands subjugated by the invading Tukano were attached to their settlements as servant groups (Coudreau 1887: II, 179). Such groups lived permanently, or seasonally, close to their masters' maloca but never within it (Koch-Grünberg 1906: 881). They retained their families and their headmen but were entirely at the service of their Tukano masters. Some of these servant groups underwent a process of Tukanoization, becoming eventually integrated into the language group of their former masters as low-ranking sibs (Koch-Grünberg 1906: 878; Nimuendajú 1950[1927]: 165).

From the late eighteenth century to the late nineteenth century, the Vaupés River basin remained quite isolated. Catholic missionaries attempted to settle in the region in 1793 and 1852, but with little success (Souza 1848: 465; Coppi 1885: 139–140). Only in 1880 were the Franciscans able to establish themselves more permanently in the region. By then, however, international demand for rubber had led many Brazilians and Colombians to engage the native peoples of the Vaupés in the extraction of this resource. Their demand for domestic servants led Tukano groups to increase their raids against the Makú (Jackson 1983: 157). So scandalous was this traffic that the Franciscans issued a decree forbidding it within their missions (Giacone 1949: 88). After the end of the rubber boom in the 1920s, the region once more fell into a period of relative isolation, with missionaries being the most important external agents. In the early 1970s, with the support of Javeriano missionaries, the Tukano created the Regional Indigenous Council of the Vaupés (CRIVA) to fight for their rights (Jackson 1999: 286). In 1975 the Colombian government granted them a reserve of more than three million hectares. Nowadays, the Tukano number about 18,500 persons, while their Makú neighbors number around 2,700 (SIL 2004).

CHIRIGUANÁ OF SOUTHEASTERN BOLIVIA

Located along the eastern slopes of the southern Bolivian Andes, the Tupi-Guaraní-speaking Chiriguaná—also known as Chiriguano, Chiliguana, or Chiriones—were newcomers to the region at the time of contact. The earliest mention of their existence places them raiding the eastern frontiers of the Inka empire during the reign of Tupac Inca Yupanqui (circa 1471–1493) (Garcilaso de la Vega 1963[1609]: 322). The origin of the Chiriguaná has been the matter of numerous traditions. Some authors say that they came from the Paraguay River around 1473 and that their aim was originally to pillage the Inka empire (Anon. 1941[1573]: 66). Other authors assert that they arrived from the Paraguay River during the reign of Huayna Capac (circa 1493–1528) with the intention of plundering wealthy Inka outposts established in the tropical plains east of the Andes (Alcaya 1961[1610]: 47–49). A third oral tradition has the Chiriguaná arriving at the eastern frontiers of the Inka empire sometime in 1526 as allies of a certain Alejo García, a Portuguese adventurer who had heard news of the Inka empire (Díaz de Guzmán 1836[1612]: 15–18). These three traditions are in no way contradictory. In fact, it is highly probable that Chiriguaná people originated as a result of several waves of migrating Tupi-Guaraní-speaking peoples that began well before Columbus's arrival in America. This would explain why the Chiriguaná did not act, as has been noted, as a single, unified front (Julien 1997: 52).

According to these different traditions, the invaders numbered between 1,000 and 8,000 people, organized into three large groups (Alcaya 1961[1610]: 52; Díaz de Guzmán 1836[1612]: 17; Techo 1897[1673]: IV, 300). These groups settled in the Upper Grande (Guapay) River in the north, the Upper Parapetí River in the center, and the Upper Pilcomayo River in the south (Map 1.4). In the process, they displaced, or subjected as servant groups or tributary populations, Inka colonists, highland frontier peoples, and the native Arawak-speaking Chané. Although there is evidence that the invaders brought with them some of their women, it is said that most took women from the Chané native population. It was claimed that for this reason they were called Chiriones, which in Tupi-Guaraní means "mixed bloods, children of Chiriguaná men and women from other nations" (Suárez de Figueroa 1965[1586]: 404). Chiriguaná call themselves Ava/Aba, or "men," in the sense of "human beings."

Chiriguaná territory lies at the interface between the tropical montaña and the Grand Chaco (Riester et al. 1979: 266). During the 1500s, Chiriguaná lived in scattered settlements composed of three to five rectangular longhouses (Arriaga 1974[1596]: 69–70; Lizárraga 1968[1603]: 83; Arteaga 1961[1607]: 177). These houses were inhabited by extended

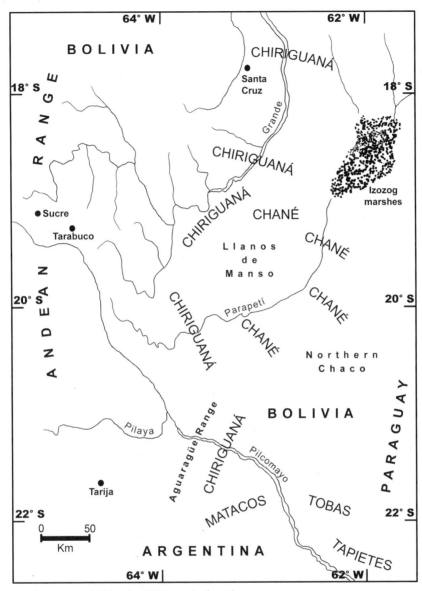

1.4. Areas occupied by the Chiriguaná of southeastern
Bolivia and their neighbors, 1500s.

families numbering between 100 and 150 people. Many Chiriguaná settlements had Chané servant groups attached to them (Arteaga 1961[1607]:
172, 176). These Chané groups lived under their own leaders in the

periphery of Chiriguaná settlements. Often, the size of the Chané servant population was much larger than that of their Chiriguaná masters (Suárez de Figueroa 1965[1586]: 405).

For defensive reasons, Chiriguaná people preferred to settle in forested rather than open areas (Arriaga 1974[1596]: 70). Chiriguaná practiced swidden agriculture. Maize was their staple food and the basis of their main fermented beverage. But they also cultivated manioc—from which they produced manioc flour—as well as squash, sweet potatoes, hot pepper, and cotton. Chiriguaná gardens were large and productive, allowing households to store sizable quantities of dry goods, such as maize, beans, and manioc flour (Lizárraga 1968[1603]: 151; Arteaga 1961[1607]: 178). Hunting and fishing made a lesser contribution to daily subsistence, except during ceremonial occasions.

During the mid-1500s, Chiriguaná warriors began stealing cattle and horses from Spanish frontier towns (Castro 1921–1926[1568]: 297). By 1616 they had become experienced horse riders and had begun to raise cattle of their own (Díaz de Guzmán 1979b[1618]: 92). The adoption of horses increased their military capacity, allowing them to wage war against distant groups formerly out of range of their raids.

In the late sixteenth century, Chiriguaná people were divided into thirteen to sixteen *parcialidades*, regional groups composed of several settlements organized under the leadership of a primus inter pares war leader (Cepeda 1918–1922b[1595]: 262–263). These groups, in turn, were consolidated into three "provinces," corresponding to the areas settled by the invading Tupi-Guaraní groups in early colonial times (Martínez 1944[1601]: 504). Although Chiriguaná warfare was mostly directed toward peoples of different languages (Anon. 1941[1573]: 66; Polo de Ondegardo 1991[1574]: 137), abundant evidence points to the existence of intratribal warfare between *parcialidades* and provinces (Cepeda 1918–1922a[1590]: 2; Arriaga 1974[1596]: 64). Chiriguaná were reputed for practicing both endocannibalism (the consumption of the bodies of deceased relatives), and exocannibalism (the consumption of the bodies of enemies killed in war) (Garcilaso de la Vega 1963[1609]: 322). Adult warriors not destined to be eaten in cannibalistic ceremonies were usually sold to the Spanish as slaves (Matienzo 1918–1922[1564]: 54). Children and young women were kept as captive slaves. In the late sixteenth century, the Chiriguaná stopped cannibalizing their enemies, preferring to sell them to the Spanish instead (Díaz de Guzmán 1979a[1617]: 78). After that, ritual cannibalism was replaced by the taking of enemy heads or scalps as war trophies (Corrado and Comajuncosa 1990[1884]: I, 46).

The first Spanish outposts in Chiriguaná lands were founded in the 1560s. In 1574 the Spanish founded Tarija as a spearhead into Chiriguaná territory, but due to the constant attacks of the Chiriguaná, the newly founded village had to be moved to its present site. The next year, the viceroy of Peru organized a large punitive expedition against the Chiriguaná that had little success. In the following centuries, Chiriguaná were the subject of numerous military and evangelizing expeditions that they rejected, often through regional or panethnic military confederations. Due to colonial pressures, the northern Chiriguaná were displaced from their lands and moved to the south. But the central and southern Chiriguaná continued to resist. It was only in 1790, after a devastating epidemic of smallpox, that the Chiriguaná finally agreed to nucleate into mission posts (Mingo de la Concepción 1981[1797]: I, 356). And it was not until 1892, when the Bolivian government ferociously suppressed the uprising of prophet Tumpa Apiayawayki, that the Chiriguaná people were finally subjugated. During this long process, the Chané groups subjected by the Chiriguaná went through a process of Chiriguanáization. By the early twentieth century, Chané people were indistinguishable from their former Chiriguaná masters in either language or cultural practices (Métraux 1930: 329). As has been noted, however, this process was not unidirectional; Chiriguaná people adopted some of the cultural traits characteristic of their former servants (Combès and Lowrey 2006). Today the Chiriguanáized Chané refer to themselves as Izoceño—inhabitants of Izozog, the area in which they concentrated—and they still bear the stigma of their previous subordinate status (Métraux 1930: 329; Riester et al. 1979: 263; Combès and Lowrey 2006: 692–693). There are, at present, 18,000 Chiriguaná in Bolivia—10,000 Chiriguaná and 8,000 Izoceño. An additional 25,000 Chiriguaná—divided into 22,500 Chiriguaná and 2,500 Chané—live in Argentina, where they migrated, starting in the 1800s.

CALUSA OF SOUTHERN FLORIDA

The earliest mention of the Calusa was made by Juan Ponce de León, the first European to explore the coasts of Florida. In 1513, while in the proximity of Charlotte Harbor, Ponce de León was attacked by a fleet of canoes belonging to a chief named Carlos (Herrera y Tordesillas

1601–1615: I, 303–304). The ethnonym "Calusa" derives from the name of this chief. Some chroniclers assert that the chief adopted it from the Spanish emperor Carlos V (Solís de Merás 1990[1565]: 123). Others claim that it was a Spanish corruption of the chief's native name: Caalus (Rogel 1991b[1567]: 248). Since Ponce de León reported the existence of chief Carlos in 1513, before the accession of Charles V to the throne (1516), the second hypothesis seems to be more plausible. If this is so, then the name "Caalus" possibly means "fierce people," as a very reliable contemporary source suggests (Escalante Fontaneda 1575[1567]: fol. 2).

Calusa lived in the tropical zone of Florida (Swanton 1946: 20). Most authors affirm that their territory extended along the western coast of southern Florida, from the southern portion of Tampa Bay to the Florida Keys (Swanton 1946: 101; McNicoll 1941: 11; Marquardt 1987: 98) (Map 1.5). Other authors, however, place the northern boundary of their territory on the northern shores of Charlotte Harbor (Rouse 1951; Hann 1991a: 10). In addition, by subjugating peoples or forming military alliances with their neighbors—the Tequesta, Pojoy, Jeaga, Jobe, and Ais—the Calusa paramount chief extended his influence as far northeast as Cape Canaveral, and as far southeast as present-day Miami. These neighboring ethnic groups were linguistically, culturally, and, at times, politically connected to the Calusa. In fact, it is reported that Calusa was a language similar to, or the same as, Tequesta (Rogel 1991b[1567]: 283). Some authors also speak of the western and eastern Calusa, to underscore not only the political but also the cultural unity of the native peoples of southern Florida (Swanton 1946: 829).

Calusa were mainly a sea-oriented people who did not practice agriculture. They combined the exploitation of coastal and maritime resources with hunting and gathering in the interior lands. As we shall see, they also exacted tribute from subjugated horticulturalist and hunting-gathering populations. Their construction of long canals linking the coast with the inland areas—probably built with labor obtained from tributary populations—permitted the rapid transport and distribution of food surpluses, one of the most important functions performed by Calusa paramount chiefs (Luer 1989: 113).

The boundaries of the Calusa polity were not fixed; they waxed and waned according to the upheavals of geopolitical affairs (Hann 1991a: 26). Calusa supremacy was not absolute. The Tocobaga, located on the northern portion of Tampa Bay, were the Calusa's main rivals, contesting their hegemony at the regional level. In turn, the Tequesta of southeastern

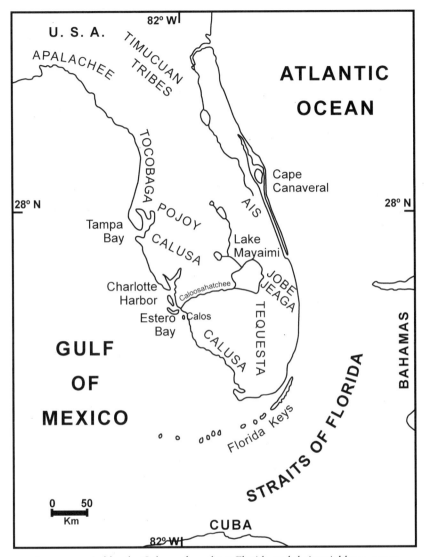

1.5. Areas occupied by the Calusa of southern Florida and their neighbors, 1500s.

Florida and the Ais of Cape Canaveral, although subjected to the Calusa as tributaries (Milanich 1998: 66), from time to time attempted to regain their political autonomy (Solís de Merás 1990[1565]: 202). This not-withstanding, it is clear that Calusa dominance in southern Florida was widespread. Before the arrival of Spanish conqueror Pedro Menéndez de Avilés in 1565, it is said that chief Carlos had authority over fifty settlements (Escalante Fontaneda 1575[1567]: fol. 5–6; see Hann 2003: 20–29 for a more detailed discussion). These included settlements belonging to tributary populations such as the Tequesta, the Florida Keys islanders, and even a group of Taino migrants from Cuba (Escalante Fontaneda 1575[1567]: fol. 4). At around the same date, the Spaniards estimated that 20,000 persons were under the control of chief Carlos (López de Velasco 1991a[1569]: 317; see also Hann 2003: 54–56). Even if this was an inflated figure, and we were to divide it into half, we would still be left with a very large number, indicating the vast extent of chief Carlos's power.

Calusa lived in sedentary villages, moving to other sites temporarily to take advantage of seasonal variations in resource availability. Sources agree that Calos, the capital town of the Calusa, was located on an island in Estero Bay, south of Charlotte Harbor, now known as Mound Key (Schell 1968; Lewis 1978; Widmer 1988; Hann 2003). Like other southern Florida coastal settlements described by early sources, Calos was composed of several human-made mounds, the largest of which, measuring up to twelve meters in height, was occupied by the chief's house and the local temple, often storing the remains of chiefly ancestors. In 1565 Menéndez de Avilés reported the presence of 2,000 people when he visited Calos (Solís de Merás 1990[1565]: 118). One hundred thirty years later, the population of Calos, estimated at around 1,000, was still very large, considering the population drop experienced by the Calusa at the time (F. López 1991[1697]: 159).

Pánfilo de Narváez and Hernando de Soto passed through Calusa territory in 1528 and 1539, respectively, but did not stay long before continuing their way north. It was not until 1565, when Menéndez de Avilés arrived in Calos after expelling the French from Florida, that the Calusa had to endure a more serious Spanish threat (Solís de Merás 1990[1565]). Following indigenous political practices, chief Carlos offered Menéndez his sister in marriage, as a sign of alliance and submission (Solís de Merás 1990[1565]: 116). But despite Menéndez's efforts to subjugate Calusa people and convert them to Christianity—including a sham marriage with chief Carlos's sister, and the recruitment of Jesuit missionaries—the Calusa managed to regain their autonomy in 1568.

The period during which Calusa were in contact with Europeans but managed to retain their independence was one of prosperity and expansion. The plunder of European shipwrecks during the sixteenth century provided the Calusa with plenty of gold, European manufactures, and European slaves, which they used to enhance their power and prestige. By 1612 it was reported that the Calusa paramount chief—a hereditary office—had increased the number of settlements under his authority to seventy (in Swanton 1922: 343). Relations with tributary populations or allied groups were reinforced through political marriages between the Calusa paramount chief and high-ranking women from these latter groups (Laudonnière 2001[1564]: 111–112).

During the rest of the seventeenth century, the Spaniards made several attempts to subject the Calusa either by the sword or by the cross, but none was successful. This did not hinder them from trading with the Spaniards. In fact, in 1689, the Calusa paramount chief visited Cuba in response to an invitation from the bishop of Havana (Compostela 1991[1690]). Despite their prosperity, and their successful resistance to colonial subjection, by 1698 the Calusa population had dropped to 2,000, one-tenth of the figure estimated a hundred years earlier (Contreras 1991[1698]: 165). The population decrease may be attributed to decimation by European epidemics, to a diminution of Calusa influence as a result of Spanish interference, or to a combination of both.

After destroying the Spanish missions of northern Florida in 1704, the British and their Creek allies started moving south, all the while attacking, displacing, and enslaving the native peoples of Florida. "By 1711," asserts Hann (1991a: 45), "the terror had reached greater proportions, moving thousands of the natives of southern Florida to request transport to Cuba." But the Spanish authorities agreed to transport only a few hundred. The Calusa and their neighbors opted to move to the southernmost regions of Florida, many of them taking refuge in the Florida Keys (Hann 1991a: 46). In 1743 the remnants of the eastern Calusa were living with members of other "nations" in a small village close to present-day Boca Raton. By then, they numbered only 180 (Monaco and Alaña 1991[1743]: 420). Franciscan missionaries attributed their population decline to interethnic fighting, alcohol, epidemics, infanticide, and slave raiding by northern, British-allied tribes. The last eastern Calusa, 80 families in total, migrated to Cuba in 1763, when Great Britain took possession of Florida (Romans 1775).

GUAICURÚ OF THE PARAGUAY RIVER BASIN

The first Europeans to enter into contact with the Guaicurú of Paraguay in 1548 already described them as having some type of dominance over neighboring populations such as the Schenne (Chané, better known as Guaná) and Tohannos (Toyana), who were said to be their subjects "in the same way as German rustics are with respect to their lords" (Schmidl 1749[1548]: 22). In subsequent centuries, Guaicurú slave raiding and dominance over tributary populations became legendary, so much so that the Guaicurú case is one of the few in which the existence of slavery and a sharp social stratification has been accepted by Americanist anthropologists (see Métraux 1946: 304; Lévi-Strauss [1955] 1974: 180; Clastres 1998a: 28).

To distinguish the Guaicurú from other Guaicuran-speaking peoples, they are sometimes referred to as "Guaicurú proper." They are also known as Mbayá, an exonym imposed on them by their sedentary Guaraní neighbors, meaning "straw mat" in reference to the mats with which the itinerant Guaicurú built their lean-tos. Here I have opted to use the term "Guaicurú," also an exonym imposed by the Guaraní, for it is the most commonly used. There is no agreement as to the etymology of this name (Sánchez Labrador 1910–1917[1760]: II, 58; Lafone y Quevedo 1896: 4). According to Sánchez Labrador (1910–1917[1770]: I, 5), Guaicurú people referred to themselves as Eyiguayegui, "people of the palm savannah," in reference to the vast palm groves characteristic of their original territory on the western margins of the Paraguay River. In later times, the Spanish and Portuguese called them Caballeros, or Cavaleiros, meaning horsemen, in recognition of their outstanding horsemanship.

The limits of Guaicurú territory changed dramatically through time in response to pressures by both Spaniards and Portuguese, but also as a response to the emergence of new opportunities for raiding European and native settlements (Map 1.6). It is said that in pre-European times the Guaicurú lived in the region of Caaguazú, east of the Paraguay River (Lozano 1733: 63). In the 1500s, however, they were located on the western margins of the Paraguay River close to where the Spanish founded the city of Asunción (Núñez Cabeza de Vaca 1585[1544]: 76v; Techo 1897[1673]: II, 159). In the following century, they moved further north to escape Spanish pressures, continuing until the early 1700s to live west of the Paraguay River between the mouths of the Pilcomayo and Yaveviri rivers (Lozano 1733: 59). In the second half of the eighteenth century, however, the bulk of Guaicurú population moved to the eastern margin of the Paraguay, and to the north, settling between the Jejuí and Mboteti (present-day Miranda) rivers (Méndez 1969[1772]: 54; Prado 1839[1795]: 25–26). By the early 1800s this move had been completed,

1.6. Areas occupied by the Guaicurú of the Paraguay River
basin and their neighbors, 1500s.

and Guaicurú were reported to be living in Brazilian territory between the Paraguay River to the west, the Apá River to the south, and the Serras de Albuquerque to the east (Serra 1845[1803]: 211).

From the very beginning, the Spanish reported that Guaicurú people did not practice agriculture, relying for their subsistence instead on hunting, fishing, and collection of forest products (Núñez Cabeza de Vaca 1585[1544]: 76v). They did not, however, lack cultivated foodstuffs, for it was said that they had an abundance of maize, manioc, and other roots (Schmidl 1749[1548]: 21). These products, as we shall see, they obtained from their tributaries. The adoption of horses in the late 1500s or early 1600s increased their mobility and thus their hunting and gathering options (Métraux 1946: 250). Horses also augmented their warring capacities. However, as Schindler (1983: 204) has argued, warring was already an important cultural practice among the Guaicurú in pre-Hispanic times, thus refuting the notion that the introduction of horses promoted warlike behavior among indigenous populations.

In the early 1700s, Guaicurú were divided into three named *cacicatos*, or chieftainships, with a total population of 700 families, or around 3,500 persons, plus more than 500 tributary families, making a total of around 6,000 (Lozano 1733: 62). These chieftainships were divided into *parcialidades*, or regional groups headed by a principal chief, and into numerous *capitanías* or *tolderías*, local settlements or camps led by lower-rank "captains." The most important among the settlement chiefs was recognized as paramount chief of the regional group, whereas the most important of the regional group chiefs was recognized as paramount of the *cacicato*.

Guaicurú livelihood was based on a scattered and mobile settlement pattern. Each chieftainship, however, had a recognized territory with access to a portion of the Paraguay River (Sánchez Labrador 1910–1917[1770]: I, 260; Jolís 1972[1789]: 301–302). Guaicurú local and family groups roamed along their territories following the seasonal availability of resources. This practice increased with the adoption of the horse, which became their most important sign of wealth (Serra 1845[1803]: 211). Always in search of pastures for their large herds, often comprising hundreds of horses, Guaicurú migrated seasonally in response to the flow and ebb of the Paraguay River.

Guaicurú raided all their indigenous neighbors except for their main rivals, the Payaguá, a hunting-gathering fluvial people living to the north of the Yaveviri River (Sánchez Labrador 1910–1917[1770]: I,

131). Guaicurú relationships with their other native neighbors varied, from annual raids for taking captives to subjection of local groups as tributaries. At the time of contact, several Arawak-speaking Guaná groups were already under their control. The relationship with these subordinated peoples softened through time, and by the late 1700s it had the character of an asymmetrical alliance rather than a tributary relation. As a result of their move to the north, closer to the Portuguese sphere of influence, in the 1800s the Guaná started to emancipate themselves from Guaicurú dominance. To compensate for this loss, Guaicurú people began to raid the indigenous peoples with whom they had recently come into contact—namely, the Bororo, Kaiwá, Guató, and Chamacoco—from whom they took children and young women.

In the early 1600s, Jesuit missionaries began to missionize the Guaicurú. Despite long-term Jesuit presence, however, Guaicurú neither converted nor stopped making war on, and taking captives from, neighboring peoples (Techo 1897[1673]: II, 375). War with the Spanish of Paraguay lasted intermittently until 1746, when a peace of sorts, which extended until 1796, was established between the opponents (Azara 1809[1781]: II, 103; but see Prado 1839[1795]: 56). This allowed Guaicurú chiefs, together with their Guaná tributaries/allies, to concentrate their attacks on Portuguese settlements and the Spanish missions of Chiquitos in southwestern Bolivia. The founding in 1775 of the Portuguese fort-prison of Nova Coimbra, or Albuquerque, located in the confluence of the Paraguay and Miranda rivers, severely hindered Guaicurú raiding and piracy (Serra 1850[1803]: 381). In the following decades, Guaicurú chiefs exploited the rivalry between the Portuguese and the Spanish in order to exact benefits from both.

In 1796–1797, the Spanish organized a punitive expedition against the Guaicurú that ended in the massacre of 11 chiefs and 300 other persons (Serra 1850[1803]: 383). This marked the beginning of a process of systematic Spanish attacks against Guaicurú, causing their gradual retreat toward Portuguese-controlled territories around the Miranda River. By 1845 most Guaicurú and Guaná lived in Brazil and had converted to Christianity (Castelnau 1850–1859[1845]: II, 391–392). Their Guaná tributaries had by then become emancipated, and Guaicurú amounted to little more than 2,000 people divided into six small chieftainships. After the Paraguayan War (1865–1870), in which the Guaicurú sided with the Brazilians against the Paraguayans, Brazil granted them a reservation in southern Mato Grosso. At the end of the nineteenth century, only one Guaicurú chieftainship survived, the Caduveo—also Kadiweu—with a population of 200 (Boggiani 1945[1892]: 243). Of the seven chieftainships into which the Guaná were divided in the 1700s (Sánchez Labrador 1910–1917[1770]: II, 255), only two survived, the Terena and Kinikinao. The demographic trajectories of these two peoples were very different, however. Today there are 1,600 Caduveo and 16,000 Terena/Kinikinao (ISA 2001).

* * *

Apart from the fact that all the above societies practiced captive slavery, they shared a common denominator—namely, that of being the most powerful societies within the regional interethnic power systems of which they were a part. These were heterogeneous regional systems comprising societies that differed substantially in terms of social complexity, demographic weight, and military capacity. Sometimes these hegemonic societies shared their position with one or two almost equally powerful neighbors. This was the case, for example, for the Calusa and Tocobaga; the Kalinago and Lokono; the Tukano and Arawak; the Conibo, Piro, and Cocama; and the Guaicurú and Payaguá. With such powerful neighbors, the relationship was one of rivalry and mutual respect. Warfare went hand in hand with trading, occasional intermarriage, and, in special circumstances, even military alliances.

Relationships with other, less powerful peoples were characterized by permanent raiding, pillaging, and the taking of captives, generally children and young women. The distinction between dominant and subordinate peoples in these regional power systems is less like that between warlike and peaceful societies than that between powerful and less powerful societies. The same societies that had been victimized by hegemonic peoples sometimes in turn victimized their weaker neighbors. It is also important to note that such interethnic power relationships did not follow any fixed pattern based on alleged "evolutionary" socioeconomic differences. In northwest Amazonia the dominant peoples were sedentary horticulturalists and fishermen living along the largest rivers who raided the nomadic hunting-gathering bands of the hinterland. In contrast, in the Paraguay River basin they were semi-itinerant hunter-gatherers who raided or subjugated village agriculturalists. In southern Florida we find a similar situation: the hegemonic people were fishermen-gatherers who lived in large permanent villages but moved seasonally to fishing and gathering sites, and who raided both fishing and farming communities. In all the other cases, the struggle was between societies with similar economies based on slash-and-burn agriculture combined with hunting and fishing in different degrees.

The only economic trait that seems to be common to these capturing societies is that all of them occupied what can be considered the richest environments from the point of view of their particular lifestyles. Calusa controlled estuarine coastal areas rich in fishing resources from which they raided or dominated their inland neighbors. Kalinago lived scattered along numerous islands possessing fertile volcanic soils and abundant fisheries. From here they could attack with relative impunity other island peoples, as well as the peoples from the mainland. Tukano, Conibo, and Guaicurú lived along the largest rivers in their respective areas, in areas of fertile soils and rich aquatic resources, from which they attacked the peoples living in the less fertile headwaters and interfluves. Finally, Chiriguaná occupied the fertile valleys of the Andean piedmont, which served as a stepping-stone for attacking the peoples living along the western fringes of the more arid Grand Chaco.

In these asymmetrical power relationships, weaker peoples were constantly harassed and placed in a position of actual and ideological subordination. In fact, as we shall see, members of captured societies were often categorized by their raiders as being closer to animals than to humans. As such, they were considered to be prey and were hunted as actual forest animals. In such regional systems of interethnic power relations, members of capturing societies saw themselves as the epitome of humanity. In their eyes, their military supremacy was an expression of their physical, mental, and moral superiority. Members of capturing societies saw themselves as more beautiful, more intelligent, and more civil—in the sense of possessing key social virtues—than their neighbors. Such sense of superiority was extended, not only to the native peoples from whom they took captives and plunder, but also to the Europeans with whom they came in contact. Again and again, European observers report in shocked tones that those whom they considered to be savage peoples saw themselves as being superior to white men (Serra 1845[1803]: 204–205; Serra 1850[1803]: 349–350; Bouton 1640: 39–40; Díaz Castañeda 2001[1912]: 348).

It is important to note that the feeling of superiority, and the asymmetry of the power relationships between capturing and captured societies, was extremely resilient to change. Captured societies, it is true, resisted the attacks of their powerful neighbors and even fought back whenever this was possible. From time to time, Amahuaca warriors raided their Conibo victimizers, and the Taino of Puerto Rico killed and ate in reciprocal cannibalistic rituals the Kalinago raiders that ravaged their island regularly. We also know that, under favorable circumstances, Tequesta and Chané local groups did not hesitate to take arms in order to shake off Calusa and Chiriguaná dominance, respectively.

What strikes the observer, nonetheless, is how these power relations survived undisturbed throughout centuries. They were broken only recently, when the societies involved were forcefully confronted with national projects of modernity. But even these radical processes of social transformation have not changed the ideology of subordination by which members of capturing societies attribute an inferior status to those belonging to former captured societies. In turn, members of captured societies accepted grudgingly but unquestioningly the inferior status their former masters attribute to them. This is all the more surprising since, as we shall see, most of the capturing societies occupying a position of supremacy within regional power systems constantly incorporated, through marriage, adoption, and filiation, large numbers of individuals belonging to the peoples they considered "inferior." This suggests that native concepts of supremacy, superiority, and purity differ in important ways from those prevailing in the Western tradition, despite their apparent resemblance.

Captive slavery and other forms of servitude can be understood only in the context of the regional power systems in which they developed. In the following three chapters I analyze the diverse forms of servitude found in the American tropics, not as isolated practices, but rather from the perspective of native regimes of capture and servitude—that is, the combination of institutionalized relations of extreme dependence that can be found within a particular regional system of interethnic power relations at any given point in time.

PART 2

Regimes of Servitude

CHAPTER 2

Captive Slaves

Variations in the organization of such violence—including raids
whose purpose was to acquire slaves, banditry, and kidnapping—
indicate that violent enslavement can be thought of as falling on a
continuum from large-scale political action, in which enslavement may
be only a by-product of war and not its cause, to small-scale criminal
activity, in which enslavement is the sole purpose of the action.

—PAUL E. LOVEJOY, *Transformations in Slavery*

In native tropical America, as elsewhere, warfare or piracy was
the matrix of slavery and other forms of servitude (Lévy-Bruhl
1931: 6). It's true that war was not the only way to obtain
slaves. They could also be acquired through trade and as tribute.
Nevertheless, slaves thus acquired were always linked to an original act of
violence, whether it was the abduction of individuals or the subjugation
of local groups by raiding and warfare. Slavery through purchase and
tribute were only derivative forms. More importantly, native slavery here
always assumed the form of exoservitude—that is, the enslavement of
people belonging to societies different from that of their captors (Lévy-
Bruhl 1931: 9). This does not mean that slaving societies did not practice
endowarfare. As we shall see, the Tukano, Chiriguaná, and Guaicurú
often raided groups belonging to the same ethnolinguistic ensemble. In
such cases, however, war prisoners were immediately assimilated through
marriage or adoption and were never kept as slaves.

Endoservitude through warfare was never an option among the native
peoples of tropical America. The reason, as we shall see, is linked to
Amerindian notions conceiving wild, different Others as significant
sources of life and as indispensable for the production and reproduction
of people, society, and self-identity (see Chapter 9). Other forms of
endoservitude such as debt slavery, criminal slavery, and voluntary
slavery resulting from personal misfortune, extreme poverty, delinquency,
or widespread famine were common in Mesoamerica but very unusual

in native tropical America. Here, pale versions of debt and voluntary slavery have been found only among Warao (Wilbert 1993: 57, 60). These forms of servitude, however, are extremely exceptional. More generally, captives were taken from alien peoples through warfare and piracy.

This in no way means, as Kopytoff (1982: 221) has pointed out, that people captured in war—or sold thereafter—always ended up becoming slaves. As we shall see in Chapter 7, even in slaveholding societies some war captives were adopted or taken as spouses or concubines almost immediately after they were captured. Thus, although it can be asserted that in tropical America all slaves were originally war captives, not all war captives were doomed to become slaves. This was particularly true in the context of homogeneous regional systems, where the societies involved had similar demographic weight and military capacity. In such systems, warfare assumed the form of a more or less balanced exchange of dead and captives within the frame of revenge and blood feuding cycles. Captives taken in such raids were promptly incorporated as concubines or adoptive children. In contrast, in heterogeneous regional systems such as the ones analyzed here, hegemonic societies engaged in large-scale seasonal raiding aimed at destroying specific enemy settlements and at capturing as many children and young women as possible. In such societies, war captives were first incorporated as slaves, and only much later—sometimes one or two generations later—were they fully assimilated as fellow tribespeople.

The distinction between slave-raiding, slave-trading, and slaveholding societies, underlying other heterogeneous regional systems, was absent in the American tropics. On the northwest Pacific coast and in adjacent regions, for instance, some Amerindian peoples acquired slaves through both raiding and trading; others took captives not to keep but to trade with neighboring peoples; and still others did not engage in slave raiding and obtained captives only through trade or debt (MacLeod 1928: 645–646; Hajda 2005: 571–572). Such specialization is absent from tropical America, where all slave-raiding societies were simultaneously slaveholding and, sometimes, slave-trading societies. In these societies, slave raiding was a permanent endeavor, since, as we shall see in Chapter 7, the descendants of slaves eventually acquired nonslave status and thus needed to be replaced with fresh recruitments. For this reason, members of capturing societies regarded the weaker populations from which they took slaves almost as slave-breeding populations, applying to them ethnonyms generally meaning "captives" (more on this in Chapter 5).

Both seasonal raiding and large-scale captive slavery were practiced by all the societies examined in this book. However, only in two of them—Kalinago and Conibo—does captive slavery appear to be the main and only form of servitude. In this chapter, I discuss the salient characteristics of the regimes of capture and servitude of these two Amerindian societies.

KALINAGO

Columbus (1991[1493]: 133, 167) first heard of Kalinago raiding against the Arawak-speaking Taino and Lucayos during his first trip to America. It was not until his second voyage (1493), however, that he came across people captured by Kalinago. In Guadeloupe and St. Martin many of the Taino captives kept by Kalinago people fled from their masters to join the Spaniards—probably enticed by the Taino interpreters that accompanied them (Alvarez Chanca 1978[1494]: 28, 34). From these captives, the Spanish learned that Kalinago warriors made long-distance expeditions of more than 150 sea leagues to take prisoners and obtain plunder from neighboring islands and even farther away (Alvarez Chanca 1978[1494]: 30). As depicted in a seventeenth-century anonymous drawing (see Figure 1), Kalinago warriors were much feared because, we are told, of their military prowess and their cannibalistic reputation. Captives suffered diverse fates. Adult men were brought back home, killed, and eaten in cannibalistic rituals. Boys were emasculated and used as slaves until they grew up, after which time they were killed whenever their captors organized a large feast requiring the sacrifice of an enemy. Young women were taken as concubines or given as maidservants to their wives (Alvarez Chanca 1978[1494]: 31).

The Spaniards were able to identify captive slaves from their captors because female captives did not wear leg ligatures, which were the most important ornament of Kalinago women, and male captives were emasculated (Alvarez Chanca 1978[1494]: 29). The first piece of data was confirmed by subsequent authors more than one hundred years later (Breton 1978[1647]; Du Tertre 1654) and is well illustrated by old colonial engravings (see Figures 15 and 16). Doubtless, it was a long-standing practice that the Spaniards understood through their informants. Guillermo Coma and other members of Columbus's second expedition to America confirmed the second piece of information concerning castration (Coma 1903[1494]; F. Columbus 1992[1539]; de las Casas 1986[1560]). By the time Europeans had renewed regular contact with Kalinago in the early 1600s, nobody mentions this practice, suggesting either that it had been abandoned or that it was a Spanish fabrication (more on this in Chapter 5).

The first reports mentioning Kalinago expeditions demonstrate that Kalinago were already engaged in large-scale pillaging and capturing at the time of contact. When Columbus arrived in Guadeloupe in 1494, Taino female captives told him that the island's paramount chief and a force of 300 men had embarked on 10 war canoes to raid the neighboring islands (Alvarez Chanca 1978[1494]: 28; F. Columbus 1992[1539]: 113). Principal among the targets of Kalinago attacks were the powerful Arawak-speaking peoples of the Greater Antilles (Taino) and Guiana (Lokono), whom they raided once or twice a year. They also raided other, less powerful Carib-speaking peoples, such as the Yao, Nepoyo, and Sapayo of Trinidad, Tobago, and the Lower Orinoco region. The regional system of interethnic power relationships in which Kalinago were involved could therefore be characterized as heterogeneous, comprising enemies of equal and unequal strength.

Most raiding was carried out during the dry season, from October to May, a time of stable and tranquil weather; the trade winds—cool winds that blow from the northeast—favored trips to the west (Greater Antilles) and southwest (Spanish Main). In colonial times, Kalinago maintained this seasonal pattern of raiding, with the only difference being that in the Greater Antilles they started attacking the Spanish instead of the Taino. The latter had been almost totally exterminated by the Spanish by 1524 (de las Casas 1986[1560]: II, 204). The first large-scale attack on Puerto Rico was reported in 1513, when 350 Kalinago navigating in a large flotilla of war canoes assaulted the city of Caparra (Alegría 1981: 50). From Spanish settlements they took plunder, as well as Spanish and African captives. The most famous among the latter was Luisa de Navarrete (1992[1580]: 40), a twenty-three-year-old African emancipated slave who spent four years (1576–1580) among the Kalinago of Dominica, leaving us her testimony about her experiences while living with them. Navarrete (1992[1580]: 42–43) claimed that she was able to escape from her captors during a war expedition against the Spanish of Puerto Rico, which was composed of 15 war canoes manned by a multi-island Kalinago raiding force.

By the early 1600s, however, the Spanish of the Greater Antilles had signed a peace treaty with most Kalinago war leaders—except those living in St. Vincent and Dominica—and the latter had stopped raiding

Puerto Rico. From then on, Kalinago raiders concentrated their attacks on the Lokono of the mainland (Anon. 1988[1620]: 20) and, later on in that same century, on the settlements and plantations that the French and English had established in islands previously in their possession. Here they also took European captives, sometimes individuals of high birth, as well as African household or plantation slaves (Pelleprat 1655: 85; Provins 1939[1646]).

Kalinago war expeditions were usually convoked by the eldest active war leader in any given island. He was recognized as the island's paramount chief and distinguished as such by the particular ornaments he wore (Anon. 1988[1620]: 184; Rochefort 1666[1658]: 15). Whenever they wished to undertake a raid, the Kalinago organized a large drinking party to which they invited people from selected settlements or from the entire island (Breton 1978[1647]: 76; Anon. 1988[1620]: 184; Bouton 1640: 120). After a few days of heavy drinking, when spirits were high, the old women present would begin denouncing the insults and sufferings they had received from the enemy, moving the audience to tears and rousing their anger (Du Tertre 1654: 443; Rochefort 1666[1658]: 318).

If the convoking leader of the feast intended to embark on a long-distance war expedition—generally to the mainland—he would send messengers to the paramount chiefs of other islands, urging them to organize multisettlement drinking parties, to exhort the people to go to war (Anon. 1988[1620]: 184). Once a date and place had been agreed upon, war leaders exhorted their followers to produce large quantities of weapons, mainly war clubs, bows, and poisoned arrows. War leaders also had their followers prepare abundant provisions, mostly cassava bread, fresh manioc tubers, and mashed manioc to mix with water when preparing manioc beer (Anon. 1988[1620]: 184).

Before departing for war, a leader would organize a second drinking party where logistics were worked out—which settlement to attack and what strategy to be followed. These tactical discussions, sometimes very prolonged, were held in a secret language, known only to well-established warriors, to prevent women, children, and captives from learning their designs (Rochefort 1666[1658]: 261). The same war language was also used in the harangues that prestigious leaders made during war-convoking feasts (Breton 1665: 376). The organization of Kalinago war expeditions demanded not only much military planning but also collective and individual spiritual preparation. In the drinking party held prior to the raiders' departure, the war leader consulted Kalinago shamans (*piayé/*

boyé) to inquire about the success of the expedition (Du Tertre 1654: 446; De la Borde 1886[1674]: 234). Individual warriors used magical substances to enhance their prowess and diminish the risks of war (Anon. 1988[1620]: 185, 192–193).

Kalinago expeditions to attack the Lokono and other mainland peoples were often composed of up to 40 war canoes, each carrying from 25 to 30 warriors, making a joint force of up to 1,200 warriors (Anon. 1988[1620]: 185). Although this figure seems excessive, it fits well with what we know of the shorter-distance expeditions to the Greater Antilles, which involved up to 350 warriors (see above). Possibly, however, the Kalinago joint force never acted in unison during the largest of these expeditions, scattering instead all along the littoral to attack different coastal and inland settlements. Be that as it may, it is clear that mobilizing such large numbers of people required a degree of planning and coordination well beyond that demanded by the raiding parties characteristic, for instance, of historical Yanomami, Jivaroan, and Tupi-Guaraní peoples.

Kalinago people had two types of boats: small dugout canoes and larger vessels used for long-distance war and trading expeditions (see Figure 2). This latter type, we are told, was fitted with masts and sails (Alvarez Chanca 1978[1494]: 30; Rochefort 1666[1658]: 320; Breton 1665: 108). War canoes could carry a retinue of 60 men and more and could travel two hundred and even three hundred leagues into the sea. Building such large canoes required the concerted effort of many men under the leadership of the man who convoked them, who accrued much prestige from this activity (Anon. 1988[1620]: 176). Some war canoes were decorated with designs of emblematic animals, as well as with body parts taken from the enemy and displayed as war trophies (Labat 1724[1705]: I, Part 2, 11–12). The use of smoked enemy body parts doubtless was intended to instill terror on whatever enemy crossed their path. War canoes were so esteemed that after a successful raid, canoe captains organized a drinking party in honor of their canoes (Anon. 1988[1620]: 186–187).

All authors coincide in that Kalinago raiders never attacked their enemies in the open but always relied on an element of surprise (Breton 1665: 375; Rochefort 1666[1658]: 321). They preferred to attack on nights with a full moon (Du Tertre 1654: 447). When they first reached an enemy village, they spied on its inhabitants to learn about their comings and goings, as well as their defenses (Anon. 1988[1620]: 186; Labat 1724[1705]: II, Part 4, 114). Once they had learned about their enemies' defenses and weak points, they waited until everybody had gone to sleep and then attacked in the middle of the night. They entered into the houses of their enemies and took as many people as possible, including newborns. If perchance they were discovered before the attack, they would shout wildly, hoping to frighten their enemies and create chaos (Breton 1665: 375). When attacking houses surrounded by palisades, they threw burning arrows on the thatched roofs, forcing people out (Rochefort 1666[1658]: 321).

Except when their lives were at risk, the Kalinago are said to have refrained from killing enemy people; the aim of their raids was to capture men, women, and children alive (Anon. 1988[1620]: 186). Other authors insist that they killed everybody who resisted them, taking as many young women, children, and adult males as possible (Breton 1665: 375). If they had had a clear victory, they stopped, according to Rochefort, to behead and skin the enemies they had killed, taking their heads and skins with them as war trophies. If the enemy resisted and wounded one of their warriors, the wounded man's companions did their utmost to rescue him, for they considered it outrageous to abandon a comrade-in-arms in the hands of the enemy (Rochefort 1666[1658]: 322; Martire d'Anghiera 1966[1555]: 80r–81v).

Kalinago raids were not aimed at abducting a few solitary women returning home from their gardens—as is the case among many historical tropical American indigenous societies. Neither were the raids intended to appropriate the land of their enemies. Instead, we are told, "all their wars had no other objective than to exterminate the enemy in revenge for injuries they believed they had received from them" (Du Tertre 1654: 449). Thus, prior to their retreat, they threw a volley of incendiary arrows on the thatched houses to set the enemy village on fire if they had not done it before. Apparently, not all the peoples that Kalinago raided were passive victims, however. Lokono, one of the Kalinago's preferred enemies, responded fiercely to attacks by the Kalinago, often taking them prisoners and subjecting them in turn to ritual killing and cannibalistic consumption (Breton 1978[1647]: 76–77). A seventeenth-century engraving from a Dutch travel report illustrates the torments to which the Carib-speaking Kalinago and Kari'na were subjected when captured by the Lokono (see Figure 3).

Once the raiders returned home, they distributed their war captives (Anon. 1988[1620]: 187). The fate of the captives varied according to gender and ethnicity. Men and boys destined to be eventually consumed in cannibalistic ceremonies were more or less equally divided between the captains who had provided the war canoes and the warriors who had taken them prisoner. Women and girls were mostly kept by war captains as household servants and concubines. African captives were retained by whoever had captured them for use as field laborers and domestics. The same applied to European captives. Thus the distribution of captives largely benefited war leaders, who, we are told, kept one of every two or three prisoners of war (Anon. 1988[1620]: 174).

Almost no demographic information exists to determine the weight of the captive population in Kalinago society. However, Alvarez Chanca (1978[1494]) provides some fragmentary data that can be used to produce at least a gross estimate. He mentions that when he and his party visited Guadeloupe, they encountered few men, most of them, numbering about 300, having departed on a raid to neighboring islands (Alvarez Chanca 1978[1494]: 32; F. Columbus 1992[1539]: 113). Only women, plus a few men, were left behind to keep watch over the captives and protect their settlements. Alvarez Chanca asserts that as soon as they had landed, captive women and boys—whom they recognized by the lack of leg ligatures or their having been emasculated—deserted their masters and joined them voluntarily. Among the captives who joined the Spanish, Alvarez Chanca (1978[1494]: 26, 28, 30, 32) lists around 40 women and young men. If we assume that each of the 300 warriors was the head of a family of 5, that would give us a total population of 1,500 inhabitants. If we also assume that not all captives were able to join the Spanish and that only half did so, then the proportion of captives with respect to the total population ($n = 1,580$) must have been around 5 percent. In later times, the percentage of slaves must have increased substantially as a result of the incorporation into the system of large numbers of captives of African origin.

After contact with Europeans, the most radical innovation the Kalinago made in their patterns of capture and servitude was to assign a special place to African and European captives. Black men were excluded from the symbolic system of reciprocal war cannibalism that linked Kalinago with their preferred enemies, the Arawak-speaking Taino and Lokono (Anon. 1988[1620]: 187). The same was true of white men (Breton 1978[1647]: 77). Kalinago also excluded African people, but not white people, as potential marriage partners (Labat 1724: I, Part 2, 26). Clearly, this is an intriguing case of adoption and adaptation of analogous European forms of servitude by an Amerindian people. Kalinago called both African and

European captives *támon*, as they called their Amerindian captives, but their rights, functions, and ultimate fate where closer to those of African slaves in French and English plantations than to those of Amerindian captive slaves. Interestingly enough, both forms of servitude, native and foreign, subsisted side by side in Kalinago society without apparent contradictions for several centuries.

The prestige of a Kalinago man and his chances of advancement within his society depended entirely on his warring abilities. High-ranking Kalinago men offered their daughters to the young warriors who had proven to be the most courageous in war (Rochefort 1666[1658]: 333). The braver a man was, the more wives he could obtain, and the larger his household would become. Doubtless, this increased his possibilities of founding a new settlement and of becoming a war leader. Cowards, in contrast, were ignored; they encountered difficulties in finding wives.

Kalinago believed that whenever a man's will to go to war wavered, Maboya, a demonic being, beat him in his dreams, both to punish him and to motivate him to go to battle (Rochefort 1666[1658]: 282). They also believed that the souls of courageous warriors went to dwell in a paradisiacal island after death, where they passed the time dancing, playing, and feasting and were served by numerous Arrouague (Lokono) and African slaves. In contrast, the vital essences of those who "were cowardly and afraid to go to the wars against their Enemies, do after death serve the Arouagues, who inhabit barren and desert Countries beyond the Mountains" (Rochefort 1666[1658]: 289). In summary, then, the capacity to wage war was a constitutive aspect of Kalinago manhood. And the taking of captives, whether as trophies, servitors, or concubines, was a key element in increasing the prestige of a Kalinago man and, with it, his possibilities of becoming a settlement founder and a war leader.

CONIBO

The Conibo were engaged in large-scale warfare against their riverine neighbors of the Ucayali basin from at least the mid-1500s, when Spanish explorers found large tracts of uninhabited lands separating Conibo territory from that of their traditional riverine enemies, the Cocama and Piro. These no-man's-lands functioned as buffer zones and resting points for raiding parties. Warfare continued to be a central aspect of Conibo life in the late 1600s, when they were recontacted by the Spanish. Conibo people formed part of a heterogeneous regional power system within which they competed for supremacy with the equally powerful Cocama and Piro and constantly raided their weaker semi-riverine and interfluvial neighbors. Fellow Panoan peoples such as the Cashibo, Amahuaca, Remo, Sensi, Capanahua, Mochobo, and Comabo, and the Arawak-speaking Campa (Asháninka, Ashéninka, Machiguenga, and Nomatsiguenga), were favorite targets of Conibo raiders. According to missionary Manuel Biedma (1981[1682]: 95), at the time Conibo were contacted by the Spanish in the 1680s, they were constantly harassing Campa people, capturing their children and killing the old men and women who could not "serve them as slaves." By then, another source stated, Conibo possessed "many slaves from other nations, which they had captured . . . in their raids" (Maroni 1988[1738]: 286). Jesuit missionaries used these captives as sources for learning more about the inland peoples and as middlemen for contacting them.

Two separate Franciscan witnesses reported the first Conibo slave raid for which we have detailed information (Beraún 1981a[1686]; Huerta 1983[1686]). After briefly visiting the mission of San Miguel—by then under dispute with the Jesuits—the Franciscan missionaries asked their Conibo hosts to take them upriver to Campa territory—along the Ucayali and Tambo rivers and up to the mouth of the Perené River—a trip of at least six hundred kilometers. The Conibo organized a large expedition of 18 to 22 canoes manned by 66 warriors armed with bows and arrows, spears, war clubs, and "shields made of bamboo covered with hides of jaguars, pigs [*Pecari tajacu*] and boars [*Tayassu pecari*]" (Beraún 1981b[1686]: 181; Huerta 1983[1686]: 123). Departing on September 19, 1686, the fleet did not arrive at the Perené River until October 12, twenty-three days later. Once the Conibo fleet entered the Tambo River, marking the beginning of Campa territory, warriors began pillaging all the settlements they encountered on both sides of the river.

The Conibo fleet advanced with great fanfare, its members shouting at each other and playing their horns, flutes, and drums (Huerta 1983[168]: 123). Wherever they landed, the Spanish reported with disapproval, they sacked the houses, taking as many captives as they could. After each raid, "one or two canoes returned home filled with clothes and prisoners" (Beraún 1981a[1686]: 177). This would explain why there were so few warriors per canoe at the time of departure (three or four men). The idea, it seems, was to be lightly loaded while navigating upriver, in order to be able to return downriver as soon as any given canoe was filled to the brim with captives and loot. In effect, by the time the fleet reached the Perené

River, where the Franciscans had to disembark, only six canoes were left to accompany them, and all were loaded with booty.

Plundered items included clothes—the male cotton tunics and female wraparounds decorated with geometric designs used by most riverine Ucayali people—as well as blankets, feather headdresses, valuable ornaments, and salt (Amich 1975: 97, 100). So abundant were the textiles pillaged from their neighbors, Franciscan friars recounted, that Conibo women no longer bothered to weave (Beraún 1981b[1686]: 181). A hundred years later, the situation had changed very little. It was still being reported that Conibo women "do not spin or work on anything else aside from their gardens; nor do they use any clothes other than those that their husbands, fathers, or kinsmen steal from their enemies in their raids" (Amich 1975: 93).

In addition to a large amount of booty, the participants of the 1686 raiding expedition took with them more than 40 captives, mostly women and children (Huerta 1983[1686]: 124). If we assume that the 66 Conibo warriors involved in the raid were heads of households composed of a minimum of 5 members—giving us a total of 330 persons—then captive slaves represented about 10 percent of the total population ($n = 370$). If we further assume that these warriors already possessed captives before engaging in this particular expedition, we must inevitably conclude that the percentage of slaves in Conibo society was probably above 10 percent. Slave raiding was thus a large-scale phenomenon and a standard feature of Conibo social landscape.

We must, however, distinguish raids against the Campa and other weaker peoples from raids against the Piro and Cocama, with whom Conibo people were engaged in a long-standing contest for dominance in the Ucayali River basin. Whereas raids against the former produced large numbers of captives, attacks against the Piro and Cocama had much more balanced results. In 1686, at the same time as the above-mentioned raid against the Campa, the Conibo of San Miguel organized an expedition against the Piro of the Urubamba River under the leadership of one of the three chiefs who shared power in this large aggregate settlement. Composed of 180 warriors in 30 war canoes, the Conibo force attacked a large Piro settlement located at the mouth of the Anapati River (Amich 1975: 108). The approximately 200 Piro living in this settlement fought fiercely against the invaders with even results: on one side, eight dead Piro and two captives; on the other side, one dead Conibo, albeit an important personage, no less than the paramount war chief. Clearly, then, raids against both powerful and weak neighbors could be large-scale endeavors, but their aims and results could also be very different. Assaults on powerful enemies were aimed at revenging past grievances and maintaining the balance of power and the status quo. In contrast, raids against weaker peoples had as their main objective the destruction of particular enemy settlements and the capture of large numbers of people, even though they were equally inscribed in a similar logic of interethnic vengeance cycles.

Conibo raiding was a seasonal affair. They attacked some interior peoples, such as the Mayoruna, at the end of the rainy season, when the latter were still living in scattered small settlements, but the Conibo avoided those peoples during the dry season, when they congregated in large numbers along the banks of the Ucayali River to fish (Sandi 1905[1865]: 252–253). Nevertheless, most Conibo carried out their raids during the dry season. These engaged numerous warriors for long periods, often all the adult men of a village (Maroni 1988[1738]: 291). Two hundred years later, this feature of Conibo seasonal raiding persisted. A contemporary observer asserted that during the dry season all Conibo people went out on raiding expeditions, with "not a living soul remaining in their houses, for they embark on their canoes not only all members of their family, but also their dogs and other domestic animals, if they have them" (Samanez y Ocampo 1980[1884]: 81; see also Sabaté 1877: 177).

Raiding parties could vary considerably in size. Expeditions against powerful enemies could invoke almost 200 men in 30 canoes. Such large undertakings were still commonly held in the last quarter of the nineteenth century. Sabaté (1877: 111) reports having seen a fleet of 31 Conibo canoes carrying numerous well-armed warriors who were "traveling at full speed, with rage and barbarian spite, to avenge themselves satisfactorily against their enemies, the Ipitineris [Amahuaca]." However, there were also smaller raiding/trading expeditions comprising 7 to 10 canoes and as few as 30 men (Huerta 1983[1686]: 118; Herndon and Gibbon 1854: I, 200; Sabaté 1877: 149). Such incursions expressed the fundamentally unbalanced nature of Conibo raiding and captive slavery. In the first of two lesser raids mentioned by Marcoy, Conibo raiders attacked an Amahuaca settlement whose inhabitants had allegedly stolen plantains from their gardens; the Conibo took loot and several captives in compensation (Marcoy 1869[1847]: I, 629, 642). In the second, they assaulted a group of Remo accused of stealing a Conibo canoe. Although they could not take any captives, they pillaged their settlement and burned it to the ground. Clearly, then, Conibo raids were not about replacing slain fellow tribesmen by captive enemies. Rather they were about taking as many persons captive and about causing as much damage to the enemy as possible.

To increase their probabilities of success, Conibo sometimes invited one or other of their powerful riverine enemies to join them in attacking the inland peoples (Wertheman 1905[1877]: 202). In the early 1800s the Franciscans reported a joint Conibo-Piro raid against the Sensi (Alcántara 1900[1810]: 455) and, shortly after, a Conibo, Shipibo, Piro, and Omagua raid against the Mayoruna (Alcántara 1900[1810]: 80). In a joint expedition that took place in 1878, the Conibo and Shipibo outfitted "hundreds of canoes" to attack a large Amahuaca group that had recently expelled the Franciscan missionaries and was thus left unprotected (Amich 1975: 424). By then, many Conibo possessed shotguns, assuring them an additional advantage over their traditional inland enemies (Samanez y Ocampo 1980[1884]: 83). Given the scale of Conibo attacks against their weaker neighbors, it is not surprising that the Remo, Amahuaca, and Cashibo were on the verge of extinction by the late 1800s (Amich 1975: 293, 373).

To ensure a victory, Conibo raids were preceded by several magic rituals. Before departing, expedition leaders—probably with the aid of Conibo shaman-diviners (*mueraya*)—consulted the *reco* (or *reccu*), a rare silkworm (unidentified, but probably the caterpillar of a large moth), which they believed could predict the outcome of future raids (Alcántara 1900[1810]: 456). Any man who had found a *reco* in the forest would carry it in a tiny basket hanging from a necklace. Before undertaking an expedition, the raiders took the *reco* in procession around the public plaza. If it wriggled within its cocoon, the claim was that they would defeat their enemies.

Conibo war expeditions could last from several weeks to four months (Amich 1975: 297). Each year, hundreds of Conibo canoes departed from the Ucayali toward the Urubamba or Tambo rivers to raid their enemies (Samanez y Ocampo 1980[1884]: 82). While away, Conibo warriors experienced many hardships, the lack of food being the most important. Raiding parties carried with them great quantities of green plantains but no other food, relying for survival mainly on what they could hunt, fish, or steal en route. Some authors assert that, for this reason, Conibo warriors sometimes waited until the beginning of the rainy season to go on raiding expeditions. At that time of the year, the gardens of their enemies were ready to harvest, and they could feed themselves by pillaging (DeBoer 1986: 233).

Along the Urubamba, Tambo, and Ene rivers, Conibo people attacked Piro and Campa riverine settlements. Along the Ucayali, however, which they dominated, they assaulted the peoples who lived on its tributaries and in the interfluves. Conibo fleets navigated upriver along the tributaries of the Ucayali in search of enemy settlements. If they could not find any riverine villages on the banks, they would send scouts to explore the interior. When they encountered jungle trails or signs of enemy activity, they regrouped and followed their enemies' tracks (Anon. 1905[1826]: 261). All attacks were carried out at night. On their way to the target settlement, the raiders would blow a magical powder in its direction, to make their enemies fall fast asleep (Alcántara 1900[1810]: 456). They walked carefully, to avoid traps such as the pits lined with sharp poisoned stakes that Mayoruna people dug along the trails leading to their houses (Sotomayor 1905[1899]: 358).

When approaching an enemy settlement, Conibo raiders walked in a row. They carried, hanging from their backs, certain sticks that glowed tenuously in the dark, allowing them to see each other (Alcántara 1900[1810]: 456). To distinguish friends from enemies, they wore elaborate headdresses made of white feathers that could be seen in the dark. They approached the enemy settlement in silence, breaking into their houses, scattering the logs in the hearth, and clubbing whoever dared to confront them. If the settlement consisted of a walled longhouse, Conibo raiders shot burning arrows into the thatched roof to force out their enemies (Alcántara 1900[1810]: 80). According to a Shipibo-Conibo oral account (Roe 1982: 84), when the enemies fled from the burning house, the raiders hastened to capture the children: "Some of our tribesmen grabbed two, some three, some only one. Those that did not get any began to fight with those who had many. Therefore, he who had two gave one to him who had none."

On other occasions, Conibo took advantage of their enemies' seasonal activities to attack them by surprise. When hundreds of thousands of giant Amazonian river turtles (*Podocnemis expansa*) started nesting along the banks of the region's larger rivers during the dry season, Cashibo family groups moved from the interior to the shores of the Pachitea River to gather them (Marcoy 1869[1847]: II, 295). Such collecting forays were generally undertaken in nights of full moon for greater visibility. They were rather simple, requiring overturning the turtles, some measuring up to three feet long and weighing over 150 pounds. Cashibo hunters also collected turtle eggs. When finished, they would make a hole on the beach and cover themselves with sand and leaves to avoid the abundant mosquitoes. Since these giant turtles frequented the same beaches year after year, the sites visited by Cashibo turtle hunters were well known to Conibo raiders. Following the forested edge along the low river, the attackers approached the site when the Cashibo were asleep. Whoever tried to escape into the forest was clubbed or taken captive. Captured men were tortured and killed, whereas women and children were kept as captive slaves. The French traveler Paul Marcoy has left us an impressive visual record of one such nocturnal raid. Whether he witnessed it personally or reconstructed it on the basis of oral information is not, however, entirely clear (see Figure 4).

Conibo raiders killed all adult males encountered, because, according to some sources, male prisoners always tried to escape. Ordinaire (1887: 288) provides an alternative explanation that expresses a more indigenous point of view. He claims that Conibo raiders killed the fathers, brothers, and husbands of the women they captured to avoid future enemy claims on the captive women and also to make it easier for the latter to put their past behind them and embrace their new life without resistance. Most authors suggest that the main objective of Conibo raids was the capture of women, attributing this practice to Conibo polygyny, which tended to concentrate women in the hands of older men, leaving younger men without eligible marriage partners (Amich 1975: 298; Buenaventura Bestard 1906[1819]: 345–346; Raimondi 1905[1862]: 219; Ordinaire 1887: 288). A nineteenth-century engraving by Marcoy shows, in somewhat idealized form, a Conibo man with what seems to be one such captive woman (see Figure 5). A careful reading of the sources demonstrates, however, that the capture of children was as important as the abduction of women, if not more so. Women, therefore, were not the Conibo's main target. In this sense, Unánue (1924[1793]: 286) was more accurate when he asserted that the objective of Conibo raiding was to capture as many persons as possible, to assimilate them, and thus to "increase the nation" (more on this in Chapter 9).

Equally important to Conibo raiding was the taking of body trophies. Although this practice seems to have been abandoned in the nineteenth century, evidence indicates that in the 1600s and 1700s the taking of body parts of slain enemies as war trophies was a key dimension of Conibo warfare. Conibo raiders allegedly mixed the blood of the enemy warriors they had killed with manioc beer and drank it, before beheading them (Biedma 1981[1682]: 95). They subjected fallen enemies to insults and ritual debasement that lasted a whole night (Amich 1975: 108). When Conibo raiders returned home, they took with them the heads and hearts of the enemies they had killed. Once desiccated, the body parts were hung from the rafters of their houses. The more heads and hearts they accumulated, the braver they were considered by their fellows (Biedma 1981[1682]: 95).

If they had been successful, Conibo raiders announced their victory with a roll of drums whenever they passed a friendly settlement on their way back home (Amich 1975: 373). No sooner had they arrived home than they heaped all the spoils they had obtained on the village's central plaza, to display them for all to see (Alcántara 1900[1810]: 456). Their wives prepared for them a special manioc beer mixed with very hot peppers, a beverage that induced heavy vomiting intended to purge any witchcraft that the enemy might have done to them (Alcántara 1900[1810]: 456). According to a more recent source, this emetic drink was also meant to purge the aggression from the raiders' bodies so they could reenter society in peace (Roe 1982: 84, 319). A drinking party that lasted several days followed, during which time the raiders recounted their deeds, boasting about their prowess and displaying the war trophies that they had taken. If any of their own raiders had been killed by the enemy, their companions did everything possible to bring their corpses back home (Amich 1975: 108). During the victory celebration, they held a funerary banquet to placate the manes of the deceased, who could otherwise come back to haunt the living (Samanez y Ocampo 1980[1884]: 81).

Courage and success in war were integral aspects of Conibo ideals of manhood. Only hardworking and courageous men, we are told, were able to secure a wife within the tribe. The lazy and cowardly had to content themselves with captive concubines (Sotomayor 1905[1899]: 356–357). Polygyny was very common, but whereas most men had no more than two wives, war leaders had three or more (Ordinaire 1887: 307; Díaz Castañeda 2001[1912]: 350; Sala 1897: 79–80). It is also affirmed that intertribal trading was in the hands of the bravest and most powerful men (Dueñas 1924[1792]: 248). The highest expression of Conibo ideals of manhood was their conception of the land of the dead as a celestial abode where they would spend most of their time fighting in tournaments and duels, while beautiful women served them heaps of food and vast quantities of drink (Marcoy 1869[1847]: I, 671).

* * *

The Kalinago and Conibo cases demonstrate that in societies occupying a hegemonic position within regional interethnic power systems, raids were not the kind of small-scale, random, and opportunistic attacks typical of societies involved in homogeneous regional systems. They were not "village affairs" that involved small parties of a few warriors belonging to the same local group and that aimed at abducting only a few women and children from a neighboring enemy settlement, whether they belonged to the same or another tribe (Boomert, in Benjamin 1987: 8).

This is not to claim that Kalinago and Conibo never engaged in small-scale raiding aimed at avenging a particular death or a theft. They certainly did. But this kind of raid—having specific objectives, requiring little organization, and lasting a short time—was unusual. More often, Kalinago and Conibo engaged in seasonal raiding, as did other societies in the sample. These were large-scale endeavors requiring the mobilization of considerable numbers of warriors from more than one settlement under the leadership of a paramount war chief. More importantly, they were not undertaken as a response to particular attacks or conflicts but were organized on an annual basis, frequently during the dry season.

Long-distance expeditions of this kind demanded a great deal of planning, gathered intelligence, and attention to logistics. The objective was the destruction of specific enemy settlements—always from a foreign tribe—singled out in advance by spies and scouts. In such attacks, the raiders killed all adult enemies, took body trophies from fallen adversaries, captured a few warriors to be ritually sacrificed, and took as many children and young women as possible to be raised as captive slaves.

Relationships between hegemonic and subordinate peoples were not, however, always hostile; at times seasonal raiding and pillaging alternated with trading. In the case of the historical societies analyzed here, these relationships can in no way be considered as being based on reciprocal exchange, as some authors analyzing blood feuding and interethnic raiding in contemporary Amazonia have proposed (e.g. Lévi-Strauss 1943; Menget 1985; J. B. Ross 1988; Erikson 2000). In capturing societies, the purpose of warfare was always conceived of as avenging past wrongs and deaths in the hands of the enemy, but there is little evidence for the existence in these historical societies of "a-captive-for-a-deceased" ideology typical of the Txicão (Menget, in Erikson 2000: 17). Vengeance was the justification rather than the ultimate end of large-scale raiding.

Moreover, in most instances, as we shall see, the warring parties were involved in an unequal balance of power in which predation and the exercise of violence was mostly unidirectional. Only in a few cases—such as the Kalinago and their Taino and Lokono adversaries—did the peoples at war consider each other as "privileged enemies" with similar military capacities (see Menget 1996: 141). Thus, rather than privileged enemies, the weaker societies on which these hegemonic groups preyed could be more precisely represented as "privileged victims."

CHAPTER 3

Servant Groups

When a people was conquered, it was by definition the conquerors who were
outsiders to the local community and the conquered who were the natives. In
this situation one of the fundamental elements of slavery—natal alienation—
was almost impossible to achieve either intrusively or extrusively.

—ORLANDO PATTERSON, *Slavery and Social Death*

The appropriation of enemy land was not usually the main
objective of Amerindian warfare in postcontact times (Evans
1971: 1416). There is evidence, nonetheless, that in precontact
times this was an important cause for large-scale wars of
conquest and defense (Roosevelt 1993: 260). The fragmentation and
broad dispersal of indigenous groups belonging to the same language
families throughout tropical America suggest that in pre-Columbian times
there was some sort of competition for land—possibly for the most fertile
and productive lands—that gave rise to out-and-out wars of expansion.
In such a historical scenario, migrating peoples were either collectivities
waging war against native populations to occupy their territories, or
displaced peoples escaping from expanding groups who had invaded their
lands. Even if we were to assume that the search for better lands was not
the main cause of all prehistoric Amerindian migrations, as Heckenberger
(2002) has suggested, we still would have to conclude that, whatever
may be the reasons behind these migrations, they must have entailed
some sort of confrontation between migrating and resident populations.
The victorious invaders often ended up displacing or subjugating native
populations during these encounters.

In historical times, these vast population movements went undetected
because early European chroniclers saw only a temporal slice of
indigenous regional power systems—a view that prompted the illusion
that these systems were in a state of equilibrium. Even in contact times,
however, evidence exists that at least some large Amerindian populations
were locked in a struggle over land and military supremacy. This was

certainly the case of Carib- and Arawak-speaking peoples in both Guiana and the Antilles. According to a tradition collected from the Kalinago of St. Vincent, their ancestors had moved from Guiana to the Lesser Antilles to escape domination by the Lokono Arawak (Rochefort 1666[1658]: 208). At the time of contact, the displaced Kalinago had in turn displaced the Arawak inhabitants of the Lesser Antilles and were expanding northward. Some Kalinago groups had even managed to settle in parts of Hispaniola, the center of the large Taino archipelagic polity (C. Columbus 1991[1493]: 329–331; Fernández de Oviedo 1851[1548]: I, 65).

In postconquest times, European presence triggered its own migratory movements, with groups trying to escape from colonial oppression clashing with more remote indigenous peoples and often subjugating them. This was the case of the Tupi-speaking Oyampi, who around 1780 left their lands along the Lower Amazon River to escape from Portuguese pressures and moved to Guiana, where they subjugated or displaced the Carib-speaking Roucouyenne and the Tupi-speaking Emerillons (Coudreau 1893: 558–563). According to Coudreau (1893: 282–283), the defeated Emerillons opted to become "vassals" of the Oyampi rather than migrating. If we disregard Coudreau's use of the term "'vassals," which brings to mind unbefitting images of feudal domination, we can assert that in tropical America the subjection of native populations, and their incorporation into the conquering society as a lowly stratum of servants, was a common outcome of indigenous wars of expansion.

The situation that resident peoples vanquished by expanding groups found themselves in differed greatly, however, from that of war captives taken in seasonal raids. In kin-based societies, captives taken in war were removed from their families, their land, and their people, a phenomenon that Patterson (1982: 5) has labeled "natal alienation." The alienation and depersonalization of war captives facilitated both their submission—they had nowhere to go and no one to go to—and their repersonalization as slaves, a first step leading to their integration and eventual assimilation. As Patterson (1982: 111) points out, conquered populations could not be alienated to the same degree as war captives. In such situations, defeated peoples could be sold as slaves in block, with colonists taking their place on the conquered lands, or they could be incorporated as subject populations. The first alternative—common in Roman times—was alien to native tropical American peoples, who did not use money and did not have a market economy. In contrast, the second alternative was widely practiced in the region, even though it has received very little attention in the specialized literature.

The subjection of the original inhabitants of the land as servant groups is a variation on the theme of captive slavery. In both forms of servitude, the basis for the relationship is warfare and the use, or threat of use, of force to oblige captives or subjects into obedience. The regime of capture and servitude characteristic of the two cases discussed below—Tukano and Chiriguaná—combines the taking of war captives with the subjection of local settlements as servant groups. The Tukano subjected small groups of hunters and gatherers, whereas the Chiriguaná subjected sophisticated horticulturalists, demonstrating clearly that this form of servitude cannot be attributed to any presumed difference in economic might or technological "evolution." At the same time, these contrasting examples provide a broad view of the flexibility underscoring this particular form of servitude.

TUKANO

The two most important nineteenth-century explorers of the Vaupés River basin—namely, Spruce (1908[1852]: I, 477) and Wallace (1853: 288)—noted that Makú and other hunting and gathering tribes were the objects of raids conducted by both Tukano and white people. It was Stradelli (1890[1882]: 445), however, who first noted that Tukano considered the itinerant Makú who roamed in the hinterland to be a "slave race." Tukano warriors, such as the ones depicted in an early twentieth-century photograph taken by Koch-Grünberg (see Figure 6), periodically raided Makú bands in search of captives. Stradelli (1890[1882]: 445) also suggested that Makú were the region's original inhabitants, having, later on, been conquered or displaced by one or more waves of invading Tukanoan and Arawakan peoples. Subsequent observers agreed with this interpretation (Coudreau 1887: II, 163; Nimuendajú (1950[1927]: 163–164).

The analysis of Makú and Tukano oral traditions has allowed modern authors to confirm this view. Giacone (1949: 88) informs us that Makú claimed to be the region's primitive inhabitants and that they were defeated by Tukano, who either enslaved them or expelled them from their lands. Knobloch (1972: 102), who collected a similar story, sees confirmation of this tradition in the fact that the Tukano name for the Vaupés River is Dya Poxsá—where *dya* means "river" and *poxsá* means "slave/servant," the exonym Tukano use to refer to Makú people. The Vaupés River would thus be the River of the Makú/Servants, its original inhabitants. Makú and Tukano myths of origin confirm oral tradition, reinforcing the notion that Makú were the region's native population, later displaced by invading Tukanoans and Arawakans who occupied the best riverine lands (Silverwood-Cope 1990: 73; S. Hugh-Jones 1988: 295).

Makú lived deep into the forest, in the headwaters of the tributaries of the Vaupés and Negro rivers during the late 1700s and early 1800s (Noronha 1862[1768]; Sampaio 1985a and 1985b[1775]). By the late 1800s, they were avoiding contact with Tukano people, who "held them in veritable captivity" (Stradelli 1890[1882]: 433). Stradelli is not precise about the characteristics of Makú "captivity," however. Other contemporary sources seem to be equally ambiguous. This apparent vagueness has created much confusion among modern authors as to the exact nature of the relationship between Tukano and Makú. The confusion, I would suggest, can be overcome through a historical approach to the problem. A closer look at the sources demonstrates, as Jackson (1983: 154) has already noted, that the relationship between Tukano and Makú varied significantly from place to place and throughout time.

According to Coudreau (1887: II, 160–164, 179), Makú people were involved in three types of servile situations. First, there were those Makú bands that had retained their autonomy but were regularly raided by Tukano in search of children captives, as exemplified by the Makú of the Upper Tiquié River. Second, there were those bands that had at some point been subjected by the force of arms and were attached to Tukano local groups as servants. This was the case with small Makú groups attached to the Cubeo and Baniwa of the Cuduiarí and Caiarí rivers, respectively. Finally, there were several groups of Makú or Makú-Tukano descent who, after adopting Tukano languages and customs, were integrated as low-ranking sibs with servant ceremonial status. The Sub-Wanano, Desana, and Juruparimira, attached to the Wanano, Tukano, and Tariana, respectively, are the best examples of such a situation.

Twenty years later, Koch-Grünberg (1906: 878–881) confirmed this social scenario but mentioned a fourth type of relationship that could be considered as a variation of Coudreau's second type. In addition to Makú captive slaves, Makú bands attached as servant groups, and Makú groups assimilated as low-ranking sibs, Koch-Grünberg encountered Makú bands on the Caiarí River who were from the Upper Papurí and who worked as client groups for the local Wanano and Desana seasonally rather than permanently. They toiled for their masters during several months every year, then returned to their lands.

These forms of servitude all have their origin in warfare and coercion. They can be considered to be transformations of each other along a temporal line. Raiding for individuals gave way to the wholesale subjugation of entire bands as attached servant groups, which in turn could give way either to relations of clientship and the prestation of seasonal services or to integration as low-ranking sibs. This progression did not, however, preclude the possibility that all four types of situations coexisted in time. The most common ties of subordination linking Makú to Tukano during the eighteenth and nineteenth centuries were captive slavery and group servitude. In contrast, the most common form of servitude in the twentieth century was group clientship.

Tukano raiding of Makú groups went hand in hand with intra-Tukano warfare. However, whereas violence against Makú people was aimed at creating or perpetuating links of subordination and servitude, intra-Tukano violence obeyed somewhat different rationales: disputes over lands and fisheries, wife capture, or theft of highly valued ritual paraphernalia (Giacone 1949: 14; Chernela 1993: 23; S. Hugh-Jones 1993: 109). The capture of people, land, resources, objects, or vitalities was common to both forms of warfare, but only warfare against Makú linked capture with the imposition of forms of servitude. Tukanoan peoples are reported to have practiced ritual anthropophagy and the taking of enemy body parts—especially hair, teeth, arm bones, genitals, and heads (Coudreau 1887: II, 177; Stradelli 1890[1882]: 436; Whiffen 1915[1908]: 122–124; Goldman 1963: 164). It is not clear, however, whether these symbolic exchanges were confined to intra-Tukano warfare or whether Makú people were also considered to be legitimate partners from which to capture vital essences.

In the mid-1800s, Makú bands attacked the villages of the riverine Tukano, searching for iron tools and other industrial goods (Wallace 1853: 508). In revenge, Tukano raided Makú camps to take women and children captives. This practice was so widespread that Wallace (1853: 508) asserted, "[I]n most [Tukano] villages you will see some of them." Even by the early 1900s, this situation had remained unchanged

(Koch-Grünberg 1906: 880). Makú captives taken in these raids worked for their masters as domestics or as laborers in their gardens. Tukano men could make use of Makú girls to satisfy their sexual desires (Whiffen 1915[1908]: 262; Biocca 1965: I, 471). Under no circumstances, however, did they marry Makú women. Tukano repugnance to marry Makú individuals has persisted until today, to the point that in a sample of 684 Tukano marriages taken by Jackson (1984: 172) in the early 1970s, only one was with a Makú partner. This did not hinder, however, sexual exchanges between Tukano and Makú. Thus Coudreau (1887: II, 161) asserts that Desana were a "mixture of Makú and other tribes." This ambivalence, pointed out by Reichel-Dolmatoff (1971: 19), is discussed in more detail in Chapter 7.

A portion of the Makú captives taken in raids were sometimes sold to white people in exchange for shotguns and other industrial goods. In fact, at the height of the rubber boom in the 1880s, some Tukano raiders were outfitted by Brazilian rubber patrons (Spruce 1908[1852]: I, 330; Wallace 1853: 362). By then, Makú boys and girls fetched high prices in the regional market and could each be exchanged for a rifle (Coudreau 1887: II, 179), a situation that has prompted some authors to suggest that Tukano people took Makú war captives mostly in response to the demands of white traders and rubber gatherers. However, Wanano oral tradition already mentions raids against Makú long before the rubber boom (Chernela 2001), and such raids were still common in the 1920s, long after the collapse of the rubber economy, casting doubt on this attribution.

In the late 1920s, Tukano continued to embark on long raiding expeditions to capture young Makú (McGovern 1927: 148). Some raids may have been undertaken in response to Makú looting of Tukano gardens, a practice common in times of famine (Kok 1925–1926: 624) and still common in more recent times (Silverwood-Cope 1990; Reid 1979). The purpose of such raids was not to take children for sale to white people but, rather, to keep them as captive slaves (McGovern 1927: 148). By then all Tukano malocas along the Papurí River had around five Makú captives each (McGovern 1927: 247). A contemporary source indicates that Tukano malocas in this region were composed of at most twelve families (Kok 1925–1926: 627). If we assume that each family had five members, this means that Makú captive slaves represented around 8 percent of the total population ($n = 65$). Probably this was a much lower figure than in earlier times, before Tukano people had been missionized.

The existence of Makú servant groups attached to Tukano malocas was as common as the possession of Makú captives. This practice must be taken into consideration when estimating the size of the servile population in Tukano society. Coudreau (1887: II, 179) reported that "[e]ach Vaupés nation has a certain number of Makú, which they treat almost as slaves, especially in the interior." The key to Coudreau's statement lies in the phrase "almost as slaves." He makes a clear distinction between war captives incorporated as slaves, and those other groups, attached to Tukano communities by links of servitude, who were not "slaves." A similar situation is reported on the Tiquié River, where Koch-Grünberg (1906: 880) found several Makú groups "living under the dominion of the Tukano and Tuyuka sedentary tribes." A photograph of a free Makú band from the Upper Tiquié River taken at around this time provides a general idea of the overall aspect of Makú servant groups (see Figure 7). Some Makú groups had been subjugated by force of arms in revenge for alleged sorcery attacks or for the pillaging of Tukano gardens and had been appended to the maloca of their captors. Others apparently surrendered voluntarily, often after long periods of being harassed or as a result of famine or other deprivations.

Koch-Grünberg (1995[1909]: II, 236) mentions one such case. In the Caiarí River he encountered a Makú band composed of twenty men, women, and children that had surrendered to the chief of a Desana maloca. The latter had kept five Makú men and their families for himself, had given two Makú to the headman of a neighboring maloca, and had distributed the remaining Makú among the other families of his maloca. If we assume that the Desana maloca was composed of the average twelve families—as indicated by Kok (1925–1926: 627)—having five members each, this would give us a total population of about sixty. If to this figure we add the average five captives per maloca mentioned above and the eighteen Makú that the Desana chief kept as servants ($n = 83$), then the proportion of persons living under servile conditions must have been around 28 percent. This is a much higher figure than the one found in societies that practiced only captive slavery.

The attached Makú servants lived not in the maloca itself but in temporary shelters in its vicinity. Here, Koch-Grünberg (1995[1909]: II, 236) says, they acted not as "domestic slaves" but rather as "day laborers," called upon only to render certain services. Voluntary submission of Makú groups to Tukanoan peoples in exchange for food, shelter, and protection from enemies persisted during the following decades (Goldman 1963:

105). In these instances, Makú groups surrendered their autonomy, but most of their members continued to live together despite having been distributed among different Tukano families. Thus, they were not alienated to the same degree as war captives.

In some areas, Makú captives and servant groups managed to regain their autonomy but maintained links of attenuated servitude—best characterized as ties of clientship—with their former Tukano masters. In the late 1800s, Coudreau (1887: II, 179) already mentions Tukano and Arawak local communities that had Makú "vassals" who did not live permanently with their masters but roamed the forests, changing dwellings frequently. Among the peoples he mentions as having Makú client groups are the Cubeo of the Cuduiarí River, the Desana of the Içana River, and the Baniwa of the Caiarí River. In the early 1900s, Makú groups living in the affluents of the Papurí River used to visit regularly the neighboring Desana and Wanano of the Caiarí River. After working several months for their hosts, they would once more disappear into the forest (Koch-Grünberg 1906: 881). These groups maintained their own leaders and a higher degree of autonomy, but even in situations of moderate servitude such as this, coercion, or the threat of coercion, continued to be a central feature of the relationship, as is reported in various sources (McGovern 1927: 177; Knobloch 1972: 106).

The position of Makú people in the Vaupés River basin in the 1940s was not uniform and was changing rapidly (Lowie 1948: 349–350). Raiding against Makú groups had become a thing of the past in most of the Vaupés region (Jackson 1983: 22). By then, all the Cubeo sibs of the Cuduiarí River had stopped keeping Makú captives (Goldman 1963: 106). On the Tiquié River small clusters of Makú continued to be attached to Tukano malocas as servant groups, obliged to render all kinds of services. But some of the groups that in past times had been linked to Desana local communities as servants had regained their autonomy and now acted as client groups (Giacone 1949: 7). On the Caiarí River also, Makú bands led an autonomous life as client groups, summoned only sporadically to perform special jobs (Lowie 1948: 349–350). By then, the relationship between Tukano and Makú had acquired a less authoritarian tenor. Makú individuals in a relation of clientship with Tukano groups began to be considered as "helpers" rather than "servants"; they were no longer "summoned" but were rather "invited" to work; and they did not work for food and shelter but were "compensated as day laborers"

(Giacone 1949: 7, 88; Lowie 1948: 349–350). One practice, however, remained unchanged: Tukano refused to intermarry with Makú, whether they be slaves, servants, or clients (McGovern 1927: 148).

The dissolution of ties of servitude between Tukano and Makú accelerated even more during the 1960s. The turning of some former servant groups into client groups continued to be quite common in this new phase (Silva 1962: 468; Biocca 1965: I, 185, 472; Reichel-Dolmatoff 1971: 19; Silverwood-Cope 1990: 29; Chernela 1993: 115). Other servant or client groups shook off Tukano dominance as soon as their masters lost power and were unable to retain them. One Makú client group, for example, abandoned the Wanano sib to which it was linked after most of the Wanano men left the village to work in the coca fields of Colombia in the 1970s (Chernela 1993: 137). Recently emancipated groups, we are told, were "resolutely xenophobic and refuse(d) all direct contacts with the rest of the world" (Terribilini and Terribilini 1961: 39; also Reid 1979). The relationship between Makú and Tukano in this new phase became one of exchange, resembling free trade, with the former providing services, forest resources, and specialized manufactures in exchange for cultivated foodstuffs and Western goods (Moser and Tayler 1963: 446; Silverwood-Cope 1990: 43, 71; Chernela 1993: 115). This latter-day transformation of the servile relationship between Makú and Tukano has provided the grounds for some authors to advance the notion that they enjoy a symbiotic relationship (Goldman 1963: 5; Reichel-Dolmatoff 1971: 18; S. Hugh-Jones 1988: 25; Ramos, Silverwood-Cope, and Oliveira 1980; Cabrera et al. 1999: 43).

However, these were not simply trading relationships between groups controlling different types of resources and dependent on each other for their subsistence. Symbiotic relations not only involved groups related to each other hierarchically but also took place within the old system of interethnic power relations. Thus most of the trading was carried out between Makú and Tukano groups linked by old ties of servitude (Silva 1962: 202). It is only in more recent times that Makú people have started trading not only with their "hereditary patrons" but also with other Tukano groups with whom they did not maintain patron-client relationships (Silverwood-Cope 1990: 71; Reid 1979). Old ties of clientship have increasingly come to resemble links of debt peonage based on *aviamento*, or *habilitación* (outfitting), common throughout Amazonia (Silverwood-Cope 1990: 71). The invading Tukano, however, continue to view and treat the native Makú as subordinates, despite the significant changes that have taken place in their relationship. This is also true of those Makú groups that, after undergoing a process of Tukanoization, were incorporated into the societies of their former masters as low-ranking sibs (see Chapter 8).

CHIRIGUANÁ

At the time of contact with the Spanish around 1526, Chiriguaná people had been settled in the Andean piedmont of southeastern Bolivia for less than fifty years. The earliest date when they are thought to have arrived in this area is sometime during the reign of Tupac Inca Yupanqui, circa 1471–1493 (see Chapter 1). Thus, in contact time, Chiriguaná were still in a process of vigorous geographical and political expansion. They had already occupied the headwaters of three important piedmont rivers and, in the process, had displaced or subjugated the native populations— a variety of mostly Arawak-speaking ethnic groups collectively known as Chané—as well as the highland Indians who had been settled by the Inkas in some of the same areas.

In some early traditions the Chiriguaná are said to have brought with them their women; in others, that they arrived in the region as an exclusively male army. These two possibilities are not mutually exclusive. Most probably, the Chiriguaná occupation of southeastern Bolivia did not take place as a result of a single migratory event. Rather, it was accomplished in various waves, some of which may have been largely male-dominated war expeditions, and others the movement of entire local groups. Most accounts, however, mention that many invading Chiriguaná took as wives women captured from vanquished native peoples. Spanish authorities estimated that by 1586 Chiriguaná people totaled four thousand men of war, half of them not pure Chiriguaná but the offspring of mixed marriages between Chiriguaná men and women from the various nations they had conquered (Suárez de Figueroa 1965[1586]: 405). Additionally, they had under their direct dominion several thousand Chané from the eastern plains, whom, we are told, "they call slaves." Under this term, the Spanish conflated both, prisoners taken in war and held as slaves, and subjected collectivities attached as servant groups. Captive slaves were eventually assimilated; with the passage of time, their descendants lost all memory of their origins. Servant groups, on the other hand, retained the stigma of their past and were not considered legitimate marriage partners, despite ultimately adopting the language and cultural practices of their conquerors.

Colonial authorities early on complained that the Chiriguaná were "unruly people" who raided the peoples of both the lowlands and the highlands to take captives either as slaves or to be eaten (Audiencia 1918–1922a[1564]: I, 133). News about Chiriguaná raids constantly appeared in subsequent governmental reports. It is claimed that some captives were killed and eaten in cannibalistic rituals. Like other Tupi-Guaraní-speaking peoples such as the Tupinambá, Chiriguaná were renowned, at least during the first decades of contact with the Spanish, for holding male captives for a while before executing them. This fueled the Spanish chroniclers' claim that war prisoners were kept alive to fatten them before eating them (Cañete 1921–1926[1560]: I, 349; Samaniego 1944[1600]: 485).

The symbolic meaning that anthropophagy may have had for Chiriguaná people remains obscure, however. Among the Tupinambá, a warrior who had captured an enemy had the right to appropriate his name as his own. His courage and prestige were measured by the number of enemy names he had accumulated during his lifetime (Abbeville 1614: 348). Possibly, the same applied to the Chiriguaná. But we will never know for sure because by the late 1500s Chiriguaná had stopped ritually eating their war prisoners. As soon as they learned in 1575 that their cannibalistic practices were the main argument Viceroy Toledo wielded to suppress them, Chiriguaná leaders hastened to send envoys to inform him that St. Jacques had beseeched them through visions not to eat human flesh (Ramírez de Quiñones 1918–1922a[1575]: I, 326).

Clearly, theirs was a stratagem used to persuade the viceroy, who was ready to head a large army and attack them, not to do so. In fact, reports on Chiriguaná anthropophagy continued to appear for years in official correspondence. The awareness that cannibalism was deeply offensive to the Spanish, and a strong ideological instrument used against them, must have, however, increased among the Chiriguaná during this period. By 1587, according to some authors (Díaz de Guzmán 1979a[1617]: 76), or by 1602, according to others (Barco Centenera 1836[1602]: 28), Chiriguaná had put an end to their exocannibalistic practices. From then onward, those captives who would have otherwise been consumed were either killed to take their heads as trophies (Díaz de Guzmán 1979a[1617]: 80) or sold as slaves to Spanish landowners and traders.

The Arawak-speaking Chané living along the Andean piedmont constituted the main victims of the invading Chiriguaná. Since before the arrival of the Spanish, Chiriguaná warriors had been expelling the Chané from their lands, pushing them toward the east, a process that continued in colonial times. Most Chané had by the mid-sixteenth century either been subjected as servant populations or displaced to the arid, sandy plains of the Parapetí River (Matienzo 1918–1922[1564]: I, 54). Chiriguaná attacks always took place at night, shortly before dawn, and always by surprise (Anon. 1941[1573]: 66; Polo de Ondegardo 1991[1574]: 136). One or more local settlements joined in the raids, with all able men participating. In times of war, entire villages were inhabited only by women and children (Lizárraga 1968[1603]: 151). To wage war, allied settlements chose a paramount war chief whose authority ended once the raid was over and the booty had been distributed (Mendoza 1976[1665]: 262). In some cases, however, war leaders were regional chiefs who had permanent authority over several local settlements.

All war activities entailed some degree of ritual preparation. Giannecchini (1996[1898]: 324) reports that before engaging in a war expedition, the paramount war chief organized a celebration to which he invited all the warriors from his and other settlements who had agreed to join him. On the day of the departure, women would perform a ritual dance, amid cries urging their sons, husbands, and brothers to kill their enemies and bring them captives (Thouar 1991[1887]: 58). Before the departure, the paramount war chief harangued his men one last time, inciting them to defend their wives and children, to be worthy descendants of their ancestors, to fight to the death, and never to allow themselves to become slaves (Thouar 1991[1887]: 58; Giannecchini 1996[1898]: 325). While the men were away, the women continued to perform daily marching around the central plaza, singing war songs entreating the Fox-God and the tutelary spirits, especially the morning sun, to help their men succeed (Corrado and Comajuncosa 1990[1884]: I, 46; Giannecchini 1996[1898]: 326–327; Thouar 1991[1887]: 57–59).

Spanish functionaries depicted Chané people, the Chiriguaná's main enemies, as "extremely docile people who pose no resistance" (Audiencia 1918–1922b[1595]: 241). This was probably more an excuse to present Chiriguaná as savage tyrants, thus justifying their enslavement, than a faithful portrayal of this Arawak-speaking group. In fact, we know that Chané people did not accept Spanish domination without resistance and that, once incorporated into Chiriguaná society, they fought as bravely as their masters. Chané society did not, however, promote military values; their men were not trained as soldiers from an early age, as Chiriguaná warriors were. Not surprisingly, they were thus easy prey for Chiriguaná groups who constantly assailed them.

After the adoption of the horse sometime along the mid-sixteenth century, Chiriguaná war parties were composed of both infantry and cavalry (Giannecchini 1996[1898]: 325). The infantry fought with bows and arrows, clubs, and long knives; the cavalry, with clubs and lances. Both infantry and cavalrymen wore tunics made of the hardened hide of a jaguar or bull, on top of the short cotton tunic or loincloth they used daily, as is depicted in a detailed engraving illustrating Thouar's travelogue (see Figure 8). To appear more ferocious, they painted their faces red or black, and their teeth blue (Viedma 1970[1788]: 757–758).

Before attacking, Chiriguaná raiders checked their enemies' routines and defenses by posting spies (Giannecchini 1996[1898]: 326–327). Once the day and time of the attack were decided, the assailants fell upon their enemies generally at dawn, amid fierce shouting and playing of war horns and war flutes that produced eerie sounds meant to terrorize the enemy. The most prestigious warriors (*queremba*) attacked first, followed by the cavalry, who killed as many enemy warriors as possible, and, finally, by the infantry, who did most of the slaying, sacking, and capturing. The attackers killed the old, the sick, and all others who could not flee. They sacked and burned their houses, destroying all things they could not carry away. They gathered all the fowl, cattle, and horses they could lay hands on, and if the enemy's maize gardens were ripe, they harvested all they could carry. Whatever they could not take with them, they smashed, killed, or burned. They also took as many captives as possible, especially children, but also young men and women. On their return, each warrior carried to their village all the possessions, animals, and captives he had managed to take. For, according to Chiriguaná custom, booty and prisoners belonged to whoever had captured them (Giannecchini 1996[1898]: 327). Whenever a Chiriguaná warrior was killed, his fellows strove to recover the dead man's body in order to carry it home with them (AGI 1735: fol. 56r).

If the settlement they had raided was close to home, they also brought back with them the heads of those enemies they had killed. If it was far from home, they brought only their *tembetá* (lip plugs) or earrings if the enemies were Chiriguaná—or their scalps if they were not (Giannecchini 1996[1898]: 328). The capture of these body trophies was as important as the taking of war captives (more on this in Chapter 9).

Captives remained the property of those who had captured them. They were handed to their wives to serve them as domestics (Thouar 1991[1887]: 59). War prisoners were insulted and maltreated during victory celebrations. On such festive occasions, many prisoners were sold, exchanged, or used as wagers in games of dice (Nino 1912: 279). After the celebrations ended, however, they were respected and provided for by their captors. Women remained the absolute owners of war captives, having the right to sell them to whomever they pleased or even to have them killed (Giannecchini 1996[1898]: 328). Chiriguaná captive slavery differed from that of other Tupi-Guaraní groups like the Tupinambá in that the latter ritually killed and consumed most captives, whereas the former kept them as domestics and eventually integrated them into their society (see Chapter 8).

Not all Chiriguaná raids ended in the massacre of the enemy and the enslavement of the survivors. Often, entire local groups chose to surrender, to avoid the loss of life and property entailed by waging war against such powerful enemies. These groups were generally resettled in the environs of the conquering Chiriguaná settlements. Chiriguaná used two terms to express the notion of subjection: *aimoauje* referred to the act of subduing an individual; *aitigc*, to the subjection of a collectivity, be it a village, enclosure, or army (Anon. 1938[1622]: 204). The latter, in turn, is related to two key verbs: *anhemõbiarijar rece*, meaning "to subject an individual or group to one's authority or lordship," and *aimõbirarijar*, meaning "to allow someone to lord over oneself, or to make someone one's lord" (Anon. 1938[1622]: 204). The existence of these two verbs indicates that the process by which entire local groups came under the influence of a given Chiriguaná chief was perceived not as a unilateral development but as a result of the merging of two wills: the Chiriguaná will to subject their enemies, and the enemies' will to make the Chiriguaná their lords. This explains why local groups subjected by Chiriguaná as servant populations often adopted the language and customs of their masters instead of adhering to their own cultural practices as a form of ethnic resistance.

The proportion of Chané servant groups in Chiriguaná society was very high. In 1586 it was reported that 4,000 Chiriguaná "men of war" (indicating a Chiriguaná population of 20,000, if we assume that each of them was the head of a family of 5) had in their service some 5,000 Chané (Suárez de Figueroa 1965[1586]: 405). This means that servile groups under Chiriguaná domination represented around 20 percent of the total population (*n* = 25,000). Another early source estimates that in five Chiriguaná settlements there were 1,500 Chiriguaná and at least 7,000 subordinates, making the servile population around 80 percent of the total (*n* = 8,500) (Arriaga 1974[1596]: 69). The great disparity revealed by these figures is not necessarily due to erroneous demographic estimates—although it is well known that European conquistadores and missionaries manipulated population figures to serve their own interests—but rather seems to express important differences at the local level.

The first detailed information by a witness to report on Chané servant groups confirms the above. In 1607 the Chiriguaná chief Cuñayurú complained to his Spanish allies that his enemies had "taken from him two slave towns and all his horses, mares, and much property" (Arteaga 1961[1607]: 174). The Spanish sent troops to support their ally. In his report of the expedition, Arteaga (1961[1607]: 175) informs that, despite heavy losses, the settlement of Cuñayurú had a population of 300 Chiriguaná and 100 "slaves." Some of these so-called slaves must have been war captives, but most were undoubtedly members of the attached Chané servant groups that chief Cuñayurú claimed to possess. Arteaga further reports that two of the Chiriguaná settlements that had joined chief Cuñayurú also had large numbers of Chané servants. Cuñayaba, we are told, had a population of 60 Chiriguaná and 150 slaves; whereas Tembero had 100 Chiriguaná and 500 slaves (Arteaga 1961[1607]: 172, 176). The proportion of servile population in Chiriguaná settlements may indeed have fluctuated between 25 and 80 percent. Unfortunately, the sources are mute on what percentage corresponded to captive slaves, and what to attached servant peoples.

The incorporation of such large numbers of people posed very different problems from those faced by societies that practiced captive slavery on a smaller scale. Chiriguaná people were extremely successful in integrating their servant Chané populations, to the point that today Chané do not exist as an autonomous, self-identified ethnic group. However, despite their adoption of Chiriguaná language and cultural practices, the descendants of former Chané servant groups still bear the stigma of their origin (see Chapter 8). Moreover, though Chiriguaná men used to take Chané women as spouses when they first arrived in the region, today the Ava-Chiriguaná (the "pure" Chiriguaná) and the Ava-Izoceño (the Chiriguanáized descendants of the Chané) distinguish between one another and do not intermarry.

* * *

The Tukano and Chiriguaná examples share numerous similarities. Both peoples were involved in processes of territorial expansion, and both were newcomers to the area where they finally settled. Both had better-trained warriors, and more experience in raiding, than the native peoples they met. In both instances, the invaders occupied the best lands, displacing those who still resisted to the periphery: the interfluves and headwater regions in the Tukano case, and the arid western fringes of the Grand Chaco in the Chiriguaná case. And, in both cases, the invaders managed to subject the local populations through the systematic and unrelenting force of arms, giving way to highly heterogeneous regional systems. Despite their marked asymmetry, however, both conquerors and conquered ideologically viewed their relationship as a confluence of wills, with the invaders perceiving themselves as imposing their dominion on the locals, and the natives viewing themselves as allowing the invaders to lord over them (see also Chapter 8). This willingness to surrender, which dumbfounded contemporary observers, apparently had little to do with the awe that the less technologically advanced are supposed to feel for the more developed. The Chané, for instance, made use of complex irrigation systems and were far better agriculturalists than the Chiriguaná (Riester et al. 1979: 263). Rather, their reactions responded to the secret admiration that warring peoples often elicit—albeit grudgingly—from those whose lives do not revolve around waging war.

Such covert admiration may explain, at least partially, why segments of the conquered population were willing quite rapidly to abandon their language and customs and adopt those of their defeaters. In this, however, the above examples differ to some extent. The Tukano never managed to completely subjugate the Makú; it is even doubtful whether this was ever their aim. Tukano language groups incorporated numerous Makú servant populations as low-ranking sibs, but many other groups became emancipated from them before becoming Tukanoized, or they never experienced direct military subjection. In contrast, the conquest of the Chané by the Chiriguaná, quite advanced at the time the Spanish arrived in southeastern Bolivia, was completed in the following centuries. As a result, by the time Chané servant groups started struggling for their emancipation in the late eighteenth century, they were completely Chiriguanáized (Mingo de la Concepción 1981[1797]: I, 368).

Servant populations differed from war captives in several respects. First, they were subjected as collectivities and not as individuals. They thus represented a large proportion of the total population; in some settlements they even surpassed their conquerors in numbers. Second, they were not displaced from their lands, although they were often resettled in the periphery of their conquerors' settlements or in areas close at hand, where their masters could easily maintain a hold on them. Finally, servant groups were allowed to retain their families, kinship networks, and even their headmen.

The circumstances that servant populations found themselves in, however, varied through time. In the earliest and harshest stages, vanquished groups were attached to the communities of the conquerors, where they were obliged to perform a variety of services for their masters (see Chapter 6). Makú servant groups provided most of the game meat consumed by their Tukano masters, whereas Chané servant groups performed most horticultural activities. In addition, a small number of individuals from these groups were assigned to live in particular households, where they worked as domestics under almost the same conditions as war captives. In exchange for their services, servant groups enjoyed the wealth acquired by their masters through war and pillaging, and they obtained protection from other capturing societies.

With the passage of time, the domination of those servants groups that had not been assimilated assumed a milder form. Subjected populations continued to be assigned to particular conquering groups, but they recovered a certain degree of political autonomy and had much more freedom of movement. They no longer were required to live next to their masters and could develop their productive activities independently. The master-servant relationship was activated either when the headman of the dominant group requested specific goods or services from the servant group or in bad times—spells of famine or interethnic hostilities—when servant groups resorted to their masters in search of food or protection. In such cases, the link between former masters and servants assumed the form of a patron-client relationship, based on the exchange of specialized products and services for shelter, food, and military safeguard. This situation has prompted some authors to characterize this milder version of the subjection of native populations as a symbiotic relationship.

In both the harsher and milder versions, the relationship between conquerors and conquered not only was markedly asymmetrical in political and ideological terms but also involved an important dose of coercion. Even in the more "symbiotic" version, where the element of compulsion was minimal, members of servant groups had to be at the beck and call of their masters; they simply could not refuse to comply with any of their demands. Generally, servant people were not ill-treated, yet they and their descendants continued to be considered inferior and were despised for having been conquered or for having been born as servants. Some servant groups adopted the language and customs of their masters; with the passage of time, they were assimilated into their masters' society. Even then, however, they were attributed a low status associated with the dishonor of having been conquered. This contempt found expression in the refusal to marry the offspring of former servants. In earlier historical stages, however, members of the conquering group felt no qualms in marrying them, as oral tradition establishes was the case of the Tukanoan Desana and the precolonial Chiriguaná. The ban against marrying former servant peoples marks an important difference from the situation that existed for tributary peoples—discussed in the next chapter—who not only allowed but in fact favored intermarriage between high-ranking members of the dominant and subordinate groups.

CHAPTER 4

Tributary Populations

Tribute relations can be understood as a form of exploitation which consists
of the regular appropriation of products from the conquered population
which for the most part retains its former economic and social structure.

—ABRAHAM I. PERSHITS, "Tribute Relations"

Seasonal raiding and wars of expansion seem to have been the main forms of indigenous warfare in the American tropics. Each of these forms of warfare gave rise to a very different mode of servitude: in one, war captives were used as domestics and drudges; in the other, subject populations were employed as servants for the collective benefit of the dominant society. Persons subjected through these two forms of warfare could not have been in more different situations. Whereas war captives underwent processes of homeland alienation, depersonalization, and social death, subordinate populations were able to maintain their lands, family ties, and customary lifeways.

Between these two forms of Amerindian warfare, we find a third modality: chronic hostility, which shares elements of the other two forms. As with seasonal raiding, the purpose of chronic hostility was to obtain prisoners and loot, but it was not to annihilate the enemy. As with wars of expansion, the aim of chronic hostility was to subject entire collectivities, but it was not directed at appropriating their lands per se. Chronic aggression was the way warring peoples forced their more numerous but weaker neighbors into capitulating and entering a tributary relationship. It was thus characteristic of heterogeneous regional systems. Chronic hostility differed from seasonal raiding in its frequency and intensity, taking place throughout the year and striking the enemies in their most vulnerable area: the need for food. The periodic destruction of their crops and gardens, and the burning of their villages, placed great economic stress upon chronically raided peoples, forcing them to surrender and accept a tributary status.

Tribute relations developed—in tropical America as elsewhere (see Pershits 1979)—between societies that had already undergone a process of internal stratification leading to the creation of an upper stratum of chiefly families, clans or lineages, and a lower commoner stratum. The societies that imposed tributary relationships on their neighbors were for the most part highly mobile nonagriculturalists. This was certainly so in the two societies discussed in this chapter: the Calusa of southern Florida, whose main subsistence pursuit was fishing and who alternated residence between winter permanent settlements and summer camps; and the Guaicurú of Paraguay, hunters and gatherers who moved seasonally from riverine to inland areas following the rains. Such societies could deploy chronic hostility to greater advantage than their less mobile horticulturalist neighbors, attacking them periodically and unrelentingly with only a minimal risk of retaliation.

Populations subjected to chronic hostility by more mobile and aggressive enemies often preferred to surrender and accept a tributary status rather than continue to resist and risk being subjected as a servant population or even being exterminated. In exchange for their submission and tribute, the conquering people assumed the task of protecting the tributaries from other enemies. Acceptance of tributary status was frequently represented as constituting an alliance between the chiefly families of the dominant and subordinate groups. Such a political alliance was usually cemented by the marriage of a chief from the conquering group with a woman of chiefly status from the tributary group. Such arrangements allowed tributary peoples to retain their economic and social structure, as well as a large degree of political autonomy, more so than if they had been subjugated as a servant group. The chiefly elites of dominant and tributary groups were represented ideologically as being of equal status, especially in the face of weaker common enemies. Despite this ideological equality, however, tributary peoples as a whole were regarded by capturing societies with the same contempt they felt for war captives and servant groups.

Tributary relationships always coexisted with captive slavery, the most widespread Amerindian mode of servitude. This also holds true for the two peoples discussed in this chapter. But whereas tribute relations among Guaicurú had as important a weight as captive slavery, among Calusa they constituted the prevailing mode of servitude. It must be pointed out, however, that distinctions between tributaries, servants, and captive slaves were not sharp and absolute. Tributary groups often had to pay their masters annual tribute not only in goods and services but also in slaves, taken either from their own people (Patterson 1982: 123) or from other groups (Meillasoux 1991: 71). More importantly, tributary populations were forced to comply with their masters' requests or face the possibility of being raided and reduced to total slavery (Burnham 1980: 49).

CALUSA

The Calusa were exceptional in the context of tropical America, for they were politically unified under the leadership of a hereditary paramount chief and had subjected many of their neighbors as tributary populations. In the mid-sixteenth century, it was reported that the supreme chief of the Calusa "was the strongest and most powerful Indian in the country, a great warrior having many subjects under his sovereignty" (Laudonnière 2001[1564]: 110). From their capital, Calos, Calusa people dominated southern Florida, as indicated in Theodor de Bry's map of the region (see Figure 9). The Calusa were also exceptional in that, although they kept captives, they did not seem to have practiced captive slavery of the kind commonly found throughout native tropical America (Goggin and Sturtevant 1964: 190).

The information we have on Calusa raiding is almost nonexistent. This is in contrast to other native tropical American peoples, for whom there are numerous first- and secondhand narrations of seasonal raids against the enemy. The evidence suggests, however, that Calusa and their enemies—the Tequesta, Tocobaga, Pojoy, Jeaga, Jobe, and Ais—did not hesitate to take captives from each other. In 1566 chief Carlos, the Calusa paramount chief, held in captivity one of the daughters of the supreme chief of the Tequesta (Menéndez de Avilés 1991[1566]: 303). And in 1567 the Tocobaga, northern enemies of the Calusa, had, according to Solís de Merás (1990[1565]: 205), ten to twelve captive Calusa, among them one of chief Carlos's sisters. What is not clear, however, is whether these captives were employed as slaves or were just held as hostages to be used as political pawns in negotiations with the enemy. Thus the daughter of the Tequesta chief may have been originally given to chief Carlos as a wife in proof of allegiance; only after the Tequesta attempted to shake off Calusa domination might she have been considered to be a "captive."

Calusa also kept European and African captives—generally castaways or wounded soldiers abandoned by their companions. By order of chief

Carlos, all foreign castaways that landed on his territories, or on those under his rule, had to be taken to Calos, his capital town, where they were kept as servants or redistributed among important chiefs (Solís de Merás 1990[1565]: 201). Captives performed lowly or dangerous tasks, such as providing wood and water for a village, carrying messages between settlements, acting as court buffoons, or guarding the bodies of dead chiefs and nobles kept in village temples (Garcilaso de la Vega 1995[1605]: 103–104; Laudonnière 2001[1564]: 111; Escalante Fontaneda 1575[1567]: fol. 8; Elvas 1995[1539]: 60). Members of the chiefly elite were constantly attended by a host of servants, generally children and young women (Monaco and Alaña 1991[1743]: 423; Solís de Merás 1990[1565]: 164). Calusa leaders and warriors were also exempted from daily subsistence activities, such as fishing, which were carried out by others (Monaco and Alaña 1991[1743]: 428). Unfortunately, no evidence exists indicating whether these servants and drudges were captives, members of the commoner stratum, or both.

Calusa may or may not have kept war prisoners as domestic slaves, but we do know that they took captives to sacrifice during annual fertility rites (Laudonnière 2001[1564]: 111; López de Velasco in Swanton 1922: 389). The Gentleman from Elvas (1995[1539]: 61) suggests that they sacrificed captives to their gods when the latter demanded it or when, after experiencing some grave catastrophe, they wished to placate the gods. On special occasions, such as the death of a chief or the establishment of peace with an enemy, they also sacrificed children (Monaco and Alaña 1991[1743]: 423). In addition, captives were important as providers of war trophies. Calusa warriors beheaded their enemies, displaying their heads or scalps, stuck on spears, in their victory dances and fertility rituals (Zubillaga in Goggin and Sturtevant 1964: 200; López de Velasco in Swanton 1922: 389).

Rather than conducting seasonal raids, Calusa engaged in chronic hostility against their powerful enemies or, as other authors describe it, they were in a state of endemic warfare (Widmer 1988: 273). The enmity between the Calusa and their neighbors made news among Spaniards and Frenchmen, whose accounts describe in more or less detail the wars they waged against each other. These were not intended to take captives, however, but to subjugate enemy settlements as tributaries, to crush rebel tributary settlements, or to recover tributary groups wrested from Calusa control by rival groups.

Calusa conducted their warfare on both land and sea. Whenever the Calusa paramount decided to embark on a war against an enemy, he sent word to his people and tributaries, commanding them to send a certain number of warriors and to manufacture a massive quantity of weapons— bows, arrows, clubs, spears, and spear throwers (Rogel 1991b[1568]: 254, 266, 288). Warriors formed a separate group in Calusa society, enjoying a status midway between that of people of chiefly descent and commoners. They were exempted from subsistence activities and could devote all their time to warfare, thus fulfilling the needs of a society permanently engaged in war against its enemies. The Calusa army was composed of highly trained and imposing full-time warriors. In 1566 chief Carlos received Menéndez de Avilés, accompanied by a personal guard of three hundred bowmen. Impressed by their demeanor, chronicler Bartolomé Barrientos (1965[1568]: 87, 95) described them as "great warriors."

Calusa were also skillful sailors. When, in 1513, Juan Ponce de León anchored his three ships in Charlotte Harbor, the center of the Calusa polity, he was attacked by a fleet of twenty Calusa war canoes, some of them tied in pairs, whose occupants tried to cut the anchors and board the Spanish ships (Herrera y Tordesillas 1601–1615: I, Década 1, 304). The attack was repelled. Next day, however, chief Carlos sent a second fleet, this time composed of eighty canoes richly decorated with banners and pennants. The Calusa paramountcy still had a powerful flotilla a century later—in 1612 a Spanish expedition sent to punish some Pojoy and Tocobaga rebel chiefs was met by sixty canoes when it set anchor in Calos (Swanton 1922: 343). Calusa war canoes were large vessels capable of carrying many warriors. The one belonging to the Calusa supreme chief was manned by sixteen rowers (San Miguel 2001[1596]: 80). These canoes were used to transport goods, warriors, and other people both along the seacoast and along the web of canals connecting the coast with the interior. They could also be used for open-sea traveling; it is reported that Calusa sailors regularly made trading expeditions to Cuba (Swanton 1946: 64).

Calusa war tactics involved spying on enemy movements and launching surprise attacks by both land and sea. Coastal settlements were therefore often located on islands having only a few safe landing sites. Such settlements could not be attacked by land and were difficult to attack by sea, provided that landing places were adequately guarded. Calusa warfare was generally aimed at terrorizing and subduing the enemy. These policies are clearly expounded in the remonstrations that Doña Antonia, chief Carlos's classificatory sister, directed at conquistador Menéndez de Avilés when he refused to aid the Calusa in defeating the Tocobaga: "Why—she reproached him—had he not killed [chief] Tocobaga and his Indians and burned their town and house of idols?" (Solís de Merás 1990[1565]: 210). Notice that there is no reference to the taking of captives and booty; rather, there is only a clear intention to punish the enemy and force it into submission. Such tactics were not exclusive to the Calusa; whenever they could, Tocobaga chiefs also attacked and burned Calusa villages (Elvas 1995[1539]: 61).

At the time of contact, Calusa ruled over a large number of villages. Castaway Escalante Fontaneda (1575[1567]: fols. 5–6) provides a list of fifty settlements that were under Calusa rule in the 1550s. These included tributary villages belonging to the eastern Tequesta, to the southern Florida Key islanders, and even to a group of Taino migrants who had come from Cuba in search of the fabled fountain of youth (Escalante Fontaneda 1575[1567]: fol. 4; López de Velasco 1991b[1575]: 312). Probably the list also included Pojoy tributary settlements; we know that these northern neighbors of the Calusa were ruled on and off by them (de la Cruz in Hann 1991a[1680]: 26; Milanich 1998: 73).

Tributary settlements were kept in check principally by the force of arms, but also by several ideological mechanisms legitimizing their rule. Calusa rule was not, however, absolute; tributary chiefs constantly strove to recover their autonomy. For example, when the Spanish visited the Calusa in 1565, the Tequesta had recently shaken off Calusa domination. Chief Carlos was at the time engaged in a bloody war to subdue the rebels once more (Solís de Merás 1990[1565]: 202). The Mayaimi of Lake Okeechobee—which some authors consider to be a distinct ethnic group (Widmer 1988: 5) but who were probably Tequesta (see Escalante Fontaneda 1575[1567]: fol. 2; Menéndez de Avilés 1991[1566]: 303)— were reported by Menéndez de Avilés (1991[1566]: 303) to be great enemies of chief Carlos. They had thus allied with Saturiva, a renowned Timucuan chief of the eastern coast of Florida, presumably to fight the Calusa jointly. Triggering the war, or at least deepening it, was the abduction of the daughter of the paramount chief of the Ais; she had been promised to chief Carlos sometime before 1565, probably as part of his obligations as a tributary chief (Laudonnière 2001[1564]: 111–112). The Ais noblewoman, together with a large retinue of her ladies-in-waiting, were abducted by the Tequesta of Lake Okeechobee while en route to the Calusa capital, where she was to marry chief Carlos (see Figure 10). The warfare that ensued between the Calusa and Tequesta weakened considerably the natives of southern Florida, favoring, at least for a while, Spanish domination over the region.

Tributary settlements would sometimes change allegiances, shaking off Calusa control and seeking the protection of the latter's enemies. This is exactly what happened after Menéndez de Avilés forced the Calusa to make peace with the Tocobaga in 1567. Seizing the opportunity provided by the *pax hispana*, the Tocobaga supreme chief, according to Father Rogel (1991b[1568]: 226), "subverted" four towns that were "vassals" of Felipe, chief Carlos's successor, persuading them to throw off the Calusa yoke and become his tributaries. These rebel tributary villages, south of Tampa Bay, were probably Pojoy, a group known to be under Calusa domination in the late 1600s (Milanich 1998: 73). It is unclear, however, whether their switch in loyalties resulted from Tocobaga armed pressures or was a genuine desire on their part to secure the protection of a less oppressive lord. Be that as it may, three of the four rebel towns asked for the Calusa paramount's pardon and pledged their obedience after the Spanish burned the Tocobaga capital in reprisal for the killing of Spanish soldiers. On this occasion, chief Felipe pardoned the rebels. But this leniency was exceptional. More often, tributary chiefs plotting to escape were simply seized and executed (Zubillaga in Goggin and Sturtevant 1964: 200).

Shortly after this event, the Calusa managed to expel the Spanish from their lands, expanding their sphere of influence greatly during the following decades. Taking advantage of the Spaniards' defeat of the Tocobaga, chief Felipe began preparing for out-and-out war against his traditional enemies. His aim was to subject or at least displace them (Rogel 1991b[1568]: 254). Chief Felipe may have succeeded in this enterprise, given that a century later the Calusa's domain is reported to have extended as far north as Apalachee territory, north of the Tocobaga's. By then, at least some Tocobaga had moved into Apalachee (Compostela 1991[1690]: 86). It was reported that by the beginning of the seventeenth century the chief of Calos had seventy towns under his rule, "not counting the very great number which paid him tribute because they feared him" (Swanton 1922: 343). This represents an almost 50 percent increase with respect to the number of subject villages reported a half century earlier. Quite possibly the Calusa managed to subjugate the Tequesta once more, since we are told that, around the mid-eighteenth century, the remaining

Tequesta and Florida Key islanders recognized him as "chief of the land" (Monaco and Alaña 1991[1743]: 421–422).

Calusa paramount chiefs received tribute in goods—mostly processed foodstuffs, fine painted deerskins, weapons, amber, and precious metals. Bread, made from starchy wild roots, and dried game meat were among the most important processed foodstuffs they obtained from their tributaries. They also received tribute in people, generally European and African captives, but also women given to the Calusa paramount as secondary wives. Whenever a new Calusa chief was proclaimed, tributary chiefs were each obliged to send him a woman as a sign of submission and alliance (Rogel 1991b[1568]: 268). Lastly, Calusa supreme chiefs received tribute in the form of various services: labor for the construction of canals, public buildings, and artificial mounds, and military aid for the undertaking of large war ventures (see Chapter 6).

After meeting Menéndez de Avilés in 1565 and realizing that he could not defeat him, chief Carlos attempted to win the latter's support against his enemies by pledging obedience and offering his classificatory sister and former wife—the above-mentioned Doña Antonia—to him in marriage (Solís de Merás 1990[1565]: 116). In other words, he sought to become a tributary/ally of the Spanish in order to obtain their protection against his enemies. By so doing, he was applying to a new historical situation a model of the relationship between peoples with uneven military power that had a long-standing tradition in southern Florida. The Guaicurú of Paraguay, as we shall see, attempted a similar strategy in their first contacts with the Spaniards.

Tributary relations among southern Florida native peoples were legitimized through ties of fictive kinship, elite marriage exchanges, and ritual claims to ownership of the land. I discuss the first two mechanisms in more detail in Chapter 8, focusing here only on the last. Calusa paramount chiefs claimed to be owners of the lands occupied by their people and tributaries. It was as titular owners of the land, in fact, that they believed themselves to have the right to exact tribute from its occupants (Monaco and Alaña 1991[1743]: 421–422). This claim to ownership of all lands is consonant with what we know, for instance, of native Amazonian leaders. Generally, they were settlement founders whom their followers referred to as "owners of the house" and/or "owners of the land" (see, for instance, Overing 1975: 30, 53). In the case of the Calusa, however, claims to ownership of the land were based, not on their status as "founders," but rather on their military supremacy and, more importantly, on their alleged ritual powers.

Subjugation of enemy peoples was certainly crucial to claiming ownership of the land. The legitimacy of such claims rested on the land rituals that Calusa paramounts performed periodically on behalf of their own people and their tributaries. Once or twice a year the Calusa supreme chief retired to a ceremonial house with two or three of his closest associates—probably the head shaman, which we know existed, and a few of his disciples—to engage in secret rituals aimed at ensuring the fertility of the land (Laudonnière 2001[1564]: 110–111). At the time of harvest, he also sacrificed a captive slave, presumably to thank the divinities for their generosity and to ensure their protection for the coming year (Laudonnière 2001[1564]: 111). Since Calusa subsistence was based mostly on fishing and only to a lesser extent on the gathering of roots, the main objective of these land rituals must have been to legitimize their claim upon their inland tributaries, who depended heavily on the collection and processing of wild roots for their own subsistence and for payment as tribute to their Calusa lords (Escalante Fontaneda 1575[1567]: fol. 2).

These ideological mechanisms, which disguised the more brutal aspects of their dominance, allowed Calusa supreme chiefs to represent their relationship with tributary chiefs as one of alliance. Tributaries fought side by side with their masters whenever the Calusa paramount requested it, a practice strengthening the notion of alliance. As a result, some authors are inclined to interpret the ties linking the Calusa to their neighbors as a confederation rather than as a tributary arrangement (Goggin and Sturtevant 1964; Lewis 1978; Widmer 1988). However, there is more than enough evidence, as we have seen, to conclude that Calusa polity was based on the constant repression of subordinate populations and on coercive methods of extracting tribute. Some authors have suggested that Calusa expansion was triggered by an increase in the availability of precious metals resulting from Spanish shipwrecks. They argue that the great wealth that Calusa paramount chiefs commanded strengthened their power and brought about a sort of Calusa "golden age" (Wheeler 2000: 7–8). Even if we accept the truth of this statement, there is no denying that the main features of the Calusa regime of servitude were already in place in pre-Hispanic times. European presence might have accentuated certain sociopolitical features, but the foundations were already there.

GUAICURÚ

Soon after contacting Guaicurú in the first half of the sixteenth century, Núñez Cabeza de Vaca (1585[1544]: 76v, 83v), the region's earliest chronicler, stated that they attacked their enemies regularly in order to take captives. Female prisoners, he wrote, were well treated and eventually were granted freedom; men were killed, except when a Guaicurú woman claimed a particular captive for herself. Around the same time, the Guaicurú apparently ruled over two neighboring groups—the Chané and Toyana—who, according to Schmidl (1749[1548]: 22), were subordinated to them as German rustics were to their feudal lords. Both sources are early enough to discard European influence as a possible cause for the development of these forms of servitude, as some authors have suggested (Radin 1946: 190–191; Métraux 1946: 301–302).

Guaicurú were indisputably the most powerful Amerindian people living in the southern portion of the Paraguay River basin at the time of contact. Despite some instances of internal warfare, most Guaicurú warfare was waged against non-Guaicurú neighbors. Revenge for past grievances—killings and theft of horses, iron tools, and weapons—was a common justification for raiding the enemy (Sánchez Labrador 1910–1917[1760]: I, 310–311; Méndez 1969[1772]: 57–58). In such instances, the prospect of seizing booty and captives was an additional incentive to take up arms. Guaicurú people also made war on enemies who were becoming too powerful and needed to be contained lest they became a threat to Guaicurú survival, as was the case of the Payaguá, renowned pirates of the Paraguay River (Sánchez Labrador 1910–1917[1760]: I, 306).

Guaicurú military power—already great at the time of contact—increased even more after the adoption of the horse sometime in the late 1500s. Guaicurú people became fearsome horsemen, as illustrated by the French painter Jean Baptiste Debret in his rendition of a Guaicurú cavalry charge in the early 1800s (see Figure 11). Horses had become such an intrinsic part of Guaicurú warrior culture by the early 1600s that dead Guaicurú chiefs were buried, not only with their weapons, but also with their favorite horses (Techo 1897[1673]: 73–74). Doubtless, the adoption of horses conferred on them a considerable advantage over those neighbors who remained horseless. It would nevertheless be mistaken to overestimate the influence of this event in the shaping of Guaicurú society and its forms of servitude, as some authors have (Métraux 1946: 301–302). At the time of contact, Guaicurú people were already dominant in the Paraguay River regional power system and already had captive slaves and tributary populations under their rule, as the earliest sources confirm. More likely, as Oberg (1949: 3) has suggested, the adoption of the horse accentuated existing social and political traits, such as Guaicurú internal stratification and the relationship of institutionalized subordination between Guaicurú and some of their neighbors.

Guaicurú raids could involve members of a single local group, or camp (*tolderia*), or members of several camps belonging to the same regional group (*parcialidad*). In extraordinary cases, all regional groups belonging to a given chieftainship (*cacicato*) would agree to join forces and wage war against a numerous or powerful enemy. Whenever a local chief wanted to organize a raid, he had his servants convoke his followers by drum signals (Sánchez Labrador 1910–1917[1760]: I, 307). When organizing a larger expedition, a headman sent messengers or smoke signals to convoke other camps from the same or different regional groups. Once they had agreed on a meeting place and date, the various local groups that had accepted the invitation pitched camp apart, under their own leaders. When two or more regional groups joined a raid against a common enemy, each of them was commanded by its own regional leader (Sánchez Labrador 1910–1917[1760]: I, 309). Regional leaders coordinated their actions but acted independently. Only in those exceptional cases when an entire chieftainship mobilized itself against an enemy did regional leaders subordinate their authority to that of the paramount chief. Before agreeing to go to war, leaders consulted local shamans to help predict the outcome of the projected incursion (Serra 1850[1803]: 369). If the omens were bad, they waited for a more auspicious occasion.

Guaicurú never attacked an enemy more powerful than themselves. The selection of the right victim was a critical aspect for waging a successful war (Serra 1850[1803]: 368). They posted spies in order to determine the position, routines, and weaknesses of their enemies. Spies communicated with each other by using special whistles (Sánchez Labrador 1910–1917[1760]: I, 309). Once a proper target had been chosen, raiders would approach enemy territory in rigorous silence, even avoiding cutting palm trees or making fires that could betray their presence. To drive away evil spirits and ensure the expedition's success, local shamans marched on the vanguard (Sánchez Labrador 1910–1917[1760]: II, 34). Often, unmarried women went along with the raiders to help them carry loads, collect foodstuffs, and bring back the loot (Lozano 1733: 71).

Guaicurú usually struck at their enemies on moonless nights, although they were also known to attack or ambush their enemies in broad daylight (Azara 1809[1781]: II, 112). To prevent the victims from fleeing, the attackers formed a semicircle at the center of which, and separated from the rank and file, stood their more important war leaders. Raiders were armed with hardwood clubs, long spears, and bows and arrows. They also carried a short knife made of sharp piranha jaws, which they used expertly to behead the enemies they slew (Núñez Cabeza de Vaca 1585[1544]: 82r). While attacking, Guaicurú raiders blew horns to create as much confusion and panic as possible. If they caught their targets by surprise, the raiders surrounded them, killing all who resisted, taking as many captives as possible, and burning their houses and possessions (Sánchez Labrador 1910–1917[1760]: I, 310). If, on the contrary, the enemy was on its guard, and resisted fiercely, the Guaicurú retreated. In all cases, they returned as rapidly as possible to their camps, which, surrounded by marshlands and scrub forests, were effectively protected against enemy reprisals.

Guaicurú raiders usually killed all adult men and women (Sánchez Labrador 1910–1917[1760]: I, 311), though they sometimes took a few adult women captive. All in all, however, there was a marked preference for children and for young men and women—so much so that Guaicurú warriors did not hesitate to abduct even babies, who were later given to their wives or female relatives to breastfeed (Prado 1839[1795]: 37–38). Older captives were tied up to prevent them from escaping and were released only after arriving at their captors' village (Lozano 1733: 65). Plunder was not distributed. Captives and loot belonged to whoever had secured them (Sánchez Labrador 1910–1917[1760]: I, 308).

The prestige of a man was measured by the amount of enemies he had killed in battle and the number of captives and servants he possessed (Techo 1897[1673]: II, 160). The pressure to make more raids and raid more peoples was therefore constant (Sánchez Labrador 1910–1917[1760]: I, 311). Guaicurú leaders raided their enemies every year (Serra 1850[1803]: 368). So intense was Guaicurú raiding that Azara (1809[1781]: II, 109), a usually austere observer, claimed that even the poorest Guaicurú had three or four captives. The privileged enemies and sometimes allies of Guaicurú since precolonial times were the Arawak-speaking Guaná. Accomplished agriculturalists and skillful weavers, the

Guaná were much valued, whether as captives or as tributaries (see Figure 12). But Guaicurú also raided other peoples, sometimes living hundreds of kilometers from their territories: the Naperú, Guaraní, Toba, Mocoví, Abipón, Chiquitos, Lengua, Kaiwá, Bororo, Guató, Sanapaná, Angaité, and Chamacoco.

Most war captives were kept by their captors to be employed as laborers in the most arduous tasks or as domestic servants. Children were raised in the language and customs of their masters. Unlike other Grand Chaco tribes, Guaicurú rarely married adult female captives. These were kept as servants, and in later colonial times they were sold to the Spanish and Portuguese (Lozano 1733: 67). Captive men were generally killed, except when they could be sold to Europeans (Techo 1897[1673]: II, 161). However, the demands of the colonial slave market do not seem to have intensified Guaicurú raiding, as in other regions of tropical America. Even as late as 1892 an observer reported that Guaicurú kept most of their captives as servants, only exceptionally trading them with the whites (Boggiani 1945[1895]: 120). In contrast, the same author affirms that there was an active trade in captives between Guaicurú local and regional groups (see Chapter 7).

The special relationship that existed between the Guaicurú and the Arawak-speaking Guaná was noticed early on by the first European chroniclers, who described it as a situation similar to feudal serfdom (Schmidl 1749[1548]: 22). Other groups mentioned as having been subjugated by the Guaicurú as tributaries were the Toyana (Schmidl 1749[1548]: 22), Naperú (Lozano 1733: 62), and Chamacoco (Serra 1850[1803]: 210). At least one author affirms that the Guaicurú themselves had been under the rule of the Enimaga (Lengua) of the Pilcomayo River in pre-European times (Azara 1809[1781]: II, 157–158). This would confirm the notion that hierarchical social arrangements of this nature developed independently of European influence.

In the early 1700s, two of the three Guaicurú regional chieftainships had control of Guaná and Naperú subordinate populations (Lozano 1733: 62). Not all Guaná chieftainships and regional groups were subordinated to the Guaicurú, however. Part of the Echoaladi—one of the six Guaná chieftainships that existed in the early 1700s—was subordinated to the Guaicurú chief Caminigo (Sánchez Labrador 1910–1917[1760]: I, 267). Another segment of them, in contrast, not only successfully resisted Guaicurú pressure but even dared to raid Guaicurú occasionally to procure horses and iron tools (Méndez 1969[1772]: 57). Military force was crucial in this subordination. It is said that the Guaná and Naperú accepted Guaicurú dominance because they were tired of the Guaicurú's constant destruction of their plantations (Serra 1850[1803]: 208), despite living in palisaded villages, as shown in a late-1500s engraving (see Figure 13). Military dominance was often accompanied by marriage exchanges between Guaicurú chiefs and high-ranking Guaná and Naperú women. These two elements—military subjection and the establishment of links of marriage and kinship—were crucial components of Guaicurú tribute relations.

Sometimes Guaicurú masters lived close to the settlements of their Guaná subordinates, in pasturelands that could feed their large herds of horses (Sánchez Labrador 1910–1917[1760]: I, 255). In other instances, Guaná tributaries lived amid their Guaicurú masters, acting as servants (Azara 1809[1781]: II, 87). When Guaicurú masters lived close by, they visited their tributaries periodically, especially at times of harvest, to collect tribute in the form of cultivated foodstuffs, tobacco, textiles, and other products. When Guaná tributaries lived among their Guaicurú masters, they cultivated their masters' lands, served them as domestics, and fought together with them whenever they organized a war expedition (Azara 1809[1781]: II, 96). Attached Guaná servants were free to come and go; they could even quit living with their masters and settle independently. However, they continued to be regarded by their masters as subordinates and could, at any time, be forced to comply with whatever their masters requested (Méndez 1969[1772]: 66–67; Azara 1809[1781]: II, 96–97).

The weight of subordinate populations in Guaicurú society was hefty. In 1733, Spanish missionaries estimated that the Guaicurú, comprising 700 families (around 3,500 people), held under their yoke 500 Guaná and Naperú families (around 2,500 people), who thus represented approximately 42 percent of the total population (n = 6,000) (Lozano 1733: 62). This percentage accords well with figures provided by Spanish missionaries forty years later. The Guaicurú population, including captive slaves and Guaná tributaries, was appraised in 1770 to be around 7,000 (Sánchez Labrador 1910–1917[1760]: II, 31). Almost simultaneously, another Spanish source advanced the figure of 3,800 Guaicurú, without counting their subordinates (Azara 1809[1781]: II, 103). This would mean that the population under Guaicurú rule amounted to around 48 percent of the total. These figures did not change significantly in the nineteenth century. Serra (1845[1803]: 211) reports that the total Guaicurú population, including war captives and tributaries, amounted to 2,600 people. Of these, 42 percent were Guaná tributaries, either living together with the Guaicurú or in their own settlements. Another 19 percent were recent war captives taken from among the Chamacoco. The rest were Guaicurú proper, or descendants of Guaicurú and former Bororo, Chiquitos, Kaiwá, and African captives. In short, estimates of the servile population (captives and tributaries) under Guaicurú control ranged between 42 and 61 percent.

Guaicurú based their dominance over the farming Guaná population not only on the force of arms but also on claims that they owned the lands. Early on, Núñez Cabeza de Vaca (1585[1544]: 81r–82v) reported that, in order to gather forces to expel the Guaná, Guaicurú convoked their allies and neighbors on the grounds that "they were few and braver than all the other nations of the land, and that they were lords of the land, of the deer, and of all terrestrial animals; and that they were lords of the rivers, and of the fish that live in them." Later sources confirmed that, indeed, the Guaicurú claimed the lands of their tributaries as their own (Jolís 1972[1789]: 319). Evidence is lacking that Guaicurú chiefs performed rituals aimed at ensuring the fertility of the land and animals, as the Calusa paramount did. Nevertheless, Guaicurú shamans were reputed for "having the keys to the rains that fertilize the fields"; they may thus have played an important role in the symbolic justification of Guaicurú domination (Sánchez Labrador 1910–1917[1760]: II, 234).

Authors vary on the subject of how Guaná subordination emerged. Sánchez Labrador (1910–1917[1760]: I, 267) asserts that he could find no evidence that the Guaná were ever conquered. He claims that Guaná subordination derives instead from marriages made between Guaicurú male chiefs and Guaná female chiefs. At the death of the latter, their Guaná followers became "vassals" of the Guaicurú chiefs and their descendants.

Other authors, like Méndez (1969[1772]: 66–68), Azara (1809[1781]: II, 109), and Jolís (1972[1789]: 318) propose similar interpretations, underscoring that Guaná seemed to serve their Guaicurú masters willingly and with pleasure. This has led some scholars to argue that the relationship between Guaicurú and Guaná was not hierarchical, that it should be understood as "some sort of trading relationship" and as a form of "symbiosis" (Lowie 1948: 349). Such a view, however, ignores at least two phenomena. First, it overlooks the fact that tributary relationships all over the world are phrased in terms of exchange, even if only the exchange of tribute for protection against third parties. The generosity of suzerain chiefs toward their tributaries has little to do with "trade," and much to do with the paternalistic reinforcement of their authority and personal prestige. Second, this interpretation omits the well-attested fact that Guaná tributaries complained constantly that, in their "many visits," their Guaicurú masters consumed much of their production, leaving them with very little to sustain their families and forcing them to gather wild fruits, grains, and tubers (Jolís 1972[1789]: 325).

That the relationship between Guaicurú and Guaná was not as idyllic as colonial authors would have it is confirmed by Méndez (1969[1772]: 66–68) himself. He reports that the Guaicurú considered their Guaná subordinates as the "lowest and most abject of plebs" and that the Guaicurú "mortally hated" them. He further adds that Guaicurú had waged bloody wars against the Guaná in the past and that "because of this they had agreed to become their subjects, serve them, and give them all they needed." Later authors describe the relationship between Guaicurú and Guaná as being very close, even though it originated in violence and coercion (Serra 1850[1803]: 208).

These different outlooks, I would suggest, derive from different temporal perspectives. Observing the relationship between Guaná and Guaicurú at a time when the system was well established and more or less in a state of equilibrium, eighteenth-century authors rejected the idea that it was based on force; they saw it as a relationship founded on mutual friendship and alliance. On the other hand, nineteenth-century authors such as Serra, who witnessed firsthand the Guaná's initial attempts to shake off Guaicurú dominance and the reprisals that followed, envisioned the relationship unadorned by the centuries-old discourse concerning alliance and mutual interest; that is, they saw it as a hierarchical relationship based on the use, or potential use, of coercion.

That the Guaicurú's chronic hostility, manifested in periodic raids, burning of villages, and destruction of gardens, was indeed the means by which they managed to subjugate some of their neighbors as tributaries is confirmed by late-colonial events. It is also indirectly supported by early-colonial evidence. Serra indicates that in the nineteenth century the Guaicurú used the same tactics to subject the Chamacoco as they had used to subjugate the Guaná in pre-European times. When the Guaná requested and obtained Portuguese protection against the Guaicurú in the late 1700s—a first step toward their emancipation—the latter reduced their exactions, underscoring the ties of friendship and alliance that united them (Serra 1850[1803]: 209). At the same time, the Guaicurú intensified their raids against the hunting-and-gathering Chamacoco to compensate for the loss of Guaná labor (Ribeiro 1970: 82). Under the pretext of buying captives from them, Guaicurú raided Chamacoco groups several times a year. To free themselves from constant Guaicurú harassment, in 1801 the Chamacoco summoned the aggressors to come to their lands and make peace. They then surrendered to the Guaicurú, accepting the status of *cativeiros*, which in this context must be understood as meaning "tributaries" rather than "captives" (Serra 1850[1803]: 210). To seal the alliance, the Chamacoco "sold" two hundred of their own people, both children and adults, to their new masters. They also offered their women in marriage to the Guaicurú and invited the Guaicurú to join them in attacking other, more isolated Chamacoco groups (Serra 1850[1803]: 210). This relation of subordination and tribute continued for more than a century (Boggiani 1945[1895]: 133), during which the subjugated Chamacoco were obliged to provide their Guaicurú masters tribute in the form of services; mainly as domestics and as warriors taking part in raids against third parties. Additionally, they were required to pay tribute in slaves, which they captured from more remote Chamacoco groups or from other peoples (Boggiani 1945[1895]: 133).

* * *

Like captive slavery and the subjection of entire enemy groups as servants, tributary relations were founded on violence and coercion—or on the threat thereof. War can therefore safely be said to have been the matrix of all Amerindian forms of servitude. Combined in different ways, these modes of servility gave rise to different regimes of servitude. Captive slavery was present in all these regimes, so it could be argued that this particular type of subordination is the basic form of servitude, the other two being but elaborations on this basic theme. Confirmation of this lies in the fact that both servant and tributary populations could be treated as enemies and raided for captives if they did not comply with their masters' requests. Such possibility is well documented for Makú and Chané servant groups (McGovern 1927: 186; Ramírez de Quiñones 1918–1922b[1573]: 282), as well as for Tequesta and Guaná tributaries (Solís de Merás 1990[1565]: 202; Cominges 1892[1879]: 239). In addition, both servant groups and tributary populations were often obliged to furnish individuals to work as family servants for their masters, under similar conditions as those of captive slaves. These unfortunate persons may sometimes have been captured as slaves from other groups but were often chosen from among the members of the servant and tributary groups themselves. The stratified Guaná serve as an example; they chose the individuals to be sent to serve their Guaicurú masters from among the *wahere-shané*, the "ugly people," or commoners (Susnik 1971: 141).

As fine a line separated servant groups from tributary populations as the one distinguishing these two forms of subordination from captive slavery. Quite possibly, servant populations gradually acquired with the passage of time greater freedom and the right to be treated as tributaries; recalcitrant tributaries, in contrast, were simply crushed and subjected as servant groups. Moreover, the distinction separating, let us say, Makú servant groups attached to Tukano malocas, and Guaná tributary groups living among their Guaicurú masters, is so tenuous as to be almost nonexistent. Rather than differing in terms of the duties they were expected to perform or the way they were treated by their masters, these two subordinate groups differed mostly in the opportunities for social advancement that were open to them. Marriages between masters and members of servant groups were generally out of the question. In contrast, intermarriage between lords and tributaries—particularly between members of their respective chiefly families—not only was accepted but was an important way to cement ties of subordination, alliance, and friendship.

Servant groups and tributary populations also differed in the options they had for preserving their identities as separate social entities. Despised because of their origins and having fewer opportunities for social advancement as individuals, members of servant populations often opted to become fully integrated into their masters' societies. Such a strategy was adopted—with mixed results—by many Makú groups and by all the Chané of eastern Bolivia. By adopting the language and customs of their masters, these peoples improved their social situation with respect to other groups who resisted foreign domination. Their assimilation, however, was never complete. Even now, the very Chiriguanáized Chané (Izoceño) continue to be accorded a lower status by the "pure" Chiriguaná. In contrast, tributary populations, who had better possibilities of integration as individuals and greater political autonomy, felt no need to relinquish their language and cultural practices. For example, no historical evidence points to tributary populations under Calusa or Guaicurú rule ever having been absorbed as collectivities into their masters' societies. Thus, even when they were on the verge of extinction, Calusa and their Tequesta tributaries maintained separate identities (Monaco and Alaña

1991[1743]: 420). And the Guaná of Paraguay not only preserved their identity but also managed eventually to emancipate themselves from their Guaicurú masters.

If we attempted to classify the three Amerindian forms of servitude identified here in terms of degrees of subordination, we would conclude that captive slavery was the harshest type, and tributary relationships the least oppressive, with servant groups somewhere in between. In the next three chapters, the more sociological aspects of Amerindian modes of servitude are examined, in an attempt to determine differences in status, obligations, and social conditions among captive slaves, servant groups, and tributary populations.

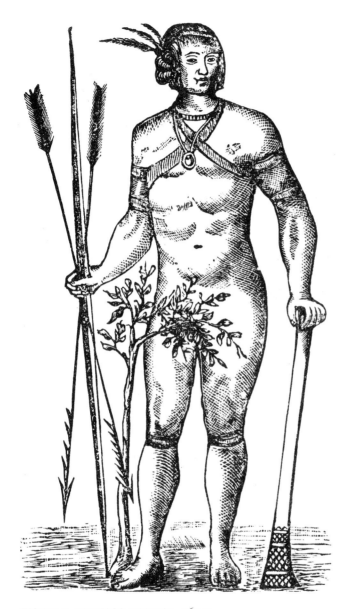

FIGURE I. KALINAGO WARRIOR, 1600S.

Kalinago men used bows and arrows to hunt and to make war. Arrowheads—made of tortoise shell, fish bones, or the shinbones of slain enemies—were often poisoned. Clubs, generally decorated with geometrical designs, were used only as war weapons. Kalinago warriors engaged in long-distance maritime expeditions to take captives and plunder from the neighboring islands and even from farther away, along the coasts of Guiana and Venezuela. *Source*: C. E. Taylor 1888: 109; based on a 1667 engraving by Sébastien Le Clerc. Courtesy of the U.S. Library of Congress.

Pagalle

Piroque

Canot a la Voile

FIGURE 2. KALINAGO CANOE AND WAR VESSEL, EARLY 1700S.

Kalinago working canoes (above) were carved out from a single trunk and propelled by short oars. War and trading vessels (below) were much bigger, being carved from the trunk of a large tree. They had a flat stern fitted with a rudder, two masts, and one or two sails. They could carry up to sixty men and were decorated with emblematic animals and bodily war trophies taken from slaughtered enemies. War canoes were used in long-distance expeditions of up to 150 sea leagues. *Source*: Labat 1724: I, Part 2, 16. Courtesy of the U.S. Library of Congress.

FIGURE 3. KALINAGO WARRIOR TORMENTED BY HIS LOKONO CAPTORS, LATE 1600S.

The Carib-speaking Kalinago and Kari'na were sworn enemies of the Arawak-speaking Lokono, with whom they were engaged in a symbolic system of cannibalistic exchange. In this engraving, a Carib prisoner, clad in a loincloth and with his hands tied on his back, is surrounded by Lokono men, who harass him with their torches. Adriaan Van Berkel claimed to have witnessed several of these cannibalistic rituals, which would explain the realistic character of his engraving. *Source*: Van Berkel 1695: 52–53. Courtesy of the U.S. Library of Congress.

FIGURE 4. CONIBO NOCTURNAL RAID, MID-1800S.

Conibo warriors, dressed in white cotton tunics and brandishing their war clubs and lances, attack a group of naked Cashibo turtle-hunters in the Pachitea River. The hunting of giant turtles was undertaken in the dry season, when hundreds of the animals would come to lay their eggs on the exposed beaches of the region's larger rivers. Conibo attacks on Cashibo turtle-hunters to take women and children were carried out in nights with a full moon to afford better visibility. *Source*: Marcoy 1869[1847]: II, 96. Courtesy of the U.S. Library of Congress.

FIGURE 5. CONIBO MAN WITH CAPTIVE WOMAN, MID-1800S.

The Conibo man depicted in this engraving is holding a blowgun and wears all the trappings typical of high-ranking Conibo men. His occiput protrudes slightly upward, the result of head elongation, which Conibo regarded as a sign of "civilization." Since Conibo women also had elongated heads, donned cotton wraparound skirts, and wore elaborate necklaces, bracelets, and waist bands (see Figure 15), the nudity, lack of ornaments, and round head of the woman behind him suggests that she must have been a recently captured foreign woman. *Source*: Marcoy 1869[1847]: I, 648. Courtesy of the U.S. Library of Congress.

FIGURE 6. TUKANO WARRIORS IN FULL CEREMONIAL REGALIA, EARLY 1900S.

These two Tukano warriors of the Tiquié River are dressed in highly ornamented ceremonial garments in preparation for a ritual dance. They hold wickerwork dancing shields—which, for warring purposes, were sometimes covered with thick tapir, jaguar, or deer hides—and long, decorated staffs indicating their chiefly status. These staffs were often ornamented with feathers and human hair taken from fallen enemies (Stradelli 1890: 436). *Source*: Koch-Grünberg 1909–1910: Plate 7.

FIGURE 7. MAKÚ FREE BAND, 1920S.

This Makú band from the headwaters of the Tiquié River—upriver from Cururu Cachoeira—was separated from their Tukano neighbors by a large tract of no-man's-land, indicating this group's resistance to enter into servile relations with Tukano people. Sometimes, however, Makú bands like this one were coerced into serving a Tukano maloca or submitted voluntarily as servants during times of famine, disease, and demographic decrease. *Source*: MacCreagh 1926: 390. Reproduced with permission of the University of Chicago Press.

FIGURE 8. CHIRIGUANÁ WARRIORS, LATE 1800S.

Chiriguaná warriors were extremely skillful with their bows and arrows, but they also used lances and shields. They wore leather bracelets on their right arms to avoid being hit by their bowstrings. Originally, they did not poison their arrows, but sometime in the late 1600s they adopted this practice from their neighbors, the Chiquitos. Notice the use of the *tembetá*, or lip plug, an exclusively male ornament that distinguished Chiriguaná from their Arawak-speaking Chané neighbors and enemies. *Source*: Thouar 1884: 235. Courtesy of the U.S. Library of Congress.

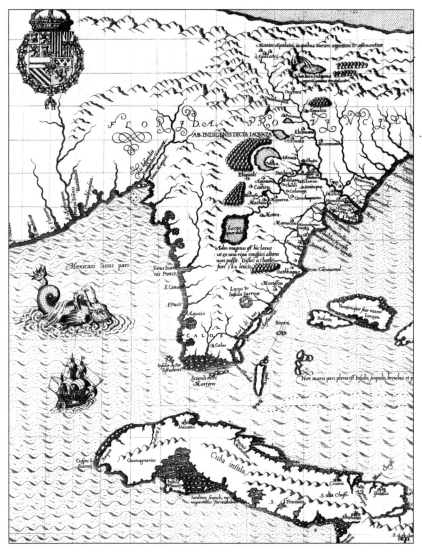

FIGURE 9. CALUSA TERRITORY, LATE 1500S.

According to this map, the domain of Carlos, the Calusa paramount chief, extended south of Charlotte's Harbor and occupied the tip of southern Florida from coast to coast. Most authors agree, however, that at the time of its maximum expansion Calusa territory stretched as far north as Tampa Bay. Calos, the capital settlement, is erroneously placed inland, along a river that flows to the south, whereas it is agreed that it was located on an island within Estero Bay. *Source*: De Bry 1591: facing p. 1. Courtesy of the U.S. Library of Congress.

FIGURE 10. TIMUCUAN CHIEFTAINESS TRANSPORTED
IN STATELY FASHION, LATE 1500S.

The pomp with which the daughter of the chief of the Ais was transported to Calos, the
Calusa capital, where she was to marry chief Carlos, was probably similar to that which
surrounded the elected wife of the Timucuan chief depicted in this engraving. Marriages
between the Calusa paramount and high-ranking tributary women were important political
events. The Ais fiancée on that occasion was accompanied by her father and a large number
of warriors and ladies-in-waiting (Laudonnière 2001: 111–112). *Source*: De Bry 1591:
Plate 37. Courtesy of the U.S. Library of Congress.

FIGURE 11. GUAICURÚ CAVALRY CHARGE, EARLY 1800S.

The Guaicurú adopted horse breeding and riding in the late 1500s. By the early 1800s,
they had also adopted saddles, which were generally made of jaguar pelts. Guaicurú raids
were usually carried out at night, but sometimes they waged war in broad daylight. The
adoption of the horse allowed Guaicurú warriors to extend their raiding much farther, thus
increasing the power they already had over their neighbors in precolonial times. *Source*:
Debret 1993[1834–1839]: Plate 17. Reproduced with permission of Villa Rica Editoras
Reunidas Limitada.

FIGURE 12. GUANÁ TRIBUTARIES, 1800S.

It is highly probable that the two Guaná men depicted in this drawing were tributary people, since we know that the illustrator, Hercules Florence, visited some of the Guaná local groups that were at the time subjects of the Guaicurú. The two men must have been commoners, for, in contrast to Guaná chiefs, they are wearing almost no ornaments. Their lack of facial paintings sets them apart from their Guaicurú masters, who spent much time painting multicolor designs on their bodies and faces. *Source*: Florence 1941: 69. Reproduced with permission of Edições Melhoramentos Limitada.

FIGURE 13. NAPERÚ PALISADED VILLAGE, LATE 1500S.

This early engraving shows the Spanish forces of Juan de Ayolas being massacred by the Paiembos (Payaguá), Peisemios, and Naperus. At the time of contact, Guaicurú had subjugated as tributaries a large number of Naperú and Guaná settlements. Despite their palisaded villages, neither Naperú nor Guaná could withstand chronic Guaicurú hostility manifested in periodic raiding and, above all, continual destruction of their fields. *Source*: Schmidl 1599: 32. Courtesy of the U.S. Library of Congress.

FIGURE 14. BARRILES CULTURE CHIEF CARRIED ON SHOULDERS, CIRCA 800.

This monumental stone sculpture (2.25 meters high) belonging to the tropical forest Barriles Culture of western Panama depicts an adorned high-ranking personage being carried by a naked underling, most probably a captive slave. In similar statues, the carried personage holds head trophies in the palms of his hands, suggesting that in this culture there was a symbolic connection between warfare, the capture of slaves, and the taking of bodily trophies. *Source*: Olga F. Linares. Reproduced with permission of Olga F. Linares.

FIGURE 15. KALINAGO HIGH-RANKING WOMAN, 1600S.

Because of her numerous ornaments, the woman depicted in this drawing must have been of chiefly rank. Note the tight leg bands, placed above and below the calves, that Kalinago women were entitled to wear only after undergoing puberty rituals. The use of leg bands was a sign of female adulthood, as well as a sign of identity as a Kalinago woman. In contrast, the prohibition of wearing such ornaments marked captive women as slaves. *Source*: C. E. Taylor 1888: 110; based on a 1667 engraving by Sébastien Le Clerc. Courtesy of the U.S. Library of Congress.

FIGURE 16. KALINAGO FAMILY WITH CAPTIVE SLAVE, LATE 1700S.

This engraving—based on an oil painting by Agostino Brunyas, drawn from life on the island of St. Vincent—depicts a Kalinago family composed of four women, two men, and two children. Whereas the women in the foreground wear leg bands and many ornaments and seem to be at leisure, the one in the background, close to the warrior holding a bow, has no leg bands and few ornaments. This, and the fact that she is the only woman carrying a heavy basket filled with garden produce, suggests that she was a captive slave. *Source*: Edwards 1793: I, 390. Courtesy of the U.S. Library of Congress.

FIGURE 17. CONIBO CHIEF AND HIS WIVES, LATE 1800S.

Surrounded by his three wives and holding his bow and arrows, Chief Mariano wears a combination of Western and Conibo clothing. His more traditional wives wear cotton wraparound skirts, shawls, necklaces, and waist bands. All have flattened heads, the result of head elongation during early infancy. Conibo considered head elongation, female circumcision, and the use of woven clothes as signs of civilization and regarded those who lacked these traits as wild peoples to be enslaved and civilized. *Source*: Sala 1897: 78. Courtesy of the U.S. Library of Congress.

FIGURE 18. CONIBO FEMALE CIRCUMCISION RITUAL, MID-1800S.

After a one-year period of seclusion, Conibo pubescent girls were circumcised in large public celebrations. Before the operation, they were stupefied by being given manioc beer and narcotic plants. The heart-shaped contraption on the right seems to be a product of the engraver's imagination. Female circumcision was seen as a civilizing practice and the utmost sign of Conibo womanhood. For this reason, uncircumcised captive women were regarded as inferior and inappropriate as prospective wives. *Source*: Marcoy 1869[1847]: I, 669. Courtesy of the U.S. Library of Congress.

FIGURE 19. CONIBO BABY UNDERGOING HEAD ELONGATION, EARLY 1900S.

The head of this Conibo baby is compressed between a soft pad and a padded board, which were periodically tightened. Conibo people believed that the procedure repressed capricious and rebellious tendencies, thus ensuring a civil disposition. From a Conibo point of view, head elongation and female circumcision were the two practices that marked them as civilized and distinguished them from animals and their less-than-human neighbors *Source*: Tessmann 1928: 192. Courtesy of the U.S. Library of Congress.

FIGURE 20. AMAHUACA MAN AND WOMAN, MID-1800S.

The round-headed Amahuaca man and woman depicted in this engraving differ greatly from the flat-headed Conibo shown in Figure 17. From a Conibo perspective, round heads were a sign of savagery or a lack of civility. Considering themselves to be the only civil (that is, human) people, the Conibo used to attack all their round-headed neighbors of the interfluvial and headwater areas—the Amahuaca among them—to take captives and loot. *Source*: Marcoy 1869[1847]: I, 630. Courtesy of the U.S. Library of Congress.

FIGURE 21. TUKANO WARRIOR IN FULL CEREMONIAL REGALIA, EARLY 1900S.

This young man, the son of a Tuyuka chief from the Tiquié River, is dressed in full ceremonial garb. The white cylindrical quartz stone (*uhtabú*) that he wears as a necklace was until recently the most important Tukano male ornament, its size indicating the status and prestige of the bearer. The absence of this much valued ornament was a sign either of affiliation to a low status Tukano sib, or of Makú servile status. *Source*: Koch-Grünberg 1909–1910: Plate 9.

FIGURE 22. MAKÚ CAPTIVE
SLAVES, EARLY 1900S.

These Makú men were captives of the chief of
the Tukano maloca of Cachoeira Pary. They
lived with their wives and children in makeshift
huts in the forest, not far from the village.
Like the free Makú depicted in Figure 7, they
wear no ornaments. Particularly significant
is the absence of *uhtabú*, the cylindrical
quartz stone necklaces that all Tukano men
wore until recently. In Tukano eyes, this
lack of ornamentation marked Makú as
alien, uncivilized, and inferior. *Source*: Koch-
Grünberg 1906: Figure 4.

FIGURE 23. CHIRIGUANÁ MEN WITH CAPTIVE SLAVE, LATE 1800S.

Four of the five men from the Chiriguaná mission of San Pascual de Boicovo depicted here
have underlip plugs (*tembetá*) of varying sizes, indicating that they were indeed Chiriguaná.
The fifth, on the far left, does not wear one, suggesting that he was either a captive or a
former captive. We know that he was not a Chané servant, for by the late 1800s the Chané
had adopted most Chiriguaná cultural practices, including the use of *tembetá*. *Source*:
Giannecchini and Mascio 1995: Photo 106. Reproduced with permission of Banco Central
de Bolivia.

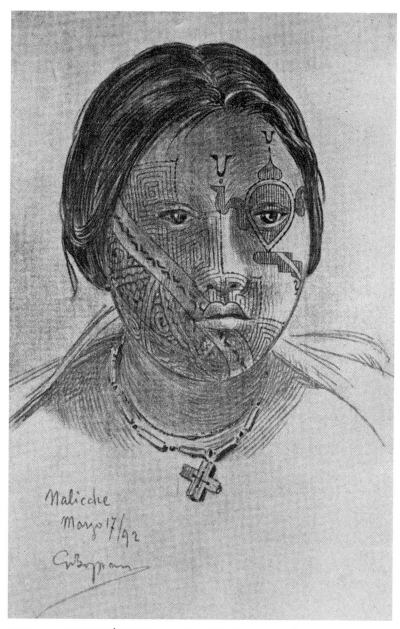

Malicche
Mayo 17/92
G. Boggiani

FIGURE 24. GUAICURÚ WOMAN OF CHIEFLY RANK, LATE 1800S.

Guaicurú women belonging to chiefly families showed their high status by decorating their faces and bodies with intricate designs. Such women never tattooed their faces, a practice reserved for female captives only. The young woman in this drawing was the sister-in-law of Joãzinho, second chief of the Guaicurú settlement of Nalique, close to the Nabileque River. *Source*: Boggiani 1945: Figure 83. Reproduced with permission of Martins Fontes Editora.

FIGURE 25. HIGH-RANKING GUAICURÚ WOMAN, 1935.

The facial designs of this Guaicurú woman betray her high rank. At the time this picture was taken, Guaicurú people had been decimated. They lived on a reservation granted to them by Brazilian emperor Pedro II in gratitude for their support in his war against Paraguay, and their lifestyle at the time differed little from that of the surrounding Brazilian peasants. In spite of this, however, Guaicurú women maintained the tradition of painting their faces with intricate designs, a tradition considered to mark their superiority with respect to their neighbors. *Source*: Lévi-Strauss 1995: 75. Reproduced with permission of Prof. Claude Lévi-Strauss.

FIGURE 26. HIGH-RANKING GUAICURÚ GIRL, LATE 1800S.

The beautiful designs that cover the face, shoulders, chest, and arms of this young Guaicurú woman are a sign of her high status. These designs were reserved for Guaicurú women or adopted captive girls. Captive women were only exceptionally allowed to use them. The complexity, precision, and extent of these designs, as well as the motifs used, conveyed important information as to the status and mood of the woman bearing them. *Source*: Frič and Fričova 1997: 132. Reproduced with permission of Pavel Frič and Yvonna Fričova.

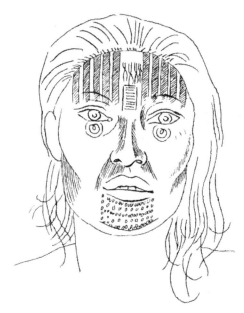

FIGURE 27. CHAMACOCO CAPTIVE WOMAN, EARLY 1800S.

This Chamacoco woman was captured and raised by Guaicurú people. Later on, around the 1820s, she was sold to the commander of the Brazilian fort of Albuquerque. Her face was tattooed with a design that Guaicurú masters used only on captive women. The simplicity and coarseness of this design contrast with the more elaborate and refined designs of Guaicurú high-ranking women (see Figures 24–26). In the center of her forehead she bears what seems to be a Guaicurú property mark. *Source*: Florence 1941: 52. Reproduced with permission of Edições Melhoramentos Limitada.

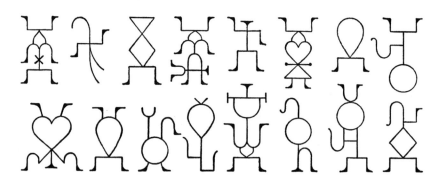

FIGURE 28. GUAICURÚ PERSONAL MARKS, LATE 1800S.

This sample of the personal signs used by Guaicurú men and women to mark their possessions was collected in the late 1800s. Such marks were painted, or branded, on material objects and animals. They were also tattooed on the faces and chests of captives. The mark in the upper left corner belonged to Capitãozinho, the headman of the Guaicurú village of Nalique. The one next to it belonged to his wife. *Source*: Boggiani 1945: 227. Reproduced with permission of Martins Fontes Editora.

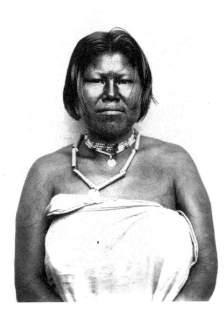

FIGURE 29. CHAMACOCO
CAPTIVE WOMAN, LATE 1800S.

The Chamacoco captive depicted here
has been painted as a Guaicurú woman.
Guaicurú mistresses painted their female
captives in such a way on the occasion of
great festivities. Her designs, however, are
less intricate and less well painted than
those of the Guaicurú women of noble
stock shown in Figures 24–26. More importantly, the Chamacoco woman bears a
Guaicurú property mark on her forehead,
between her eyebrows, a mark that may
have been that of her master or mistress.
Source: Frič and Fričova 1997: 73. Reproduced with permission of Pavel Frič and
Yvonna Fričova.

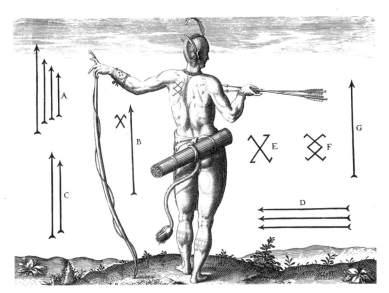

FIGURE 30. NATIVE VIRGINIAN CHIEFLY MARKS, LATE 1500S.

Native Virginian people bore on their backs the personal marks of their chiefs. Although
these tattoos indicated political affiliation rather than ownership, they demonstrate that the
marking of people with personal signs was a precolonial practice. A is the mark of Wingino,
chief of Roanoac; B is that of Wingino's brother-in-law; C and D are those of chiefs from
Secotam; E, F, and G are the marks of chiefs from Pomeiooc and Aquascogoc. *Source*: De
Bry 1590: Plate 23. Courtesy of the U.S. Library of Congress.

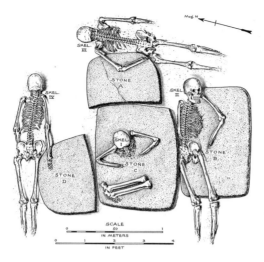

FIGURE 31. SACRIFICED SLAVES IN SITIO CONTE TOMB, CIRCA 450–900.

This tomb, found in the tropics of central Panama, contained the bodies of a seated high-ranking personage (skeleton I) surrounded by three sacrificed men (skeletons II–IV)—presumably captive slaves—and a large number of gold ornaments and personal utensils. Two of the slaves (III and IV) were elderly men buried facedown, together with a few possessions. The third slave was a younger man buried faceup, along with a richer cache of utensils and adornments. Since some of them were female objects, it has been suggested that he might have been a highly appreciated *camayoa*, or man-woman slave. *Source*: Lothrop 1937: I, 213. Reprinted courtesy of the Peabody Museum of Archaeology and Ethnology, Harvard University.

FIGURE 32. KARI'NA BURIAL, MID-1800S.

This engraving, depicting the burial of a Kari'na man, can be used to illustrate similar Kalinago practices, given the linguistic and cultural proximity of these two peoples. Kalinago people buried their dead, wrapped in their hammocks, in holes dug in their houses. Buried with the dead were all their possessions, including their captives, who were executed and interred beneath their masters in order to continue serving them in the afterlife. *Source*: Benoit, c. 1858: 85. Courtesy of the U.S. Library of Congress.

FIGURE 33. GUAICURÚ CHIEF WITH PERSONAL ATTENDANT, EARLY 1800S.

This Guaicurú chief (center) is attended by a servant—most probably a captive slave—who holds his horse and long bow. The horse, saddled with a jaguar pelt, has two brands in its rump, the personal marks of its owner. Guaicurú chiefs were always accompanied by a retinue of followers and captives. In the 1800s the chiefs also showed their high rank by wearing some criollo items of clothing, such as ponchos, shirts, and boots. *Source*: Debret 1993[1834–1839]: Plate 15. Reproduced with permission of Villa Rica Editoras Reunidas Limitada.

FIGURE 34. KALINAGO WARRIOR AND CRESCENT-SHAPED ORNAMENT, EARLY 1700S.

In the bottom left corner of this idealized portrait of a Kalinago warrior, the artist has depicted a *caracoli*, the most important Kalinago male ornament. These crescent-shaped jewels, made of an indigenous metal alloy that glittered like copper or gold, were worn as both pectorals and earrings. They were the most prized possessions of Kalinago men, so much so that one large *caracoli* could be exchanged for a captive slave. *Source*: Labat 1724: I, Part 2, 3. Courtesy of the U.S. Library of Congress.

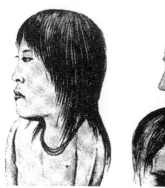

FIGURE 35. MAKÚ CAPTIVE GIRLS, MID-1800S.

These two Makú girls, aged nine (left) and sixteen (right), were captured by Arawak-speaking peoples in a raid on the Upper Içana River. They were later sold to the Brazilian commander of the Fort Marabitanas, on the Upper Rio Negro. In the 1800s the trade in Makú children was very active among both the Arawak and the Tukano. In intertribal networks, Makú captive children could be exchanged for an *uhtabú*, a highly valued Tukano quartz pendant; in extratribal markets, they were worth a rifle. *Source*: Spruce 1908: I, 345. Courtesy of the U.S. Library of Congress.

FIGURE 36. KARI'NA ANTHROPOPHAGOUS RITUAL, EARLY 1600S.

The two Kari'na men in this woodcut are engaged in the ritual consumption of a war captive. Kalinago people also practiced war cannibalism. This image depicts, not an actual cannibalistic feast, but rather the way Europeans imagined such feasts to be. Most sources indicate that Kalinago ate only small morsels of the smoked flesh of their enemies or dabbed their food with small quantities of their enemies' fat. Kalinago anthropophagy had nothing to do with hunger but was aimed at debasing the enemy and capturing its fertilizing vitalities. *Source*: Mocquet 1696: 133. Courtesy of the U.S. Library of Congress.

FIGURE 37. CHIRIGUANÁ HEAD-TROPHY VICTORY DANCE, LATE 1800S.

This engraving depicts Chiriguaná women celebrating the return of a group of victorious warriors. It is not clear whether it is imaginary or drawn from life. The mounted Chiriguaná warrior on the left holds an enemy head from each of his hands, while carrying two others tied to his saddle. Other warriors have stuck the heads of slain enemies on their lances. Chiriguaná victory rituals revolved around the abuse and mistreatment of spoils taken from the enemy. But it also involved dancing and the promenading of head trophies throughout the village, a ceremony that was probably connected with the appropriation and incorporation of the vital forces of the enemy. *Source:* Thouar 1884: 237. Courtesy of the U.S. Library of Congress.

FIGURE 38. MUNDURUCÚ HEAD TROPHY, EARLY 1800S.

One of the main objectives of Amerindian raids was the taking of enemy heads. Believed to be the repository of a person's vitality, such head trophies were treated ritually so as to preserve their generative force in favor of the captor and his family. Some Amerindian peoples kept only the skulls; others kept the outer skin and hair; and still others—like the Mundurucú and Conibo—dried the entire head, preserving both the skull and the skin. In most cases, however, the orifices of the head were sown, closed with thorns, or plugged with resin—as in this case—so as to prevent the enemy's vital force from escaping. *Source:* Helbig 1994: 64. Reproduced with permission of the Brasilien-Bibliothek der Robert Bosch GmbH.

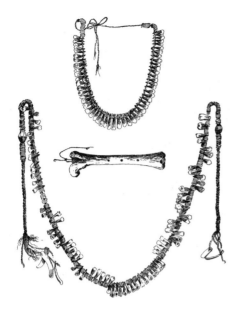

FIGURE 39. BORA HUMAN TEETH AND BONE WAR TROPHIES, EARLY 1900S.

The Bora necklace (*top*) and belt (*bottom*) depicted in this drawing are made of the teeth of enemies killed in war; the flute is made of a humerus bone. Similar objects were made by Tukanoan peoples living south of the Vaupes River. Human teeth and bones were considered to contain an important portion of the vital force of a person, a generative force that could be appropriated and recycled by the warrior who had obtained them, for the benefit of himself and his family. *Source*: Whiffen 1915: Plates 16 and 23. Courtesy of the U.S. Library of Congress.

FIGURE 40. TIMUCUAN RITUAL SCALPING OF FALLEN ENEMIES, LATE 1500S.

Timucuan warriors of northern Florida scalped and dismembered their enemies as soon as they had fallen. They smoked the captured scalps in situ and removed the flesh from the broken limbs in order to keep only the long bones. These bodily trophies were tied to the tip of their spears and carried proudly during victory rituals. Amerindian peoples, as well as other peoples throughout the world, believe that hair is an important container of life force or strength—a belief expressed, for example, in the biblical story of Samson. It is thus probable that the purpose of scalping was not only to exact revenge and debase defeated warriors but also to capture important life forces from the enemy. *Source*: De Bry 1591: Plate 15. Courtesy of the U.S. Library of Congres.

PART 3

Sociologies of Submission

CHAPTER 5

Markers of Servitude

Masters all over the world used special rituals of enslavement upon first
acquiring slaves: the symbolism of naming, of clothing, of hairstyle, of
language, and of body marks. . . . The objective of the rituals was the same:
to give symbolic expression to the slave's social death and new status.

—ORLANDO PATTERSON, *Slavery and Social Death*

That most Amerindian raiding was aimed at taking women as
wives, and that other captives—mostly children—were promptly integrated into their captors' societies, is a widespread but
misleading notion based mostly on twentieth-century ethnographic information. Many tropical forest societies during contact times
did not incorporate war captives into their households as concubines or
adopted children. On the contrary, captors marked captives as being alien,
inferior, and subordinate, and hence not eligible for full membership in
their society. In this chapter, I examine the many ways in which war
captives were marked as servitors through what Patterson (1982: 52) has
called "rituals of enslavement."

It has been argued that captives became slaves because of their fear of
death, that, to avoid annihilation, they simply allowed themselves to be
captured (Taussig 1999: 40). Their lives were thus spared because they
offered no resistance—that is, because they acted in what was perceived
as a cowardly manner. As a result, captives owed their captors their most
prized possession: their lives (Condominas 1998: 545). For this, they
paid a heavy price: a life of dishonor, a loss of autonomy, and, worse still,
an existence that no longer belonged to them. Captive slavery in native
tropical America, as elsewhere, not only brought with it alienation but
also converted captives, as Patterson (1982) has skillfully argued, into
"socially dead" individuals, a condition of uprootedness, loss of identity,
and disenfranchisement violently imposed upon them by war, capture,
and ritual debasement. The transformation of captives into slaves was
accomplished symbolically by means of elaborate rituals of enslavement

and desocialization. Aimed at depersonifying captives—depriving them of their previous identities and social personas—and re-personifying them as generic dependents (Meillasoux 1975: 21), these rituals involved various symbolic acts. These included the rejection by captives of their past lives and kinship ties, the imposition of new names, the marking of their bodies, and the assumption of a new status within the capturing society (Patterson 1982: 52).

Despite their new status, war captives found themselves in a "limbic condition," no longer a part of their societies of origin, nor fully assimilated into the society of their captors (Vaughan 1979: 100). The fear of death that led them to captivity, and the fact that they owed their lives to their masters, marked captives as both inferior and marginal in the eyes of their captors. This stigma, expressed in a variety of linguistic and bodily markers, generally persisted long after captives had lost their slave status and had been assimilated into the capturing society.

Terms used by members of capturing societies to refer to captive slaves—and sometimes also to servant groups and tributary populations—were multivocal; they could designate "strangers," "enemies," and "captives." This suggests that, at least in some Amerindian worldviews, all strangers were considered to be potential enemies, and all enemies potential slaves. Noting that a similar logic operated in ancient Rome, where the term *hostis* meant "stranger," "enemy," and "virtual slave," Lévy-Bruhl (1931: 7, 10) argued that slavery should not be regarded simply as a juridical relationship, for it also contained an ethnic dimension that made the servile relationship indelible. This holds true in native tropical America, where exoservitude became the predominant form of extreme dependency. Captors expressed the lack of humanity of their enemies by using a series of reference terms, metaphors, and myths to justify raiding and enslaving them. Sometimes these Amerindian representations were accompanied by a hierarchical gendered imagery that portrayed masters as occupying a masculine position, and subordinates a feminine one. In other instances, these representations went hand in hand with metaphors that equated war captives with the offspring of slain game that had been adopted as "pets" (see Chapter 8).

The depersonification and re-personification of war captives—and to a lesser degree, of servants and tributaries—often entailed the imposition of special markings on their bodies. This is a reflection of the Amerindian propensity to use the body as the main instrument through which to convey social and cosmological meanings (Seeger et al. 1979; Viveiros de Castro 1979; Turner 1995), as well as the privileged means for imprinting and preserving the memory of changes in status (Clastres 1998d). It is precisely for this reason that Amerindians have privileged bodily transformations to mark and denote the passage from personal autonomy to servility.

The imprinting of servile status through what Mauss (1936) has called *les techniques du corps* was achieved through several means: by emphasizing those bodily marks that betrayed the foreign, less-than-human condition of war captives; by underscoring the lack of bodily marks characteristic of their captors, considered to be signs of full humanity; by prohibiting the use of items of clothing or ornaments that were the prerogative of full members of the capturing society; and, lastly, by imposing on them debasing ornaments, body marks, and corporeal mutilations. As long as they retained their servile status, such corporeal markings labeled captives—and to a lesser extent servants and tributaries—as being different and inferior.

KALINAGO

Kalinago had a rich vocabulary to refer to enemies taken in war and kept as servitors or concubines. The Kalinago term for "enemy" is *etoutou*, or *itoto* (Rochefort 1666[1658]: Appendix). Among the related, Carib-speaking Kari'na of the mainland, this term is not only used to designate foreigners and enemies but is also extended to prospective *poito*, or sons-in-law (Whitehead 1988: 225). Here I will dwell only on the first meaning, leaving the examination of the second meaning for the discussion on Amerindian modes of assimilating servants and captives (in Chapter 8). Since the preferred enemies of the Kalinago were the Arrouague (present-day Lokono), the terms *etoutou* and *arrouague* (also *allouague*) were often used synonymously (Breton 1665: 223).

Kalinago described the action of taking captives in war as *katámoni láyem*, or *catámonihánum loróman*, meaning "he renders them slaves" or "makes them captives" (Breton 1665: 450). Breton (1666: 152) translates the root *támon*, found in these two expressions, interchangeably as "slave" or "captive," though the basic meaning of *támon* possibly is "seized in war." However, Breton (1665: 45) presents another term for "captive" or "prisoner of war," *libínali etoútou*, which designated those destined to be killed and consumed in anthropophagous rituals. This suggests that Kalinago distinguished between adult male captives destined to be executed (*libínali*) and female and infant captives meant to be kept alive as concubines and servitors (*támon*).

It should be noted that Kalinago also had a term for servants not captured in war, or "hired servants, such as the Christians have": *nabouyou* (Rochefort 1666[1658]: Appendix; Breton 1666: 362). We are told that in the past this kind of servant, who might have been low-ranking Kalinago attached to a chief's household, was in charge, for instance, of carrying renowned chiefs on their shoulders (Rochefort 1666[1658]: 208–209; Breton 1665: 230), a practice with a long tradition in native tropical America (see Figure 14). Such a linguistic distinction should dispel the notion that European chroniclers mistook Kalinago "servants" for "slaves."

Several sources report that once they arrived at their captors' village, all war prisoners were subjected to the fury, insults, and beatings of the local people, a much-dreaded prospect (Du Tertre 1654: 450; Labat 1724[1705]: I, Part 2, 11). Almost immediately, Kalinago masters proceeded to shear the hair of the female and infant captives they had taken (Anon. 1988[1620]: 187–188; Du Tertre 1654: 421). Never again were they allowed to grow their hair long, as both Kalinago men and women normally wore it. Since Kalinago people cut their hair on only two sorts of occasions (at around the age of two, when children were weaned and allowed to eat fish, and whenever a spouse or close relative died), the shearing of female and infant captives must be seen as marking the end of the captives' past lives and the obliteration of their previous social ties. Thus, long hair came to be perceived as a sign of "independence and liberty," whereas short hair was seen as a sign of servitude (Breton 1978[1647]: 60–61).

From then onward, captives were addressed not by their names but by the term *támon*, "male slave," or *oubéherou*, "female slave" (Breton 1665: 450, 417; Anon. 1988[1620]: 187–188). French sources assert that young male captives were sometimes also addressed as "my barbecue," in reference to the fate that awaited them (Chevillard 1659: 118) (more on this in Chapter 8). These appellations contributed to the process of depersonification of war captives and their re-personification as subordinates. By refusing to use their names, Kalinago masters deprived war captives of their past identity, and even of their humanity, since the naming of Kalinago boys and girls one month after their birth marked the beginning of their existence as human and social beings (Anon. 1988

[1620]: 167). By addressing them as "my (male or female) captive slave," their captors provided them with a new, generic identity as servitors.

In addition to being deprived of their names and having their hair cropped, in contact times captive boys were also emasculated. Reporting on Columbus's second voyage to America, Alvarez Chanca (1978[1494]: 31) remarked that when Kalinago "take any boy prisoners, they dismember them", and he claimed to have seen "three of these boys . . . thus mutilated." Other authors who participated in this trip confirm Alvarez Chanca's report (Coma 1903[1494]: 250; Cúneo 1928[1495]: 280). Vespucci (cited in Schwerin 2003: 48) provides an independent confirmation of this practice. In 1499 he intercepted a canoe manned by seventy warriors on the southern coast of Trinidad. The raiders were transporting four emasculated male captives. When interrogated, they asserted that their genitals had been cut off and eaten by their captors, whom they called Camballi (Caniballi), the term used by the Arawak speakers of the Greater Antilles to refer to the dreaded Kalinago. Later, but generally reliable, sources confirm these reports (de las Casas 1986[1560]: I, 370; F. Columbus 1992[1539]: 117).

It is difficult to assess the veracity of this information, but it is telling that these allegations were not directed at any other indigenous peoples within the region. We do know, however, that castration of slaves was a well-known practice in ancient Rome, China, India, Byzantium, and the Ottoman empire and would not have scandalized the Spaniards. In fact, in the early sixteenth century, the Spanish still found it legitimate to cut the genitals of Indian servants and African slaves as punishment for being disobedient or rebellious (Loaisa 1885–1932: 473ff.; Porcallo de Figueroa 1522: fols. 274–274v). Emasculation of slaves in the Old World entailed either the removal of the testes or the excision of both testes and penis, leaving the man with only an orifice for urination. Among Kalinago people, captive boys seem to have been subjected to this latter procedure (Alvarez Chanca 1978[1494]: 31; F. Columbus 1992[1539]: 117). If emasculation was indeed an important practice in Kalinago rituals of enslavement, it had been abandoned by the seventeenth century; it is not reported in any other source. However, evidence exists that Kalinago continued to cut off and throw into the sea the penises of slain enemies (Anon. 1988[1620]: 189).

Female captives not only were forbidden to grow their hair but also were not allowed to wear the *echépoulátou*, the leg bands used by Kalinago women (Alvarez Chanca 1978[1494]: 29; Breton 1978[1647]: 62) (see Figure 15). *Echépoulátou* were ligatures made with cotton thread that were placed right above and below the calves, so that the calves looked swollen. Kalinago girls were given their first leg bands after undergoing puberty initiation rituals (Labat 1724[1705]: I, Part 2, 5). These cotton ligatures were never removed unless they rotted or were damaged as a consequence of some grave accident. According to Breton (1665: 197), Kalinago women valued their leg bands "as the most beautiful of their ornaments and the most infallible sign of their freedom, and because of this they do not stand any slave to wear them." Female captives also differed from Kalinago women by having a lack of ornamentation and being given heavy tasks that they were expected to carry out. An eighteenth-century engraving based on an oil painting of a Kalinago family of St. Vincent shows the differences in ornamentation and activities between Kalinago women and female captives (see Figure 16).

Deprived of their names, addressed only as captives, with their bodies marked by mutilations, and prohibited from wearing ornaments that were the sole prerogative of their masters, war captives in Kalinago society were forced—at least during the years immediately after their capture—to lead a suspended life of alienation and marginality.

CONIBO

Conibo people regarded all their neighbors as *nahua*, meaning both "foreigner" and "enemy" (Anon. 1927: 413). Taking captives was described by the term *yadtánqui*, "to make captives," where *yadtá* means "captive," and *áqui*, "to make" (Marqués 1931[1800]: 143, 160). Since *yadtánqui* also means "to grab" or "to seize" (Marqués 1931[1800]: 145), the literal meaning of the root *yadtá* (captive) must be "the seized one." Conibo people had a second term to refer to war captives, to wit, *hiná*, which had the double meaning of "household servants" and "domesticated wild animals" (Marqués 1931[1800]: 143; Anon. 1927: 405). I explore the implications of the simile between captives and pets in more detail in Chapter 8. Here I only want to stress the idea that Conibo people regarded most of their neighbors as being less human than themselves or, at least, as representing a different form of humanity, one closer to animality (DeBoer 1986: 238).

Peoples who did not wear tunics and who did not practice head elongation and female circumcision—cultural practices that Conibo people regarded as the utmost signs of civilization—were especially perceived as nonhuman. Head elongation and the use of cotton tunics are depicted in a drawing of a Conibo headman and his three wives made by Father Gabriel Sala in the late 1800s (see Figure 17). From a Conibo point of view, their most savage neighbors were the Panoan-speaking Cashibo, Amahuaca, Remo, Sensi, Mayoruna, and Capanahua, who went around naked, had round heads, and, except for the Cashibo, did not practice female circumcision. These backwoods peoples were considered to be cannibalistic, dirty, and savage. Slightly less savage were the Arawakan-speaking Asháninka, who wore tunics but did not practice head elongation and female circumcision, and the Piro, who wore tunics and practiced female circumcision but did not elongate their heads. The Panoan-speaking Shipibo and Setebo, peoples who engaged in all these practices, were considered enemies but not savages. At the other extreme of this continuum were the Conibo, who viewed themselves as the epitome of civilized beings.

Most Conibo raids were directed at peoples with round heads, a situation reminiscent of that found on the Pacific northwest coast, where the southern Wakashan-speaking peoples who practiced head elongation took captives only from the coastal peoples of northern British Columbia, who did not; and vice versa (MacLeod 1928: 645–647; Ruby and Brown 1993; Hajda 2005). Conibo were very aware of the difficulties inherent in the process of *hináqui*, the raising or making of captives and pets. Adult males were killed immediately, for Conibo warriors knew that they would attempt to escape, no matter how far away they were taken, or that they would otherwise languish and die soon thereafter (Ordinaire 1887: 288). To avoid revenge or any future proprietary claims, Conibo warriors also killed all close relatives of the young women and children they abducted (Ordinaire 1887: 288). To lessen the feeling of regret that captives might experience after being removed from their villages, Conibo raiders torched their homes. Having no family or place to go back to, female and infant captives were expected to submit and integrate more readily into Conibo society.

As soon as Conibo raiders returned home, they dressed whatever captives they had brought with them in the Conibo manner: wraparound skirts for the women, cotton tunics for the men (Roe 1982: 84). Since most inland peoples wore only string belts that left their genitals exposed—something that Conibo people abhorred as a sign of immodesty and savagery—the dressing of war captives must be considered as a civilizing act, as well as a first step in their process of integration. Captive women had their hair bangs cut two fingers above their eyebrows. This practice was meant to distinguish them from true Conibo women, whose bangs reached their eyebrows, as well as to denote their status as "half-civilized" people. Young captive men had their long hair cut short, to differentiate them from their masters, who wore their hair long (see Figures 5 and 17).

In some cases, the youngest female captives were circumcised (DeBoer 1986: 238). Female circumcision of Conibo nubile girls was carried out in large celebrations known as *ani shreati*—"the great libation"—taking place after having undergone a one-year-long period of ritual seclusion (Morin 1998: 392). Circumcision consisted in the removal of the clitoris and labia majora and the perforation of the hymen (Stahl 1928[1895]: 161–163). Conibo people argued that clitoris excision impeded women from developing "uncivil desires" and thus made them more "civilized." Female circumcision, depicted in a nineteenth-century engraving from Marcoy's expedition, was considered to be a sign of true Conibo womanhood (see Figure 18). For this reason, captive women who were past their puberty and could not be circumcised were regarded as being inferior and unsuitable as prospective wives.

Conibo rituals of enslavement had the purpose of marking war captives both as outsiders and insiders—as ugly foreigners but also as prospective concubines or adoptive children. Most captives had physical characteristics (round heads) or cultural decorations (facial tattoos, as with the Remo, Capanahua, and Mayoruna) that marked them indelibly as foreigners and captives, no matter how Coniboized they became. The lack of an elongated head was especially significant. Head elongation was achieved by compressing the forehead and occiput of babies between a soft pad and a padded board during the first months of their lives, as shown in an early 1900s photograph taken by Günter Tessmann (see Figure 19). According to Stahl (1928[1895]: 164), head elongation was considered to be as important a feature in the definition of legitimate Conibo men and women as female circumcision, for it was believed that the flattening of the head repressed capriciousness and rebelliousness, and thus induced a civil disposition in those who had undergone the procedure. In such a context, having a round head was a sign both of captive status and of irremediable incivility (Morin 1998: 390–391). Thus the round-headed Amahuaca, such as those depicted in a mid-1800s engraving, were the target of constant Conibo raiding (see Figure 20).

TUKANO

Tukano regard Makú as being their opposites—the absolute Others, the anti-Tukano (Jackson 1983: 158). From a Tukano point of view, Makú people live deep in the forest instead of along the open riverbanks; they are nomads dwelling in fragile lean-tos instead of large, sturdy malocas; they subsist on hunting and gathering instead of fishing and agriculture; they are incapable of feeding themselves instead of being well provisioned; they are small and have ugly features and unclean habits instead of being tall, well built, and clean; they go about unadorned instead of donning rich ornaments; they speak an awful gibberish instead of the beautiful Tukanoan languages; and, worst of all, they marry within their language group instead of marrying exogamously.

All these characteristics lead Tukano people to consider Makú as not quite human. Some even assert that Makú are not *mahsá*, or true people (Jackson 1991: 25; Reichel-Dolmatoff 1971: 18). Barasana believe that Makú are primitive, uncivilized, and closer to the natural order, and they often compare Makú to monkeys (C. Hugh-Jones 1979: 5). This analogy is based not only on alleged facial and bodily similarities but also on the notion that Makú are the servants of Tukano people, just as monkeys were the servants of Yeba, the first man (Århem 1981: 127). Some Barasana even claim that Makú people are "children of the jaguar," recalling a widespread Tukano myth that recounts how Makú were magically made by Yeba, the son of Jaguar Woman and the Primal Sun, and were thus not true people (Giacone 1949: 88–89; S. Hugh-Jones 1988: 295).

Tukano, Pirá-Tapuya, and Wanano peoples call Makú *pohsá*; Desana call them *poyá*, whereas Barasana and Makuna call them *hosa* or *josa* (Reichel-Dolmatoff 1996: 83; C. Hugh-Jones 1979: 57; Århem 1981: 121). Most authors translate the expression *pohsá*, or any of its variants, as "servants" or "servant people." Giacone (1965: 96) goes even further, rendering it as "slave of others, the one who works without remuneration." According to Reichel-Dolmatoff (1971: 19), however, the term *poyá* derives from *poyári*, which denotes "something incomplete or abnormal" or "something that is almost-but-not-quite," in reference to the fact that Tukano regard Makú people as "not entirely people."

Giacone (1965: 142, 150, 181, 188) claims that Tukano express the relation of servitude by the term *petocángue*, which he renders as "servant," "slave," or "serf," but also as "neighbor." This expression derives from the root *petoáca*, "nearby," and the causative suffix *cángue*, "to be" or "to be made to be" (Giacone 1965: 94, 28). The term *petocángue*, "to be made into neighbors/servants," would refer to the action of forcing Makú people to reside as servant groups close to the malocas of their Tukano masters. The Barasana describe this same action through the verb *hoso*—from the root *hosa*, or "servant"—which, according to S. Hugh-Jones (1992: 68), can be translated as "to be made into Makú" or "to be made into servants." Both terms—*petocángue* and *hoso*—also seem to denote the action of transforming wild forest peoples into civilized but subordinated neighbors.

Little information about Tukano rituals of enslavement is available. In contrast, much more information exists on the markers of servitude that distinguished Makú from their Tukano masters. Makú people in general differed from their masters because of their lack of ornamentation (Jackson 1983: 152). In Tukano thought, ornamentation was a basic requisite of human status (Goldman 1963: 153). From birth, Tukano children were decorated with facial designs, arm bands, and seed necklaces. One of the main reasons Makú people were derided as "not human" was precisely because they lacked ornaments.

The absence of proper humanity was even more clearly manifested in the case of Makú men, who did not wear the *uhtabú*, the white cylindrical quartz stone that all Tukano men wore hanging from their necks. The length and width of these stones revealed the status of their bearers, the larger stones being worn only by the most powerful *tushábua*, or headmen (Sampaio 1985b[1775]: 117–118; Souza 1848: 467). Thus, for instance, the *uhtabú* worn by the Tuyuka headman of a Tiquié River maloca photographed by Theodor Koch-Grünberg in the early 1900s is not as large as those possessed by more powerful headmen, indicating that he was a man of high rank but not a chief (see Figure 21). Likewise, Makú men lacked the complex feather headdresses, which were "the minimum ornamental requirement for full standing as an adult male" among the Cubeo (Goldman 1963: 153). Not only did Makú subordinates lack these ornaments, but their masters forbade them to wear them (McGovern 1927: 248). The three Makú captive slaves photographed by Koch-Grünberg in the early twentieth century are a good example of the stark austerity in dress and ornamentation of the Makú, so maligned by their Tukano masters (see Figure 22).

Because they were not considered true people, Tukano viewed with abhorrence the possibility of marrying a Makú person (McGovern 1927:

184). This was an important obstacle preventing the assimilation of Makú captives as individuals—not so as collectivities—into the society of their captors. However, Reichel-Dolmatoff (1971: 19) argued that for Desana people the Makú were "not only servants but represent the female element, a sexual object, upon which very ambivalent ideas and emotions are projected." Tukano babies were often breast-fed by Makú women, generating close emotional relationships between Tukano and Makú. And although no Tukano man would take a Makú woman as a wife, they allowed their sons to have sexual access to Makú servant girls (Koch-Grünberg 1995[1909]: I, 277). In some cases, they would even take a Makú concubine, using the precaution, however, not to have children by them (Silva 1962: 409). In contrast, no Tukano woman would ever enter into a relationship with a Makú man.

Makú servant peoples were not subjected to the kind of extreme bodily modifications imposed on war captives by Kalinago and Conibo people. Yet some of their physical and cultural traits, as well as the prohibition to use ornaments considered to denote Tukano identity, set them apart as inferior and servile peoples in the eyes of their Tukano masters.

CHIRIGUANÁ

Chiriguaná language—which shares 96 percent of lexemes with Tupi-Guarani (Dietrich 1986: 194)—distinguished between two types of subordinate peoples: captive slaves and domestic servants. This distinction accords well with what we know of their warring practices, which included raiding for captives and subjugating entire non-Chiriguaná settlements as servant groups. The terms for war captives forced into slavery were *miauçuba* (also *tembiara*, "human prey") and *tapui* (Anon. 1938[1622]: 218, 169, 408). The first term, also rendered as *mbiaîhú* or *tembiaîhú*, was used to refer to actual, individual captives (Ruiz de Montoya 1876[1639]: 337v, 139v). It was made up of the terms *tembiâ*, meaning "that which I seized while hunting, fishing, or warring," and *ha–hubá*, "to gain someone's goodwill through love." These apparently contradictory expressions convey the paradoxical positioning in which war captives in Chiriguaná society found themselves. Initially forced violently into slavery through raiding and capture, they were eventually loved and taken care of, either as wives or adoptive children. This ambivalence was possibly more marked in the early days of Chiriguaná invasion of eastern Bolivia, when the mostly male invaders were in search of wives, than in later times, when their society became more stable and raiding was no longer the main means of obtaining a spouse. Be that as it may, Chiriguaná warriors clearly equated ideologically the violent taking of war captives with the seduction and taming of reluctant women and children.

The second term, *tapui*—from which are derived the terms *tapuipera* (male slave) and *tapuigya* (female slave)—was used to designate actual captive slaves but, above all, to refer to generic, potential captives (Anon. 1938[1622]: 218). According to Ruiz de Montoya (1876[1639]: 355v), the root *tapui* (or *tapĩi*) is composed of the nouns *tapĭ*, "purchased thing," and *teĩi*, "generation." The latter expression has a broad range of meanings, being used to designate troops, companies, parties, and genealogies; in other words, to refer to collectivities, whether of animals or of people (Ruiz de Montoya 1876[1639]: 376r). Thus, the term *tapĩi*, which Chiriguaná people used to refer to all their neighbors, could be translated as "slave peoples." The term *tapĩi*, however, has a second, more complex level of meaning. According to an earlier author, the term *tapijara* meant "native or inhabitant of the land" (Anon. 1938[1622]: 306). If this were so, then the expression *tapĩi* would convey the double condition sustained by the Chané, the Chiriguaná's most significant neighbors, who were natives of the land but also enemies and potential slaves. This equation between enemies and potential slaves marks an important difference with respect to other Tupi-Guaraní peoples, like the Tupinambá, who equated enemies with brothers-in-law, thus treating them as potential affines (Combès and Saignes 1991: 66).

Newly taken war captives suffered a violent underscoring of their foreignness. They entered the village of their Chiriguaná captors tied up, trailing on foot the individual warrior who, having captured them, would advance proudly, mounted on his best horse. Once they arrived in the village, captive children and young women were handed over to the wives, mothers, and daughters of the victorious warriors (Giannecchini 1996[1898]: 327). Amid insults, spitting, and beatings, the enraged women blamed the captives' dead parents and husbands for instigating the war and mocked their memory for having failed to defend them (Nino 1912: 279). Meanwhile, captives were forced to witness how the heads and scalps of their older male relatives and spouses were dragged around the village, kicked, and insulted by the local women and children.

Chiriguaná rituals of enslavement and the imposition of markers of servitude are not well documented. We learn only that, after the abuse proffered on them during the victory rituals, captives were respected and kept as the property of the wife of the warrior who captured them (Giannecchini 1996[1898]: 328). We know, however, that male war captives were easily identified as such because they did not wear the *tembetá*, the underlip plug characteristic of Chiriguaná men but absent among most of their neighbors. One of the five men portrayed in a late-1800s photograph taken by Franciscan missionaries at the Chiriguaná mission of San Pascual de Boicovo illustrates this distinction (see Figure 23). *Tembetá* were a sign of virility, conferred on boys when they were six or seven years old during elaborate initiation rituals. The lower lips of the initiates were perforated by the local shaman or by a respected elder, an act considered to mark the boys' passage from an ambivalent gender to full manhood (Giannecchini 1996[1898[: 305–306).

Tembetá were originally made of wood, but after contact with Europeans, Chiriguaná men started making them of metal, generally tin (Nino 1912: 228). They were cylindrical in shape, with a small cavity in the front and two small wings in the back to hold them in place. The hole in the front was filled with wax and decorated with a small colored stone— green Andean stones being the most prestigious and coveted. The kind of material from which the plugs were made, their size, and the quality of the colored stones indicated differences in the social status and prestige of the bearers (Sanabria Fernández 1949: 40). The *tembetá* was not only the Chiriguaná's foremost sign of virility, but it was also an important ethnic marker. An origin myth claimed that the Chiriguaná obtained the *tembetá* from the Fox divinity, who wanted to distinguish them from the white men and other native peoples (Nino 1912: 234–235).

Chané servant groups adopted the Guaraní language of their masters with the passage of time, as well as many of their cultural practices (Thouar 1991[1887]: 311). Foremost among these was the male initiation ritual centered on the implanting of the *tembetá*. The *tembetá* used by the Chiriguanáized Chané, however, was smaller than those of the Chiriguaná (Nino 1912: 233), encouraging the latter to call their Chané peers *cuñareta*, or "women," an extremely demeaning insult in a society that took such pride in manliness (Nordenskiöld in Combès and Saignes 1991: 109). Adoption of the *tembetá* by the Chiriguanáized Chané did not help breach the gap separating them from the Chiriguaná, but it certainly contributed to perpetuating the latter's contempt for their former servants.

CALUSA

Very little information, either linguistic or ethnographic, exists on the rituals of enslavement performed by the Calusa. In fact, data on Calusa language is so meager that there is still disagreement as to their linguistic affiliation. Thus, it is difficult to reconstruct how Calusa viewed war captives and tributary peoples, the two main categories of subordinate peoples in their society. After a victorious war expedition, Calusa people apparently brought back to their villages the severed heads of enemies they had killed, together with whatever captives they had been able to take. They might have also scalped their enemies (RAH 1549: fol. 107). All that is known about the victory ceremonies that ensued is that head trophies—and scalps?—were the focus of ritual dances, where they were publicly displayed (Rogel 1991b[1568]: 265; Goggin and Sturtevant 1964: 200).

According to at least one source—Father Gregorio de Beteta, who in 1549 landed in "Juan Ponce's Bay" (Charlotte Harbor)—war captives were called *yague* (RAH 1549: fol. 108v). During victory rituals, captives were forced to witness the abuses heaped upon the remains of their kin and companions. They were also forced to dance and sing, making clowns of themselves, for the amusement of the local people (Escalante Fontaneda 1575[1567]: 8). This accords well with what we know about the ritual debasement undergone by war captives in other capturing societies. The "education" of war captives among the Txicão, according to Menget (1988: 68), involved two imperatives: to ridicule their ethos of origin and to praise the acquisition of the qualities of their captors.

The evidence suggests that Calusa people marked their war captives. It is said that Juan Ortiz, a Spanish captive held by the Calusa of Tampa Bay for twelve years, "had his arms tattooed after the manner of the Indians" (Elvas 1995[1539]: 59). The imposition of Calusa tribal garments and markings on war captives was a widespread practice. Solís de Merás (1990[1565]: 111) asserts that the Spanish captives held by Carlos, the Calusa paramount chief, "went about naked [and] turned into savages, like the Indians themselves"; and referring to one of these captives, Barrientos (1965[1568]: 85–86) states that "he came naked and painted, turned into Indian."

The assertion that Spanish captives were tattooed and painted in the same way as their captors suggests that Calusa people imposed their tribal markings on their war captives. This practice has been reported by Erikson (1993: 52) as being common among the interfluvial Pano-speaking peoples of the Ucayali River basin, who tattooed the faces of war captives with their tribal designs "to signify and materialize their social incorporation within the group of their abductors." More often than not, this painful operation was practiced against the will of the young captives (Erikson 1986: 192). I would argue that in the case of the Calusa the imposition of tribal markings on war captives should not be seen only as an indication of their social incorporation into the society of their captors. It was, above all, a means to mark the end of their past kinship links and social personas, and the beginning of a new life as captive slaves.

The rituals of enslavement devised by capturing societies were intended to alienate, depersonify, and re-personify individuals or collectivities subjugated by the force of arms. The contradictions and ambiguities posed by the integration of captives and subject peoples into the societies of their captors made it imperative that they be marked in some way—linguistically or physically—as both outsiders and insiders. Tributary populations were in a very different situation. In such cases what was important to stress was not that subordinates owed their lives to their captors and should therefore meekly accept a servile position within the latter's society. Rather, what had to be emphasized was that they owed their autonomy to their masters/protectors and should never forget their superiority. This capitulation was accomplished by demanding the proper ritual gestures of acquiescence and obedience, not by the ritual imposition of bodily markings.

The procedure followed by Carlos, the Calusa paramount chief, in his attempts to persuade conquistador Menéndez de Avilés to become his suzerain and protector, provides a glimpse of the ritual gestures that he himself expected from his tributary chiefs. It is reported that when chief Carlos welcomed the Spanish conquistador, he knelt and extended his hands palms up, waiting for the visitor to place his hands over his own. According to the chronicler, this was "the greatest obeisance that they perform for their principals" (Barrientos 1965[1568]: 88). Later on, Carlos ordered his people to carry the Spanish on their shoulders as a sign of homage (Barrientos 1965[1568]: 89). We are told that he did so in order to make it easier for his men to ambush them, but it is clear that this was a customary practice by which commoners honored their chiefs, and tributary chiefs honored their suzerains (see Figure 14). When Menéndez de Avilés visited chief Carlos in his large house, the latter received him surrounded by his sister-wife, his closest kin, and members of the highest-ranking Calusa families. They all proceeded to stand up and to render obeisance "in the way vassal Indians do with their chiefs" (Barrientos 1965[1568]: 92). Once Menéndez de Avilés and his men were comfortably seated, chief Carlos asked the highest-ranking men and women of his entourage to sing and dance in their honor, which "was the greatest rejoicing, respect, and obedience that this chief, or any other in that land, could have rendered to the Governor" (Solís de Merás 1990[1565]: 118).

In the political interplay between suzerains and tributaries it was more important for suzerains to mark themselves as being superior than to mark their tributaries as being inferior. Thus a Calusa paramount, we are told, "stood out from the rest in the spirit and the nobleness of his person and in the respect that they all showed to him, and in the many beads with which he adorned his body, circling, with strings [that were] four or six fingers wide, his throat, upper arms, wrists, below the knees, ankles, above the ankles" (San Miguel 2001[1596]: 80). In this way, the chronicler concluded, "the king distinguished himself from his vassals." If, like the Guale of northern Florida (AGI: 1577, fol. 256r), Calusa used pearl strings as a form of native "money," such a display might have also been meant to underscore the paramount chief's wealth and power. Profuse ornamentation and elaborate rituals of submission were thus employed to stress the supremacy of Calusa suzerain chiefs and the acquiescence of tributary populations.

GUAICURÚ

Guaicurú people considered all other indigenous peoples as their *cativeiros*, or captives, who "owed them tribute and vassalage" (Florence 1941[1829]: 62–63). The Guaicurú term that Portuguese authors glossed as *cativeiros* was *nibotagi* (sing.) or *nibotagipi* (pl.). Spanish sources rendered this term as "servant," "page," "subject," "vassal," "serf," and "slave" (Sánchez Labrador in Unger 1972: 89). The term was also translated as "inferior," indicating that it denoted not only asymmetrical sociopolitical relations but also ethnosocial valuations (Unger 1972: 89). Its most basic meaning, however, was "captive" or "captured in war" (Unger 1972: 70). The opposite of *nibotagi* was *agica nibotagodi*, meaning "exempt of master, that is, neither servant nor slave" (Unger

1972: 89). Possibly, then, *nibotagi* had the double meaning of "people captured in war" and "people who have a master/owner."

Guaicurú considered Guaná subordinate populations to be not only *nibotagi*, in the sense of "subjects," but also *noyed'ogodi*, which Sánchez Labrador (in Unger 1972: 92) translates as "he who pays tribute," or "tributary" ("tribute" = *noyedi*). In turn, Guaná people called Guaicurú *oquilidi*, or "masters." Guaicurú were thus well aware that war captives and subject populations may have all been "servants" in the sense that all had "masters," but their political situation varied significantly. Tributary peoples retained their political and economic autonomy, their chiefly families were related to Guaicurú chiefly lineages, and in the affairs of war they were considered to be friends and allies. In contrast, captives were an acquisition; they were part of *conoelogodipi loguodape* ("things of our enemies"), the term Guaicurú used to designate spoils taken in raids against the enemy (Unger 1972: 69).

Victory rituals included parading handcuffed captives and displaying head trophies or scalps. Village women danced and sang, holding these remains while praising the valor of their fathers, brothers, and husbands (Jolís 1972[1789]: 314). Doubtless, one of the aims of these performances was to mark captives as despised foreigners. In addition, war captives were marked as such and were differentiated from their Guaicurú masters, using several methods. Guaicurú men wore a variety of feather ornaments—headdresses, arm bands, and leg bands—made of many kinds of colored feathers (Prado 1839[1795]: 29; Lozano 1733: 65). They refused, however, to use headdresses made from feathers of the greater rhea (*Rhea americana*). These were reserved for making shamanic feather fans and women's parasols and were the only feathers that captives were allowed to use (Sánchez Labrador 1910–1917[1760]: I, 214). Given that greater rheas symbolized animality in the Guaicurú worldview (see Lozano 1733: 64), their use by captives must be regarded as marking their animality and, thus, their less-than-human condition. In addition, male captives were allowed to paint their bodies only with black charcoal, whereas Guaicurú men preparing to go to war painted their bodies with rich designs in red annatto (*Bixa*), black genipapo, and the white flour of the *namogoligi* palm (unidentified) (Sánchez Labrador 1910–1917[1760]: I, 286) (see Figure 11).

Female captives and servants differed from their mistresses by their facial designs and by the techniques used to apply them. Guaicurú women painted elaborate designs on their faces and bodies, much like the woman in a late-nineteenth-century drawing by Guido Boggiani (see Figure 24), and the woman in the photograph taken by Claude Lévi-Strauss a half century later (see Figure 25). The higher their rank, the more elaborate the designs. As a mark of extreme nobility, they even sometimes tattooed their arms from their shoulders to their wrists (Sánchez Labrador 1910–1917[1760]: I, 285)—like a young girl depicted by Boggiani (see Figure 26). No high-ranking Guaicurú woman would, however, tattoo her face under any circumstance. Facial tattoos were considered to be "the mark of their inferiors and servants," meaning captives and Guaná household servants, but also, probably, Guaicurú commoners (Sánchez Labrador 1910–1917[1760]: I, 285). Guaicurú tattooed the foreheads of low-ranking women "from the hairline to above their eyebrows with thick black lines resembling the keys of an organ," using a fishbone and the ashes of the leaves of a certain palm (Sánchez Labrador 1910–1917[1760]: I, 285). In addition, they sometimes tattooed their chins. This custom, indicating servile status, was still in use fifty years later, when Hercules Florence visited the region around 1825 and drew the portrait of a Chamacoco captive woman (see Figure 27).

Apart from these differences in personal ornamentation, evidence points to the Guaicurú having placed their personal marks on their captives. These marks were applied to all personal belongings, be they animals (horses and dogs) or objects, such as combs, smoking pipes, weaving utensils, gourds, and boxes (Boggiani 1945[1895]: 228). Guaicurú chiefs sometimes displayed their personal marks on flags planted in front of their tents. Apparently, personal marks were also applied to people, especially women. Confused about this practice, some authors reported that Guaicurú women bore the brands of their horses on their bodies (Prado 1839[1795]: 30). Other authors asserted that most Guaicurú women bore these marks on their chests, the signs of the male heads of family, who "applied them to everything they possessed" (Castelnau 1850–1859[1845]: II, 394). Boggiani (1945[1895]: 228), who lived many years among Guaicurú people, affirmed, however, that both Guaicurú chiefs and their wives had their own personal marks (see Figures 28 and 33). Thus, personal marks were not solely a male prerogative. Boggiani's statement also suggests that Castelnau's interpretation is wrong and that only certain women—namely, captive women—were marked by their masters in such a way. This seems to have been the case for a Chamacoco slave woman photographed by Boggiani in the late 1800s; she bore the personal mark of her "owner" between her eyebrows (see Figure 29).

Apparently, the custom of marking people derived from the Spanish and Portuguese practice of branding their horses; it would have been adopted by Guaicurú people in the late 1500s, together with the horse. However, strong evidence indicates that the practice of marking people existed in America prior to contact. Reporting on the native peoples of Virginia, Thomas Hariot (in Lorant 1965[1588]: 271) asserted: "All inhabitants of this country have marks on their backs to show whose subjects they are and where they come from." Theodor de Bry immortalized some of these marks in one of his famous engravings on the New World (see Figure 30). Among native Virginians, chiefly marks signified personal allegiance and local affiliation rather than personal possession. Elsewhere, such as in lowland Costa Rica and Panama, they denoted slave status (Fernández de Oviedo 1851[1535]: I, 204; Lothrop 1937: 23). This suggests that Guaicurú marking of war captives was a precolonial practice. If true, then the elaborate marks that Guaicurú branded their horses with in colonial times were inspired by the tattooing of captives rather than the other way around (see Figure 33).

* * *

The previous discussion should dispel the idea that the manner in which the capturing societies examined here handled war captives is in any way similar to that found among the ancient Tupinambá (Carneiro da Cunha and Viveiros de Castro 1985) or, more recently, among the Txicão (Menget 1988), Matis (Erikson 1993), or Parakanã (Fausto 2001). In these societies captives were neither executed gloriously in cannibalistic rituals nor assimilated promptly into their captors' societies. On the contrary, they were marked—linguistically and physically—as both captives and servants, a status that often persisted until the end of their lives and, in some cases, was even transmitted to their children (see Chapter 7).

An analysis of the terms used by capturing societies to designate subordinate or dependent people allows me to draw a second important conclusion, to wit, that the native terms translated by European authors as "slave" would almost invariably be better translated as "captive" or, more specifically "captured in war." The Kalinago *támon*, the Conibo *yadtá*, the Chiriguaná *tembiaĩhú*, and the Guaicurú *nibotagi* all convey the notion of "someone seized in war, hunting, or fishing," that is, the notion of prey. They also imply notions of inferiority and servitude, which would explain why Europeans rapidly equated these native terms with their concept of "slave." Whether these captives can be analytically considered as slaves or not is something that I will address further on. Here, I would like to stress that, apart from these basic terms, Amerindian capturing societies possessed a rich vocabulary to describe situations of subordination and extreme dependency.

All these terms, including those that do not allude to the condition of war captive, imply some sort of coercion. This is the case of the Tukano terms *petocángue* and *hoso*, "to be made into servant/neighbors," used to designate Makú servant peoples. It also applies to the Guaicurú term *noyed'ogodi*, "those who pay tribute," employed to refer to Guaná tributary populations. Once more, these examples confirm that actual war—or the threat of force—lies at the origin of all these situations of extreme dependency. Even if both captors and captives sometimes represented their relationship as one of alliance or symbiotic reciprocity, the expressions that captors used to describe them belie their peaceful or consensual nature.

Notably, in all the above examples, capturing societies singled out specific neighboring peoples as enemies and potential captives. They did so by referring to them using terms that evoked notions of inferiority, enmity, and servility. Members of capturing societies apparently regarded their preferred victims as being marked with the stigma of servitude even before they were actually defeated and subjugated. Ushique, a late nineteenth-century Conibo headman, offered an interesting rationale for this particular conception. He asserted: "Cashibo are mostly our maroon servants who have taken to the woods; they speak our language, although badly, and we go from time to time to retrieve their offspring as they reproduce" (Stahl 1928[1895]: 150). Similar notions were present among Chiriguaná (Arriaga 1970[1594]: 447), Tukano (Giacone 1949: 87), and Guaicurú (Serra 1845[1803]: 204), indicating that capturing societies saw their preferred enemies as slave-breeding or servant-breeding populations. If this was actually the case, then markers of servitude imposed on war captives during rituals of enslavement would only confirm a preexisting condition.

Indeed, among native tropical American societies the reinforcement of the social distance separating masters from subordinates—whether captive people, servant groups, or tributary populations—through a variety of ritual mechanisms seems to have been only a way of giving material expression to what captors viewed as an original, almost essential dissimilarity. Marking captives' bodies—whether actually or symbolically, by imposition or default—set them apart as less-than-human and inferior foreigners. This is true even in those cases in which the markings imposed were those of the capturing society.

The marking and mutilation of bodies were not, however, the only physical means of underscoring the social distance that separated masters from subordinates. The imposition of rituals of acquiescence and obedience was also an effort to discipline and master the bodies of subordinates, to instill in them a sense of inferiority and submissiveness. But if the direct marking of the body was the ultimate affront to individuals already demoralized and defeated—a sort of final debasement prior to their acquisition of a new identity and status as an insider—the imposition of ritual gestures of acquiescence was meant as a reminder of the tenuous equilibrium on which the life and fortunes of servant groups and tributary populations depended. It allowed them to maintain a certain degree of autonomy so long as they willingly complied with their masters' requests. The rich ornamentation worn by Tukano, Chiriguaná, and Guaicurú chiefs of old, and the almost regal splendor of Calusa paramount chiefs, are the stark counterparts of these rituals of obeisance. Whereas the latter were meant to instill discipline, the former was meant to inspire awe and fear.

CHAPTER 6

Servile Obligations

> Most social scientists seem to think that people are worth
> acquiring and controlling only or mainly for the labor or the wealth
> that they bring. . . . People can be acquired and controlled for a
> great variety of purposes, and many of these are not economic.
>
> —IGOR KOPYTOFF and SUZANNE MIERS,
> "African 'Slavery' as an Institution of Marginality"

It has been argued that native tropical American war captives cannot be defined as slaves because they were not central to the productive system of their masters' societies. Some contend that no Amerindian society had developed an economy sophisticated enough to depend on the labor force of a slave class (Langebaek 1992: 145; Clastres 1998b: 70). Others assert that captive slaves had little economic importance (Goldman 1963: 106) or did not provide a significant volume of surplus labor (Steward and Faron 1959: 188). Most authors, however, agree on the important point that the existence of captives did not liberate their masters from the necessity to work.

Arguments such as the preceding ones are based on a venerable tradition within the social sciences that views slavery as a means of obtaining surplus labor and enhancing the economy of the capturing society. In a short but influential essay on slavery, Finley (1968) differentiates between "slave owning societies" and "genuine slave societies" on the basis of the centrality of slavery to the economic reproduction of the slaveholding society. Lovejoy (2000: 9) perpetuates this view by distinguishing slavery as a "minor feature of society" from slavery as an "institution." Both of these authorities insist that in societies where only a few people own slaves, and the latter are not crucial to the productive process, slavery can be considered to be an incidental segment of its social and economic structure. The transformation of slavery from an incidental to an institutional feature of society is always accompanied, they claim, by the development or consolidation of a "slave mode of production" (Lovejoy 2000: 10).

Kopytoff and Miers (1977: 55) have criticized this economistic outlook on slavery, arguing that people can be acquired and controlled for a multiplicity of purposes and that "many of these are not economic." Lévy-Bruhl (1931: 13) goes even further, suggesting that the practice of slavery precedes the notion that slaves can be useful in economic terms. From the point of view of these authors, productive functions and economic relevance are not defining elements of slavery. Slaves, they argue, can carry out a broad range of social, political, and economic activities. In some societies, they represented a chief form of economic capital; in others, their economic function was insignificant, but they had great importance as social and political capital. As Patterson (1982: 33) contends, "In many primitive societies where there was little differentiation in the possession of wealth, slaves were usually the major (sometimes the only) form of wealth that made such differentiation possible." In short, the existence of slavery was not confined to societies based on a slave mode of production.

In this chapter, I examine the great variety of activities that slaves, servants, and tributaries were expected to perform, in an effort to determine the extent of their economic role. I argue that, in native tropical America, captive slaves and other subordinate peoples rarely replaced their masters in the sphere of production. They were required, however, to perform the heaviest, dirtiest, and lowest-ranking activities, thus making an important contribution to the economy of slaveholding households. In addition, they were required to provide a large number of small, noneconomic personal services. Such personal services were valued, not because they contributed to their masters' economy, but rather because they enhanced the prestige of their owners and, with it, their political standing vis-à-vis their followers, neighbors, and rivals. Often these subordinates were also expected to fight alongside their masters, sometimes as allies, sometimes as cannon fodder in the vanguard of their masters' army.

Servant peoples and tributary populations sometimes provided services and goods for which they were considered specialists and in which they excelled. Often these services were rewarded, leading some authors to describe such situations as an indication of symbiotic exchange. Such a characterization obscures the fact that these relationships were not economic but, above all, sociopolitical, and that these links were based on the actual defeat (or the fear of defeat) of one of the parties by the other. In so doing, the notion of symbiotic exchange downplays the coercive aspects inherent to such relationships—aspects that are absent, for instance, from intertribal trading relationships such as those reported for the Guiana Highlands (Butt-Colson 1973), eastern Peru (Bodley 1973, 1984), eastern Ecuador (Kelekna 1991), and the Orinoco River basin (Arvelo-Jiménez and Biord 1994).

Captives also played an important role in the ceremonial life of their captors. They were frequently the preferred victims in sacrificial rites focused on increasing the fertility and regeneration of the earth, animals, and plants. In such capacity, they became living war trophies (more on this in Chapter 9). Additionally, they were important elements in life-cycle ceremonies and particularly in funerary rituals. Captives belonging to a man or woman were sacrificed in some societies when their masters died, and were buried together with them to serve them in the afterlife. As attested by AD 450–900 tombs found in central Panama, this practice had a long tradition in native tropical American societies (see Figure 31).

Servile duties included doing chores that had little economic importance but great symbolic significance. Male captives were frequently obliged to perform menial tasks that were considered to be in the women's domain. And female captives were often required to provide sexual satisfaction to their masters or their masters' sons. These services were forced upon captives to remind them that they were alien and inferior and that their masters could do with them whatever they pleased. It is this power that constitutes the very foundation of slavery—whether under the form of a minor social feature or of a central institution—and not the economic functions of slaves (Testart 1998: 32).

KALINAGO

Chronicles written in the early sixteenth century already report that not all Kalinago war captives were destined to be consumed in collective cannibalistic ceremonies. Martire d'Anghiera (1966[1555]: 3r) states that this was mainly the fate of adult men. Boys were kept, he asserts, to be fattened and, when they reached adulthood, to be ritually executed and eaten. In the meantime they were supposed to serve their masters. Girls and young women were kept as concubines and also as servants. In contrast, old women were kept mainly as workers. Luisa Navarrete (1992[1580]: 40), an African former slave taken captive by Kalinago raiders, also reported that those war captives who were kept alive were forced to work for their new masters.

Boys and girls performed light household chores, such as serving food and beverages. One source asserts that the greatest sign of respect for a high-ranking guest was to have him served by the host's wife rather than by his male or female captives (Anon. 1988[1620]: 141–142). This suggests that captive children performed the day-to-day care of household members and guests. Captive children were also charged with bringing food to male initiates, confined in a hut deep in the forest during the second stage of their initiation (Anon. 1988[1620]: 171).

Female captives were sometimes kept as concubines. If they were not attached to any particular man, however, they were obliged to grant sexual favors to whoever requested them (Navarrete 1992[1580]: 40). Captive women were an important economic addition to a Kalinago household. They performed two of the most onerous food production activities in a society whose staple was bitter manioc, to wit, making cassava bread and brewing manioc beer (Navarrete 1992[1580]: 40; Anon. 1988[1620]: 130). In addition, they did much of the cooking. Old women were given the most tedious chores; one source asserts that they were used as "drudges" (Martire d'Anghiera 1966[1555]: 3r). Captive children and women were also required to prepare food and serve those Kalinago men who were engaged in large collective tasks, such as the building of a war canoe or a new longhouse (Anon. 1988[1620]: 171, 176). In later times, African captive men—who were excluded from the cannibalistic ritual exchange system that joined the Kalinago and their preferred enemies, the Lokono—were forced to do much of the planting and tending of manioc gardens (Anon. 1988[1620]: 187).

Kalinago war captives were expected to perform services for their masters and mistresses even after the latter's death (Anon. 1988[1620]: 191). The earliest existing source on this subject states that only some of a dead person's captives were killed (Navarrete 1992[1580]: 40); other sources assert that all of them were slain (Anon. 1988[1620]: 151). All accounts coincide, however, in stating that captives were executed so they could continue to serve their masters and mistresses in the afterworld. Even if a Kalinago warrior died far from home, his captives were executed in the belief that their souls would travel far to join that of their master (Anon. 1988[1620]: 192). Kalinago believed that, after dying, courageous warriors went to live on "certain Fortunate Islands, where they have all things at their wish, and that the Arouagues are their slaves; that they swim unwearied in great rivers; that they live deliciously, and spend the time in dancing, playing and feasting, in a land which produces in abundance all sorts of excellent fruits without any cultivation" (Rochefort 1666[1658]: 289). The slaves mentioned in this narrative seem to be those whom Kalinago warriors captured during their lifetimes and who were executed after their masters' death so that their souls could join those of their masters in the land of the valiant dead.

One source contends that, originally, slaves were buried alive together with their masters in a mass grave dug in the latter's house, similar to that depicted in a late engraving made by the French traveler, Pierre Jacques Benoit (see Figure 32). Dead Kalinago were supposedly buried with all their possessions, including their hammocks, weapons, domestic utensils, and even their dogs (de la Borde 1886[1674]: 252). Later on in time, captives were first executed, then laid on the bottom of the grave and covered with rags (Anon. 1988[1620]: 151). Over their heads a clay vessel was placed so that they could continue cooking fish for their owners. The body of the deceased, generally wrapped in his or her hammock, was placed on top of the executed captives. Other sources assert that after a person was buried, a big fire was lit on top of the grave, and his or her captives were beheaded over it, supposedly to be cremated (Breton 1978[1647]: 80, 138). More often than not, however, as soon as captives heard that their master or mistress was about to die, they fled to the mountains or to a neighboring island; although they were bound to be recaptured by another Kalinago man, they could save their lives (Breton 1978[1647]: 80; Rochefort 1666[1658]: 350).

Captive men also performed important ritual functions. Adult men captured in war were executed soon after the return of their captors, in spectacular ceremonies organized by the chief or by successful warriors (Du Tertre 1654: 450). Captives chosen for sacrifice were obliged to fast for several days. On the day of their execution, they were brought into the longhouse, where they were insulted and beaten by everyone. An old man then executed the prisoner by delivering a sharp blow to his head. The body of the dead man was summarily dismembered, and selected parts were grilled in a large fire. It was said that Kalinago ate this meat "out of rage and not appetite, to revenge and not to feast themselves, neither for the pleasure they found on its taste; for most of them fall ill after this execrable meal" (Du Tertre 1654: 451). Captive boys were emasculated and kept as servants until they became adults, at which time they were also executed and eaten (Alvarez Chanca 1978[1494]: 31). As we shall see, these ceremonies had important implications for the fertility and abundance of Kalinago women and gardens. We may thus conclude that the contribution of captive slaves to the Kalinago economy went far beyond their value as laborers.

CONIBO

The earliest European sources to report on Conibo slave-raiding practices indicate that they "killed or beheaded the old men and women who could not serve them as slaves" (Biedma 1981[1682]: 95). Almost all sources insist that Conibo slave raids were prompted by the institution of polygyny and the generalized scarcity of women (Buenaventura Bestard 1906[1819]: 345–346; Ordinaire 1887: 308; Sotomayor 1905[1899]: 356–357). Young single Conibo men were thus encouraged to raid neighboring groups in search of wives. Captured young women were taken as concubines, whereas girls were raised as prospective spouses for the sons of their captors (Dueñas 1924[1792]: 249; Raimondi 1905 [1862]: 218).

At first sight, the above would suggest that female captives were almost immediately integrated as full members into the families of their captors, as some authors have suggested (DeBoer 1986: 233). However, this interpretation is erroneous. That captive women taken as concubines did not have the same rights as legitimate Conibo wives was spelled out by more detailed sources. In fact, they did not even enjoy the same status as polygynous secondary wives of Conibo origin. Their status remained that of a household servant (Stahl 1928[1895]: 150) who was obliged to perform a variety of tasks, including providing sexual services, whenever her master demanded them (see Chapter 7 for a more detailed discussion of the status of female captives).

Adult captive women were expected to work under the direction of the female household head, who was generally the first legitimate wife of the male head of the household. Although Conibo women were not exempted from working, more than the average share of a household's female work fell on the shoulders of female captives. According to some authors (Stahl 1928[1895]: 150), this would explain why captive concubines often tried to escape. Planting, weeding, harvesting, and carrying loads of agricultural produce were among the most important tasks female captives were expected to perform (Amich 1975: 93). Among household chores, the most salient duty was the preparation of large quantities of manioc or maize beer. For a man trying to build up a following, this beer was an indispensable product; its frequent and generous distribution considerably increased a man's prestige and, eventually, his power (DeBoer 1986: 237). Captive women were also expected to weave mosquito nets, male tunics, female wraparound skirts, bags, and other woven products. Conibo women were able to avoid this extremely tiresome activity, thanks to their servants' labor or to the acquisition of textiles taken from enemy peoples by their husbands as booty (Beraún 1981b[1686]: 181).

That the capture of women was not the main objective of Conibo raiding is confirmed by the fact that a large proportion of war captives were children. Captive children were usually charged with taking care of the older members of their captors' household (Stahl 1928[1895]: 150). When the children grew older, however, they were expected to assume more laborious, time-consuming tasks. Conibo men generally possessed one or more of these young captives (Stiglich 1905: 344). Captive men were expected to perform the heaviest menial tasks, including clearing gardens and carrying loads of firewood (DeBoer 1986: 233; Amich 1975: 93). One such demanding task was making canoes, something that required a large investment in time and energy. This was such a burdensome undertaking that at least one author mentions it as one of the main reasons why male captives sought to escape (Stahl 1928[1895]: 150). Similarly, when Conibo men went on a trading or visiting trip, their male captives were expected to do all the heavy work, including paddling, loading and unloading the cargo, and carrying the canoe on their shoulders whenever necessary (Stiglich 1905: 344; DeBoer 1986: 233).

The labor of captives did not exempt Conibo men and women from working. Doubtless, however, it constituted a significant proportion of the total work required by a household. A surplus supply of female labor reduced the amount of work that Conibo wives had to do, and it boosted their husbands' political careers. In turn, a surplus of male labor allowed Conibo men to devote more time to trading and raiding.

TUKANO

The activities of Makú captives and servants did not, on the whole, differ substantially. However, they did differ significantly from the activities expected of client groups. An analysis of the servile duties of each of these categories of dependents should help scholars reconsider some of the more common views on the nature of Makú dependency.

Makú captives were forced to do all the heavy and unrewarding work (McGovern 1927: 209). They were employed to carry out farming activities and do household chores (Koch-Grünberg 1906: 877). In certain areas the availability of a Makú captive labor force freed its Tukano masters from the need to perform most daily subsistence activities. Koch-Grünberg (1995[1909]: I, 276) asserts that the Tukano "lords" of the Upper Tiquié River led a very comfortable life: "they scarcely knew the way to their gardens," because they had Makú captives who did all the work for them. Latter-day sources confirm this view. Referring to the Tukano of the Upper Papurí River, McGovern (1927: 249) affirms that Makú female captives had to perform most of the agricultural activities so that "their mistresses could lie at ease in their hammocks." Often the female captives were even in charge of breast-feeding their mistresses' children (Reichel-Dolmatoff 1971: 19). In turn, male captives were expected to do the rougher work about the maloca and to provide their masters with game meat. These statements should nevertheless be taken with caution. Tukano chiefs may have had a larger than average number of captives, but there is little evidence that their purpose in holding captives was ever to liberate themselves from work (Goldman 1963: 106; Jackson 1983: 155–156).

Makú captives carried out other heavy tasks not related to subsistence, such as serving as paddlers on long-distance fluvial trips (Koch-Grünberg 1995[1909]: II, 246). On certain occasions they were required to perform activities usually reserved to women. When their masters undertook long-distance trips or trekking expeditions, Makú captives were expected to help the women carry the provisions, a task that no Tukano man would ever perform (Stradelli 1890[1882]: 440).

An important part of the duties of Makú captives consisted of attending to the personal needs of their masters. Tukano chiefs and their wives had a larger number of captives, some of them designated as personal attendants (Koch-Grünberg 1995[1909]: II, 62). These were in charge of holding the large cigars that Tukano chiefs smoked during special ritual occasions (McGovern 1927: 249). They were also in charge of preparing the coca powder that only Tukano men could consume (Koch-Grünberg 1995[1909]: I, 310).

Captive children were used as babysitters for their masters' younger children. So common was this practice that, according to oral tradition, Tariana chiefs often organized raids with the only aim being that of procuring Makú servants for their children (Biocca 1965: 481). Young, unattached female captives were supposed to be freely accessible to Tukano youngsters. And, according to some sources, even older married men occasionally requested their sexual services (Koch-Grünberg (1995 [1909]: I, 277; McGovern 1927: 249). Little evidence exists, however, to substantiate some authors' claims that Makú women played the role of "tribal prostitutes" (Whiffen 1915[1908]: 262).

The duties that members of Makú servant groups performed were similar to those of captive slaves. According to Goldman (1963: 105), Makú bands often attached voluntarily to Cubeo groups, working for them in return for food, shelter, and protection against enemies. In such cases, the Makú servants did most of the everyday work, such as fishing, tending the gardens, and fetching water and firewood. Makú servant groups attached to Tukano, Desana, and Tariana malocas performed similar services (Reichel-Dolmatoff 1971: 19, 161). In addition, they provided their Tukano masters with game (Knobloch 1972: 106), curare (Silva 1962: 202), and baskets (Reichel-Dolmatoff 1971: 119).

Differences existed between Makú captives and servant groups (Koch-Grünberg 1995[1909]: II, 236), but the line separating them was far from clear-cut. Members of Makú servant groups not only were distributed among the different households that composed a maloca but sometimes were even given away as presents to the chiefs of neighboring malocas (Koch-Grünberg 1995[1909]: II, 236; Goldman 1963: 105). Makú servants could be hired out to third parties, including itinerant Europeans (Wallace 1853: 342; McGovern 1927: 248). In extreme cases, they could even be sold as captive slaves to other Tukano malocas "in exchange for ceremonial objects, such as wooden dancing staffs" (Goldman 1963: 105–106). The ease with which Makú captives could be turned into servants, and Makú servants into captive slaves, demonstrates the shifting nature of dependency and servitude in native tropical America.

Client groups were not obliged to dwell in the proximity of their patrons' maloca. They retained a larger degree of autonomy; either they were approached by their Tukano patrons to carry out a particular task, or they periodically visited their patrons to offer their services (Silverwood-Cope 1990: 48; also Reid 1979). Rather than being forced to perform certain tasks, as servant groups were, client groups were "invited" to do so. These tasks consisted of burdensome activities such as clearing and weeding gardens, preparing house materials like thatching, building malocas, paddling canoes, or carrying loads (Koch-Grünberg 1995[1909]: I, 271; Giacone 1949: 7; Biocca 1965: 472; Silverwood-Cope 1990: 37). More frequently, they were asked to provide their Tukano patrons with fish and, especially, game meat, for Makú were renowned for their skills as hunters (Silverwood-Cope 1990: 63, 70; Ramos, Silverwood-Cope, and Oliveira 1980: 148). In addition, they supplied their Tukano patrons with forest resources, such as wild fruits, resins, bamboos, pelts, feathers, and other raw materials for making ritual ornaments, as well as manufactured goods considered to be Makú specialties, such as blowguns, curare poison, hallucinogenic shamanic snuff, and heavy-duty carrying baskets (Silverwood-Cope 1990: 70–71; C. Hugh-Jones 1979: 169–170; Jackson 1983: 153; Chernela 1993: 111).

In exchange for their services, Makú clients received cassava bread, manioc flour, manioc beer, chili peppers, tobacco, coca, and a few industrial goods (Silverwood-Cope 1990: 36–37, 48; S. Hugh-Jones 1988: 25; Jackson 1983: 154; Chernela 1993: 115). The acquisition of iron tools seems to have been one of the greatest incentives for Makú groups to continue providing client services to Tukano malocas. As recently as the late 1960s, many Makú bands did not possess any iron tools, and those who did had paid for them dearly in game meat and services to their Tukano patrons (Silverwood-Cope 1990: 43). The services of Makú clients were occasionally paid for with several day-long festivals in which they were given abundant manioc beer and food (Jackson 1983: 155). Coercion, however, was not totally absent from these transactions. It is thus reported that Tukano chiefs often bullied client groups into working for them or giving them some of their offspring to serve their own children as "servants or pages" (McGovern 1927: 186; Giacone 1949: 88). Makú client groups might have had a greater degree of autonomy and power of negotiation than Makú servant groups or captive slaves, but their servile origin was neither forgotten nor allowed to be forgotten.

CHIRIGUANÁ

As soon as they were captured, Chiriguaná war captives were put to work carrying the booty taken by their captors (Castro 1921–1926[1568]: III, 297). Those who could not do so, in their large majority the elderly and infirm, were put to death (Giannecchini 1996[1898]: 328). Once in the village of their captors, the most important task assigned to both captive men and women was farming. According to an early source, Chiriguaná men did little agricultural work, spending most of their time fishing and hunting when not waging war (Polo de Ondegardo 1991[1574]: 136). Chiriguaná were proud horticulturalists; they showed visible contempt for those peoples who did little or no farming (Giannecchini 1996[1898]: 296). However, they considered agriculture to be mostly a female task (Susnik 1968: 33). Thus, most of the farming was done either by Chiriguaná women or by their Chané captives and servant groups.

Chané people were renowned farmers. Given that between 20 and 80 percent of the population of Chiriguaná settlements consisted of Chané captives and servants, Chiriguaná masters had at their disposition a large stock of surplus labor, allowing an increase in productivity to levels that surprised even Spanish chroniclers. Spanish sources from the sixteenth and seventeenth centuries marveled at the vast extent of the lands planted with manioc, maize, beans, squash, and cotton that they found in Chiriguaná settlements (Arriaga 1974[1596]: 70; Lizárraga 1968[1603]: 151). They also called attention to the high productivity of Chiriguaná gardens and the large amount of stored food (mainly maize and beans) and fermented beverages (maize beer) that were kept in their houses. Some sources report that in good years Chiriguaná production of maize was so abundant that much of it was left to rot in the fields (Viedma 1970[1788]: 757). Although Chiriguaná women and men never completely stopped performing agricultural activities, the high productivity must be largely attributed to the surplus labor provided by Chané captives and servant groups.

Captive women were often taken as concubines by their captors, but their status remained that of servants. Besides performing agricultural tasks, they were burdened with the heaviest household chores (Lizárraga 1968[1603]: 84). These included the preparation of maize beer and the care of their masters' children (Combès and Saignes 1991: 80). Captive women and children were also charged with serving food and beverages to their masters and guests (Arriaga 1974[1596]: 65). On special occasions, captives were sent, as a kind of reception committee, to welcome foreign visitors before they entered the settlement (Arteaga 1961[1607]: 172). They did so, carrying food and beverages to regale the guests. Sometimes captive women also served as personal attendants, caring for the clothes of their masters and dressing them on special occasions (Arriaga 1974[1596]: 66). Captive women also did most of the spinning and weaving of cotton textiles, for Chiriguaná women were little inclined to perform these demanding tasks (Polo de Ondegardo 1991 [1574]: 137).

Captive men and boys were expected to do the heaviest agricultural tasks. They also had menial obligations, such as kindling the fire during the night to keep their masters warm (Arriaga 1974[1596]: 70). In addition, captive men were expected to accompany their masters as porters and personal attendants whenever they traveled. In fact, carrying loads seems to have been a sign of servitude. Farming and household chores were not the only activities performed by captive men, however. Chiriguaná masters taught their Chané slaves and servants the arts of war (Polo de Ondegardo 1991[1574]: 136). When attacking the enemy, either in the open or at night, Chiriguaná war leaders placed the Chané captive-soldiers in the front line (Suárez de Figueroa 1965[1586]: 241). Chané warriors, Suárez de Figueroa asserts, "knew that if they did not fight to the death, they would die at the hands of their masters, and to escape from this peril, they fought even harder than the Chiriguaná." Another Spanish chronicle adds that if the Chané captive-soldiers did not fight well, their masters shot them from behind (Lizárraga 1968[1603]: 84). The use of Chané captive-soldiers was a permanent feature of Chiriguaná warfare; according to some sources, the proportion of captive-soldiers in Chiriguaná armies was often very large (Arteaga 1961[1607]: 173). Despite the grave danger entailed by being employed as shock troops, soldiering was one of the few paths open to Chané male captives and servants to rise above their servile status (more on this in Chapter 7).

Farming and soldiering were the two most important servile obligations carried out by male Chané captives and servants, but they had an important additional role to play as personal attendants and retainers. Chiriguaná chiefs in particular always traveled with a retinue composed of their eldest sons, their most famed warriors, and a large number of captives (Arriaga 1974[1596]: 25; Lizárraga 1968[1603]: 142). Indeed, the prestige of a Chiriguaná chief was in large measure judged by the number of captives he possessed (Giannecchini 1996[1898]: 345; Susnik 1968: 35). The conspicuous display of a large number of servant-concubines, captive-soldiers, and children attendants was apparently an important way to build up and consolidate Chiriguaná leadership. For this reason, captives were even more important as symbols of personal courage and political prestige than as laborers or warriors.

CALUSA

Captives do not seem to have contributed in important ways to the Calusa economy, at least not in terms of labor. Female captives served their mistresses as personal attendants. High-ranking Calusa women had many of these servants, who tended to their needs and accompanied them wherever they went (Solís de Merás 1990[1565]: 124, 164). Male captives also acted as personal attendants to high-ranking Calusa men (Solís de Merás 1990[1565]: 199). The Calusa paramount had many of these captives, some of whom were Spanish men taken in battle or castaways (Laudonnière 2001[1564]: 110–111). On special occasions, these personal attendants carried their master on their shoulders or were ordered to carry important guests in the same manner (Barrientos 1965[1568]: 89). Sometimes they were used as messengers in communications with allied chiefs or enemy peoples (Laudonnière 2001[1564]: 111).

As elsewhere, captive men were also employed in the heaviest menial tasks. According to Garcilaso de la Vega 1995[1605]: 117), they were often in charge of providing all households with firewood and fresh water. They were likely to have been also employed as rowers in the war canoes of the Calusa paramount and other principal chiefs during formal or ceremonial occasions (San Miguel 2001[1596]: 80). Captive men were additionally charged with guarding burial houses, a lowly assignment insofar as it entailed close contact with the polluting dead along with burdensome nightly vigils to prevent wolves and other predators from devouring the corpses (Elvas 1995[1539]: 60; Garcilaso de la Vega 1995[1605]: 104).

Evidence indicating that captives performed basic subsistence activities such as fishing, hunting, or collecting food is completely lacking. Spanish chroniclers reported that Calusa chiefs and warriors were exempted from most subsistence tasks, but it seems that these were carried out mostly by commoners—perhaps former servant populations who had been Calusaized and incorporated as low-ranking retainers, as was the case among the Tukano and Chiriguaná (Monaco and Alaña 1991[1743]: 428).

Captives played a far more important role in Calusa ceremonial life than in the economy. Garcilaso de la Vega (1995[1605]: 103) reports that "at the time of their special festivals" captives were forced to run in the main plaza of the village from sunrise to sunset. If they stopped, they were shot with arrows. This report seems to refer to the fall festival mentioned by López de Velasco (1991a[1569]: 316), in which Calusa shamans disguised as their "idols"—representations of divinities, ancestors, and spiritual beings—ran around day and night, howling as wild animals. No mention is made of the purpose of this ceremony, but captives were necessary to its success.

The central role played by captives in Calusa rituals emerges clearly from descriptions of fertility ceremonies performed by the Calusa paramount chief. It is said that at harvest time the Calusa paramount chief, in his role of life dispenser, sacrificed a captive slave "whom he kept expressly for this purpose, picked from a number of Spaniards who by ill fortune were cast upon the coast" (Laudonnière 2001[1564]: 110–111). After the execution, the sacrificed person was beheaded and his eyes were offered by the officiating shaman to "their idol," after which all those present performed a ritual dance, parading the head of the victim through the village (López de Velasco 1991a[1569]: 316).

The life of service endured by captives belonging to chiefly families continued even after the death of their masters. According to López de Velasco (1991a[1569]: 316), whenever a Calusa chieftain or chieftainess died, all of their servants were killed and buried with them to serve them in the afterworld. In addition, when a chief or one of his sons died, some families also sacrificed their servants' children so they could accompany the high-rank deceased to the abode of the dead (Rogel 1991b[1568]: 245; Monaco and Alaña 1991[1743]: 423).

In contrast to war captives, tributary populations were central to the reproduction of Calusa material economy. Tribute owed to the Calusa paramount included a variety of goods and services. The Tequesta, who were under Calusa domination in the early 1550s, were obliged to pay tribute in plant roots, game meat (mostly deer, alligators, trout, and birds), and tanned deer hides used to manufacture breechclouts and other items of clothing (Escalante Fontaneda 1575[1567]: fol. 3). The roots mentioned by Escalante were starchy tubers obtained from wild plants that grew abundantly in the marshlands around Lake Okeechobee, in Tequesta territory. With the flour obtained from them, the Tequesta made a kind of bread, which was their staple food as well as their main item of tribute (Escalante Fontaneda 1575[1567]: fol. 2). Tequesta also paid tribute in other, unprocessed wild roots. Other subordinate peoples paid the Calusa paramountcy tribute in the form of feathers, straw mats, fruits, and other foodstuffs (Rogel 1991b[1568]: 237), among which cocoa beans were especially important (Alonso de Jesús 1993[1630]: 96).

Foodstuffs flowed into Calos, the Calusa administrative center, from the inland tributary villages through a web of man-made canals controlled by the Calusa paramount. These canals, some authors speculate, were constructed by Calusa tributary laborers and functioned as a sort of "king's highway" (Luer 1989: 113). The produce thus accumulated seems to have been used to feed the Calusa elite and the warrior class, who, as noted above, were exempted from subsistence tasks. Tributary chiefs were also obliged to send military aid in the form of warriors, weapons, and provisions whenever the Calusa paramount requested it (Rogel 1991b[1568]: 254, 266).

The Calusa head chief also received tribute in gold, silver, and amber salvaged from Spanish shipwrecks by the natives of eastern Florida—namely, the Tequesta, Jobe, and Jeaga (Escalante Fontaneda 1575[1567]: fol. 5; Hann 1991a: 23). These precious materials were manufactured into ornaments that only members of chiefly families could wear. Chief Carlos's store of gold and silver was reported to have been so large that it could "fill to the brim a hole to the height of a man and as wide as a barrel" (Laudonnière 2001[1564]: 110). At least once a year, subordinate chiefs went in person to Calos to pay their tribute in precious metals during certain special celebrations (Rogel 1991b[1568]: 267). Archeological finds confirm this piece of information, since most of the gold and silver artifacts discovered in southern Florida appeared in Calusa territory rather than on the east coast or in the Keys, where the majority of shipwrecks occurred (Goggin and Sturtevant 1964: 188).

Tributaries of the Calusa were obliged to pay tribute not only in goods and services but also in people. All Spanish and African people captured by Calusa tributaries had to be sent to the Calusa paramount chief, who might redistribute them afterward. In addition, whenever a new paramount chief was proclaimed, each tributary chief had the obligation to send him a woman of chiefly descent, who was taken as one of several secondary wives (Rogel 1991b[1568]: 268). Unilateral marriage exchanges of this nature reinforced hierarchical relations between the Calusa and their tributaries, while at the same time cloaking a relation of domination as one of affinity.

GUAICURÚ

Two kinds of subordinates existed in Guaicurú society: captive slaves and tributaries. The latter, who were mostly Guaná, were divided into two groups: those living autonomously in their own villages, and those acting as domestic servants attached to their masters' households. The duties of captives and tributaries were clearly different. In contrast, the duties of attached Guaná servants resembled those expected from captives. Thus, here I will consider the duties of captives and attached servants as being basically the same unless otherwise specified and will also refer to both categories of subordinates as captives.

Captive men and women performed most of the subsistence and domestic tasks necessary for the sustenance of wandering Guaicurú households. Captive women tended the small gardens opened in the environs of Guaicurú settlements (Azara 1809[1781]: II, 110; Serra 1850 [1803]: 354; Boggiani 1945[1895]: 133). In addition, they did much of the gathering, especially of palm hearts and palm sap for making wine (Sánchez Labrador 1910–1917[1770]: I, 286). In turn, captive men did much of the hunting and fishing, the main tasks, apart from war, that Guaicurú men occasionally engaged in.

Captive women and girls did almost all of the household work. They provided their masters' households with basic daily necessities, such as firewood and fresh water (Sánchez Labrador 1910–1917[1770]: I, 291–292). They had to keep the fires lit, cook and serve their masters and their guests, and bring water to their masters for washing their hands after eating (Sánchez Labrador 1910–1917[1770]: I, 273, 275; Boggiani 1945[1895]: 135, 151). Female captives also helped their mistresses to weave straw mats (which served as both flooring and roofing), to prepare vegetable fibers, and to manufacture pottery (Sánchez Labrador 1910–1917[1770]: I, 292).

Captive boys helped their masters care for their horses, taking them to graze and to drink water in the river (Sánchez Labrador 1910–1917[1770]: I, 289). They were also forced to carry large loads, especially during camp moves, when male and female captives dismantled and assembled the straw mat lean-tos, as well as loaded and unloaded their masters' possessions on and off their horses (Sánchez Labrador 1910–1917[1770]: II, 27–28; Azara 1809[1781]: II, 109; Serra 1850[1803]: 352). If deemed courageous, captive boys were sometimes trained as soldiers, often accompanying their masters in raids (Serra 1850[1803]: 354).

In addition to the above duties, both male and female captives acted as personal attendants to their masters and mistresses. High-ranking Guaicurú women made a point of being always attended by numerous servants, which was one of their main sources of pride (Sánchez Labrador

1910–1917[1770]: II, 267). During important celebrations, captives accompanied their masters and mistresses in order to wait on them (Boggiani 1945[1895]: 191; Azara 1809[1781]: II, 109). Guaicurú chiefs were also permanently attended by captive women and men, especially when visiting other chiefs or Spanish and Portuguese authorities (Ferreira 1974[1791]: 77). An early nineteenth-century painting by Jean Baptiste Debret shows one such proud Guaicurú chief attended by a personal servant (see Figure 33). Personal attendants took care of the smallest needs of their masters and mistresses, to the point that if one of the latter fell ill, a captive stood by his or her bedside and chased the flies away (Sánchez Labrador 1910–1917[1770]: II, 38). As among the Calusa, captives were often used to carry messages within and between settlements (Ferreira 1974[1791]: 77; Boggiani 1945[1895]: 189).

Whenever a Guaicurú chief or chieftainess died, some or all of the deceased's captives were sacrificed to keep them company. Various sources confirm this practice, adding that in some cases captives offered voluntarily for such sacrifice to "demonstrate the love and esteem they [felt] for their masters" (Techo 1897[1673]: II, 376–377; Lozano 1733: 70). If the deceased owned horses, they also killed a few, "so that in its new state the soul can ride and amuse itself in better pastures and hunting grounds" (Sánchez Labrador 1910–1917[1770]: II, 47). Although some authors assert that killing a dead person's slaves had been abandoned by the 1760s (Sánchez Labrador 1910–1917[1770]: II, 47; Jolís 1972[1789]: 315), this custom seems nevertheless to have been maintained for a longer time in some places (Serra 1850[1803]: 361).

Guaná tributaries living autonomously played an important role in the Guaicurú economy, for they were the purveyors of most of the cultivated foodstuffs consumed. Every year, at the time when different staples were harvested, Guaicurú chiefs made the rounds among their various Guaná tributary settlements. They stayed in each tributary settlement for two or three days, during which time their Guaná subordinates were obliged to feed them and their followers. Guaná tributaries offered their masters products from their gardens—namely, maize, beans, sweet potatoes, and squash—and whatever they had collected, such as wild rice, honey, fruits, and tubers (Jolís 1972[1789]: 319). They also acted as their masters' personal servants during these visits, fanning them to keep them cool and free of mosquitoes and other insects. Before their masters left, Guaná gave them, "willingly or by force," a portion of whatever they had harvested (Sánchez Labrador 1910–1917[1770]: I, 305). The tributaries also offered their masters gifts of cotton blankets, processed tobacco, and rolls of red annatto paint (Sánchez Labrador 1910–1917[1770]: II, 23). These latter gifts amounted to little, and Guaicurú chiefs immediately redistributed them among their followers. In contrast, it is said that tribute in foodstuffs "consumed great part of their efforts," and Guaná tributaries complained bitterly that their masters "deprived them and their poor wives and children of their sustenance" (Sánchez Labrador 1910–1917[1770]: I, 305; II, 270; also Jolís 1972[1789]: 320).

In exchange for the gifts received from their Guaná tributaries, their masters gave them knives, glass beads, needles, fishhooks, and other small gifts of European manufacture (Sánchez Labrador 1910–1917[1770]: II, 268). Guaná people had no direct access to European sources of trade; most of the European manufactures they possessed were thus obtained from their Guaicurú masters. Whenever a Guaná tributary wanted something from a master or mistress during tribute-collecting visits, we are told he or she would ask for it and often obtained it. It is claimed that the generosity of Guaicurú masters was such that some female chiefs would give away all their ornaments to their tributary women. Some authors have argued on the basis of these exchanges that the relationship between Guaicurú and Guaná was not hierarchical but should be understood as a form of symbiosis (Lowie 1948: 349). This view ignores, however, the coercive aspects of the relationship, of which, if we are to trust the sources, Guaná people were very aware.

Another obligation of Guaná tributaries was to aid their Guaicurú masters whenever they required military assistance (Serra 1845[1803]: 209). Indeed, the Terena, one of the Guaná regional groups controlled by the Guaicurú, were so quick to adopt their masters' militaristic lifestyle that their status was reported to be more like that of allies than that of tributaries (Susnik 1971: 160). They accompanied their Guaicurú masters in raids against the Chamacoco and, sometimes, even against other independent Guaná regional groups. Despite enjoying a privileged status as war partners, however, the Guaicurú never considered the Terena as their equals, showing their scorn toward their subjects by declaring that they were inclined to lying (Susnik 1971: 161).

Among Guaicurú, the large number of captives and tributaries possessed by chiefs and other high-ranking men and women allowed them, unlike other capturing societies, to delegate most subsistence activities to their subordinates, thus freeing them to devote their lives to warring and leisure (Sánchez Labrador 1910–1917[1770]: I, 251, 286;

Azara (1809[1781]: II, 109). Their aversion to perform menial tasks was vividly expressed by a Guaicurú chief, who, after being invited by the Portuguese commander of Fort Coimbra to move near the fort and build houses and plant large gardens, asked the commander how many slaves would he provide to carry out these tasks, for Guaicurú people were not captive and did not engage in such activities (Serra 1850[1803]: 349).

***

The analysis of the servile duties of captive slaves, servant groups, and tributary populations demonstrates that the contribution of dependents to the overall economy of the above societies varied greatly. Such variation is not, however, random. In all these societies, captives and other subordinates performed important subsistence activities. However, in societies in which captive slavery was combined with other forms of dependency, thus increasing the number of surplus laborers available, the proportion of daily subsistence activities performed by subordinates was much larger than in societies where it was the only form of servitude. This is reflected in the amount of work performed by masters. In Kalinago and Conibo societies, where slavery was the only form of dependency, it is reported that masters were not exempted from working; they engaged in the same subsistence activities as their subordinates. In such societies, servile work complemented rather than substituted for the labor inputs of the masters. In societies where captive slaves coexisted with servant groups, such as the Tukano and Chiriguaná, subordinates carried out a larger proportion of basic subsistence activities. In these societies, masters, and especially those chiefs possessing large numbers of captives, worked very little. The tendency to shy away from agriculture was even more marked in societies where captive slavery was combined with tributary populations. Among Calusa, chiefs, members of chiefly families, and warriors were supposedly exempted from daily subsistence activities. And although high-ranking Guaicurú men and women were not totally exonerated from these tasks, the general consensus is that they worked hardly at all, spending most of their time warring or enjoying leisurely activities.

In none of the above-mentioned societies, however, did captive slavery by itself entirely free masters from working. If the contribution of captives to their masters' economy was not essential, their input as household servants and personal attendants nonetheless was. Instead, what the above analysis suggests is that in all these societies captives performed the heaviest menial tasks necessary for the daily functioning of their masters' households. These were the chores that even nowadays Amerindian peoples often complain about: carrying firewood, fetching water, grating and squeezing bitter manioc for the preparation of cassava, or chewing sweet manioc for the elaboration of beer. In addition, they carried out other heavy tasks, such as building canoes, weaving clothes, making mats, or manufacturing pottery—all items with a high exchange value. In short, the work that captives did enhanced a household's pool of laborers and, thereby, its wealth without necessarily being crucial for its survival. Chiefly, or high-ranking, families, who had the largest numbers of captives, benefited the most from the extra labor. One could even argue that in some of these societies it was this extra labor that increased a chief's power.

The contribution of dependents was not confined to subsistence and household chores. Captives, and to a lesser extent other subordinates, played an important role as personal attendants. Whether as squires, retainers, cupbearers, and pages, or as lady's maids, maidservants, nurses, and babysitters, they provided a range of personal services mostly meant to enhance the reputation and prominence of their masters. Here again we find a similar difference between societies in which captive slavery was the only form of servitude and societies in which it coexisted with other forms of dependency. Whereas captives among the Kalinago and Conibo played no role as personal attendants, among the Tukano and Chiriguaná, and especially among the Calusa and Guaicurú, they were a central accoutrement of the chiefly position. In these two latter societies, the refinement of the etiquette required to attend properly to the needs of high-ranking men and women reached levels similar to those usually attributed to complex polities. Servile practices such as bringing water for their masters to wash their hands after eating, receiving presents from guests on behalf of their masters, dressing and decorating their masters, or waiting on their masters and mistresses during important public ceremonies bring to mind the sophisticated etiquette of courtly societies.

An equally important sign of social stratification, and the enhancement of chiefly authority, was the practice of sacrificing the slaves of deceased high-ranking men and women. With the exception of Kalinago, this practice was absent from societies where slavery was the sole form of servitude, or where it was combined with the presence of servant groups. In contrast, it was a central practice among the Calusa and Guaicurú, societies that combined captive slavery with the subjection of numerous tributary groups. The execution of captives belonging to deceased high-ranking personages should be viewed as resulting from the deeper social distance that separated masters from subordinates in these latter societies. As we shall see in Chapter 8, the integration of captives was much slower among these peoples than in less stratified societies, perpetuating for longer periods the social differences that set apart masters and slaves and enhancing chiefly authority in ways that are absent in other capturing societies.

In summary, captive slaves, servant peoples, and tributary populations certainly contributed greatly to their masters' economy, but their duties extended well beyond the economy. Their activities as household servants, personal attendants, and soldiers were as significant as their economic functions, if not more so. More importantly, captive slaves and other subordinates played a central role in the political economy of life characteristic of native tropical America, as we shall see.

CHAPTER 7

Dependent Status

No profession, no social role, no task, no way of life, is typical of the
slave condition; that which is typical is neither what slaves do nor how
they live, because that depends on the goodwill of their masters; it is
not what the master does to his slaves, but rather that he can do
whatever he pleases, that he has the right to do whatever he pleases.

—ALAIN TESTART, "L'esclavage comme institution"

For native tropical American societies, the slave condition was
not so much a contrast between freedom and lack of freedom
as one between humanness and nonhumanness, or between
sociality and nonsociality. As Kopytoff and Miers (1977: 17)
have argued in relation to African societies, "the antithesis of 'slavery' is
not 'freedom' qua autonomy but rather 'belonging.'" Slaves in kin-based
societies are foreigners, 'others' who do not belong because they are
considered to be less than human, and thus are believed to lack the arts
of civility and social life (Lévy-Bruhl 1931: 14). People "like us" cannot
be enslaved. They can be fought against, and even captured, as we know
was occasionally the case among Tukano, Chiriguaná, or Guaicurú local
groups, but they cannot be enslaved. Only others "different from us" can
be assigned the status of captive slaves and be subjugated as such.

From this perspective, then, the slave condition of foreigners precedes
their capture, which is seen only as a confirmation of their essential status.
Capture, and the rituals of enslavement that follow, confirm this virtual
status by uprooting the foreigners, which deprives them of social ties, and
by depersonifying them, which deprives them of their social personas.
The result is people who lack the basic rights accorded to full members
of capturing societies—not only the right to have control over their own
persons but also the right of being a person. Again, their lack of rights is
conceived of as a preexisting condition. From an Amerindian viewpoint,
then, foreigners are enemies and potential slaves who lack all rights and
are entirely at the disposal of their virtual masters. The only exceptions

were peoples subjugated as tributaries, a class that was accorded many of the rights denied to war captives.

In this chapter, I analyze the status of captive slaves, members of servant groups, and tributary peoples, and spell out the rights they had and, more importantly, those they lacked. These rights were not encoded in well-established sets of rules—which native tropical American peoples seemed to be greatly averse to make—but were expressed through a number of more or less loose social prescriptions and proscriptions. These terms of engagement situated captives as individuals having fewer rights than anyone else within their masters' societies. Servant groups and tributary populations enjoyed a number of rights that captives lacked, but their status was nevertheless precarious; they were always forced to comply with their masters' demands. If they did not, they could be swiftly punished and turned into captive slaves.

Captives were denied the most important right—namely, that of being considered a person. Regarded as less than human, owing their lives to the clemency of their masters, and being deprived of their previous identities through rituals of enslavement, the status of captives differed only slightly from that of personified objects. Their condition goes against received wisdom. Authors have previously argued that in native tropical American societies war captives could not be characterized as slaves because "they could not be bought, sold, or traded as in chattel slavery" (Steward and Faron 1959: 138). Other scholars have argued more cautiously that "the 'alienability' of war prisoners in precolonial contexts is not well established" (A. C. Taylor 1999: 213).

The notion that slaves are only such if they have the status of chattel is misleading, as Patterson (1982: 17) has rightly pointed out. It is true that slaves are often treated as property, but this in no way is a defining element of slavery. In native tropical America, abundant evidence indicates that captives were alienable. In this chapter, I analyze Amerindian notions of ownership and property revolving around the status of captives and other subordinates. I argue that Amerindians viewed captives—and, to a lesser extent, servants and tributaries—as the product of their efforts. As such, captives were considered as much their property as the produce of their fields or the produce of their hunting and fishing activities. Captives, servants, and, occasionally tributaries could be transferred to third parties in exchange for goods, as part of bride-price payments, as gifts, or under the rules of inheritance. The emergence of dynamic slave trading networks and regional slave markets was the result. What ultimately expressed their condition as chattel was, however, that captive slaves could be executed in generative rites, as well as in funerary rituals performed in honor of high-ranking men and women.

Captives were thus considered to be the property of their masters and as such could be traded, given away, or even executed. Paradoxically, however, they were seldom treated cruelly or inhumanely. A relationship of intimacy often developed between masters and their subordinates by virtue of co-residence, commensality, and conviviality. As a result, subordinates were well treated and even considered to be integral members of their masters' households. This partial incorporation did not obliterate their position as subordinates and inferiors, and it certainly did not endow them with the rights of full members of the society. Nonetheless, it ameliorated their personal situation.

Because captives were often well treated, and their Amerindian masters were reluctant to sell them to Europeans, some authors question the existence of native forms of slavery in tropical America. I contend, together with other scholars, that such an argument mistakes slavery as a *situation de fait* (actual state), with slavery as a *condition juridique* (juridical condition) (Lévy-Bruhl 1931: 2–3; but also Meillasoux 1975: 22; Kopytoff and Miers 1977: 49; and Vaughan 1979: 99). In other words, it confounds the slaves' lifestyle, and the way people treat them, with their social status. Such a view assumes that slaves are always ill-treated and always lead miserable lives. It derives from Western images of slavery, often based on the model of plantation slavery as it developed in the American South and the Caribbean. The enormous weight of such images prevented even colonial administrators from describing certain African forms of servitude as slavery (Meillasoux 1975: 12).

What determines the slave condition, however, is not how masters treat their slaves but rather, as Testart (1998: 32) has contended, that they can treat them as they please. Slaves have no rights, either as foreigners or virtual slaves, and they have even fewer rights as war captives or actual slaves. Thus, what determines the slave condition is not whether slaves are exploited, maltreated, or obliged to perform lowly activities. It is that their masters have total power over their lives: power to assign them a servile status or emancipate them, to treat them well or badly, to put them to work in the fields or as personal attendants, to exploit them or grant them favors.

KALINAGO

Kalinago society was relatively unstratified. The main social division was between Kalinago people and captives taken in war or obtained through trade. The fate and status of individual captives varied widely, however. Adult male Amerindian captives were tormented, executed, and eaten in cannibalistic celebrations shortly after their capture. In contrast, African and European male captives were excluded from this symbolic system of exchange with the enemy and were put immediately to work. Amerindian boys were emasculated and raised as household servants. They were well treated, but their position remained that of servants. They could be punished if they disobeyed, and were considered to be too inferior to even touch their masters' hands (Chevillard 1659: 117–118). More importantly, captive boys had little hope of ever being integrated into Kalinago society.

Young captive women were kept as concubines by their captors or given as maidservants to their wives (Coma 1903[1494]: 251). Older women were kept as drudges, forced to perform the heaviest field and household tasks (Martire d'Anghiera 1966[1555]: 31). All captive women were obliged to provide sexual favors to their captors whenever required (Navarrete 1992[1580]: 40).

Captive concubines enjoyed a lower status than Kalinago consorts. They were at the total mercy of their masters, who, it was said, "treat them very badly and sometimes kill them" (Bouton 1640: 110). Kalinago mistresses were not less harsh toward them. Jealous Kalinago wives often shot captive concubines if the latter attracted more than a normal share of their husbands' attention (Navarrete 1992[1580]: 40). These are not isolated, idle claims. Reliable authors, such as Du Tertre (1654: 421), report that Kalinago masters could dispose of the lives of their concubines as they pleased. Female captives could be taken as concubines, and some, we are told, were even loved dearly (Du Tertre 1667: 379), but all sources concur that they were "still accounted Slaves" (Rochefort 1666[1658]: 332). Their situation seems to have improved in later times, however (Labat 1724[1705]: II, Part 4, 108–109).

Most authors agree that after an initial stage when war captives were insulted and beaten, they were generally well treated (Labat 1724[1705]: I, Part 2, 11). Even captive boys destined to be executed once they became adults were treated, we are told, "as they treated their own" (Anon. 1988

[1620]: 187). In no way, however, did this treatment obliterate the stigma of foreignness and inferiority surrounding war captives.

Kalinago captives seem to have possessed few belongings. And if the captive woman represented in Figure 16 serves as an example, they also possessed very few ornaments. It is not clear whether captive slaves were allowed to own property. We do know, however, that Kalinago masters could seize whatever goods fell into the hands of their captives (F. Columbus 1992[1539]: 113). Not only did Kalinago masters have full control over their captives' possessions, but they also had power over their selves, being able to trade them or sell them as they pleased. In the period immediately after their capture, when war captives had still not been incorporated into their captors' households, this total "ownership" was especially true. During this liminal stage, many captives were exchanged in intra- or intertribal networks (Navarrete 1992[1580]: 40; Chevillard 1659: 131). Not all transactions involving captive slaves had a commercial purpose, however. Some captives were given away as gifts. Victorious warriors would sometimes give their young female captives as presents to their fathers and grandfathers (Breton 1665: 279). Captives could also be given away as a sort of bride-price (Chevillard 1659: 118).

Recently secured war captives not only circulated in intra- and intertribal trading networks but also were sometimes sold to Europeans. In early colonial times Kalinago sold most of the African slaves captured in raids or seized when they sought refuge in their islands after running away from their masters (Labat 1724[1705]: II, Part 4, 148). Later on, Kalinago began to keep them as slaves, rarely parting with them. Most of the captives sold to Europeans were of African or European origin; nonetheless, from time to time, Kalinago would also sell some of their Amerindian captives (Rochefort 1658: 477). They sometimes even sold Amerindian males who had been condemned to be ritually eaten, including captive boys they had raised, who would otherwise have been executed and eaten after reaching adulthood (Labat 1724[1705]: II, Part 4, 108).

Trade in captives along Amerindian commercial networks was so common that there were fixed exchange rates. A captive slave was worth one *calloúcouli* or *caracoli*, a crescent-shaped ornament worn by Kalinago men as both earrings and pectorals (Breton 1665: 106; de la Borde 1886[1674]: 247). These ornaments were made of an indigenous metal alloy that glittered like polished copper or gold and did not rust (see Figure 34). Captives were sometimes exchanged with European agents for *caracoli* ornaments. In such extratribal networks, however, the most common goods exchanged for all kinds of captives—men, women, or children, or Amerindians, Africans, or Europeans—were iron tools. Nevertheless, the slave trade between Kalinago and Europeans never attained the intensity and volume of that between the Kari'na— the Kalinago's mainland Carib-speaking associates—and the Dutch (Whitehead, forthcoming). Among Kalinago, most people captured in war went to satisfy indigenous needs.

Kalinago men and women were buried with all their personal belongings, or "riches" (Anon. 1988[1620]: 191), which included not only material possessions, such as weapons, feather headdresses, ornaments, baskets, and vessels but also their dogs and captives (Rochefort 1666[1658]: 351; de la Borde 1886[1674]: 252). The practice of killing the slaves of deceased Kalinago men and women confirms that war captives were entirely owned by their captors, who could dispose of them as they pleased. In this respect, the status of captives varied according to ethnic origin. Amerindian and African captives were executed so that they would serve their masters and mistresses in the land of the dead, whereas European captives were apparently spared this fate. Differences also existed between Amerindian and African captives. The former were buried alive, whereas the latter were executed before being interred (Anon. 1988[1620]: 151). Later on in time, hardworking African captives were spared from being sacrificed when their masters died (Anon. 1988[1620]: 152). In contrast, Amerindian captives were never spared this fate.

CONIBO

Stratification was mostly expressed in Conibo society as an opposition between Conibo people and alien captives. The low status of war captives went hand in hand with their being deprived of most of the rights enjoyed by true Conibo. Captive females were usually taken as concubines or raised to be future concubines for their captors' sons (Stahl 1928[1895]: 150; Anon. 1905[1826]: 261). Captive girls were forced to have sexual relations at a very early age, unlike Conibo women, who could marry only after having completed their sexual development and achieved a certain maturity (Stahl 1928[1895]: 150, 153–154). Those female captives that were not taken as concubines by Conibo men were given to male captives, preferably of their same tribe (Fry 1907[1888]: 474). Under no circumstances, however, were female captives assimilated as proper wives. They always retained their status as servants, obliged to perform the most exhausting tasks (Ordinaire 1887: 307).

Male captives were also kept as servants and assigned the heaviest chores. Their marginal status was permanent; they had few prospects to improve it. Marriages between captive men and Conibo women were rare. Described as "elusive and disdainful," Conibo women were portrayed as being extremely proud "of the purity of the race" and never having affairs with non-Conibo men (Fry 1907[1888]: 477). Only those male captives who stood out because of their good behavior and great valor were given Conibo wives (Stahl 1928[1895]: 150). Even then, however, their round heads betrayed their origin and continued to stigmatize them.

All sources coincide on the impression that Conibo people treated their war captives kindly. Dueñas (1924[1792]: 249) and Girbal y Barceló (1924a[1790]: 161), for instance, assert that Conibo treated captive children "as if they were their own children." One hundred years later, another observer (Fry 1907[1888]: 474) claimed that Conibo people treated their captives "with affection and equality," meaning, presumably, without making distinctions between them and Conibo people of the same gender and age. This did not mean, however, that Conibo masters ceased demanding more work from their captives than from other members of their households. Hence, when Stahl (1928[1895]: 150–151) rebuked a Conibo headman for exacting too much work from captives, the latter answered that "servants had a better life with their masters, who are their parents, and that doubtless white people could not have servants without forcing them to work."

That war captives led a "better life" among their Conibo masters than at home cannot be considered as anything but a piece of Conibo "civilizing" propaganda (more on this in Chapter 8). This same kind of obfuscation is found in the narration of an old Shipibo-Conibo informant, who claimed that, after experiencing captivity for some time, a Cashibo captive man had expressed his desire to bring his son and sister to his master's settlement (Roe 1982: 84). The assertion by the same Conibo headman that Cashibo captives often sought to escape from their masters because they abhorred hard work clearly exposes this blatant piece of propaganda as being a lie (Stahl 1928[1895]: 150). Their main reason for escaping, according to Stahl (1928[1895]: 150), was different: captives, he claimed, "never forgot the total freedom they could enjoy in their land, and . . . had no hope of improving their condition among Conibo people."

The good treatment of captives, in fact, depended very much on their being submissive. Captives who did not comply with their masters' wishes were publicly punished in yearly multivillage meetings in which quarrels between people and cases of insubordinate or disrespectful servants were presented, discussed, and dealt with (Stahl 1928[1895]: 159). If found guilty, Stahl asserts, the insolent slave had to kneel and was admonished and punished by the local chief, sometimes with a few club blows on the head. Briefly, then, captives were generally well treated, but their status of servants, deprived of most rights accorded to Conibo people, always remained.

Captives were not allowed to possess personal property. Whatever goods they owned could be taken away by their masters (Castelnau 1850–1859[1847]: IV, 350). Likewise, they had no control over their own lives. Victorious raiders returning home with numerous captives kept some of them for their own service, trading the rest with fellow tribesmen or with Europeans. An early source reports that Conibo raiders preferred to keep all captive girls for themselves, selling only some of the boys (Anon. 1905[1826]: 261; Raimondi 1905[1862]: 218). Intertribal trade in war captives was quite extensive. Conibo people obtained slaves not only by raiding for them but also by exchanging iron tools for captive children with the interior tribes (Fry 1907[1888]: 474). Recent captives provided the bulk of the trade. But there is evidence that Conibo people sometimes traded captive children they had raised and even captive women they had kept as concubines. These unfortunates, we are told, were exchanged with other Conibo men or sold "as mules" to foreigners (Marcoy 1869[1847]: I, 629; Ordinaire 1887: 308).

A sharp increase in the Peruvian demand for a "civilized" labor force to collect rubber led Conibo people to engage in an active slave trade with rubber extractors in the late 1800s. Conibo raids were intended to capture children and young women who, after being sold to Peruvians, would be raised in the "civilized" mores of their masters, eventually to be incorporated as disciplined laborers (Santos-Granero and Barclay 2000: 41). Little is known about the rates of exchange of captive slaves during precolonial times. For later years, sources mention that captives were exchanged for iron tools or valuable indigenous goods. A canoe, an ax, or even a few knives sufficed to buy a captive child (Marcoy 1869[1847]: I, 468, 629; Castelnau 1850–1859[1847]: IV, 352).

Notably, however, Conibo raiding never became exclusively oriented toward the regional slave market. All authors, even those writing at the height of the rubber boom, stress that Conibo people sold only those captives whom they did not want to keep as servants (Sandi 1905[1865]: 252; Samanez y Ocampo 1980[1884]: 82). This demonstrates that native slaving practices were never totally effaced by their European equivalents. Doubtless, European demand for native slaves intensified Conibo slave raiding, but European forms of capture and servitude never superseded the native ones. On the contrary, Europeans not only relied on these native forms to satisfy their demands for a labor force but even readily adapted to them. Whereas the European slave trade in Africa involved mostly adult male slaves, raids conducted by Peruvian rubber extractors were modeled on indigenous forms of raiding; thus, they were always focused on the capture of young women and children.

TUKANO

The relationship between Tukano and their Makú captives and servants was decidedly ambivalent. Despite the taboo against marrying Makú women (McGovern 1927: 148; Terribilini and Terribilini 1961: 39; Silva 1962: 408–409; Biocca 1965: 471; Knobloch 1972: 105; Silverwood-Cope 1990: 117), Tukano men often engaged in clandestine sexual affairs with Makú servant girls (Koch-Grünberg 1995[1909]: I, 277; McGovern 1927: 249; Goldman 1963: 96; Jackson 1991: 31). A similar ambivalence underscores the rights Makú servants had as household members. Goldman (1963: 105) asserts that Makú servants "were to all intents and purposes members of the household." All sources agree, however, that Makú subordinates were not allowed to live in their masters' malocas; instead they occupied small makeshift huts on the periphery of Tukano settlements (Koch-Grünberg 1995[1909]: I, 276; McGovern 1927: 248; Giacone 1949: 88). Attached servant groups, as well as client families performing temporary work for their Tukano masters, were similarly lodged (Biocca 1965: 472; Reichel-Dolmatoff 1971: 19; Silverwood-Cope 1990: 37).

Makú subordinates were expected to eat in their own houses, apart from their masters (Knobloch 1972: 105). And Makú female servants were not allowed to participate in the final stages of cooking or to serve food to their Tukano masters (Jackson 1983: 155). On the few occasions when Makú servants ate with their masters, they did not dare eat until their masters had finished and did not talk unless they were invited to join the conversation (McGovern 1927: 186; Jackson 1983: 156). The refusal to allow Makú servants to cook, serve food, or eat together with their masters seems to relate to Amerindian notions of kinship, determined as they are less by blood than by the daily sharing of food and drink (Gow 1989, 1991; Belaúnde 2001). By interdicting all aspects of commensality with their Makú servants, Tukano masters made it clear that they had no intention to establish any kind of kinship relationship with them (more on this point in Chapter 8).

Makú captives were allowed to participate in small drinking parties (Koch-Grünberg 1995[1909]: I, 276), but they were prohibited from attending larger tribal festivals (Knobloch 1972: 105–106). In fact, during such drinking parties, they behaved less as participants than as spectators and servants charged with preparing coca snuff and lighting their masters' cigars (McGovern 1927: 248; Giacone 1949: 88). They were not permitted to dance or to wear feather ornaments. Most of the time they sat in a dark corner. Their masters, from time to time, handed them a bowl of manioc beer, a cigar, or a small quantity of coca snuff, but this was all.

Makú subordinates were not forbidden from holding property, especially if they belonged to servant or client groups (McGovern 1927: 248). Their masters, nevertheless, had the option to deprive them of any of their possessions on a whim (Silverwood-Cope 1990: 72). Whenever subordinates worked for the missionaries, Tukano masters usually took away whatever goods they had earned (Biocca 1965: 472; Giacone 1949: 89). The right that Tukano masters had to seize their servants' property extended to their children. Frequently, Tukano masters would force their Makú servants to hand over their offspring to them, so that they could serve as pages and nannies to the masters' children (Knobloch 1972: 106). Tukano mothers considered it degrading, however, for their children to play with Makú captive children or servants (McGovern 1927: 248; Koch-Grünberg 1995[1909]: I, 276; Jackson 1983: 156).

Generally, Tukano people treated their Makú subordinates well, and even with a certain degree of "compassion" (Koch-Grünberg 1906: 877; 1995[1909]: I, 310; II, 62; Kok 1925–1926: I, 628). Some authors even assert that it was because subordinates were well treated that they seldom attempted to escape (McGovern 1927: 247–248). The information provided by other authors indicates, nonetheless, that the good treatment Makú subordinates experienced never excluded a deep-set contempt toward them or a large dose of coercion. For example, Makú captives and servants were never formally greeted (Jackson 1983: 156). And although Makú clients bringing smoked game meat, baskets, and other products were received ceremonially, Chernela (1993: 115) asserts that they were remunerated immediately, indicating a lack of interest on the part of Wanano masters in establishing symmetrical relationships that could eventually lead to marriage exchanges.

In addition, Tukano often made fun of their Makú subordinates behind their backs (Jackson 1983: 156). Tukano mockery was generally targeted at Makú language, which, from their point of view, was gibberish (Silverwood-Cope 1990: 72; Koch-Grünberg 1995[1909]: I, 277), and at Makú physical traits, which they despised (Koch-Grünberg 1995[1909]: II, 92). In addition, Tukano often insulted their Makú servants by calling them *si'i pé*, a term that can be literally translated as "anus" but also means "stubborn" or "stupid" (Reichel-Dolmatoff 1971: 121).

Coercion loomed large in the relationship between Tukano masters and their Makú subordinates. It is said that when Makú servants refused to comply with their masters' wishes, the latter did not hesitate to maltreat them (Giacone 1949: 88; Knobloch 1972: 105). Servant groups and client populations could expect to suffer retaliation in the form of raiding and enslavement (Koch-Grünberg 1995[1909]: I, 277). Makú subordinates were acutely aware of this possibility, as is revealed by the shy, reluctant, and servile attitude they adopted in the vicinity of Tukano people (Silverwood-Cope 1990: 72; Ramos, Silverwood-Cope, and Oliveira 1980: 167).

The possibility of raiding, enslavement, and sale was not a meaningless Tukano threat. Tukano people were certainly engaged in an active intertribal trade in war captives long before the rubber boom (Wallace 1853: 300–301). Such trade increased considerably as a result of the demands made by a burgeoning rubber industry beginning in the 1870s. Tukano raids at this time gave rise to two distinct slave trading networks. The intertribal slave trade was based on the exchange of war captives for prestige goods—namely, personal ornaments and ceremonial objects. Kok (1925–1926: II, 922) states that the price of a captive woman was an *uhtabú*, the white cylindrical quartz stone that male Tukano most valued as an ornament. War captives were also exchanged for other highly valued traditional objects such as weapons, feather headdresses, ceremonial staffs, and necklaces of jaguar teeth (Wallace 1853: 288, 300; Goldman 1963: 105–106).

In the extratribal trading network, river merchants paid Tukano and Arawak raiders a rifle for each Makú boy or girl they bought (Coudreau 1887: II, 179). The two Makú girls drawn by Spruce in 1853 were sold thusly to the Brazilian commander of the Fort Marabitanas, on the Upper Rio Negro (see Figure 35). In the early 1900s, Makú captives fetched even higher prices. Koch-Grünberg (1995[1909]: I, 57) reports that by then a young Makú could be exchanged for a repetition rifle. Trade in Makú children with Brazilians and Colombians continued well into the twentieth century (McGovern 1927: 248). It never displaced, however, the capture of Makú individuals and the subjugation of Makú bands to be used as slaves and servant groups.

CHIRIGUANÁ

Chiriguaná society showed important signs of social stratification from early colonial times. The Chiriguaná elite was composed of the families of the *tubichá*, the "great men," or leaders, of local and regional groups, and the families of the great *ipayé*, or "shamans" (Giannecchini 1996[1898]: 302). The *queremba*, or "great warriors," also enjoyed a high status. Most people, however, belonged to the commoner stratum. Differences between the high- and low-status strata were not breached; the *abâ moacára*, "noble people," refused to intermarry with the lowly *abâ teitê*, "humble people" (León de Santiago 1985[1794]: 225). The status of captives and servant groups was even lower than that of commoners, but this had not always been the case.

During the first stage of the Chiriguaná invasion of eastern Bolivia in the late fifteenth century, when Chiriguaná women were scarce, Chané female captives seem to have been incorporated on an even status with Chiriguaná wives (Polo de Ondegardo 1991[1574]: 138). The passage of time, and the massive subjection of Chané people as both captive slaves and servant groups, made it impossible for this egalitarian mechanism of integration to operate. Thus, during the second stage of Chiriguaná establishment in the region, captive women continued to be taken as concubines, but this time with the status of captive slaves (Lozano 1733: 58; Susnik 1968: 38). The fate of male captives also changed. Whereas in the first stage captive men were destined mostly to be consumed in cannibalistic rituals, in the second stage they became the object of an intensive slave trade with the Spanish. In the following paragraphs I discuss the status of slaves and servant peoples during this second stage.

Captive women and children lived together with their Chiriguaná masters in their longhouses, but instead of sleeping on hammocks as the latter did, they slept on the ground (Arriaga 1974[1596]: 70). Captives may have been considered members of their master's household, but their status remained that of servants charged with the most burdensome tasks. Members of attached servant groups slept in their own houses, located generally on the periphery of their masters' settlement (Métraux 1930: 324–325). They kept their own fields and made their own family arrangements, yet they were always at the beck and call of their masters.

Immediately after their capture, war prisoners were insulted, beaten, and in many other ways maltreated. After this initial explosion of anger, however, they were generally respected and well treated (Giannecchini 1996[1898]: 328). This in no way implied that captives enjoyed the same rights as Chiriguaná. Captives and servants could be punished if they refused to comply with their masters' wishes. In fact, this happened so often that captives used to prepare magical charms known as *moçangaiba* to prevent their masters from thrashing them (Anon. 1938[1622]: 234). Chiriguaná masters frequently addressed their subordinates in derogatory terms, calling their male servants *cuñareta*, or "women," implying they were effeminate and cowardly (Sanabria Fernández 1949: 41).

More importantly, Chiriguaná masters and mistresses held the power of life and death over their captives (Arriaga 1974[1596]: 63). According to some authors, captive women who refused sexual favors demanded by their captors could be killed (Nino 1912: 279). In turn, captive children were considered to be the property of the wife of the man who captured them. As their "absolute owners," their mistresses "could sell them to whomever they pleased and, if necessary, also kill them" (Giannecchini 1996[1898]: 328).

Two indications that captives were considered to be the property of their captors are that the latter had the right to dispose of the lives of captives and that slaves could be inherited by the children of their captors (Susnik 1968: 35). We know little about the circumstances and mechanisms through which this type of transferal took place. We do know, however, that masters had the right to pass their captives on to their descendants or, on the other hand, to emancipate them (Díaz de

Guzmán 1979a[1618]: 93). Moreover, we know that captives could and were bartered in intra- and intertribal networks.

After a victorious raid, Chiriguaná warriors used to gamble some of the war prisoners they had captured, particularly "old women, children, and infants less than seven years old, and a few girls for whom the master has no need" (Nino 1912: 279). It is also reported that when Chiriguaná masters got tired of their captive concubines, they "bartered them, or sold them for almost nothing, a sheep, a goat, or a hat" (Nino 1912: 279). Sometimes, however, captives could fetch high prices. A man who inherited a Chané captive from his father, an important headman, later sold him to another chief for the considerable amount of four cows and two horses (Susnik 1968: 35). Such intratribal trade often took place not within the same locality but between distant settlements (Nino 1912: 279). The alienability of war captives was inscribed in the term *tapui* (or *tapïi*), which can be translated as "purchased people" or, perhaps more accurately, "bartered people" (Ruiz de Montoya 1876[1639]: 355r). It also appears in the distinction that Chiriguaná people made between *tembiaĩhú*, "captive slave," and *tembiaĩhú bó*, "purchased slave" (Ruiz de Montoya 1876[1639]: 377v).

Intra- and intertribal trading of war captives was very rapidly reoriented during colonial times to satisfy the demands of the Spaniards. When discussing the fate of war captives, the earliest Spanish chronicles assert: "[Some] they eat immediately after their capture, others they fatten for the same purpose, others they sell, and still others they keep as slaves" (Matienzo 1918–1922[1564]: 54). In later phases of the colonial period, and as a result of Spanish demand for slaves, Chiriguaná began to spare the lives of most of their captive men, in order to sell them to the Spanish (Díaz de Guzmán 1836[1612]: 18; Techo 1897[1673]: IV, 300). Chané captives were taken to sell in the highlands or were sold in situ to Spanish slave traders in exchange for swords, machetes, iron tools, horses, saddles, and textiles (Audiencia 1918–1922b[1595]: 241; Díaz de Guzmán 1979a[1617]: 214).

All sources agree that the Spanish presence and demand for slaves intensified Chiriguaná slave raids on their neighbors (Samaniego 1944 [1600]: 485; Díaz de Guzmán 1836[1612]: 18; Anon. 1965[1570]: 399). The colonial slave trade experienced ups and downs in the relationship between the Chiriguaná and the Spanish in the Andean borderlands, intensifying in times of peace, diminishing in times of conflict (Polo de Ondegardo 1991[1574]: 140; Díaz de Guzmán 1836[1612]: 79). In contrast, the intra- and intertribal slave trade was an ongoing activity throughout the colonial period and even later, in republican times.

CALUSA

Calusa society was highly stratified, with the paramount chief and his extended family occupying the highest position. The head shaman and the leading war captains belonged to the same chiefly family or to interconnected ones. Together they formed the ruling elite. The warrior stratum retained a slightly lower status, but its members could improve their position by demonstrating valor in the field and by marrying chiefly women. Commoners followed in rank order; they performed most subsistence activities, since members of the chiefly and military strata were exempted from manual work. War captives occupied the lowest status and had few rights. Tributary peoples were in a better position but were also considered to be subordinates.

Captives were given the heaviest household chores and the most ritually polluting duties. Their movements were also very much restricted; they were not allowed to go too far away from their captors' settlements (Elvas 1995[1539]: 62). Notwithstanding, this condition could change; if slaves gained their master's trust, they could travel everywhere, as exemplified by a Spanish captive who was appointed official messenger by chief Carlos (Laudonnière 2001[1564]: 111). In fact, captives could achieve a certain degree of prestige in recognition for outstanding service. Thus the status of a Spanish captive owned by chief Ucita, who was in charge of guarding the settlement's burial house, improved greatly after he prevented a wolf from carrying away the corpse of a child. From then onward, chief Ucita "showed him great honor" (Elvas 1995[1539]: 60).

Captive women were usually taken as concubines by their Calusa captors. Treatment of captive concubines must not have been excessively harsh, for it is reported that two of the five Spanish captive women liberated by conquistador Menéndez de Avilés refused to abandon their Calusa husbands and children (Solís de Merás 1990[1565]: 124). That three of them did decide to go back to Spain, leaving behind their Indian children, is a sign, on the other hand, that Spanish women faced considerable difficulties in adapting to their captors' society. We can only wonder whether indigenous captive women had the same trouble in adapting to Calusa society.

Most sources indicate that Calusa maltreated their captives (Swanton 1946: 101). The life of the Spanish captive found by De Soto seems to have been quite miserable before he regained some honor (Elvas 1995[1539]: 60). He was forced to work unceasingly and was cuffed or lashed if he refused to do so (Garcilaso de la Vega 1995[1605]: 103). Calusa masters had total power over their captives, including over their lives, and could exert that power even upon esteemed slaves, such as the one owned by chief Ucita. It is reported that when his settlement was attacked and burned by a neighboring chief, chief Ucita sought to placate the divinities by sacrificing his Spanish slave (Elvas 1995[1539]: 61). The latter managed to escape, thanks to the intervention of the chief's daughter. Despite the happy ending, what this story confirms is that even well-integrated and esteemed captives did not lose their slave status and were at the mercy of their masters, who could dispose of their lives on a whim.

Such power also entailed the paramounts' privilege of giving captives away as gifts or in exchange for prestigious goods. We know that Mocoço, the Tocobaga chief, had asked his Calusa colleague, Ucita, to give him or sell him his Spanish slave (Elvas 1995[1539]: 61). We also know that after the Tequesta abducted the daughter of the Ais paramount chief, who was en route to Calos to marry the Calusa paramount, the latter gave his ally and future father-in-law one of his esteemed Spanish captives (Laudonnière 2001[1564]: 112). Such gifts seem to have been expected among allied chiefs, as well as between tributaries and suzerains. Thus, when Menéndez de Avilés asked chief Carlos to give him the Spanish captives he had under his control in exchange for showering him with European gifts, the Calusa paramount must have thought that the Spanish captain was seeking to establish an alliance with him. I could find no evidence, however, that captives were routinely traded in either inter- or extratribal commercial networks. In addition, there is little evidence that European presence intensified slave raiding among the peoples of southern Florida.

Members of tributary populations occupied a higher status than captive slaves. Tributaries enjoyed a greater autonomy and experienced none of the constraints on their movements that captives bore. Still, the position of tributaries very much depended on their willingness to comply with their suzerains' demands. These were quite onerous. They included tribute in goods, the performance of a variety of services, the provision of secondary wives for the Calusa paramount, and the constant expression of acquiescence in the form of ceremonial salutations, ritual dances, and other signs of obeisance. Any breach of their servile duties was meted with harsh punishment. This happened to three former tributary chiefs. After changing their allegiance from the Calusa to their archenemies, the Tocobaga, they shifted their loyalties back when the Calusa obtained the support of the Spanish against the Tocobaga. Fearing chief Carlos's punishment, the dissident chiefs implored him to pardon them (Rogel 1991b[1568]: 262). The Calusa paramount granted them his pardon, but not before demanding from them that they vowed "to return to their obedience and vassalage."

Carlos's successor was not less imperious in his behavior. Finding that some of his tributary chiefs had attempted to kill him, "some by treachery and others with witchcraft," chief Felipe had them punished (Rogel 1991b [1568]: 240). Rogel is vague about how the conspirators were punished. If we are to trust another sixteenth-century story concerning chief Felipe, in all probability the punishment was death. This source reports that when chief Felipe found out that four of his tributary chiefs "wanted to revolt and go over with their towns to others of his enemies," the Calusa paramount had them captured and decapitated (Goggin and Sturtevant 1964: 200). He then proceeded to celebrate his victory over the rebel chiefs by parading their heads while people danced around them. Much later, in 1680, a Pojoy tributary chief begged the commander of a Spanish force coming from the north not to continue on to the Calusa capital, stating that if "the said Cacique of Calos learned that he had consented to let them pass on, he would order him to be killed" (de la Cruz in Hann 1991a: 26). In general terms, Calusa tributaries might have been better off than captive slaves. Notwithstanding, their position was extremely shaky and their well-being very much dependent on their unwavering obedience and fidelity.

GUAICURÚ

From their first contacts, European chroniclers alluded to the high degree of stratification that characterized Guaicurú society (Schmidl 1749[1548]: 21). Guaicurú were divided into people of chiefly status, warriors, and ordinary freemen (Lowie 1948: 348; Steward and Faron 1959: 422). Among the *eleg'ipi*, "noble people" (Unger 1972: 89), there were those who belonged to the group by descent and those who were awarded this status for their lifetime, as a reward for outstanding acts. Warriors, called *aguitideg'ipi* (Unger 1972: 69), enjoyed a lower status than chiefs and principal people. Originally, membership in this category depended on military prowess, but as social differences became more marked, warrior status became mostly hereditary. Ordinary freemen, or commoners, known as *noiga icatinedi* (Unger 1972: 90), occupied a lower status. Not surprisingly, captives, *nibotag'ipi* (Unger 1972: 89), had an even lower status than did commoners. The social status of tributaries was that of subordinates. But being themselves highly stratified, the status of particular tributaries varied according to their position in their own society.

The fate of war captives in Guaicurú society varied greatly. It is reported that the most beautiful girls and young women were adopted as daughters or taken as concubines, whereas the more homely were treated as servants and assigned the rough chores (Serra 1850[1803]: 372, 206). This has led to many apparent contradictions surrounding the status of captives in the historical literature. In this chapter, I will focus on the status of this latter category of captives.

Guaicurú people always kept a measure of distance between themselves and their captives. The master and mistress of the household slept on one side of the lean-to, together with their children and relatives; their captives and tributaries who worked for them part-time occupied the opposite side (Sánchez Labrador 1910–1917[1770]: I, 272–273). Captives ate only after their masters had finished, and in a separate area within the abode (Sánchez Labrador 1910–1917[1770]: I, 273). During drinking parties and public festivals, captives were expected to tend to the needs of their masters and mistresses and were not allowed to drink (Boggiani 1945[1892]: 191). Similarly, Guaicurú men never shared their pipes with captives, for, we are told, "they considered such familiarity to tarnish their dignity" (Sánchez Labrador 1910–1917[1770]: I, 278).

Guaicurú had no explicit or implicit rule against marrying people from other ethnic groups. But the higher-ranking they were, the more reluctant they were to marry outsiders, especially captives. Guaicurú women, in particular, refused to "taint their generous blood with that of aliens" (Sánchez Labrador 1910–1917[1770]: II, 28; Méndez 1969[1772]: 63). This does not mean that such marriages never took place, but when they did, they were generally ill-regarded (Prado 1839[1795]: 28). Guaicurú men were more inclined to take captive women as concubines, but they would never take them as legitimate wives (Méndez 1969[1772]: 62). And it is said that even those whom they took as concubines always retained their servant status (Sánchez Labrador 1910–1917[1770]: II, 28-9).

All chroniclers agree that Guaicurú treated their captives with great consideration and even "with great love" (Prado 1839[1795]: 27), especially those persons incorporated as family members (Núñez Cabeza de Vaca 1585[1544]: 76v, 83v; Méndez 1969[1772]: 62). They seldom scolded or punished them (Azara 1809[1781]: II, 110). And they shared everything with them, so much so, it is said, that it seemed as if they and not their masters were the lords (Méndez 1969[1772]: 64–65; Azara 1809[1781]: II, 97; Taunay 1931[1866]: 21). Moreover, the intimacy between masters and slaves was such that masters had no qualms about sharing their concubines with their most esteemed captives (Azara 1809[1781]: II, 96–97). For this reason, we are told, captives seldom ran away.

Some authors explicitly compare the good treatment that Guaicurú meted their captives to the cruelty with which Europeans treated theirs (Azara 1809[1781]: II, 110; Ferreira 1974[1791]: 81). However, the same authors that describe Guaicurú kindness toward their captives inform us that they also exerted total control over them, which, arguably, is the essence of slavery. Guaicurú masters seldom punished their captives physically, but when they wanted to punish a disrespectful or lazy slave, they took away all the property they had given him (including his captive wife), expelled him from their settlement, and totally ignored him (Serra 1850[1803]: 372). Without a wife, horses, weapons, or clothes, such slaves had little chance of survival in the harsh environment of the Grand Chaco. Boggiani's cutting statement (1945[1892]: 133) summarizes well the Guaicurú attitude toward captives: "They generally treat them kindly, without ever letting them forget their duties."

All authors agree that captives could own property. They were even allowed to keep all the loot and captives that they took in war (Serra 1850[1803]: 371; Sánchez Labrador 1910–1917[1770]: I, 308–309). As we haven seen, however, captives could also be dispossessed of all they had, if they did not comply with their masters' wishes. In addition, Guaicurú masters could hire out the labor of their captives and keep the proceeds for themselves (Boggiani 1945[1892]: 183). They could even exchange the sexual favors of their captive concubines for necessary goods (Boggiani 1945[1892]: 120). More importantly, they could devolve their captives on their children (both male and female) under rules of inheritance (Prado 1839[1795]: 31; Serra 1850[1803]: 372).

Captives could also be traded among other Guaicurú and with other neighboring peoples (Lozano 1733: 67). In such intra- and intertribal dealings, captives were exchanged for horses, oxen, rifles, annatto (*Bixa orellana*) paste, weapons, and other valuable objects (Boggiani 1945 [1892]: 133). It is reported that even captives who were considered to be household members were sometimes "sold with extreme ease" (Taunay 1931[1866]: 21). Guaicurú not only sold some of their war captives but often bought captives from other tribes, especially from their Chamacoco tributaries (Prado 1839[1795]: 38; Serra 1845[1803]: 206, 209–210; Boggiani 1945[1892]: 133). Evidence that Guaicurú slave trade increased with the presence of Europeans is lacking. In fact, until the second half of the nineteenth century, there are almost no data to suggest that Guaicurú sold war captives to the Spanish or Portuguese. Even as late as the 1900s, captives were only exceptionally sold to white merchants (Boggiani 1945[1892]: 120). One such exception was the Chamacoco woman depicted in an early 1800s drawing, who was sold to a Brazilian commander (see Figure 27).

The maximum expression of the power that a high-ranking Guaicurú master had over his slaves was their execution at the time of his death so that they could serve him in the netherworld (Lozano 1733: 70). Captives were killed, together with the deceased's horses, hunting dogs, and parrots (Techo 1897[1673]: III, 74). This suggests not only that they were regarded as the property of the deceased but also that their status was that of privileged pets, an analogy I will discuss in more detail in the next chapter.

Although Guaicurú referred to both as *nibotag'ipi* or "captives," the social status of Guaná tributaries was slightly higher than that of captives. Guaicurú chiefs and members of chiefly families often married Guaná women of chiefly status. Such ranked marriages, however, still belied the asymmetrical character of the relationship, insofar as Guaicurú always appeared in the role of wife takers. Marriages with Guaná tributary women also took place among people of lower status (Ferreira 1974[1791]: 78; Serra 1850[1803]: 356). When this happened, Guaná women went to live in the settlement of their Guaicurú husbands. Only Guaicurú men of chiefly status possessed Guaná tributaries. Guaicurú commoners could own war captives, but they seldom had tributaries.

Guaná tributaries frequently spent part of the year serving their masters in their settlements. On such occasions, even Guaná chiefs adopted a submissive attitude and gladly acted as servants (Méndez 1969[1772]: 66–67). In fact, despite the links of affinity between Guaicurú and Guaná chiefly families, Guaicurú chiefs regarded Guaná chiefs not as peers, but as inferiors (Serra 1845[1803]: 209). Disrespectful Guaná tributaries, especially those who failed to address their masters by this title, were often chastised with a few blows (Serra 1850[1803]: 372). Only when Guaná tributary groups began being emancipated with the support of the Brazilian authorities did Guaicurú masters curb their despotic treatment of them (Serra 1845[1803]: 209).

* * *

Lévy-Bruhl's dictum (1931: 2) that "the slave is a being deprived of rights" holds true in the context of native tropical America. The common denominator of captive slavery in all the societies examined here is that captives were deprived of rights and were thus at the total mercy of their captors, who could decide their fate. Such fate was not always that of becoming slaves. Some war captives were adopted as legitimate children or married as legitimate spouses, immediately becoming family members, and with the passage of time were treated as such. Others, however, were immediately bartered with fellow tribesmen or taken to intertribal markets such as those reported by early chroniclers in other regions of tropical America (López de Gómara 1946[1552]: 206; Sparrey 1625[1595]: 1249). Those who were kept as slaves retained the lowest status in their masters' societies.

Servant groups, incorporated but not fully assimilated into the dominant society, occupied a spatially and socially peripheral position with regard to their masters. With respect to their rights, they differed little from captives, the main difference being that they were not totally uprooted and disenfranchised. They were allowed to maintain their family, their kinship ties, their local authorities, and even some degree of personal autonomy. However, they were always marked as being inferior and were subjected to similar social proscriptions as captive slaves.

Tributaries were allowed to retain their tribal rights and personal autonomy. Their situation was much better than that of captives and servant peoples, especially because their relationship with their overlords was frequently represented as one of friendship and alliance. Such favored status, nevertheless, was contingent upon their compliance with the conditions imposed by their overlords. These included the prestation of domestic services, periodic tribute in specified goods, and military aid. The status of tributaries also implied expressions of personal and collective obeisance in their dealings with their overlords and, above all, when present at public ceremonies.

Generally, captives were well treated by their masters. But this treatment varied substantially depending on the social context. In societies where captive slavery was the only form of servitude, and the proportion of captives was relatively small, captive slaves received a tolerable treatment. In societies where captive slavery was combined with other forms of servitude, and the percentage of subordinates was considerably larger, they were often mistreated. Decent treatment toward captives did not obviate the fact that they, and other subordinates, were expected to discharge certain obligations and to observe a certain etiquette of submissiveness. More importantly, it did not obliterate the fact that masters had the power of life and death over captives and, to a lesser degree, members of servant groups and tributary populations.

The ideological basis for this Amerindian conception rests on three considerations. First, being less-than-human foreigners, enemies could be the object of enslavement. Second, having allowed themselves to be captured, they owed their lives to their captors and thus belonged to them. But above all, they were considered to be property, insofar as they were the product of their masters' productive agency.

This latter Amerindian notion assumes that the action of "giving origin to," or "causing something to exist," grants rights of ownership over that which is produced (Dumont 1976: 34; Jackson 1983: 57; Wright 1998: 296; McCallum 2001: 7). Productive agency can assume a variety of forms. It can be the production of material things with one's own hands, or it can be the production of extraordinary things made to appear through one's ritual activities, such as fasts, vigils, or the ingestion of psychotropic substances. It involves all things that are obtained as the result of one's negotiating abilities to barter, purchase, or engage in gift exchange—including, in some societies, wives (Dumont 1976: 40; Y. Murphy and Murphy 1985: 133). In addition, it concerns the social production of bodies, especially those of one's own children. Lastly, it involves all collective initiatives originating from one's abilities as a leader and organizer. This explains why in Amerindian societies one can own pots and weapons, houses and gardens, sacred songs and spirit familiars, children and captives, ritual ceremonies, and fishing expeditions, but one cannot own the land, the rivers, the forests, or the wild animals—none of which are of human creation.

From an Amerindian perspective, however, being the owner of something does not necessarily grant exclusive rights of property over it. This clearly applies to things that result from collective efforts under the guidance of a leader. In maloca-based Amerindian societies, the man and woman who take the initiative of building the longhouse are considered to be "owners of the house" (C. Hugh-Jones 1979: 46; Århem 1981: 83; Chaumeil 1983: 248–249; Londoño Sulkin 2004: 93–100). They can thus have the last word about who can or cannot live in the maloca. They cannot, however, destroy, barter, or in any other way dispose of the maloca, for it is the outcome of collective effort by the inhabitants, and for this reason they all have some claim over it. The same is true of other collective enterprises such as fishing expeditions, drinking parties, or collective gardens.

The partial disjuncture between rights of ownership (being acknowledged as the owner of something) and property rights (having the right to dispose of the thing owned) explains why, even though Amerindian war leaders were considered to be "owners of the raid" or "lords of the war" (Mader and Gippelhauser 2000: 79), they were not entitled to keep the loot and captives. These belonged to the warriors who had seized them as the result of their personal courage.

The notion that captives belonged to those who seized them was reinforced by an underlying Amerindian perception that equates the production of captives with the production of children. From an Amerindian viewpoint, children are brought to life through the expenditure of their parents' bodily fluids and energies (Wagley and Galvão 1949: 69; McCallum 2001: 16). They are endowed with social identity through the ritual bodily practices their parents perform on their behalf. And they are kept alive through the productive activities their parents conduct so as to provision them with their daily needs for food and drink. For this reason, children are frequently said to be "owned" by their parents, whereas orphans are considered to be "without owner" (Rivière 1969: 243; Santos-Granero 1991: 211; Belaúnde 2001: 121). Similarly, captives come into being through the efforts of their captors, who spend energy, and even risk their lives, to capture them. They are given a new social identity through rituals of enslavement organized on their behalf by their captors and their wives. And they are nourished with food and drink nominally produced by their masters and mistresses. Captors own the people they have captured—and parents own the children they have given birth to—because they are responsible for causing them to exist. This is confirmed by the Carib-speaking Wayana, who refer to all the things that are the product of a person's efforts, including children, hunted animals, and captured enemies, as "my made things" (Van Velthem 2003: 141). Such is the deeper sense of the Kalinago, Conibo, Chiriguaná, and Guaicurú terms for captive slaves, which convey the notion of "prey," something created through one's efforts and for this reason amenable to being "owned." This notion extends to bodily trophies taken in war, which explains why Jivaro warriors who have taken an enemy head are referred to as "lord of the head," in the sense of "owner of the head" (Karsten 1923: 29).

It should be noted, however, that not everything that is the result of one's productive agency—and is therefore "owned"—can be bartered or sold or, even less so, can be destroyed or killed. Children and wives may be "owned" in the sense of being the product of one's exertions or exchanges, but they are rarely bartered or sold, and only under very special circumstances can they be legitimately killed (Santos-Granero 2002b, 2004). In contrast, captives could be exchanged in indigenous and European markets, they could be branded with the markings of their owners, and they could be killed with total impunity in a moment of rage. More importantly, they could be destroyed, together with the horses, dogs, parrots, and other items of property owned by their deceased masters, to serve them in the afterworld and to hinder them from haunting the living. What entitled captors to dispose of their war captives' lives was not only that captives were conceived of as being the property of their captors but also that they were considered to be less than human and to owe their lives to their captors.

PART 4

Ideologies of Capture

CHAPTER 8

Civilizing the Other

The basic problem in 'slavery' is not the impossibility of
dehumanizing a person into property, for the newly acquired
alien is already a mere object. Rather, the central problem of 'slavery'
is the "rehumanization" of the nonperson in a new social setting.

—IGOR KOPYTOFF and SUZANNE MIERS,
"African 'Slavery' as an Institution of Marginality"

Rather than being a fixed status, captive slavery in native tropical America was a process—a process in which slaves shifted from a marginal condition as recent war prisoners to their integration as subordinates and, eventually, to their (or their descendants') assimilation into their masters' kinship networks. Cut off from their kin, alienated from their territories and collectivities, war prisoners occupied a liminal position similar to that of initiates in rites of passage (Kopytoff and Miers 1977: 15). Captives who were destined to be traded immediately remained in this liminal condition. The few who were chosen to be adopted or married off were promptly marked as such through more or lesser formal rituals of assimilation. In contrast, captives selected to be kept as slaves were integrated into the society of their captors, all the while preserving their foreignness. As discussed in Chapter 5, integration was achieved by a number of rituals whose main objective was to re-personify war captives by imposing on them both tribal markings (underlining their proximity) and markers of servitude (underscoring their distance).

Marked as both insiders and outsiders, captive slaves occupied a limbic position of institutionalized marginality, a position that they often retained throughout their lives (Vaughan 1979: 100). In these societies the basic problem was not so much the making of, but rather the unmaking of, a slave and his/her transformation into kin (Kopytoff and Miers 1977: 22). The incorporation of war captives into their masters' households as subordinates, and the increased intimacy that this conviviality presupposed, generated its own contradictions (Patterson 1982: 13). Such contradictions could be bridged only via a second process of incorporation whereby captives were gradually assimilated into the society of their captors by way of marriage and kinship. This would explain the good treatment granted to captives in this type of society, for, as Testart (1998: 46) suggests, "it would be illogical to maltreat in excess those who one day will have to be considered as relatives." In some capturing societies the process of assimilation was accomplished during the captive's lifetime; in others, it was deferred, being attained only by their children or even grandchildren.

Recruitment, enslavement, and manumission were therefore closely related aspects of slavery as a process of status formation. Central to this process was how the condition imposed on war captives, characterized by a lack of rights and a set of duties, was transformed, abolished, or transferred to their descendants with the passage of time (Kopytoff 1982: 221). When viewed as a status, slavery can be defined as "a means of denying outsiders the rights and privileges of a particular society" (Lovejoy 2000: 2–3), but when regarded as a process, it can be characterized as a means of systematically incorporating alien outsiders as familiar kin— that is, endowing foreigners with the rights of fellow tribespeople. To distinguish these two stages in the process of incorporation, I will refer to the first stage as *integration* (incorporation without rights) and to the second as *assimilation* (incorporation with full rights).

In this chapter, I examine the different pathways through which captive slaves, servant groups, and tributary populations were integrated, and eventually assimilated, into their masters' societies. In native tropical America, this process often took the ideological form of "familiarization" with war captives conceived of as pets (Viveiros de Castro 1992; Menget 1996; Fausto 1999). In such contexts, the pet analogy is not a mere metaphor. Rather, it is a logical outcome of interethnic systems of classification by way of which powerful capturing societies classify their weaker neighbors as game animals (C. Hugh-Jones 1979: 223–224). Enemies are equated to affines and game meat, whereas captive children are associated with consanguines and pets (Descola 1994: 339). This ideology was also present among native groups outside tropical America; Cherokees are a good example of a group that perceived the enemy in such a way (Perdue 1993: 16).

Following this Amerindian logic, captives are not likened to orphan children belonging to one's group—who are often rejected and mistreated as bearers of ill fortune—but rather to the progeny of killed animals. They must be treated kindly but raised as pets—that is, as exotic family additions. Given that Amerindians often attributed animals with the capacity for sociality, while denying such capacity to their human enemies, war captives were seen both as quasi animals to be domesticated and as quasi humans to be civilized. Thus, in native regimes of capture and servitude, the pet analogy serves the triple purpose of stressing the predatory nature of captive slavery, naturalizing interethnic power differences, and underscoring the ambiguous status held by slaves and servants—who, like pets, occupied a position midway between animals and humans.

Slavery, therefore, is but a temporary status in a process through which enemy Others are civilized and transformed into intimate consanguines. Such a transformation generally entails the use of fictive kinship terms, which, at least in the first stages of incorporation, do not fully conceal the hierarchical and subordinate nature of the master-captive relationship. The notion of civilizing the Other by way of intermarriage, conviviality, and consanguinization is not, however, the only means of dealing with subordinate enemies. This will hopefully become apparent from my analysis of the three broad regimes of capture and servitude identified in the region.

It should be emphasized that assimilation of captives and other subordinates via the creation of kinship and marriage ties did not necessarily put an end to their marginality. Captives thus assimilated could cease to be marginal to their masters' kinship networks, but they often continued to be marginal to the capturing society as a whole (Kopytoff and Miers 1977: 16). The stigma of their captive origins frequently continued to haunt them and even their descendants. However, prolonged co-residence, sharing of food and drink, and the development of affective ties gradually conspired to obliterate the stigma of captivity. And although the social amnesia that facilitated this process could be reversed if sociopolitical conditions required it, it was a powerful enough force to guarantee the constant enfranchisement and assimilation of enemy Others into their captors' societies.

KALINAGO

The process of assimilation of war captives among Kalinago differed substantially depending on an individual's ethnic origin, sex, and age.

Indigenous captives—mostly Arawak-speaking Lokono, their preferred enemies—were never fully assimilated during their lifetime. Captive women could be taken as concubines. And they could be greatly loved by their elderly masters. They nevertheless always bore the marks of their slave condition—short hair and a lack of leg ligatures—and were treated accordingly (Du Tertre 1654: 421).

Children born from unions between Kalinago men and captive concubines were known as *tíoüe* (Breton 1665: 464). They were brought up under the same conditions as Kalinago children (Du Tertre 1667: 379). Their fate, however, varied according to sex. Whereas captive girls were raised to marry Kalinago men, captive boys were kept as sacrificial victims to be eaten in cannibalistic ceremonies when they reached adulthood (Alvarez Chanca 1978[1494]: 31; Anon. 1988[1620]: 187). This led Martire d'Anghiera (1966[1555]: 3r) to assert that "such young women as they take, they keep for increase, as we do hens to lay eggs," an image that, despite the prejudice it betrays, is not totally incorrect, as we shall see.

The practice of sacrificing captive boys when they became adults, which to this day seems too cruel to be true, has been rejected by some contemporary scholars as a coarse Spanish slander (Cassá 1992: 168). We do know, however, that similar customs were found among the Tupinambá of coastal Brazil, where abundant evidence supports their existence (Viveiros de Castro 1992: 374). In this latter case, it was the children begotten by captive men and local women who were raised, executed, and consumed after coming of age. European sources attributed this Tupinambá practice to a patrilineal bias whereby children of enemy captive men were considered to be enemies in themselves. Given that among Kalinago it was the children of captive women who were consumed, the explanation for this practice probably has less to do with lineality and the gender of captives than with the gender of the children they begot, with boys always doomed to be executed as potential enemy warriors, and girls destined to be assimilated as potential mothers of fellow warriors.

Captive boys, as well as boys begotten by female slaves, bore the mark of servitude—namely, short hair—and were addressed as *támon*, "captive" (Anon. 1988[1620]: 187–188). According to Chevillard (1659: 118), who unfortunately is the only chronicler to report this practice, Kalinago masters also called such boys *lixabali*, or "our barbecue," in a vivid allusion to their fate. Du Tertre (1654: 449–450) asserts that Kalinago ate not only the sons of their captive women but even their grandsons—that is, the sons of female descendants of captive women. Other sources, however, call this assertion into question (Rochefort 1666[1658]: 326). In a later edition of his book, Du Tertre (1667: 405) eliminated the passage to the effect that Kalinago people ate the sons of captive women, suggesting that perhaps by the time he wrote his report, these practices had been abandoned, so he was unsure about their veracity. Breton (1665: 278–279), around the same time, seems to confirm Du Tertre's revised opinion when he affirms that the children of female slaves "are esteemed and treated as legitimate." Also confirming this important change is the fact that Kalinago abandoned ritual cannibalism around the second half of the seventeenth century, preferring instead to sell their male captives to European traders (Rochefort 1658: 477; Labat 1724[1705]: II, Part 4, 108).

Be that as it may, enough evidence supports the idea that, early on, at least the sons of female slaves were thus consumed. Further support for this practice is found in Kalinago representations of war captives. Whether men condemned to being cannibalized (*libínali*), or women and children destined to be kept as concubines and servants (*támon*), Kalinago equated their war captives to animal prey. Rochefort (1666[1658]: Appendix) asserts that one of the terms by which Kalinago masters called their captives was *nïouitouli*, which he translates as "my prisoner of war." But in his dictionary, Breton (1665: 390) renders the root of this term, *ioüítouli*, as "the capture that I made," in the sense of "the prey that I have hunted." Thus a better translation of the term *nïouitouli* would be "my prey that I have captured in war."

Kalinago classification of enemies as potential game, and of war captives as actual prey, is consonant with Amerindian ideologies of predation, which regard enemies as being on the side of animality and thus liable to be hunted and eaten (Overing 1986; Viveiros de Castro 1993, 2001; Århem 1996; Fausto 1999; Vilaça 2002). This analogy, which Descola (1994: 339) has synthesized in the structural formula "affines = enemies = game meat :: consanguines = captive children = pets," does not apply easily to the Kalinago, however. In effect, some enemies (women, but also Africans and Europeans) were not considered good enough to be eaten, whereas some domesticated captives (captive boys and male descendants of captive women) were not assimilated as consanguines but, rather, were raised to be eaten.

African and European captives underwent a completely different process of assimilation. To begin with, they were excluded from the system of cannibalistic exchange linking the Kalinago to their Arawakan enemies. Both men and women were integrated as slaves (*támon*), and put to work as such. In a few cases, captive men who excelled as workers or warriors were rewarded by being given Kalinago women (Gage 1992[1648]: 85). In such situations, their children were considered to be Kalinago.

However, since Kalinago were reluctant to marry African captives, the latter tended to marry among each other. With the passage of time, these Kalinagoized African captives acquired greater autonomy (Le Breton 1998[1722]: 4). Indeed, during the 1600s, former African captives and their descendants formed their own independent settlements in both St. Vincent and Dominica. During a greater part of the century, these two groups—the Black and the Red (or Yellow) Caribs—lived side by side and were engaged in a system of reciprocal prestations (Le Breton 1998[1722]: 4). By the late 1600s, however, the Black Caribs not only had surpassed their former masters in numbers but also raided them often in search of wives and plunder. The assimilation of these Black Caribs was thus only partial. They may have acquired the language, culture, and ethos of their Kalinago masters, but they had retained a different ethnopolitical identity and organization. More importantly, their former masters regarded them as occupying a lowly status and continued to call them *támon* long after they had ceased to be captives.

CONIBO

Among the Conibo, war captives had little chance of being fully assimilated during their lifetimes even if they had been taken as children. All sources concur that captive children soon learned the Conibo language, aesthetics, and social etiquette (Girbal y Barceló 1964[1794]: 282). They were nevertheless prevented from being considered to be fully Conibo because they had not undergone head elongation, which from the point of view of the Conibo was the main trait signaling their condition as "civilized" people. In addition, captive girls, though integrated, were not considered to be true Conibo, because they were uncircumcised. This latter condition could sometimes be remedied if the captive girl had been taken before puberty. On the other hand, it was not imposed on fully developed captive women, who were thus stigmatized as remaining "wild" and "uncivilized."

The wildness attributed to war captives is linguistically expressed by the term *hiná*, one of the two words Conibo used to refer to them. An early Conibo-Spanish dictionary translates *hiná* as "captive," "slave," or "live-in servant," but also as "animal tail" (Marqués 1931[1800]: 143, 145, 148, 155). A later dictionary renders the term *hiná* as "domestic animals," "household servants," "adoptive children," and "animal tail" (Anon. 1927: 405, 457). More recently, the Summer Institute of Linguistics rendered the term *iná* as both "the domesticated offspring of an animal or bird" and "wild Indian" (Tournon 2002: 172). In addition, the first two dictionaries register the term *hináqui* as meaning "to raise slaves and animals" (Marqués 1931[1800]: 148), although this term would be better translated as "to make slaves or pets," since it is made up of *hiná*, "slave or domestic animal," and the causative suffix *ácqui*, "to cause to be."

The likening of captives to pets, resulting from the customs of Conibo warrior-hunters to kill the progenitors of enemies and animals and to keep their offspring, is further underscored by the second term by which Conibo referred to war captives. Translated as "captive," the term *yadtá* actually means "the seized one," suggesting that Conibo viewed enemies as animal prey (Marqués 1931[1800]: 143, 145, 160). From a Conibo perspective, therefore, enemies were equated with animal prey, whereas war captives were likened to the young of killed animals, which were captured and kept as household pets.

The notion of *hináqui*, "to make slaves," is further associated to that of *rágue áqui*. Translated as "to tame" or "to domesticate" (Marqués 1931[1800]: 134), this expression can be broken down into the term *rag*, "friend," and the causative suffix *ácqui*, yielding "to cause someone to be a friend." Frank (1994: 182–185) translates a similar term, *raëati*— used by the Cashibo, the archenemies of the Conibo and also Panoan speakers—as "to civilize or pacify." According to him, Cashibo people used this term to describe their attempts to persuade enemy Cashibo groups to enter into peaceful relationships of exchange with them, relationships that they viewed as "civilizing," or "pacifying," the Other. The cognate Conibo term *rágue áqui* has a similar meaning, but it applies to civilizing or pacifying captive wild Others.

The process of civilizing or pacifying the Other entailed the use of filial kinship terms to refer to captive children. Eighteenth-century sources indicate that Conibo treated captive boys and girls "as their children"

(Girbal y Barceló 1924a[1790]: 161). The latter, in turn, treated their masters as "parents" (Fry 1907[1888]: 474; Stahl 1928[1895]: 150–151). The use of kinship terms suggests that captive children were adopted by their captors and given the same rights as their biological children. As scholars of African slavery have already noted, however, in kin-based societies paternal-filial kinship terms are often used to express relationships of hierarchy rather than ties of intimacy and affection (Kopytoff and Miers 1977: 23–25; Patterson 1982: 19; Kopytoff 1982: 215). The use of such terms in the context of captive slavery should be regarded, they argue, as metaphors of authority and subordination rather than as indicating the actual adoption of captive children. Fictive kinship ties were used to "humanize" a relationship that was intrinsically inhuman, insofar as it related proper humans with less-than-human beings, from a native perspective.

The Conibo, among whom, as we have seen, the term *hiná* means simultaneously "captive," "slave," "pet," and "adoptive child" used fictive kinship terms in this manner. The wild, animal-like nature attributed to war captives persisted even after they had successfully undergone cultural integration through adoptive filiation. Even familiarized captive children, treated as "sons" and "daughters" by their Conibo captors, were sometimes sold or exchanged along indigenous or foreign trading networks (Marcoy 1869[1847]: I, 629). More importantly, when they grew older, captive children were generally prevented from marrying Conibo men and women because the captives lacked the marks of "true" Conibo people. Sources indicate that captive women could be taken by Conibo men as concubines for themselves or their sons, and meritorious captive men could sometimes be given a Conibo woman in marriage (Stiglich 1905: 344; Stahl 1928[1895]: 150). Nevertheless, the general tendency was for captives to marry other captives, preferably from their own society of origin (Fry 1907[1888]: 474). Captive couples continued to live together with their masters as members of their households— probably according to the uxorilocal postmarital residence rule to which Conibo people adhered.

The children born from unions between captives were subjected to head elongation and raised as "legitimate" Conibo (*legítimo Conibo*) (Stahl 1928[1895]: 164). They were taught the Conibo language and cultural practices, and the girls were circumcised after puberty. Having thus been marked as true Conibo, these children were allowed to take Conibo spouses. They were entitled to all the rights enjoyed by the Conibo and led a life almost undistinguishable from them. This would explain why some authors assert that, from a Conibo perspective, "Conibos are those who are born in the tribe bearing that name" (Fry 1907[1888]: 474). It also explains why early sources report that in the lapse of two generations the descendants of captives became part of the general Conibo population (Girbal y Barceló 1964[1794]: 282).

First-generation captives, however, continued to be treated as slaves even after giving birth to true Conibo children. Only at the death of their masters did they regain autonomy and freedom to live wherever they wanted (Fry 1907[1888]: 474). Most captives chose to live close to their master's relatives. However, even those captives who had adopted Conibo language and mores retained throughout their lives the stigma of their backwoods origins, a stigma that, under certain circumstances, could even taint their offspring (DeBoer 1986: 243).

TUKANO

The process of integration of Makú people into Tukano society differed, depending on whether they had been captured individually in war or subjected collectively as a servant group. Given the almost universal Tukano refusal to marry Makú people, female Makú captives were rarely taken as concubines. Most often they were integrated as household servants. Whenever requested to do so, they had to be sexually available to the men of the maloca (Koch-Grünberg 1995[1909]: I, 277; Goldman 1963: 96). If these furtive relationships led to pregnancies, the children of such unions were not recognized as legitimate Tukano. Stradelli (1890[1882]: 433) asserts that, in fact, the fathers of such children considered their progeny to be "scarcely more than slaves and ceded them or sold them without much difficulty."

More recent sources assert that Tukano men sometimes took Makú captives as concubines but avoided having children with them (Silva 1962: 409). If they did have such children, however, the latter were recognized "as legitimate and belonging to the father's tribe." This seems to be a late development resulting from missionary pressures, since the same source informs us that when the Tukano father of a mixed Makú child presented the child for baptism, the man at first denied being the father (Silva 1962: 409). More importantly, even those who had been recognized by their Tukano fathers were often dismissed as being "only a Makú" (Biocca 1965: I, 469).

Makú captive men had even a lesser possibility of being assimilated through marriage, for no Tukano woman would accept marrying a Makú. As a result, Makú captives married among themselves in most cases. Such captive couples, according to McGovern (1927: 248), "were allowed to live a family life so that they could breed further slaves for their masters." Whether captured in war or born to Makú captives, Makú children were regular items of commerce. This confirms Stradelli's observation (1890[1882]: 433) that captives were still treated as slaves—people without rights—irrespective of the degree to which they had adopted Tukano language and customs. If they were not sold or given away as presents, the children of Makú captive couples were inherited by the children of their captor (Ramos, Silverwood-Cope, and Oliveira 1980: 174).

The only chance that Makú captives had of overcoming their condition was through emancipation. One such case was reported by McGovern (1927: 177), who says that a Makú captive was granted freedom after saving the life of his Tukano master in a hunting accident. His dependence on his former master persisted, however, even after the captive had founded his own Makú band.

Several sources suggest that Tukano treated their Makú captives as pets, but there is no linguistic evidence that this is what the Tukano themselves had in mind. Koch-Grünberg (1995[1909]: I, 276) states that Tukano treated their Makú captives well, "as if they were pets." But McGovern (1927: 248) asserts, more specifically, that they treated them "as a particularly useful sort of dog." Although not a native distinction, this semantic divergence is significant, for we know that native tropical American peoples treat wild animals adopted as pets very differently from household dogs. Pets are well taken care of and even regaled, whereas dogs are usually treated with extreme cruelty (unless they are good hunters) and have to scavenge for themselves (Rivière 1969: 41; W. Crocker and Crocker 1994: 137; Cormier 2003b: 115). Tukano seem to have regarded Makú captives as lesser beings than dogs. Thus, it is reported that whereas Tukano mothers allowed their children to play with dogs, they thought it very degrading if their children played with Makú children (McGovern 1927: 248).

Makú servant groups had a better opportunity to be assimilated into their masters' societies than Makú captives. Early on, Koch-Grünberg (1995[1909]: II, 91) pointed out that there were several sibs among the Cubeo that were originally Makú servant groups forced to abandon their nomadic life and settle down. By the time he met these groups, they had adopted Cubeo language and cultural practices; in other words, they had been "civilized." However, although they considered themselves to be *mira*, "people," their true-Cubeo neighbors regarded them with contempt and still called them Makú, although not to their face (Koch-Grünberg 1995[1909]: II, 91–92, 99).

The existence of Makú groups assimilated by the Tukano was also reported by Nimuendajú (1950[1927]: 165). More recently, Silverwood-Cope (1990: 74) mentioned the existence of a Makú group that spoke only Cubeo but was considered Makú by all its neighbors. He asserted that the process of assimilation had not yet reached the point that the two groups, Cubeo and assimilated Makú, had cemented their alliance through intermarriage. Once such marriage exchanges had taken place, the Cubeo often chose to forget the ancestry of their forest affines.

This affinal (rather than genealogical) amnesia seems to play a large role in the assimilation of Makú servant groups as Tukano low-ranking sibs. The Tukanoan Desana had assimilated so many such groups that in the late 1800s they were considered to be of mixed Tukano-Makú heritage (Coudreau 1887: II, 164). In the early 1900s, Koch-Grünberg (1995[1909]: I, 251) noted that the Desana were still one of the few Tukano groups that allowed marriages with Makú people. However, less than twenty years later, McGovern (1927: 184) recounted that a Desana friend of his "went into hysterics" when he mentioned a Tukano rumor indicating that the Desana had once or twice married Makú people. This anecdote shows how Tukanoan groups could choose to forget that they had assimilated Makú servant groups even if they had done so recently. By the same token, according to Jackson (1983: 159), a "low-ranking sib's origin can always be impugned by suggesting that it was originally a Makú band."

In all Tukano societies, in fact, the lower-ranking sibs occupying the symbolic role of "servants" have been frequently likened to Makú servant groups (Goldman 1963: 91; C. Hugh-Jones 1979: 54; Århem 1981: 121; Jackson 1983: 152; Reichel-Dolmatoff 1996: 84). In no way should this be taken as meaning that all sibs classified as servants were originally Makú servant groups. Rather, the comparison of low-ranking sibs to Makú servant groups functions to reinforce their subordinate position in the Tukano social universe. Given that assimilated Makú groups have been reported not only among the Cubeo and Desana but also among the Tukano proper (Reichel-Dolmatoff 1996: 42), the Bará (Jackson 1983:

159), and the Makuna (Århem 1981: 13), I would argue, however, that the structural resemblance between Tukano low-ranking sibs and Makú attached servant groups reinforces the subordination of the former but, above all, enables the assimilation of the latter.

CHIRIGUANÁ

The manner in which Chiriguaná people integrated and assimilated their war captives varied along a time dimension. During the first stage, when the eastern slopes of the Bolivian Andes were conquered by the invading Chiriguaná, who were still not very numerous, they increased their population by taking Chané women as their wives and by giving their daughters in marriage to Chané captive boys who had proven their courage as warriors (Polo de Ondegardo 1991[1574]: 138). The children of these mixed marriages were raised as Chiriguaná and were assimilated as fellow tribespeople (Díaz de Guzmán 1979a[1617]: 72–73). Their acculturation was so complete that the assimilated Chané not only shared in the Chiriguaná cannibalistic rituals but also became, it is said, "as cruel and pitiless" with their own people as their captors (Polo de Ondegardo 1991[1574]: 138).

As the intensity of Chiriguaná attacks increased later on, and with it the number of Chané people taken as captives, it became more difficult for the captives to rapidly assimilate into Chiriguaná society. Captive children continued to be raised as Chiriguaná, but they were not immediately adopted by their captors. They were still considered to be *tembiau*, "captives," and were treated as such. This term is related to both *tembiara*, "human prey taken in war," and *mîmbâba*, "domestic animal," suggesting that Chiriguaná equated enemies to animal prey, and war captives to wild animals kept as pets (Anon. 1938[1622]: 352, 100, 146; Dietrich 1986: 307, 316; also Viveiros de Castro 1992: 280). Midway between humanity and animality, war captives occupied a liminal position with little possibility of being fully assimilated even though they had been integrated.

In the second stage, captive children raised as Chiriguaná were seldom allowed to take Chiriguaná spouses and thus were usually forced to marry among themselves. In such cases, their children were "like objects" and "the property of their master as long as they live under his dominion" (Giannecchini 1996[1898]: 328). Captive women continued to be taken by Chiriguaná men, but as concubines (*guasá*) rather than wives (*emirekó*). An old Chané man recounts that the children of such mixed unions retained the stigma of their captive origin and were called and treated as *tapui*, "real or potential captives" (Métraux 1930: 328). Mixed Chiriguaná-Chané children, however, stood a better chance of becoming assimilated than did the children of captive Chané couples. Thus, young captive men who stood out as brave warriors were rapidly recruited into Chiriguaná mainstream society as *queremba*, or "mature warriors."

Outstanding or favored captives who were chosen to be assimilated were treated no longer as *tapui* but rather as "grandchildren." In turn, former captives stopped addressing their master-owners as *cheya*, "my master," and began treating them as *chirámui*, "my grandfather," or *chiyari*, "my grandmother" (Susnik 1968: 32). The use of the grandparent-grandchild idiom, rather than the parent-child relationship, as a means to assimilate captive children may have originated in the extended Chiriguaná practice by which grandparents raised the children of their divorced or widowed daughters in order to avoid their mistreatment by their stepfathers (Giannecchini 1996[1898]: 301). At least some of the children taken captive by Chiriguaná were assimilated into their society through the creation of fictive relations of consanguinity. From a Chiriguaná perspective, therefore, captive slavery was a process rather than a fixed status. Captives were regarded as "people in the making." They began as less-than-human beings, and through a process of familiarization in which they were compared to pets, and a process of consanguinization by which they were adopted as grandchildren, they finally achieved the condition of civilized, true human beings.

The fate of unassimilated captives once their masters died is unclear. Some were inherited by the children of the deceased (Susnik 1968: 35). In such cases, the inheritor acquired all the rights held by the previous master-owner, including the right to sell his or her captives to a third party. Some captives may have been automatically freed at the death of their masters, but evidence to support this is lacking. We do know, however, that Chiriguaná masters and mistresses had the right to liberate their captives whenever they pleased.

During the second stage of Chiriguaná settlement of eastern Bolivia, the invaders not only raided the Chané and other neighbors in search of captives but also subjugated entire Chané local settlements, subsequently attaching them as servant groups living in the periphery of Chiriguaná villages. Members of these groups were treated as servants or as subordinate members of the household. But at a more general level they were considered to be *tapui*, "real or potential captives," as much as actual captives. For more than three centuries, Chané servant groups underwent a process of Chiriguanáization. This was achieved partly through direct contact with the language and culture of their captors, and partly through the incorporation of Chiriguanáized but unassimilated Chané captives who, after emancipation, had married into these groups.

The gradual emergence of two groups that shared the Chiriguaná language and hybrid cultural practices, but distinguished themselves in terms of their origin and a few minor linguistic and cultural elements, resulted from these processes (see Combès and Lowrey 2006). With the passage of time, intermarriages between the two groups decreased, so that each acquired an almost endogamous character. Assimilation of the Chané was completed in the late 1700s. By then, the Chané spoke, acted, and behaved in everything "almost identically to the Chiriguaná" (Mingo de la Concepción 1981[1797]: I, 116–177). The only difference between them was that the Chané were fewer in number and were still regarded by the Chiriguaná as being their "servants or boys."

In effect, both groups claimed to be Ava—that is, "real people"—but those who considered themselves to be of pure Chiriguaná stock (Ava-Chiriguaná) looked upon those who descended from Chané captives or servant groups (Ava-Izoceño) as somehow inferior. In a very Amerindian twist of perspectives, however, the Ava-Izoceño claim that it was they who enslaved the Chiriguaná, which in a sense is true, insofar as the Chiriguaná were as much Arawakized as the Chané were Guaraní-ized (Combès and Lowrey 2006: 696). The distinction was more ideological than biological—the invading Chiriguaná had mixed with the local Chané since their arrival in the region during the fifteenth century. In any case, all the Chané had been assimilated as low-ranking Ava by the end of the eighteenth century.

CALUSA

The avenues for assimilation open to captives in Calusa society also varied according to gender. Captive women were often taken as concubines or perhaps even as wives—sources are somewhat vague about the character of these unions. French sources report that four shipwrecked Spanish women who were taken captive in 1549 were living fifteen years later "with the king of Calos together with their children" (Laudonnière

2001[1564]: 110). In turn, Spanish sources tell us that the five Spanish captive women who Menéndez de Avilés forced chief Carlos to release were married to Calusa men and had children by them (Solís de Merás 1990[1565]: 114–115). That the Calusa did not allow the released women to take their children with them suggests that the children did not have the status of slaves but were regarded as legitimate and free members of their fathers' families.

European sources provide several examples of captive women married to Calusa men. Yet they offer little evidence of the reverse— namely, captive men married to Calusa women. Marrying into the group was therefore not an option open to male captives. None of the Spanish captive men for whom we have personal testimonies—Juan Ortiz, captured around 1527 (Elvas 1995[1539]), the two unnamed Spanish captives interviewed in 1549 by Laudonnière (2001[1586]), and Hernando de Escalante Fontaneda (1575), captured in 1551—ever mentioned having married native women. That captive men were the preferred sacrificial victims in yearly fertility rituals and in rituals of propitiation of local gods may account for why they seldom formed their own families (Laudonnière 2001[1564]: 110–111; Elvas 1995[1539]: 61; Solís de Merás 1990[1565]: 201). But the absence of such marriages could also be traced to a certain reticence on the part of Spanish captive men to acknowledge the existence of their native and, from their point of view, illegitimate families. Be that as it may, we cannot at this point assert with any certainty whether captive men could be assimilated into Calusa society or whether they were always destined to be sacrificed. We do know, however, that Calusa masters could choose to emancipate their captives. In contrast to practices in other capturing societies, emancipation did not necessarily lead to assimilation among Calusa. Rather, it was a mechanism allowing masters to grant permission to their captives to go back to their own people (Elvas 1995[1539]: 61).

Evidence that Calusa people ever attempted to assimilate their tributary populations is lacking. The Tequesta, Tocobaga, Pojoy, and Ais, the Calusa's main enemies and on-and-off tributaries, always maintained their own languages and identities. Even when all the native peoples of southern Florida were decimated by epidemics and wars of resistance in the mid-1700s, the Tequesta (Boca Raton), Florida Keys islanders, and other former tributaries of the Calusa kept their own identity and were regarded by the Spanish as constituting distinct "nations" (Monaco and Alaña 1991[1743]: 420). If the Calusa were not interested in assimilating their tributaries, they were nevertheless certainly eager to integrate them into their polity in such a way as to disguise the coercive nature of the tributary relationship.

Two mechanisms were put into play to achieve this integration. First was the creation of fictive kinship ties of the older brother–younger brother type. The recognition of another chief as an older brother was the way in which chiefs in southern Florida rendered "obedience" (Barrientos 1965[1568]: 125). That this was the way to cement relationships of alliance with more powerful peoples is confirmed by the fact that both the Calusa and Tequesta chiefs proposed to Captain Menéndez de Avilés that he become their elder brother, thus recognizing him as their superior (Solís de Merás 1990[1565]: 116, 202). As younger brothers, tributary chiefs acknowledged the suzerainty of a dominant chief by uttering special salutations and by having their closest relatives perform dances and songs for him (Solís de Merás 1990[1567]: 116, 118). Such fictive kin ties had the advantage of representing suzerain and tributary chiefs as equals, while simultaneously preserving the hierarchical character of their relationship. Furthermore, suzerain and tributary chiefs, as consanguines and brothers, were morally compelled to avoid fights and to develop a relationship based on mutual reciprocity and respect. Doubtless, such behavior served the interests of Calusa paramounts, who could thus appeal to the obligation of siblingship to preserve peace while at the same time benefiting from the steady reception of tribute.

Marriage was the second mechanism by which Calusa paramount chiefs integrated tributary peoples into their sociopolitical networks. Tributary chiefs were obliged to give their daughters in marriage to the Calusa paramount as a sign of alliance and allegiance. The most famous instance of such a pact was that between the Calusa and their Ais tributaries (Laudonnière 2001[1564]: 111–112). That this was considered to be a very important political act is confirmed by the fact that the bride was escorted to Calos, the Calusa capital, by the Ais chief himself. The same marriage mechanism was put into play whenever a new Calusa paramount was appointed. On such occasions, all the villages under his dominion were under the obligation to send one woman each (Rogel 1991b[1568]: 268).

Such marriages disguised the coercive nature of tributary relationships by encouraging the perception that Calusa suzerains were affines and thus potential kin. However, the asymmetrical nature of such marriage exchanges—with tributary chiefs always standing as wife-givers, and

Calusa paramounts as wife-takers—indicates that the relationship between suzerain and tributary chiefs was represented as one of equality within hierarchy. Further underscoring the imbalance of the relationship was that, in contrast to most wife-takers, Calusa chiefs were not expected to comply with bride service and uxorilocality, two of the most pervasive features of marriage exchanges in native tropical American societies. Additionally, the women that tributary groups gave to the Calusa paramount chief as wives possibly served not only to cement political relations of subordination but also to act as potential hostages in case their fathers decided to challenge Calusa hegemony (Menéndez de Avilés 1991[1566]: 303).

That tributary chiefs could stand as both younger brothers and fathers-in-law with respect to the Calusa paramount is in line with what we know of Calusa marriage practices. According to the long account of Calusa dynastic conflicts provided by Father Rogel (1991b[1568]: 266–269), Calusa chiefs married both their maternal and paternal cousins. This kind of marriage ensured that political power remained in the hands of only a few chiefly lines. Links of consanguinity and affinity between the Calusa paramount and his numerous tributary chiefs contributed to reproducing this model at an interethnic level. Such links ensured a greater level of sociopolitical integration without requiring the total assimilation of tributary peoples.

GUAICURÚ

War captives were assimilated into Guaicurú society considerably faster than into any other society in the sample. Emancipation among them was an option open even to recently captured men and women. Guaicurú women had the right to free any of the men captured by the warriors of their settlement (Núñez Cabeza de Vaca 1585[1544]: 83v). Such manumitted men could neither be killed nor treated as slaves. If they wished to stay among their captors, they were treated as one of them. Otherwise, they could go back to their own people. Attractive captive girls and boys were usually adopted by their captors and cared for as if they were their own children. This was not a fictive adoption; the Guaicurú had a specific term for this formalized procedure: *yibàà tame y'onigi*, "to adopt as a son" (Unger 1972: 82). Adoptive captive children were regaled and spoiled, probably because Guaicurú women avoided bearing children when young, and when they decided to do so, they never had more than one or two (Sánchez Labrador 1910–1917[1760]: II, 30; Méndez 1969[1772]: 61; Ferreira 1974[1791]: 80; Prado 1839[1795]: 31). When adoptive captive children grew up, they were considered to be fellow tribespeople, enjoying full rights, including the right to inherit their adoptive parents' possessions (Méndez 1969[1772]: 62).

Other types of captives, however, were not quite as swiftly assimilated. Attractive young women could be taken as concubines. As such, they were not treated as drudges, but they retained their servile status throughout their lifetimes (Sánchez Labrador 1910–1917[1760]: II, 28–29). Homely children and ugly women had even a harder time, with few possibilities of assimilation into their captors' society during their lifetimes. According to Métraux (1946: 308), who does not cite his source, this kind of slave addressed their masters as "fathers." I have not been able to confirm this assertion through other sources. But if this was indeed an extended practice, it differed from the practice of adopting captive children, insofar as it only established fictive links of filiation, entailing none of the rights enjoyed by adoptive children. This primary process of consanguinization signaled, nonetheless, the transformation of war captives, from wild nonpersons into persons in the making, thus contributing to their gradual assimilation. The depth of this assimilation is confirmed by the Guaicurú practice whereby members of a household changed their names "whenever a kinsperson or slave died" (Prado 1839[1795]: 37).

One of the few doors to achieving social mobility open to captives not assimilated through marriage or adoption was prowess in war. Young captive men raised in the Guaicurú tradition were frequently trained as warriors. Brave captive men were allowed to keep whatever plunder they could take from the enemy—who were often their own people—including not only horses and goods but also prisoners (Serra 1850[1803]: 371). Their status continued to be that of *nibotagi*, "war captive," yet bold captive warriors were included in community councils, and in some instances their opinions carried as much weight as that of their "more prominent masters" (Serra 1850[1803]: 371–372). Occasionally they even managed to marry a Guaicurú woman, an expeditious means of becoming fully assimilated into Guaicurú society (Boggiani 1945[1892]: 163).

Not all captive men stood out as brave warriors, however. And not all captive women were taken as concubines. Persons not assimilated as adoptive children or as spouses retained their slave status. They were married to other captives in a similar condition so that, we are told, "they would produce more hunters, fishermen, and servants" (Serra

1850[1803]: 356; also Boggiani 1945[1892]: 135). At the death of their masters, they could devolve on their masters' children or other close relatives (Serra 1850[1803]: 372). With the passage of time, even the children of captive couples were "included without distinction into the main body of the Guaicurú," thanks to their personal merits and marriage links (Serra 1850[1803]: 372). Emancipation of faithful captives was also possible (Boggiani 1945[1892]: 117, 186; Prado 1839[1795]: 32).

In contrast, children of mixed Guaicurú-captive parentage were always considered to be fully Guaicurú (Sánchez Labrador 1910–1917[1760]: II, 28). The assimilation of mixed Guaicurú-captive children was so complete that they could themselves become chieftains and chieftainesses, provided they came from chiefly stock (see Serra 1850[1803]: 372; Wilbert and Simoneau 1989: 6). The descendants of mixed Guaicurú-captive unions were extremely proud of their Guaicurú ancestry; being members of the most powerful people in the region, their living standard was much better than that of their non-Guaicurú forebears (Serra 1850[1803]: 375).

The relationship between Guaicurú and their Guaná tributaries was one of alliance and subjection, friendship and mutual distrust. The emphasis on one or the other of these aspects depended on external conditions. In times of drought, when resources were scarce, Guaná tributaries complained about the demands their Guaicurú masters placed on them. The latter, in turn, accused their tributaries of being lazy. In times of successful raids, when both the dominating Guaicurú and their subordinate allies benefited from the loot and captives, all parties were satisfied.

At all times, Guaicurú stood in a parent-child relationship with respect to their Guaná tributaries. Guaicurú chiefs who controlled Guaná or other tributaries were known as *inionigi eliodi*, where *inionigi* means "captain," in the sense of "chief," and *eliodi* means "father" (Unger 1972: 90, 84). This fictive consanguineal relationship disguised the underlying verticality and asymmetry of the relationship. Such asymmetry was simultaneously confirmed and obliterated by the practice of ranked marriages. Guaicurú chiefs, we are told, often married Guaná women of chiefly rank.

Such marriages legitimized Guaicurú authority over their tributaries and disguised the coercive dimension of the relationship. Intermarriage between the chiefly elites of the suzerain and subordinate groups provided a semblance of equality in what was otherwise a clearly hierarchical relationship. Notably, however, intermarriage between the Guaicurú and their Guaná tributaries involved not only the elites of both groups but all kinds of people. Members of the warrior and commoner groups also took Guaná tributary women as wives (Serra 1845[1803]: 209). In such cases, their children enjoyed the same rights as Guaicurú tribespeople. The intensity of intermarriages between suzerains and tributaries was such that it almost led to the near assimilation of entire Guaná settlements into Guaicurú regional groups (Azara 1809[1781]: II, 87). In other cases, like that of the Terena, it led to the adoption of many Guaicurú cultural practices by the subordinate group, without relinquishing its own identity (Susnik 1971: 160).

In a highly stratified society like that of the Guaicurú, which placed great importance on rank, descent, and noble blood, having a captive or tributary ancestry, or even marrying captives or tributaries, was always a handicap (Sánchez Labrador (1910–1917[1760]: II, 28; Serra 1845[1803]: 207). And even though mixed-blood children were considered to be fully Guaicurú insofar as the rights they enjoyed, "pure" Guaicurú continued to regard them as *nibotagi*, all the while acknowledging them to be their children and relatives (Serra 1850[1803]: 371). In Guaicurú society, therefore, captives and tributary peoples could be integrated and even assimilated through mechanisms of adoption, marriage, or emancipation. Nevertheless, their lowly origins were never allowed to be totally forgotten.

* * *

In native tropical American capturing societies, the integration and assimilation of war captives were as important as, if not more important than, the act of capture itself. Incorporation of war captives necessitated as much ideological and ritual management as the marking of war captives as slaves. Prisoners of war occupied a liminal position. This was often expressed by their being characterized as prey animals turned into pets. In some cases (Conibo and Chiriguaná) this analogy is explicit; in others (Kalinago and Tukano) it is implicit, insofar as enemies were equated with animal prey, or captives were treated "as pets." In still other cases (Calusa and Guaicurú), there is not enough evidence to determine whether they regarded captives as pets. Nevertheless, the pet analogy is widespread enough throughout native tropical America to be considered emblematic of the relationship between captors and captives.

The incorporation of captives-cum-pets was a gradual process. In its first stages, captives, like pets, were considered to be neither fully animal nor fully human. They were probably attributed the same status as were unnamed newborns, who, when they died—among the Bororo, at least—were buried with little ceremony, "as pets," because they were thought not to possess a soul yet (J. C. Crocker 1985: 53). In later stages, according to some authors, Amerindians equated captives-cum-pets to adoptive children, while simultaneously likening the taming or familiarization of pets to the assimilation of captives by the creation of consanguineal ties and, more particularly, by adoptive filiation (Descola 1994: 339; Menget 1988: 71; 1996: 141; Fausto 1999: 938).

These same authors have pointed out that pets are designated by the same term as captives and adopted children in many Amerindian societies (Erikson 2000: 18). This is confirmed by the aforementioned Conibo examples and, to a lesser extent, by examples from the Chiriguaná and Guaicurú, among whom masters often treated captive children "as if they were their own." Like pampered pets, captive children were "mothered and socialized" (Descola 1994: 337–378). They were given new names—and with them new souls—chosen from among those belonging to the kindreds of their adoptive fathers or mothers (Menget 1988: 68). And often they were treated as kin and addressed by appropriate kinship terms.

The familiarization of pets and, by extension, of war captives was not always accomplished through processes of consanguinization, however. Taylor (2000: 324; 2001: 54) suggests that the taming and familiarization of wild pets and alien captives involve a process of "de-affinization." Instead of being turned into consanguines, captives and pets are adopted as "affinal children," that is, as a brother's children from a female perspective or as a wife's brother's children from a male perspective. Cormier (2003b: 93, 114) has adopted a similar stance, asserting that among the Guajá, who trace consanguineal ties through males, the relationship between pets and owners is one of affinal or matrilateral siblings, by which she means siblings that are not consanguines, because they share the same mother but not the same father. In turn, Halbmayer (2004: 161) reports that among Carib-speaking peoples adoption may assume a filiative form (when captives are adopted as consanguines) or an affinal form (when they are adopted to become future in-laws). In either case, he contends, the original filiation of the adoptee is never forgotten, with captives always retaining their affinal condition.

If true—and there is some evidence to indicate that this was so in all societies in the sample—this would explain why captives maintained the stigma of their captive origin throughout their lives even after being adopted as children or taken as spouses. This stigma was often passed on to their descendants, especially if the latter were the offspring of unions between captives. The devolution of captive status took place even when children had been brought up in the language and customs of their captors and were regarded as fellow tribespeople for all other purposes. Only the offspring of mixed captor-captive marriages were considered to be full members of the captor society by virtue of having become true consanguines through descent by either the paternal or maternal side. Therefore the main avenue for the assimilation of war captives in Amerindian societies may have been, not familiarization through adoptive filiation, but familiarization through affinal consanguinity. In both instances, however, the long-term result was the same: the gradual consanguinization and assimilation of enemy Others.

Despite the many similarities existing between pets and captives, one should be careful not to place too much emphasis on the pet analogy as the sole model with which to understand the status of captive slaves. One should be especially cautious not to extrapolate the feelings of affection, caring, and empathy that pets and consanguines elicit among Westerners to the situation of captives-cum-pets-cum–adoptive children in Amerindian societies. Although some authors have rightly indicated that Amerindian peoples were often reluctant to sell their captives to Europeans and preferred to sell their relatives rather than part with their captives (Carneiro da Cunha and Viveiros de Castro 1985: 192–193; Whitehead 1999: 402), this does not necessarily mean that they regarded captives as family members.

If Amerindians were reluctant at first to part with their captives, it was not necessarily because they were attached to them by affective ties, but rather because such an exchange involved different "regimes of value" (Appadurai 1986). Insofar as trading with Europeans was not embedded in ongoing reciprocal relationships, its social or political appeal to them was limited. Note that most situations where Amerindians were reported to have refused to sell their slaves correspond to periods of initial contact. We know, however, that in subsequent years, many Amerindian capturing societies engaged in the European-induced slave trade once their mutual trading interests coincided. It should also be noted that in those exceptional cases in which relatives were sold to Europeans, it was because they were orphans thought to bring ill fortune, children of mixed captor-captive unions treated as pseudo-orphans, or children accused of witchcraft (Pineda Camacho 1985; Guyot 1984; Santos-Granero 2002b,

2004). It is true that once they were selected to be adopted, married, or kept as slaves, captives were seldom sold, either internally or externally. But there is also plenty of evidence indicating that such "singularized" captives could be, under certain circumstances, "de-singularized" and put back into the trading circuits (see Kopytoff 1986).

The pet analogy is not exclusive to native tropical America, being also present in ancient Rome (Gardner and Wiedemann 1991: 76; Adkins and Adkins 1994), later Imperial China (Anderson 1990), African Muslim societies (Bonte 1998: 158), and even the American South (Stirling 1969). Nevertheless, it reveals three fundamental aspects of how Amerindians conceived of, and represented, relations of capture and subordination. First, from an Amerindian perspective, enemies and animals shared the condition of being wild and less than human and, as such, could be preyed upon. Second, because captives and pets were the product of their captors' agency, their captors had total power over them. Captors decided whether the offspring of a slain animal should be eaten or kept as a pet, and they decided whether a captive should be killed, traded, married, adopted, or kept as a slave. Lastly, because they were wild and less than human, both captives and pets had to be tamed or civilized in order to be incorporated into the sphere of civilized humans. This process—which entailed equal doses of force and persuasion, coercion and seduction—was achieved through the humanization of both captives and pets. One could thus affirm that in native tropical America captive slaves were always "people in the making."

CHAPTER 9

Warring Against the Other

Intertribal warfare assumes a principle of asymmetry and a structural imbalance. In effect, it is founded on the idea that the possibilities of human existence are finite and dependent on a chronically insufficient stock of virtualities of persons, a stock from which all tribes participating in the Jivaro ensemble can draw upon.

—ANNE CHRISTINE TAYLOR,
"Les bons ennemis et les mauvais parents"

In native tropical America, the institution of slavery originated largely from warfare. More specifically, it originated from exo-warfare—that is, waging war against peoples with different languages and cultural practices. And yet the enslavement of enemy Others figures only marginally in the literature discussing the causes of warfare in native America, a rich and extensive literature that goes far back in time. Authors have tended to explain Amerindian warfare as originating from a combination of social and psychological features. Murphy (1957), for instance, argues that Mundurucú warfare is the result of the repressed hostility between kin and affines that often builds up in matrilocal societies. Other authors contend that Amerindian warfare is determined by ecological factors: competition for lands covered by secondary growth, which are easier to clear (Vayda 1961); for fertile, riverine areas (Lathrap 1962, 1970; Carneiro 1970; Morey and Marwitt 1975); or even for scarce protein resources (Harris 1974, 1979, 1984; Gross 1975; Harner 1977; E. Ross and Ross 1980). Still other researchers attribute the origin of warfare to demographic causes, as a means to regulate population growth in the absence of less costly options. They explain the existence of warfare by the presence of a male supremacist complex that engages in capturing women in war to compensate for a scarcity of women due to female infanticide and other female-reduction practices (Divale and Harris 1976). Finally, some other authors explain indigenous warfare as the consequence of certain historico-economic changes—namely, the disruptive influence of the colonial situation.

Newcomb (1950) contended that warfare among the Plains Indians of North America was triggered by the adoption of horses and firearms from Western agents. These innovations generated vicious competition for access to buffalo and deer herds. More recently, Ferguson (1990, 1995) has explained Amerindian warfare as resulting from a generalized competition for access to Western-made goods, especially iron tools.

These sundry theories have generated considerable discussion, as authors have questioned, negated, or defended the various opinions (H. C. Wilson 1958; Evans 1971; Hallpike 1973; Hirschfeld, Howe, and Levin 1978; Norton 1978; Chagnon and Hames 1979; E. Ross and Ross 1980; Dow 1983; Sponsel 1983; Menget 1985; Chernela 1997; Valentine and Julien 2003; Chacon and Mendoza 2007). It is not the place here to attempt a detailed evaluation of the merits or shortcomings of each of these theories. A few comments on their applicability to the cases examined here, however, seem indispensable.

Clearly, warfare in the societies included in our sample was not motivated by economic objectives, such as those we have come to associate with archaic and modern forms of warfare. Above all, war was not about conquering land, although, as we have seen (Chapter 3), land, or at least certain types of lands—hunting grounds, fisheries, certain tree stands—could become an important cause of war under certain historical circumstances. Neither was warfare in these societies fueled by a desire to acquire material wealth. Even when pillaging allowed raiding societies to stop manufacturing their own products—witness the Conibo, who acquired all their clothing by robbing neighboring peoples—certain limiting facts emerged. First, the loot they obtained consisted of more or less the same kinds of products that they could manufacture themselves. Second, in the absence of money, pillaged products could not be converted into economic power. And third, booty was not accumulated in quantities large enough for it to be conspicuously redistributed in potlatch fashion, thus converting it into political prestige.

Protein deficiency does not account either for the kind of warfare practiced by the societies examined here. As the argument goes, in order to prove this theory it is necessary only to link village fissioning and dispersion to a severe decline in the standards of protein consumption and the cost-benefits of protein capture (Harris 1979: 130–131). On the contrary, what we see in the regional power systems analyzed here is a tendency toward social agglomeration and the emergence of large villages. Certainly, the Conibo, Chiriguaná, and Calusa illustrate this trend. Among the other three societies in our sample, village fissioning might have been connected to ecological factors, but not to protein deficiency, for the Kalinago, Tukano, and Guaicurú occupied maritime or riverine areas with abundant aquatic and terrestrial fauna. It may still be argued that the main objective of warfare in these cases was the protection of these areas rich in proteins from protein-hungry enemies, but this alternative simply does not fit the available data.

Similarly, there is little evidence for the contention that warfare was motivated by a male supremacist complex, which made the capture of women from the enemy necessary. Only among the Guaicurú, only one of the six societies of the sample, is there any evidence for the practice of infanticide, and this affected both male and female babies (Sánchez Labrador 1910–1917[1770]: II, 30–31). In fact, we are told that it was the Guaná victims, rather than the Guaicurú raiders, who practiced female infanticide (Azara 1809[1781]: II, 93–94). More importantly, it is said that among all these societies, with the exception of the Calusa, raiders killed all fertile adult women, keeping only the younger girls. This suggests that the capture of fertile, marriageable women was not their main objective for warfare. Further confirmation for these observations comes from the fact that the abduction of children—both girls and boys—was as desirable as the capture of young women, if not more so.

Their marginal situation on the fringes of European-controlled state formations could explain why the societies in the sample developed supralocal forms of authority and why they also engaged in constant defensive wars (see Ferguson and Whitehead 1992: 12–13). The presence of Western intruders certainly seems to have increased the intensity of warfare and enslaving among some groups. Among others such as the Kalinago, Calusa, and Guaicurú, however, no evidence indicated that this was so. The surge in hostilities might be attributed to the ever-increasing demands for slaves by the colonial slave market, as well as to such technological innovations as the adoption of the horse and, much later on, firearms. In some instances, it might also be attributed to competition for the monopoly of access to Western goods. However, for none of the societies discussed in this book can we state that the existence of indigenous forms of servitude was a direct by-product of the colonial situation. Their presence was reported very early on, at least among the Kalinago, Conibo, Chiriguaná, Calusa, and Guaicurú, so they cannot be attributed to Western influences.

Finally, it cannot be asserted either that warfare in these societies was simply about "making slaves," at least not in the same sense as the Western notion—namely, that of acquiring a free labor force using violent means. In fact, all adult men and most adult women who could have served as laborers were killed by the raiders. Moreover, even if the young people abducted were made to perform certain services, they could hardly have become a significant source of labor from which to extract surplus value, at least not in the short term. Captive children were mostly assigned domestic chores or symbolic functions, such as serving their masters on formal occasions.

Here I would like to introduce new elements in the discussion on Amerindian warfare by considering slavery, not as a self-contained social phenomenon, but rather as a social practice that acquires meaning only when it is analyzed in the context of the set of cultural notions that, for the sake of brevity, I have called the *slave machine*, and only when it is considered within the broader frame of what I define as the Amerindian *political economy of life*. In the following pages, I explore these two critical factors; together, they present an alternative view of the issue of warfare in native tropical America.

* * *

The notion of slave machine—a term inspired by the notion of *war machine* developed by Deleuze and Guattari (1987)—involves both representations and actions. At one level, it can be seen as a set of notions—and concomitant military practices—relating to the Other in the guise of enemy, an Amerindian ideology justifying the inferiority of Others and encouraging their enslavement. At another level, however, it can be regarded as a set of notions—and concomitant ritual practices—relating to the Other as an indispensable part of Self, an ideology legitimizing the value of Others and inducing their full assimilation. Let us begin with the first set of notions.

Central to the notion of slave machine is the assumption that Others are wild and less than human. Conceived of as being closer to the sphere of animality than to that of humanity, Others are perceived as enemies and as game that can be preyed upon. This widespread conceptualization of the Other is revealed by the use of terms to refer to them that have the simultaneous meaning of "enemy" and "prey." Associated with this notion is another that regards Others as dangerous affines. Not potential affines—those marked in Dravidian kinship terminologies as marriageable consanguines—but rather meta-affines, total strangers uncontaminated by links of consanguinity, with whom, according to Viveiros de Castro (1993: 179), one does not intermarry but rather makes war. With such meta-affines one exchanges, not women, but other things, such as bodily trophies, names, and vitalities.

In making this assertion, Viveiros de Castro probably had in mind the Tupinambá, Jivaro, Mundurucú, and Nivaclé, all of whom were renowned for practicing endowarfare—that is, warfare against peoples sharing similar languages and mores. Warfare among these peoples had the purpose of capturing enemies to extract from them symbolically valuable parts, substances, or essences. Relationships between the warring parties were more or less symmetrical and involved the destruction of the enemies thus captured. In contrast, in the societies examined here the capture and incorporation of actual people was as important as the capture of war trophies, or even more so. And the relationship with the Other, far from being reciprocal, was markedly hierarchical and asymmetrical.

Warfare and raiding are defining aspects of the slave machine. These were not chance activities, taking place intermittently in response to external aggressions in the form of either actual killings or shamanic attacks—as among the Txicão (Menget 1988). And though informed by the logic of revenge, these activities did not assume the form of feuding cycles, in which revenge becomes an aim in itself and avengers are satisfied with the death of even a single individual—as among the Jivaro (A. C. Taylor 1985) or Tupinambá (Carneiro da Cunha and Viveiros de Castro 1985). In contrast, in slaveholding societies, warfare and raiding were critical activities carried out on a regular basis and on a large scale. The slave machine mobilized hundreds of warriors in expeditions that could last several months at a time and often could target peoples located hundreds of miles away. The purpose of these raids was not to kill one or two enemies or to capture a few women and children. These were expeditions aimed at killing, or capturing, as many enemies as possible. Some of these captives were consumed in cannibalistic ceremonies, a few were married or adopted, and a large number were kept as servants. In such societies, waging war and capturing enemies defined not only maleness and adulthood but also collective identities. In addition, it defined which men would make better marriage partners and, above all, which would make the best leaders.

The slave machine is responsible not only for the development of captive slavery but also for the emergence of other forms of servitude, such as servant groups and tributary populations. Without proposing for a moment an evolutionary scheme, I would suggest that these latter forms of servitude are derivative. They originated in large-scale warring and raiding with the initial aim of capturing individual enemies. These other forms of servitude, which increased exponentially the number of subordinates available to capturing societies, had the effect of liberating captors from their subsistence duties, allowing them to devote more time to raiding the enemy. This was particularly true among peoples who combined captive slavery with the subjugation of enemy populations as tributaries, such as the Calusa and Guaicurú. In these societies, the development of the slave machine led to the emergence of a stratum of nobles and warriors exempted from productive activities, thus giving rise to more rigid forms of social stratification.

The slave machine, however, was not oriented solely to the production of slaves and other types of subordinates. Its final objective was to transform war captives, first into people and, later on, into kin. This transformation was achieved thanks to another set of related notions and practices. In line with the concept that enemies were game and prey, Amerindians regarded war captives, and especially captured children, as pets, positioned midway between animality and humanity. The assimilation of war captives was thus conceived of, as Fausto (1999, 2001) has argued, as a process of "familiarization." As quasi animals, captives had to be tamed; as quasi humans, they had to be civilized. This notion, expressed in native terms meaning simultaneously "to make slaves, pets, or friends," is central to the slave machine. Hence, it could be said that Amerindian slavery was as much about turning people into pets as about turning pets into people.

In the logic of the Amerindian slave machine, the unmaking of slaves was at least as important as the making of slaves, if not more important. Such a process involved a continuum that progressed from predation to familiarization, then to integration as outsiders, and finally to assimilation as insiders. It entailed a combination of force, persuasion, coercion, and seduction. Assimilation was achieved via adoptive filiation and gradual consanguinization or, more often, through affinal consanguinity—that is, by the adoption of children as future in-laws. In either case, the ultimate aim was the production of kin. In short, in native tropical America, the slave machine was not merely about civilizing the Other—that is, making

people out of Others. Above all, it was about assimilating the Other—
that is, making Others into kin (see Vilaça 2002).

The sociosymbolic incorporation of captives as pets and, eventually,
as kin took place within the frame of a recurrent Amerindian notion that
posits that society can exist only so long as there is a proper mixing between
entities and forces different from one another (Overing 1984: 129). As
Clastres (1998c: 169) long ago suggested, Amerindians are engaged in a
constant struggle against the "one"—a notion that comprises everything
conceived of as imperfect, evil, ugly, and corruptible—favoring instead
not the "many" but the "dual." Thus, from an Amazonian perspective,
social existence is the result of a delicate balance between dangerous
but fertile difference and safe but sterile sameness. In symbolic terms,
this implies that self-identity can be ensured only by way of the periodic
incorporation and taming of enemy substances, whether they be souls,
names, bodily trophies, sacred chants, or other tangible or intangible
aspects of self. As Viveiros de Castro (2004: 480) has so insightfully put
it, in Amerindian societies "the self is the gift of the other."

In sociological terms, the implication is that social life becomes possible
only through the constant incorporation of dangerous Others, whether
affines or captives, and by their gradual transformation into full members
of the incorporating society, accomplished via symbolic processes of
consanguinization, de-affinization, co-residence, and commensality. In
other words, social collectivities and identities are not given; rather, they
are in a permanent process of construction via the "positive and necessary
use of alterity" (Viveiros de Castro 1993: 182), a procedure requiring the
ritual incorporation of enemy Others by outright or symbolic acts of
predation in what Descola (1994: 339) has characterized as a process of
"sociological cannibalism."

Are the above considerations sufficiently inclusive for us to understand
the Amerindian obsession with incorporating enemy Others? Are native
tropical American peoples interested in the wild and different Others only
as a source of substances necessary for the construction of self and self-
identity? Or, put differently, are enemy Others viewed only as building
blocks for the construction of bodies and persons in one's own society?
At a first glance this seems to be the case. Ritual anthropophagy among
the Tupinambá (Carneiro da Cunha and Viveiros de Castro 1985), head-
hunting and incorporation of enemy blood among the Jivaro and Wari'
(A. C. Taylor 1985; Conklin 2001, 2003), and wife raiding among the

interfluvial Pano (Erikson 1993) seem to respond to this logic. In the first case it is done by the killer's acquiring new names; in the second case, it is accomplished via a symbolic impregnation of the killer thought to cause the real impregnation of his wife; and in the third case, it is done by the actual incorporation of enemy Others into the social fabric. A closer look at these processes, however, undermines the notion that enemy Others are only sources of new identities. The names acquired by Tupinambá captors/killers were often not those of the enemies they had captured, but other names (Carneiro da Cunha and Viveiros de Castro 1985: 200). Rather than appropriating the identity of a killed and beheaded enemy, among the Jivaro the latter's vitality was ritually trapped in his head and granted a new name, identity, and kin ties (A. C. Taylor 1993: 671). The identity that Jivaro warriors tried to preserve by shrinking the heads of their victims was not their original identity but one bestowed on them as fictive kin after being killed (A. C. Taylor 1993: 672). Additionally, the interfluvial Pano seem to have been intent on securing the presence of enemy Others into their societies—to the point of artificially classifying part of their population as "alien captives" after the cessation of intertribal warfare—yet the first thing they did to war captives was to re-tattoo their faces with their own tribal markings, a clear negation of the captives' former identities.

If what attracts Amerindians to enemy Others is their difference and wildness, it does not seem to be because of the possibility of acquiring their identities in order to construct their own—or, at least, it does not seem to be the only reason. As Overing (1999: 90) has already noted, the final objective in capturing enemy Others, or their substances, was not to preserve their difference and wildness, but rather to tame and civilize them so as to make them "of the same nature" as that of their captors. If anything, Amerindians are not in search of concrete individual identities but, rather, seek to appropriate generic subjectivities. What they wish to acquire and preserve is not the Others' identity but something that, from their perspective, is an attribute of different wild Others—whether wild gods, wild spirits, wild peoples, or the wilderness in general. Simply put, I contend that what they are seeking is life itself.

In native tropical America, human life and life within society are considered to be under constant threat, not only from sorcery attacks, social conflicts, and demographic accidents (Y. Murphy and Murphy 1985: 111; J. C. Crocker 1985: 57; Mentore 2004: 142; Santos-Granero

2007), but, above all, from scarcity of life itself. That Amerindian peoples uphold the notion that all forms of life share the same reserve of generative force, which—in the form of energy, souls, substances, vitalities, or identities—flows in a closed circuit throughout the universe has become increasingly apparent to most scholars. Menget (1985: 137) was one of the first to underscore the importance of this cosmological notion for the understanding of native Amazonian warfare. Details concerning the origin of this vital energy, its nature, its material manifestations, and how it is transferred between different living beings, or world planes, vary from people to people. All of them, however, agree that this cosmic source of life is finite, generally fixed, scarce, unequally distributed, and in constant circulation.

The Yagua, for instance, believe that the source of all life is the cosmic energy known as *hamwo*, which resides in the celestial fire (Chaumeil 1985: 153–154). Each time the Sun passes through this earth, it releases a limited amount of *hamwo*. This energy is absorbed by plants and then passed on to animals and humans participating in the same food chain. *Hamwo* is unequally distributed among different living beings, according to their capacity to absorb it or to their predatory success. Once people die, a part of their energy goes to replenish the original solar source, another part goes to increase the energy of animals and plants that have fed them, and the final part remains in their teeth and bones, to be reused or returned to its original source.

For the Bororo, the vital force that animates all living beings is *raka*, manifested organically in people and animals as blood (J. C. Crocker 1985: 41). It is this élan vital that enables birds to fly, jaguars to kill, plants to grow and yield, and humans to work and procreate. Each living being is born with a limited amount of *raka*, the quantity depending on the input of his or her genitors at the time of conception. *Raka* is the energy that fuels every activity, so it is constantly being spent, especially during the act of procreation, when large quantities of *raka* are required to form a new being. *Raka* can also be lost through injuries inflicted by plants and animals (J. C. Crocker 1985: 57–58). In such cases, the Bororo avenge the victim by killing an individual of the offensive species; an act that does not restore the lost *raka* but is believed to maintain the equilibrium among the different kinds of beings animated by the same vital energy. Briefly, *raka* is passed on from parents to offspring in an eternal flow; never diminishing but scarce, unequally distributed, and in constant circulation.

These notions are not exclusive to Yagua and Bororo peoples. Similar ideas have been reported for the Jivaro-Candoshi (Taylor 1985: 161; 1993: 671; Descola 1992: 118; Mader 1999; Surrallés 2000, 2007; Uriarte 2007), Arawak (Santos-Granero 1991: 89, 205), Pano (Erikson 1986: 197), Carib (Rivière 1997; Butt-Colson 2001: 223–224), Tupi-Guaraní (Fausto 1999: 948–949), and, in general, societies characterized by "animic ontologies" (Ingold 1998: 183–186; Strathern 1999: 48–49). Thus, we can safely assume that the Kalinago, Conibo, and Chiriguaná of the sample, who are Carib, Pano, and Tupi-Guaraní, respectively, entertained similar ideas. The same can be said of the Calusa and Guaicurú, whose war rituals were very similar to those of the other collectivities in the sample. And it was undoubtedly the case for the Tukano, who developed ideas concerning the cosmic circulation of vital forces to a high degree of sophistication.

The Tukano-speaking Desana believe that all life comes from the Creator Sun, who is not the present-day sun (Reichel-Dolmatoff 1971: 42). Its generative power is made of male and female energies that complement and replenish each other constantly but have a limited capacity to energize. Since the same solar energy vivifies humans, animals, and plants, all living beings compete to secure access to it. The Makuna, also Tukano speakers, believe that all beings share a generic vitality that flows throughout the different lived worlds of the cosmos (Århem 1996: 188). All have a human nature and are interconnected as "eaters" or "eaten," in a cosmic food web ruled by principles of predation and exchange. Cosmic energy is finite and fixed. Therefore, predatory exchanges between different natural realms can generate profound energy imbalances. To avoid this situation, shamans have the task of regulating the flow of generative force between different natural domains to guarantee the proper reproduction of all living beings (Reichel-Dolmatoff 1971: 218–219; see also Chiappino 1997: 261–263).

The analysis of Amerindian "eco-cosmologies," as Århem (1996) has aptly named these indigenous theories of life, demonstrates that life, or life substance, is considered to be a scarce resource from a native point of view. In turn, human life is conceived of as both rare and fragile because it depends on a scarce resource that has to be shared with scores of other living beings. This has led Rivière (1984) to propose that the scarcest resource in Amerindian economies is neither land nor natural resources, but the labor to render them productive; in other words, people. In his view, Amerindian societies are based on a "political economy of people."

Since wealth depends on the number of people that Amerindian groups are able to mobilize, they compete with each other to attract as many people as possible. And since leadership is a function of the number of followers a leader and his wife are able to persuade to join them, Amerindian leaders are in a constant struggle to outrival each other and to gather around them as many people as possible.

Following the same line of thought, Fausto (2001: 417–418) argues that Amerindian societies are based on a "generalized economy for the production of people." People are not only scarce, but they are never totally complete. They are always in a process of becoming, a process that requires the incorporation of alien substances, vitalities, or identities. Amerindians obtain these generative substances, indispensable for the production of people and society, by warfare and shamanism. The vital parts or substances—heads, teeth, scalps, blood, souls—wrested from the enemy are not, however, important in themselves. Rather, they are consequential because they have rippling and multiplying effects on the fecundity and energetic capabilities of those who capture them. The production of people, Fausto argues, is a phenomenon that belongs not to the sphere of consumption—as Marx would have it—but to the sphere of production. It is not achieved in the domestic domain, but in the violent sphere of relationships with Others.

Rivière and Fausto are both correct in asserting that people are a scarce and valuable resource in Amerindian societies and that the production of people is one of the most important goals of such societies. Yet the scarcity and high value placed on people are only manifestations of something even more universal and imperative: the dearth and unequal distribution of life energy, without which humanity and society would be impossible. Early on, Overing (1976: 391) hinted at this when asserting that whereas in the "jural-political domain" labor is the scarce resource, in the "ceremonial domain" the scarcest resources are soul stuff and names. More recently, she has taken this argument further, stating that Amerindian social systems could be characterized as "generative cultures" insofar as they are very much focused on notions of fecundity and reproduction (Overing 1999). By definition, every political economy is organized around the resource that is perceived to be the scarcest and most indispensable for its functioning—for instance, land in feudal societies or capital in capitalist societies. I argue, therefore, that we could more aptly characterize Amerindian societies as being based on a political economy of life. The aim of predation and warfare in these societies is not simply to kill enemy Others. It is to capture what, borrowing from Taylor (1985: 167; 1994: 97), I would label *potentialities of life*—a process described by Conklin (2001) as the "conquest of vitality."

The notion of potentialities of life, understood here as the biological and mystical conditions necessary for the furtherance of human life, comprises a wide range of things and entities, to which authors have attributed different weights in the reproduction of Amerindian societies. It includes forces of culture (Overing 1986: 139), virtualities of persons (A. C. Taylor 1985: 161), spiritual elements (Menget 1996: 133), vital bodily substances (Conklin 2003), cosmic generative forces (Reichel-Dolmatoff 1971: 50; Chaumeil 1985: 153; J. C. Crocker 1985: 41–42; Århem 1996: 188), and actual people (Turner 1979: 158–159; Rivière 1984: 93; Morton 1984: 228). It also comprises a wide range of spiritual forces encased in sacred images, charms, and other magical objects thought to possess the capacity to infuse life or to capture life forces (Cassá 1992: 137–138; Brown 1993: 86–87). These sources of life are always conceived of as belonging to wild enemy Others, whether these be wild gods that own the generative forces of culture, or human essences of wild animals and plants that control extraordinary shamanic knowledge and powers, or wild spirits that possess extremely effective magical charms, or enemy peoples believed to have powerful virtualities of existence. Thus, the taking of war captives, as well as the co-optation of persons through alternative native forms of servitude, results in the appropriation of Others not only as a "labor force" but also as individuals who, once "civilized," "domesticated," and more or less integrated, contribute to enhancing the wealth of social relations and potentialities of life of the capturing society to the detriment of the stock of generative forces of captured groups.

This brings us to the most central aspect of the Amerindian political economy of life. All political economies entail competition and strife, to the extent that they are linked to the possession of what is considered to be the scarcest resource in each particular historical instance. In Amerindian eco-cosmologies, life itself is defined as the scarcest resource. Because it is in constant circulation and unequally distributed among different types of beings and cosmic planes, demand for such life assets always surpasses supply (Reichel-Dolmatoff 1971: 218–219; A. C. Taylor 1985: 161; 1993: 671; 1994: 74; Chaumeil 1985: 155–156). As a result, human groups compete with each other and—because of their "animic" worldview and the "law of universal sociability" (Descola 1992, 1996)—

also with nonhumans (animals and plants) and former humans (the dead) to secure through capture as many potentialities of life as possible. Which beings are involved in this competition, how this struggle is manifested in the world, and how these antagonisms are resolved are questions that receive different answers in diverse Amerindian societies.

Among the Desana, for instance, humans affect the possibilities of reproduction of other beings in the world by having too many children or by hunting too many animals (Reichel-Dolmatoff 1971: 218–219). Animals thus affected retaliate for the excessive use of generic vitality by humans by sending them illness and death, appropriating their souls, or refusing to be hunted, to the point of human starvation. The Desana solve this predicament by assigning shamans the task of negotiating with Vaí-mahsë, the Master of Animals, the exchange of human souls taken from enemy groups, for game animals belonging to diverse edible species. The underlying idea is that only a certain amount of vital energy is available, so it is necessary to maintain an equilibrium between the stocks of generative energy of animals and humans.

Whereas Desana advocate reciprocity and balance in connection with animals, they follow principles of asymmetrical predation in their dealings with other humans. They show little concern, for example, with the fact that most souls their shamans capture to exchange for animals with Vaí-mahsë are taken from the Makú (Reichel-Dolmatoff 1971: 131). And they are certainly not worried that in their relationship with Makú—at least in the past—they always took on the role of predators whereas the latter appeared as victims. Wife abduction between Tukanoan-speaking groups might have been reciprocal and balanced, but slave raids against Makú bands were mostly unilateral and asymmetrical.

The above notions point to another key aspect of the Amerindian political economy of life. At certain levels, and in relationship with certain beings, these economies might be reciprocal. Overall, however, they are based on a predatory philosophy that ensures the continuity of one's own life, even if it is accomplished at the expense of the death of others. A central tenet of Bororo cosmology, for instance, is that "the sustenance of any organic life requires the diminution of other life" (J. C. Crocker 1985: 54). For the Yagua, in turn, "the surplus of energy that an individual or group could store throughout its existence as additional life potential depended directly on its capacities to subtract for its own benefit the energy stored by the enemy, whether in the form of dead people or the capture of teeth, game, or souls" (Chaumeil 1985: 155).

This pervasive notion has led Fausto (2001: 328) to observe that the flux of alien potentialities of life generated by warfare and shamanism takes place not in a closed, reciprocal cycle of energy exchange but rather in an open cycle, which is always asymmetrical even if momentarily balanced. It is precisely these features—a ruthless competition for scarce resources (potentialities of life), and the recurrent despoiling of some groups for the benefit of others—that allows me to characterize native tropical American peoples as being engaged in a political economy of life.

The "symbolic economy of alterity," which Viveiros de Castro (1996) considers central to the construction of Amazonian sociality and selfhood would, in the interpretation offered above, constitute the superstructural or ideological dimension of the political economy of life. The notion of *capture* is the material counterpart—the concrete realization, so to speak—of the more generic and symbolic notion of *predation*. The concept of predation indicates the general tenor of relationships between Self and Others, whereas the notion of capture denotes the objective of predatory processes that are both interethnic and generalized. Native tropical American societies are capturing societies—that is, societies involved in a political economy of life whose intention is to capture life resources from others so as to enhance their own *vital capital*. In such a political economy, the survival of one's group is paramount, even if it leads to the extinction of enemy groups. This way of thinking is evidenced by such indigenous conceptions and practices as the "Piaroa bomb" (Overing 1986: 134) or the stealing of the enemy's fertility (Brown 1993: 119), game animals (Descola 1996: 259), magical charms (Brown 1993: 84), and ritual paraphernalia (S. Hugh-Jones 1993: 109). It is also expressed in the numerous cases of near extermination of enemy groups reported in historical and ethnographic records (Maybury-Lewis 1974: 26–27; Y. Murphy and Murphy 1985: 30; Vilaça 1992: 96; Basso 1995: 18; Chernela 2001: 186).

The societies examined in this study are conspicuous examples of the underlying logic that informs the Amerindian political economy of life. In them, the capture of women and children proceeded hand in hand with the appropriation of enemy body parts, substances, and essences that were either consumed or kept as life-giving trophies. It also involved the capture of powerful life-giving ritual objects.

Four of the six capturing societies in the sample—the Kalinago, Conibo, Tukano, and Chiriguaná—practiced some kind of war anthropophagy. The parts of the enemies' bodies considered to be suitable for consumption, however, varied from group to group. Kalinago reserved the heart for the men (Du Tertre 1654: 451). The arms and legs were reserved for the women, but the limbs, as well as the remaining organs, could be eaten by all those present at the victory celebrations. A rather fanciful seventeenth-century engraving demonstrates one such cannibalistic ceremony (see Figure 36). Tukano kept the head, limbs, liver, and heart for the men, with only the genitals given to the women (Goldman 1963: 164; Whiffen 1915[1908]: 123). Among the Chiriguaná, the hearts were eaten only by men, whereas the rest of the bodies were consumed by all members of the collectivity (Garcilaso de la Vega 1963[1609]: 323; Corrado and Comajuncosa 1990[1884]: I, 47). Conibo people did not eat the flesh of their adversaries but, as we shall see, did drink their blood (Biedma 1981[1682]: 95).

Some authors claim that consuming the flesh of slain enemies was meant as a form of revenge, a means to degrade the vanquished enemy and, above all, to appropriate his qualities (Whiffen 1915[1908]: 121; Coudreau 1887: II, 177; Du Tertre 1654: 451–452). That Amerindians believe that by eating the flesh of certain animals they may acquire some of their positive or negative physical qualities is commonly known. No evidence exists, however, to indicate that they believe also that the consumption of human flesh allows for the transfer of personal virtues and moral qualities. Even if this were true, it begs the question of why a victorious warrior would want to incorporate the qualities of someone whom he has just defeated and who consequently is, in his eyes, a less able fighter than himself. Many Amerindian peoples believe that a person's vital energy is concentrated in certain parts of the body, particularly in certain organs and limbs, so it is much more plausible to think that the aim of ritual cannibalism was the appropriation of the generative force of a slain enemy rather than his personal qualities.

The aim of capturing alien generative forces is more clearly articulated with reference to the genitals of killed enemies. Among Tukano, these parts were smoked and worn by the triumphant warriors on top of their own genitals in a ritual dance central to the victory celebrations. Subsequently, the smoked genitals were given to the chief's wife, according to Whiffen (1915[1908]: 123), or to the women in general, according to Goldman (1963: 164), to be eaten. The consumption of the enemies' genitals was explicitly believed to promote female fecundity. In contrast, among Kalinago people the genitals of killed enemies were thrown into the sea, a not so subtle symbol for the removal of the enemies' procreative powers (Anon. 1988[1620]: 189). Captive boys were also deprived of their genitals, both penis and testicles, presumably to prevent them from procreating with Kalinago women (Alvarez Chanca 1978[1494]: 31; Cúneo 1928[1495]: 283). Chiriguaná also cut the genitals of fallen enemies, but it is not clear whether or not these were consumed (Díaz de Guzmán 1979b[1618]: 112). In such cases, captors did not benefit directly from capturing the generative force of their enemies; rather, captors benefited indirectly by reducing their enemies' procreative capacities.

Enemy heads seem to have been considered particularly desirable war trophies. All the societies in our sample took heads, but their treatment varied widely. The Tukano stuck the heads of slain warriors on pikes and danced around them during postwar celebrations (Whiffen 1915[1908]: 122). Then they removed the hair, teeth, and brains, roasted them, and served the fleshy parts to the men. The skulls were subsequently left to dry in the killer's garden and be cleansed by ants and other scavenging insects, after which they were hung from the rafters of the victor's house. Kalinago tossed enemy heads into the ashes and gave them out as choice offerings to the first guests arriving from neighboring settlements for the victory celebrations (Anon. 1988[1620]: 189). The clean skulls were later hung under the roofs of their houses.

Chiriguaná people beheaded their enemies and took the heads home to give to their wives or female relatives (Díaz de Guzmán 1979b[1618]: 112; Jolís 1972[1789]: 265; Corrado and Comajuncosa 1990[1884]: I, 46). The women kicked around the severed heads, tossed them into the air, and insulted them while celebrating the victory of their men. A nineteenth-century engraving illustrates one such celebration witnessed by French explorer Emile Arthur Thouar (see Figure 37). Later on, they paraded the enemy heads, stuck in staves, along the entire village, "showing them" the houses and pots of fermented drink (Giannecchini 1996[1898]: 328). Whether they ate the heads or not is unclear, but we do know that they kept the skulls and scalps as war trophies. In some cases they fashioned drinking bowls out of enemy skulls (Giannecchini 1996[1898]: 324).

Calusa warriors also displayed the heads of fallen enemies during victory celebrations (Goggin and Sturtevant 1964: 200). A similar ritual was performed during the annual sacrifices held by the Calusa paramount chief and his head shamans (Laudonnière 2001[1564]: 110–111). On such occasions, a captive slave was sacrificed and beheaded. His head became the central piece in a ritual dance in which everybody participated. His eyes were given as an offering to the divinities, who were supposed to feed on them (López de Velasco 1991a[1569]: 316). The objective of such yearly celebrations was to ensure the fertility of the land, as well as the fecundity of animals, plants, and humans (Laudonnière 2001[1564]: 110–111). The Calusa believed that one of the three vital essences every person possessed resided in the pupil of the eye, and that this was the only part that remained with the body once a person died (Rogel 1991b[1568]: 237–238). Thus, it is likely that the capture of enemy heads—and, above all, their eyes—was a means of stealing the potentialities of life from the enemy. During the annual fertility festivals, these vitalities were shared with the creator gods, the ultimate origin of all life.

Guaicurú warriors beheaded their enemies with knives made from the sharp teeth of the piranha. They skinned the heads, threw away the skulls, and kept the dried skins with the mane of hair still attached (Lozano 1733: 71, 79; Schmidl 1749[1548]: 19). Then the warrior offered them to their wives (Techo 1897[1673]: III, 140). On special ritual occasions, Guaicurú women paraded the head skins, stuck on long poles, throughout the village, dancing around them while singing the praises of their husbands (Lozano 1733: 71).

Conibo did not eat the heads and hearts of slain enemies. Rather, they smoked, desiccated, adorned, and hung them from the roof of the captor's house. Such head trophies, still retaining both skull and skin, probably looked very much like the Mundurucú head trophy portrayed in an early-1800s drawing (see Figure 38). It is asserted that these trophies were kept as a sign of a man's courage and that the more heads and hearts a man had managed to accumulate, the more he was esteemed as a great warrior (Biedma 1981[1682]: 95).

Insofar as Amerindians often believe that the head and heart are the seats of potent generative forces (A. C. Taylor 1993: 660; Goldman 2004: 348), I would favor the interpretation that these societies hoarded the heads of slain enemies as a potential source of fertility, to be used in benefit of the killer and his family. By ritually displaying and parading the heads of their enemies around their gardens and villages during victory rituals or special festivities, successful warriors sought to spread the vivifying power contained in them so as to increase the fecundity of the land, plants, animals, and family members. Fashioning enemy skulls into drinking bowls was probably meant as a way to ingest part of the vitality of the slaughtered warriors. In many of these societies head trophies were presented to women, so it is quite probable that a further aim for capturing enemy heads was to transform their potentiality for life into female procreative power—a notion common, for instance, among Jivaro people (Harner 1973: 192–193; A. C. Taylor 1993: 671–672).

Cannibalistic rituals in these societies involved not only the consumption of the enemies' flesh but also the ingestion of powerful bodily substances such as blood and fat. Chiriguaná warriors collected the blood of beheaded war captives and drank it during celebrations held after a successful raid (Lizárraga 1968[1603]: 84; Garcilaso de la Vega 1963[1609]: 323). Conibo people also bled executed prisoners, pouring part of the collected blood over their own heads and drinking the rest mixed with manioc beer (Biedma 1981[1682]: 95). When asked why they did so, they answered that that was the way jaguars treated their prey (Maroni 1988[1738]: 299). We know, however, that Panoans—like many other Amerindian peoples (Conklin 2003; Belaúnde 2007)—believe that blood contains part of a person's soul or vitality. By drinking the blood of their enemies, Conibo warriors sought to appropriate the latter's generative powers. With it, they also appropriated their powers of aggression, thus becoming the "angry ones." Such powers had to be purged if the control of antisocial emotions, and with it a harmonious social life, was to be achieved (Roe 1982: 84; Erikson 1986: 195). The Kalinago considered fat to be an even more important vehicle for the transfer of vitality than blood. Kalinago warriors conscientiously collected the fat of slain enemies into little gourds and kept it for many years to be licked or added to food during special ritual occasions (Rochefort 1666[1658]: 330; Labat 1724[1705]: II, Part 4, 108).

Bones and teeth were also much sought-after war trophies. Kalinago cleansed the arm and leg bones of executed enemies of all traces of flesh and fashioned small whistles—some say flutes—from them, which they played every morning before dawn (Anon. 1988[1620]: 140, 154; Breton 1978[1647]: 61). They also used the long bones to make the handle of a ritual knife called *acoulari* (Anon. 1988[1620]: 156). Made from sharp agouti teeth, these knives were used by Kalinago elders to scarify the bodies of boys and girls undergoing initiation rituals, as well as to incise the bodies of adult men and women during other important life-cycle rituals (Anon. 1988[1620]: 156, 161–163; Breton 1978[1647]: 67; Rochefort 1666[1658]: 341). Such bloodletting was believed to make the initiates fierce and to prolong their lives. Kalinago also knocked out the teeth of dead enemies to string necklaces, like the ones shown in an early twentieth-century drawing by Thomas Whiffen (see Figure 39). These were worn as a sign of their courage in war (Drake 1992[1586]: 54). The remainder of the bones were burnt, pounded into ash, and kept in small gourds that were made into necklaces and given to boys at the end of their initiation ritual (Anon. 1988[1620]: 169). Tukano people also made necklaces out of the teeth of captured enemies (Whiffen 1915[1908]: 124). The arm bones of killed warriors were utilized as well: out of the humerus, they made flutes; from the radius, ulna, and the desiccated hand, they made a utensil with which they stirred *cahuana*, a drink made of manioc starch (Whiffen 1915[1908]: 123–124).

The Amerindian notion that bones and teeth are the loci of an important part of the vital energy or soul stuff that makes a person alive is widespread (C. Hugh-Jones 1977: 190, 1979: 116; Chaumeil 1985: 154; Erikson 1986: 198), favoring the view that the above-mentioned practices are attempts to appropriate, recycle, and transmit this energy so as to benefit the killer and his close family. This intention is quite explicit in some instances. Kalinago believed, for example, that the scarification of initiates with the *acoulari* ritual knife prolonged their lives, suggesting that they considered that through this action they transferred the vitality contained in the knife's handle—made of enemy bones—to the initiates. In other instances, such as the Kalinago habit of playing flutes made out of enemy bones or the Tukano use of an arm bone to stir manioc beer, the intention seems to be to disseminate the generative energy of the deceased either through the breath of his killer—energy and breath being two common metaphors for life in Amerindian thought—or through a drink that is usually consumed in large collective rituals. In other societies, such as the Yagua, the teeth of captured enemies were used to make female belts. Worn as a sign of their husbands' courage, these were utilized primarily during the planting of new gardens, to infuse the cuttings and seedlings with the generative power contained in the teeth of enemies (Chaumeil 1985: 152). The Nivaclé attributed similar potency to the belts they made out of enemy teeth (Menget 1996: 138).

Less important than bones and teeth, hair was nevertheless another much sought-after war trophy. After beheading their enemies, Tukano warriors removed not only the teeth but also the hair, which was used to embellish the staffs wielded by renowned warriors and chiefs (Stradelli 1890[1882]: 436). If unable to capture alive an enemy, Chiriguaná warriors attempted to bring with them at least his scalp, ears, or any other easily transportable body part (Corrado and Comajuncosa 1990[1884]: I, 46). These trophies were exposed to the fury and insults of the victors.

When they began to decompose, they were thrown away, except for the hair, which was given to the dance masters (Giannecchini 1996[1898]: 328). Guaicurú warriors kept the dried head skins of captured enemies, as well as the mane attached to them (Lozano 1733: 71, 79). Scalping was quite common in native America, as illustrated by Theodor de Bry in an early engraving of a Timucuan raid (see Figure 40), but the sources are mute on why scalps and hair were considered to be important enough to capture and keep. We know, however, that hair is often used in Amerindian sorcery attacks as a metonymic representation of the person. Furthermore, in some Amerindian societies such as the Jivaro, the *muisak*, or avenging spirit of killed enemies, is believed to reside, not only in his shrunken head, but also in his hair (Karsten 1923: 32; Harner 1973: 147). We can therefore safely assume that enemy hair, kept in the form of scalps or as ornaments for staffs and other ritual paraphernalia, was also considered to be a source of enemy vital energy.

The Amerindian political economy of life entailed more than the capture of people and the appropriation of enemy body parts and substances. It frequently involved less tangible things, such as names. It is said that when Kalinago warriors killed an enemy of renown, they were entitled to assume the latter's name (Rochefort 1666[1658]: 339). When they did not know the name of the captured warrior, they would choose someone to provide them with a new name during the victory celebrations. If Chiriguaná warriors followed the same practices as the Guarayo, their close neighbors and relatives, it is quite probable that they also adopted a new name each time they killed an enemy (Anon. 1929[1589]: 933).

The capture of enemy sources of life also involved the capture of personal or collective life-containing ritual objects. Tukano people, for instance, raided their enemies not only to capture people but also to steal their ritual paraphernalia, such as feather headdresses, masks, and Jurupari sacred flutes, all of which were believed to represent or contain the identity and powers of their enemies' ancestors (S. Hugh-Jones 1993: 109). Other native tropical American peoples, such as the ancient Taino, competed for the possession of powerful collective and family gods, represented in idols made of stone, wood, clay, or cotton fibers. This competition often led to interlocal wars and to the theft of the enemies' deities by the victorious group (Pané 1999[1498]: 21; de las Casas 1992[1566]: II, 872). Believed to be *turey*, or "heaven sent," these representations were thought to promote female fecundity, ensure the fertility of the land, and produce benefic rains (Fernández de Oviedo 1851[1548]: I, 138; de las Casas 1992[1566]: II, 869; S. M. Wilson 1990: 86–87). Some effigies were buried in the gardens to encourage plant growth and abundance (Pané 1999[1498]: 36)—as Jivaro women still do today when they bury magical stones in their gardens (Brown 1993: 120). By stealing their deities, Taino raiders deprived their enemies of owning crucial sources of generative forces, while at the same time increasing their own.

A similar logic lies behind the extreme importance that these societies placed in retrieving the bodies of dead fellow warriors. Early sources report that the Kalinago (Rochefort 1666[1658]: 322) and Chiriguaná (AGI 1735: fol. 56r) did everything they could to recover the bodies of fallen companions. Although we lack the evidence, it is probable that this was also true of the other societies in the sample, since, as Chaumeil (2007: 262–263) suggests, this is a widespread Amerindian practice. The sources insist that leaving the body of a fellow warrior behind was perceived as a shameful act. And this might have been the case. More crucial, however, seems to have been the idea of preventing the enemy from keeping the vitalities of the fallen. In a political economy where life is the scarcest resource, success is measured, not only by capturing from rival groups as large an amount of potentialities of life as possible, but also by preventing the enemy from reducing one's own stock of life forces.

Some European chroniclers were well aware that one of the most important goals of Amerindian raiding was to increase the human resources at their disposal. Dueñas (1924[1792]: 249) asserted that Conibo raiding was mainly about "increasing the number of individuals of their nation" by the capture of women taken as concubines and by the abduction of children who eventually married into the group. The capture of women and children in other societies seems to have served as an attempt to counterbalance cultural practices that hindered natural population growth. This might have been the case of Guaicurú. Being a hunting-and-gathering society that was constantly on the go to ensure its subsistence, Guaicurú sought to reduce the number of births to one or two per woman, so that babies would not hinder their mobility. They achieved this by using contraceptives and by practicing abortion and infanticide (Sánchez Labrador 1910–1917[1770]: II, 30–31; Méndez 1969[1772]: 61). Guaicurú raiding was meant to augment their own numbers by the capture of alien young women and children (Lozano

1733: 67). Acquiring older children was a way of ensuring their freedom of movement, as well as their capacity to circumvent the dangers posed on babies and infants by unceasing displacement throughout a harsh environment such as the Grand Chaco.

The desire to increase one's own population by using a variety of strategies, including the capture of women and children from enemy groups, is consistent with Amerindian notions surrounding social success. In tropical forest societies, the success of a local group is measured by both the number of people it manages to recruit and the amount of potentialities of life that it can wrest from Others. A group's vital capital includes generic life forces, vitalities, and virtualities of existence contained in war trophies, bodily substances, effigies, and magical charms. It also comprises the capabilities of actual men and women—namely, the reproductive power of female captives, the warring abilities of captive boys brought up as members of their masters' society, and the labor force of slaves, servants, and tributaries who contribute services or goods. From an Amerindian point of view, a beautiful settlement is one in which large numbers of people coexist harmoniously; a good leader is one who manages to capture, whether by peaceful or violent means, as many life assets as possible and uses them wisely to benefit his or her followers.

In short, I suggest that in native tropical America, warfare, raiding, and pillaging can be understood only within the framework of the Amerindian political economy of life. In turn, indigenous forms of slavery constitute an extreme instance of the basic idea that the survival of one's own people requires wresting from the enemy as many potentialities of life as possible, whether in the form of actual people or as life forces contained in bodily trophies, magical charms, ritual paraphernalia, idols, and so on. Native tropical American societies can be generally characterized as capturing societies insofar as they all see themselves as being engaged in a political economy of life that involves predatory competition for generative forces and life-giving knowledge and powers, against a series of human and nonhuman rivals, including animals, plants, gods, free spirits, and the dead. It is important to keep in mind, however, that whereas all slaveholding societies are capturing societies, not all capturing societies practice slave raiding or other forms of recruiting people by force.

Conclusions

Scholars who deny the existence of slavery in native tropical America base their arguments on certain distinctive features surrounding the capture and handling of enemies in the region. A brief recapitulation of these arguments, and a discussion of how they fit, or not, with the information provided about the societies in our sample, should help to determine whether the Amerindian practices revolving around the capture and subjection of war prisoners can legitimately be described as forms of indigenous slavery.

The first assumption made in these arguments is that war captives cannot be properly characterized as slaves, because they were eventually incorporated into the families of their captors through marriage or adoption. In point of fact, however, many capturing societies existing at the time of contact practiced raiding and warfare with other aims in sight than the abduction of women to be taken as wives, or children to be adopted. Some women were indeed taken as concubines, and some were even taken as wives—the distinction between both categories being difficult to determine in societies that place little emphasis on marriage rituals. A considerable number of other women were nevertheless kept as drudges, and even those taken as concubines were often treated as servants placed under the authority of legitimate wives. Such women retained their servile status throughout their lives, even after giving birth to their masters' children. In turn, the most attractive, or fittest, captive children were sometimes adopted by their captors, but most were brought up as household servants. After they grew up, they often retained their servile status and were married to other captives. The diversity of fates awaiting war captives was also common in other areas of native America, such as among the Cherokee (Perdue 1993: 12) or in the southwest borderlands (Brooks 2002: 180–181).

War prisoners not intended to be immediately assimilated into their captors' families and kinship networks were forcefully marked as inferior aliens. Such markings—including tattoos, bodily mutilations, and particular hairstyles and items of clothing—were not simply minor indicators of social or ethnic difference. Rather, they were powerful statements of the servile condition the captives found themselves in, written—as is usually the case in Amerindian societies—on their bodies. In capturing societies that practiced bodily deformations and mutilations as powerful signs of self-identity, the lack of such ethnic markings was an additional means to set aside war captives as strangers and subordinates. Whether marked by imposition or default, captives were invariably ascribed a liminal status midway between that of outsiders and insiders.

Another argument made in support of the absence of slavery is that the labor of Amerindian war captives was not indispensable for the reproduction of the economic system of capturing societies—in short, that their existence did not free their masters from their productive obligations—and for this reason such captives cannot be labeled as slaves. The first of these assertions is partially true, at least from a Western point of view. In native tropical America, there were no "genuine slave societies" in the sense of societies based on a slave mode of production. And yet the economic contribution that war captives made to the households and overall economies of their masters was far from negligible. This was particularly true in those societies in which captive slavery was associated with other forms of dependency, such as servant groups or tributary populations.

War captives never totally liberated their masters from the need to work. Nonetheless, this domain admitted differences in degree, depending on the diverse regimes of servitude and on the demographic weight of subordinates with respect to the total population. In societies where the holding of captives as servants was the only form of servitude, and subordinates represented no more than 10 percent of the total population (Kalinago and Conibo), captives worked side by side with their masters. However, captives were usually expected to perform the lowliest and most burdensome household chores. In contrast, in societies where captives coexisted with servant groups and represented more than 20 percent of the population (Tukano and Chiriguaná), subordinates did most of the work, while their masters did almost none. Finally, in societies in which war captives and tributaries represented at least 40 percent of the total population (Guaicurú and probably Calusa), members of the chiefly and warrior strata were exempted from the performance of productive tasks. They were therefore free to devote most of their time to warfare and leisure.

More importantly, captives had a large number of duties that had great social significance even though they may not have been economic in nature. The main function of captives who were personal attendants, retainers, ladies-in-waiting, and pages was to enhance the prestige of their masters, rather than their fortunes. In fact, it could be affirmed that the economic value of captive servants lay not in the surplus labor they could furnish but in their existence as personal attendants. As in other parts of indigenous America (see, e.g., Brooks 2002: 16, 34), captives in native tropical America did not *produce* wealth; they *were* items of wealth. As such, they could be sacrificed as propitiatory victims in fertility ceremonies or in funeral rituals to serve their masters in the afterworld. Whether or not their labor force was central to the reproduction of their masters' societies, war captives had a crucial symbolic significance; their role as personal servants far transcended their economic utility.

Some authors have argued further that captives were well treated and that their masters were reluctant to sell them to Europeans, so they should be considered dependent household members rather than slaves. It is true that after an initial expression of rage toward war captives—mostly during the victory rituals held after a successful raid—they were generally treated kindly. As so many scholars of slavery have pointed out, however, to make the way captives were treated the defining element in the practice of slavery is to mistake their "situation" for their "condition" (Lévy-Bruhl 1931: 3). The salient issue is not how captives were treated but, rather, that their masters could treat them in any way they pleased (Testart 1998: 32). This was so because, from an Amerindian point of view, all enemies were "captives"—that is, they were people without rights—and this state applied to them even before they were captured. Actual capture only materialized their virtual status as captives.

Indeed, Amerindian war captives enjoyed few or no rights. Their movements were restricted. They were made to perform the lowliest and most undesirable tasks. They were not allowed to keep any possessions, and if they did, their masters could take them away whenever they wished. They were forbidden to participate in collective ritual activities other than in their role as personal servants. They were not allowed to occupy political positions. And, with the exception of those who had stood out as brave warriors, they could not even participate in low-level decision-making processes. Often, first-generation captives were not permitted to marry a full member of their captors' society. More importantly, captives were well treated only when they unhesitatingly complied with their masters' wishes. If they resisted, they could be punished physically or even killed. Otherwise, they could be disowned and left on their own, a situation that could only lead to a slow death or to further captivity in the hands of other enemies.

The treatment of captives differed considerably, depending on the particular regime of servitude identified in any one region. In societies where captivity was the single form of servitude and subordinates were relatively few, captives received better treatment than in societies where captivity was combined with other forms of servitude and subordinates represented a large proportion of the total population. In societies of the first type, the intimacy that developed between captives and masters as a result of co-residence and commensality acted as a deterrent against treating captives unkindly. In contrast, in societies with larger numbers of dependents, where relationships between masters and captives were less personal and intimate, subordinates were not treated very well at all. What is important here, however, is not whether captives were treated kindly or unkindly, but that they were at the total mercy of their masters, who could do whatever they wished with their captives' lives.

Another salient objection against characterizing Amerindian captives as slaves is that they were not treated as chattel and thus could not be sold or bought. Whether individuals are the object of property, however, is not what defines them as slaves, as several scholars of slavery have already argued. Rather, what defines them as slaves is that they cannot be the subject of property; that is, that they cannot own anything other than what their masters allow them to possess (Patterson 1982: 17, 28). Yet even if we were not to take into consideration this distinction, the above statement is not entirely true. If we take chattel to mean a commodity, then Amerindian captives were not chattel. If, however, we adopt the usual definition of chattel as "an article of movable, personal property," then Amerindian captives were indeed chattels. Captives were classed—together with animals, plants, and certain objects—as other than real persons. As such they could be preyed upon. Because they owed their lives to their captors, who had spared them, captives were understood to be totally indebted to their masters, who could thus dispense with their lives at their whim.

Above all, captives were conceived of as being the property of their captors. This was an extension of another pervasive Amerindian notion that regards property as the outcome of the productive agency of individuals, so that one can own only what one has produced, or what one has "caused to be." Thus, because war captives were "caused to be" by their captors, they were understood to be the latter's property. As such, they could be bartered, given as gifts, or destroyed. This gave rise to an active trade in captive slaves and even created the conditions for the emergence of annual interethnic fairs, where captives from various societies were brought in to be exchanged. There is historical evidence specifying indigenous rates of exchange for war captives—who were generally traded for other native prestige goods—indicating that this kind of commerce developed long before the arrival of Europeans.

Captives were especially vulnerable to being traded immediately after their capture, before they were integrated into the society of their captors through rituals of enslavement. Once they had been marked as alien subordinates and integrated as members of their captors' households, their chances of being traded diminished considerably. In no way did this situation mean that captives were no longer considered as property. Rather, as the result of prolonged conviviality, some captives were "singularized"; that is, they were set apart as nontradable (Kopytoff 1986). Here we find the cause for why Amerindians were not always willing to sell their captive servants to European slave traders. As is well known, however, processes of "singularization" were not definitive. As the historical evidence indicates, captives could be de-singularized and reintroduced into the sphere of trade for a number of reasons, the most important being a rebellious disposition.

That the status of war captives was not hereditary raises the last denial by scholars as to the existence of slavery in native tropical America. Thus, they argue, captives in these societies never constituted a social class. The first part of this assertion does not always hold true. Children born from mixed captor-captive unions acquired all the rights of full members of the capturing society in most societies included in the sample. The only two exceptions were among the Tukano, who placed strong prohibitions against marrying subordinate Makú and thus strongly stigmatized the offspring of mixed unions, and the Kalinago, who assimilated the female offspring of mixed marriages but extended the mother's captive status to her sons. As such, the sons were destined to be consumed in cannibalistic ceremonies as soon as they reached adulthood.

Nevertheless, captives were not always allowed to marry members of the capturing society in at least four of these societies. Hence, they were limited to marrying people of similar captive origin. The offspring of such unions often inherited the captive status of their parents even if they had been raised in the language and mores of their captors and had received the appropriate tribal markings. The only advantage these children enjoyed was that they were allowed to marry members of the capturing society because they had been brought up as "civilized" people. Additionally, their offspring were often recognized as fellow tribespeople. One can only conclude, therefore, that captive status could be inherited and that full assimilation could be delayed until the second or third generation. In the end, however, war captives or their descendants were assimilated into the societies of their captors through processes of consanguinization (adoptive filiation), or de-affinization (adoption as affinal children).

The above leads us to the debate on the relationship—or lack thereof—between slavery and kinship, a debate that has been central to studies on slavery and that data on Amerindian captive slavery might help to clarify. In the 1960s, British anthropologists first argued that kinship and slavery were antinomic. Adherents of this position regarded slavery as a status rather than as a process (Bohannon 1963; Leach 1967). They argued that the defining element of slavery is the kinlessness of slaves. Servile relationships are not only "nonkinship," they claimed, but "antikinship," insofar as slaves are violently cut from their previous kin ties, becoming associated with their masters' households through nonkinship links. An absence of kinship relationships between masters and slaves is precisely what distinguishes chattel slavery from other forms of servitude.

In contrast, scholars who insist there is a connection between slavery and kinship regard slavery as a process rather than a status (Kopytoff and Miers 1977). They argue that in African lineage societies slavery is an extension of kinship ties; it is an extreme form of the rights-in-persons legal form—that is, the rights that family and lineage heads have over family and lineage members. Like marriage or adoption, slavery should be treated as just another mechanism through which a society incorporates outsiders. Captive or purchased slaves go through a gradual process of incorporation into the society of their masters, a process of transition that Kopytoff and Miers (1977: 22) labeled as the "slavery-to-kinship continuum." Recently acquired slaves, they argue, are alien and kinless. Unless they are immediately traded or passed on, however, their owners face a problem—namely, how to incorporate them while at the same time maintaining their status as strangers. This dilemma triggers a process by virtue of which slaves are increasingly integrated, first as quasi kin and later on as full kin. Thus, they conclude, slavery and kinship may be antithetical, but they do not constitute separate realms (Kopytoff and Miers 1977: 17).

Scholars have questioned Kopytoff and Miers's conclusions from two fronts. On the one hand, there are Patterson (1982) and Lovejoy (2000[1983]), who took a similar stance as Bohannon and Leach. On the other hand, there is Meillasoux (1991[1986]), who introduced the notion of "class" into the debate. According to Patterson (1982: 19), in premodern societies it is common to disguise relationships of domination by the use of fictive kin terms; but, he adds, "kinship, whether real or fictive, is at most a veil, never a cloak." Neither the dominated, nor the dominant person and his true relatives, lose sight of the fact that they are involved in a hierarchical power relationship. Lovejoy (2000[1983]: 2), in turn, states that slavery "is a means of denying outsiders the rights and privileges of a particular society so that they could be exploited for economic, political, and/or social purposes." The two elements that define an individual as an outsider are ethnic differences and the absence of kinship ties. From this point of view, therefore, slavery is the antithesis of kinship.

Meillasoux (1991: 40), in turn, contested the notion of the slavery-to-kinship continuum, arguing that "real slavery" exists only in societies in which slaves compose a social class and are vital to the economic reproduction of the society at large. In such societies, slaves are totally excluded from the kinship networks of their masters. They are the absolute alien non-kin, who reproduce themselves as a social category through endogamous same-class marriages. Slavery is not an extension of kinship, he asserts, because the rights-in-persons characteristic of African societies has nothing to do with "property," as Kopytoff and Miers assume, but has to do with "patrimony" (Meillasoux 1991: 13).

Meillasoux (1991: 32) admits that forms of servitude analogous to real slavery are found in kin-based societies, where the taking of captives from enemy groups was a regular activity. He nevertheless argues that war captives do not reproduce their alien, non-kin status—a condition that, from his point of view, is the essence of slavery as an institution—because in these societies captive women and children are eventually incorporated through adoption or marriage. Meillasoux insists that there is not a continuum between slavery and kinship, but rather a qualitative change. Slavery, he concludes, is outside the realm of kinship; in fact, it is the negation of kinship. As an absolute alien and non-kin, the slave is a product of class relationships.

The discussion outlined above has important implications. If slavery is the antithesis or negation of kinship, what do we make of those cases in which acquired servants are treated in the idiom of kinship and eventually integrated as kin? And if slavery is only a stage in a continuum leading to the establishment of actual kinship relations, what do we make of the fact that in most capturing societies acquired servants and their descendants continue to bear the stigma of having been "acquired," long after they have been integrated through ties of actual kinship? One solution to this conundrum is to negate, à la Meillasoux, the existence of slavery in contexts where acquired servants are eventually integrated as kin. This solution is unsatisfactory, however; it imposes artificial limits around an institution that has been reported from widely different ages and places.

Watson (1980) proposed what I consider to be a satisfactory way out from this conundrum. He contends that the contradiction between slavery and kinship is more apparent than real, resulting as it does from our dealing with two different types of kinship systems (Watson 1980: 6–7). Advocates of the proposition that there is a connection between slavery and kinship base their arguments on the analysis of African lineage societies, whose kinship systems are mostly "open" and inclusive and thus are amenable to the incorporation of outsiders. In contrast, those who claim that slavery and kinship are antinomic have in mind either Asian societies—which are based on "closed," exclusionary kinship systems that refuse to integrate outsiders—or class societies in which slaves are denied any possibility of becoming integrated into their masters' circle. In open kinship systems, the trend is for slaves to be gradually integrated into their master's kinship networks. In closed kinship systems, on the other hand, slaves retain their status and transmit it to their descendants. Watson concludes that "the eventual fate of the person who enters society as a slave is not relevant when one is constructing a definition of slavery as an institution" (1980: 9). Although I am in agreement with this statement, the part that follows—namely, that to conceive of slavery as an institution for the incorporation of outsiders is "less than helpful"— is, to my thinking, unsatisfactory.

In native tropical America, capturing societies have open, inclusive kinship systems that facilitate the incorporation of outsiders—whether individuals or groups, nonrelatives from the same ethnic group, or total strangers—via the extension of classificatory kinship terms, the conferral of younger-sibling sib status, or the attribution of exogamic moiety status. Amerindian war captives also pass through a slavery-to-kinship continuum. Sometimes this process is completed during their lifetimes; sometimes it is deferred and accomplished during the lives of their children or grandchildren. In this region of the world, slavery is neither an extension of kinship nor the negation of kinship. It is neither a distorted transformation of the rights-in-persons legal form—which is mostly absent from tropical America—nor is it totally outside the kinship domain. It is, however, a means for incorporating outsiders—alien enemies—as kin.

In Amerindian capturing societies, captives never constituted a slave class, even though they were a permanent feature of the social landscape. Villasante-de Beauvais (2000: 21) criticizes scholars who view Saharan slave groups as social classes and insists that "status stability" should not be confounded with the "fixity of status appurtenance." In other words, the permanent presence of slaves in any given society should not be taken a priori as an indication that their status is fixed or that they constitute a social class. Here I would like to stress the other side of this formula—namely, that the lack of fixed slave statuses in Amerindian societies should not be accepted as an indication that slavery is absent.

On the contrary, demographic data show that the Amerindian slave machine was extremely efficient. According to my estimates (Chapters 2–4; but also Santos-Granero 1992: 12), the proportion of captive slaves in native tropical American capturing societies fluctuated between 5 and 19 percent of the total population: Kalinago (5 percent), Tukano (8 percent), Conibo (10 percent), Omagua (16 percent), and Guaicurú (19 percent). These percentages are certainly lower than the estimated 30 percent of slaves that existed in Athens during the classical period, the 40 percent of slaves in imperial Rome, or the 34 percent of African slaves in the American South in 1860. But they are similar to the 10 percent of slaves registered in the Domesday Book in eleventh-century England. More importantly, they coincide with the range of 3 to 26 percent of slaves reported for the Amerindian societies of the Pacific northwest coast and Lower Columbia in the early 1800s: Bellabella (3 percent), Tsimshian (3 percent), Salish (4 percent), Kwakiutl (5 percent), Kitkatla (5 percent), Tlingit (8 to 14 percent), Lower Columbia (20 percent), Chinooks (22 percent), Haida (26 percent) (Ruby and Brown 1993: 291–295; Donald

1997: 185–188). And they also coincide with the estimates of 5 to 20 percent for the proportions of captives in Plains Indian societies during the same period: Kiowa (5 to 7 percent) and Comanche (10 to 20 percent) (Brooks 2002: 184, 191).

If we add members of servant and tributary groups to these figures, the relative weight of subordinates in native tropical American capturing societies increases even more. The combined population of war captives and attached servants represented 28 percent of the Tukano population and between 20 and 80 percent of the Chiriguaná population. In turn, the joint population of war captives and tributaries in Guaicurú society represented between 42 and 61 percent of the total. Even if we were to accept only the lower end of these ranges, this would still mean that in societies combining captive slavery with other forms of servitude, the proportion of subordinates could be as high as 20 to 40 percent of the total population. These percentages are quite substantial for societies consistently described as small-scale and egalitarian.

So, can we affirm with full confidence that slavery existed in native tropical America? The answer is an unqualified yes. If we take the notion of slavery to mean the condition originating in the violent capture and removal of people from their families and societies—a condition entailing their subjection to ritual processes of desocialization and depersonification, their compulsory inclusion into the society of their captors while marked as inferior people without rights, and their total subjection to the power and personal whims of their masters, to whom they owed their lives and who could dispose of their life and limb—then slavery was indeed present in native tropical America.

Was slavery in this region of the world comparable to forms of slavery in other times and other places? Comparable, yes; identical, no. Amerindian slavery was very different from slavery as practiced in the ancient societies of the Western world (Greece, Rome, feudal Europe), the Middle East (Israel, Egypt, Persia), and the Far East (China, India, and Southeast Asian kingdoms). It was crucially different from the plantation slavery practiced in the American South, the Greater Antilles, and Brazil during colonial and postcolonial times. Nevertheless, it was similar to slavery as it developed in much of Africa and in many regions of North America, such as the northwest Pacific coast, the eastern woodlands, the greater Lower Columbia region, the Great Plains, and the southwest borderlands. My suggestion, then, is that peoples native to these other regions of the world probably entertained similar eco-cosmologies and might have also been engaged in a similar competition for precious potentialities of life. If this turns out to be true, then captive slavery and other forms of servitude present in these regions must also be regarded as a powerful if extreme means—one among other possible social strategies—to enhance a group's vital capital within the highly competitive framework of indigenous political economies of life.

Appendix
Assessment of Main Sources

ALVAREZ CHANCA, DIEGO (1452–1501)
Spanish physician who was appointed by the Spanish crown to accompany Columbus on his second voyage to the New World (1493–1496). His *Letter* to the municipal council of Seville (1494) is the first document to describe aspects of the flora, the fauna, and the ethnography of the New World. His detailed report is all the more remarkable since it was the result of only three months of observation. Some of the more controversial information he presents was confirmed by subsequent independent authors, making his *Letter* one of the earliest, richest, and most reliable sources on Amerindian life in the Caribbean islands.

ANONYMOUS 1620
The anonymous author of this document traveled to the West Indies in 1619 with Captain Charles Fleury, a French captain-merchant-pirate dedicated to trading and plundering in the Caribbean. The merits of this recently discovered document are that it precedes by fifteen years the studies that the French missionary and pioneer linguist Raymond Breton made of the Kalinago and that it is based on observations made during a ten-month sojourn in Martinique and Dominica. Many of the author's assertions are confirmed by other seventeenth-century sources, but few contain as much detail and internal consistency.

AZARA, FÉLIX DE (1742–1821)
Spanish officer appointed Commissar of Limits of Paraguay in 1781, after the signing of the San Ildefonso Treaty between Spain and Portugal in 1778. He lived in the region for twenty years. A no-nonsense military engineer, Azara states upfront that since he dislikes writers who, after seeing a dozen Indians, make a description of them more detailed than the one they could make of themselves, he will confine his observations to those native peoples that he knows well. He presents a quite balanced view of the indigenous peoples of Paraguay and the River Plate, although he does not always escape from the prejudices of his time. And when discussing Guaicurú captive slavery, he is quick to note how different it is from European enslavement of African people.

BARRIENTOS, BARTOLOMÉ (1520?–1580)
Spanish professor of Latin and mathematics at the University of Salamanca. His biography of conquistador Pedro Menéndez de Avilés—who was his contemporary

—is based on the official reports, personal testimonies, and letters written by the conquistador and his higher officers. The document was completed in 1568, but it was not published until 1902. The information that Barrientos provides on the Calusa is very similar to that presented by Gonzalo Solís de Merás (see below). This has prompted some authors to assert that both narratives must be based on a third, common source. The value of Barrientos's biography is that it provides a detailed referent with which to check other narratives of Menéndez de Avilés dealing with Calusa.

BOGGIANI, GUIDO (1861–1901)

Italian aesthete who visited the Chaco region as a landscape painter in 1887. He returned to Italy in 1893, carrying with him a large ethnographic collection. There he trained himself as an ethnographer and linguist. After writing two books on the Caduveo—one of the surviving Guaicurú regional groups—and the Chamacoco, he returned to America in 1896. During his second stay in the Chaco, Boggiani took hundreds of photographs of its native inhabitants, leaving a rich visual legacy of their lifeways (see Frič and Fričova 1997). Although not formally trained, Boggiani made very fine observations of the social mores and cultural practices of Guaicurú people. In addition, unlike most scholars, he had no qualms about admitting that he was wrong. In his footnotes he regularly corrects himself and introduces nuances into his previous ethnographic observations.

BRETON, RAYMOND GUILLAUME (1609–1679)

French Dominican missionary who arrived in Guadeloupe in 1635. He was assigned to Dominica, where he stayed until 1654, when he returned to France. Back home, he published a Carib-French (1665) and a French-Carib (1666) Dictionnaire. These not only contain many entries but also include phrases showing how the terms were used, as well as a wealth of ethnographic notes explaining otherwise obscure details. He also wrote the second part of the Relations de l'Ile de la Guadeloupe (Breton 1978[1647]), devoted to the origin, customs, and religion of the Caribs (Kalinago). Breton hesitates between his condemnation of Kalinago for being godless cannibalistic savages and his admiration for their dignity, pride, and valor. Although his prejudiced views of the Kalinago have been questioned (Whitehead 2002: 60), his works continue to be considered an invaluable source of ethnographic knowledge on Kalinago people.

CASTELNAU, FRANCIS DE (1810–1880)

French naturalist and diplomat, commissioned by the French government to organize a scientific expedition to South America. Between 1843 and 1847, he traversed the continent twice, first from Rio de Janeiro to Lima, and later on from Lima to Para along the Ucayali and Amazon rivers. His work, Expédition dans les parties centrales de l'Amérique du Sud, was published in seventeen volumes. Modern authors have argued that Castelnau's perceptions of indigenous peoples mark a transition from the prevalence of racial prejudices and an emphasis on exotic topics, to a more scientific perception that prefigured the emergence of ethnology as a science. Thus his work illustrates the passage from the travelogue to the ethnographic record.

CHEVILLARD, ANDRÉ (EARLY SEVENTEENTH CENTURY)

French Dominican priest who worked as a missionary in Guadeloupe and recorded the activities of his order in the Lesser Antilles during the first half of the seventeenth century. In writing the third part of his work, entitled *Du naturel, religion, moeurs & funerailles des sauvages Caraïbes, Galibis, Aloagues & Oüarabiches*, he relied heavily on Raymond Breton's *Relations de l'Ile de la Guadeloupe*, written in 1647 but unpublished until the twentieth century, and also on Du Tertre's *Histoire Generale* (1654). This part of Chevillard's chronicle is an impoverished, distorted, and abridged version of the rich works of his predecessors. In the first part of his work, however, he presents several moral stories narrating the miraculous conversion of indigenous peoples that contain important ethnographic information on Kalinago raiding and treatment of captive slaves.

COLUMBUS, FERDINAND (1488–1539)

Son of Christopher Columbus who accompanied his father on his fourth voyage to America (1502–1504). The account he provides of Columbus's second voyage to America in his *Life of the Admiral Christopher Columbus* was based on his father's diary. Because the earliest surviving version of his biography was an Italian version published in 1571, more than thirty years after his death, historians at first doubted that he was the author. Nowadays, broad consensus exists that he was indeed the author and that Bartolomé de las Casas had in his hands the Spanish original of his work. Ferdinand Columbus is a sober writer, not much given to the exaggerations characteristic of some of his contemporaries. He based his writings on original documents, witnesses' reports, and his own knowledge of the region.

COMA, GUILLERMO (LATE FIFTEENTH CENTURY)

Spanish physician(?) who accompanied Columbus on his second voyage to the New World (1493–1496). In 1494 he wrote one or more letters to Nicoló Syllacio, an Italian who had worked in Spain. Syllacio published Coma's *Relación* in Pavia, Italy. Since Columbus's *Diary* of his second voyage to America has disappeared, Coma's work, together with those of Diego de Alvarez Chanca and Miguel de Cúneo, are the most important independent sources on that trip. Despite the sensational—and sometimes sensationalist—nature of his descriptions of Kalinago and Taino peoples, Coma's information is consistent with contemporary and subsequent sources.

COUDREAU, HENRI ANATOLE (1859–1899)

French traveler who explored the French Guiana and other areas of Amazonia in 1881–1885 and 1887–1891. During his second voyage, he visited the Tumuc-Humac Mountains, an area disputed by France and the empire of Brazil.

Coudreau was an acute observer, an indefatigable explorer, and a meticulous writer. Combining a thorough knowledge of the writings of previous explorers with extensive interviews conducted with key indigenous informants, he provides detailed information on the ethnography and history of French Guiana. His writings sometimes manifest the prejudices of his time—as when he claims that Roucouyenne mythical accounts are deprived of imagination and poetry—but his works nevertheless possess a quality and richness seldom achieved by other nineteenth-century travelers.

CÚNEO, MIGUEL DE (LATE FIFTEENTH CENTURY)

Italian gentleman who claimed to have accompanied Christopher Columbus on his second voyage to the New World (1493–1496). His *Letter* contains interesting information on the inhabitants of the Greater and Lesser Antilles. But his frequent exaggerations—for instance, that Kalinago used to make cannibalistic expeditions that lasted up to ten years during which time they depeopled entire islands—and the fact that neither Ferdinand Columbus nor Bartolomé de las Casas mention him in their writings have led some historians to doubt whether he ever traveled to America. However, on the issue of the emasculation of captive boys, Cuneo's claims are confirmed by other more reliable sources, suggesting either that he saw what he narrates or that he got the information from someone who witnessed the events.

DE LA BORDE, SIEUR (SEVENTEENTH CENTURY)

French layman who worked with Jesuit missionaries in the conversion of the Kalinago of the Lesser Antilles sometime during the second half of the seventeenth century. His work, *Relation exacte de l'origine, moeurs, coûtumes, religion, guerres & voyages des Caraibes*, published in 1674 together with other similar accounts, relies heavily on the writings of Charles de Rochefort, whom he sometimes simply paraphrases. He also seems to be indebted to the works of Father Raymond Breton. His main contributions to Kalinago ethnography are his description of Kalinago mythology and his observations about Kalinago sorcery, which he scorned but describes in some detail. In general terms, he confirms what other authors had observed before him, yet he often adds details of his own that enrich our knowledge of Kalinago cultural practices.

DÍAZ DE GUZMÁN, RUI (1558?–1629)

Spanish officer born in Paraguay, the son and son-in-law of two of the first conquistadores of Paraguay and Bolivia. He wrote his history of the discovery and colonization of the rivers Plate, Parana, and Paraguay on the basis of information collected directly from indigenous informants (he spoke Guaraní perfectly well) or from fellow conquerors. Although in his writings he deplores the extermination of the natives and denounces the genocidal policies of the conquerors, in practice he did not hesitate in crushing indigenous revolts. His work has been praised for its detail and accuracy by both Nordenskiöld and Métraux (1927: 19–20).

ELVAS, GENTLEMAN OF (EARLY SIXTEENTH CENTURY)

Portuguese officer who participated in Hernando de Soto's 1539 expedition to Florida. The latest consensus is that de Soto landed in Tampa Bay, which, many agree, was the northernmost boundary of Calusa territory; farther north were located the Tocobaga, one of their bitterest enemies (Clayton, Knight, and Moore 1995: I, 185). The information provided by the Gentleman from Elvas about chief Ucita and his settlement, as well as the data he collected from Spanish captive Juan Ortiz, is crucial to understanding Calusa religious customs and local politics at the time of contact.

ESCALANTE FONTANEDA, HERNANDO DE (1536–AFTER 1575)

Spanish youth who shipwrecked on the coast of Florida in 1549, at the age of thirteen, and was kept as a captive slave by the Calusa until 1567, when he was rescued by conquistador Pedro Menéndez de Avilés. After serving as interpreter and guide on several missions headed by Menéndez de Avilés, he returned to Spain in 1569. In 1575 he wrote his *Memoria de las cosas i costa i indios de la Florida*, which was used by contemporary historians and is still considered to be one of the most important and authoritative early sources on the political and economic life of the native peoples of southern Florida, especially the Calusa, at the time of contact.

GARCILASO DE LA VEGA, INCA (1539–1616)

Son of a Spanish conqueror of Peru and an Inca princess. In *La Florida* he recounts the adventures of Hernando de Soto's 1539 expedition to Florida. It is based on the information he obtained forty to fifty years after the events from a soldier who accompanied de Soto. *La Florida* is the longest account of the de Soto expedition. However, scholars regard it as one of the less faithful to the facts, being tainted by a too rich literary imagination. Despite its romanticism, Garcilaso often mentions details that make sense in the light of what we know about other native tropical American capturing societies, even though not confirmed by other sources.

GIANNECCHINI, DOROTEO (1837–1900)

Italian missionary who joined the Franciscan monastery of Tarija in 1860, where he stayed until his death. He was fluent in Chiriguaná, so much so that, together with other missionaries, he wrote a Chiriguaná-Spanish and Spanish-Chiriguaná dictionary. The information he presents in his *Historia natural, etnografía, geografía y lingüística del Chaco Boliviano* was thus obtained firsthand from Chiriguaná informants. Giannecchini was an acute observer; the ethnographic information he provides reveals a deep knowledge of Chiriguaná social and cultural practices. He held a favorable vision of Chiriguaná people. His remarks on the "cruelty" of Chiriguaná war practices cannot, therefore, be dismissed as the exaggerations of a moralistic European missionary.

KOCH-GRÜNBERG, THEODOR (1872–1924)
German ethnographer and linguist who visited the Vaupés region in 1903–1905. He is arguably the first ethnologist of the northwest Amazon. His work *Zwei Jahre unter den Indianern: Reisen in Nordwest-Brasilien (1903–1905)* demonstrates a deep understanding of the indigenous peoples of the Vaupés River basin, probably derived from his linguistic studies. His rigorous humanist training accounts for his precise scientific descriptions, as well as for his lack of ethnocentrism. He approaches indigenous peoples, not as abstractions, but as individuals, and thus his works contain rich information about the daily lives of actual people.

LABAT, JEAN-BAPTISTE (1663–1738)
French Dominican missionary who lived in Guadeloupe and Martinique between 1694 and 1706. In 1722 he published his *Nouveau Voyage aux Isles de l'Amérique*, in which he provides a history of the region and an ethnography of its inhabitants. Labat is very critical of previous works on the Kalinago and expounds in detail what he considers to be the failings of these works. Although much of the information he provides on the Kalinago can be found in writings of previous authors, his work presents an integral view, in that it combines the information provided by his predecessors with eyewitness accounts and information he obtained from local and native informants.

LAUDONNIÈRE, RENÉ (C. 1529–1582)
French officer who participated in three expeditions to colonize Florida. In 1564, as leader of a group of Huguenots, he founded Fort Caroline, near the mouth of the St. Johns River. He was one of the few survivors of the 1565 Spanish assaults and seizure of Fort Caroline by Pedro Menéndez de Avilés. Back in France, he wrote a narrative of these three French expeditions, which was published in 1586. Although he never visited Calusa territory, Laudonnière obtained valuable information on the Calusa from two Spanish castaways who had been captured and for many years were employed as servants by the Calusa paramount chief.

LIZÁRRAGA, REGINALDO DE (1545–1615)
Spanish Dominican priest who was appointed to several posts in Peru, Chile, Bolivia, and Paraguay. His work *Descripción breve de toda la tierra del Perú, Tucumán, Río de la Plata y Chile*, which remained unpublished until 1908, is the result of half a century (1555–1600) of traveling around these regions. Apart from his frequent condemnation of indigenous "idolatry," his work is of great value because it is based on firsthand information on the geography, ethnography, and history of these lands. Particularly important for the present book are the

chapters he devotes to describing the campaign of Viceroy Francisco de Toledo against the Chiriguaná.

LÓPEZ DE VELASCO, JUAN (SIXTEENTH CENTURY)

Spanish cosmographer. In 1571 he was appointed official cosmographer and chronicler for the Consejo de Indias. As such, in 1574 he wrote the *Geografía y descripción universal de las Indias*, which was not published until the nineteenth century. He is also reputed to have authored the questionnaire that served as the basis for the writing of the famous *Relaciones geográficas de Indias*. In both works there is as much emphasis on the physical geography as on the cultural landscapes of the New World. Because he had access to official documents and collected witness oral reports, his information is generally considered to be very reliable.

LOZANO, PEDRO (1697–1752)

Spanish Jesuit assigned to the Paraguay missions in 1714. He was appointed professor in the College of Córdoba in Tucumán, becoming in time the official chronicler of the Jesuit province of Tucumán. Twelve of the eighty-three chapters of his *Descripción chorographica del Gran Chaco* are devoted to the ethnography of its native inhabitants. Because he was extremely critical of Spanish treatment of the indigenous peoples in early colonial times, and because he wrote about the mythical city of the Caesars, his opponents accused him of being too credulous. Later Jesuit authors, such as José Sánchez Labrador, criticized Lozano for his ethnographic errors, such as, for instance, attributing certain inhuman practices to native peoples that his opponents considered had never existed. The first accusation is more telling of the moral integrity of Lozano than of his flaws as a historian. The second is countered by the existence of other sources that confirm Lozano's information.

MARCOY, PAUL (1815–1888)

Nom de plume of Laurent Saint-Cricq, a French traveler who visited Peru with the intention of traversing the continent from the Pacific to the Atlantic Ocean. In 1847 he joined a French-Peruvian expedition led by the French naturalist Francis de Castelnau and the Peruvian Navy officer, Captain D. F. Carrasco. Because he was not a scientist but was very critical of the scientists who had explored the Peruvian Amazon in his time, Marcoy was accused of being an unreliable plagiarist. However, after comparing Marcoy's report with those written by Castelnau and Carrasco, Jean-Pierre Chaumeil (2001: 24) concludes that this is not true and that Marcoy's work contains more extensive and detailed ethnographic observations than the other two.

MARTIRE D'ANGHIERA, PIETRO (1457–1526)
(AKA PETER MARTYR D'ANGHIERA)

Italian scholar employed at the court of the Catholic kings of Spain. In 1511 he was appointed official chronicler in the newly formed Consejo de Indias and was commissioned to describe the Spanish endeavors in the New World. That same year he published the first of his eight *Decades*, describing the voyages of Columbus and his partners. His work acquired its final form in 1530, when his eight decades were published under the title *De orbe novo*. Martire, who never was in America, obtained most of his information from the discoverers themselves or from other members of their expeditions. He was also able to consult the letters of Columbus and the official reports of the Consejo de Indias. For these reasons, his work is considered to be one of the most important sources of information on the early history of America.

McGOVERN, WILLIAM MONTGOMERY (1897–1964)

American professor and traveler. He was lecturer in Oriental studies at the University of London and assistant curator of the Anthropology Department of Chicago's Field Museum of Natural History. In 1925 he visited the Vaupés River basin, where he stayed two years. His book, *Jungle Paths and Inca Ruins*, is written in the form of a travelogue and book of adventures. Thanks to his long stay in the region, his writings show a familiarity with indigenous social organization and cultural practices that is seldom matched by other contemporary sources. At times, however, he betrays his racial prejudices—as when he describes the appearance and character of Makú people (pp. 179–180). For this reason, the reader should take some of his theories and interpretations with a grain of salt.

NAVARRETE, LUISA DE (SIXTEENTH CENTURY)

Former African slave who spoke Spanish and had converted to Christianity. In 1576 she was captured in Puerto Rico by Kalinago raiders from the island of Dominica, becoming the servant of the Kalinago chief who had captured her. She managed to escape from her captors when she was participating in a raid against Spanish farmers in Puerto Rico. After being liberated, the Spanish authorities asked her to render testimony of her captivity among the Kalinago. The document that has reached our hands is not a verbatim transcript of her testimony but a rendition by the procurator general. In spite of it being secondhand, Navarrete's testimony is invaluable, for it is one of the few early witness accounts of Kalinago society and forms of servitude.

ORDINAIRE, OLIVIER (1845–1914)

French vice-consul in the port of Callao, Peru (1882–1885). When his appointment finished, he decided to go back to France, crossing South America through the Amazon region. According to Renard-Casevitz (1988: 11), although Ordinaire shared the preconceptions of his time, he had a critical mind and humanistic spirit that prevented him from being blinded by them. As a result, he provides readers with "an interesting synthesis of the knowledge of his time about the places he traversed and the peoples he encountered."

ROCHEFORT, CHARLES CESAR DE (1630–1691)
Protestant Frenchman who traveled twice to the Lesser Antilles in the mid-1600s.
His *Histoire naturelle et morale des Îles Antilles*, first published in 1658, was
considered by Dominican missionary Jean-Baptiste Du Tertre (1667: Preface)
to be both plagiaristic and unreliable. Some contemporary scholars argue that
this judgment should be reconsidered, since it is clear that Du Tertre, Raymond
Breton, and other Catholic chroniclers had their own political agendas (Hulme
and Whitehead 1992: 117). This might well be true, but it is equally true that
Rochefort often provides information not confirmed by any other source—
missionary or otherwise—and, therefore, must be handled with caution. This
applies to information such as the taking of bodily trophies. Whereas the taking
of heads of dead enemies is a well-attested Kalinago practice, the taking of skins
as war trophies is mentioned only by Rochefort.

ROGEL, JUAN (SIXTEENTH CENTURY)
Spanish Jesuit missionary who settled in Fort San Antonio, built by conqueror
Pedro Menéndez de Avilés in Calos, the capital of the Calusa polity. He remained
in Calos between March 1567 and July 1568, when the hostilities of the Calusa,
Tequesta, and Tocobaga against the Spanish forced all missionaries to abandon
Florida. His long *Letter* was written in April 1568. It narrates the difficulties he
found in converting the Indians. Despite sharing the prejudices of his time against
Indian peoples and being a strong opponent of Father Bartolomé de las Casas,
whom he accused of inciting hatred against the Spanish, Father Rogel provides
invaluable information on Calusa leadership, regional politics, and religious
practices, much of which is confirmed by other sources.

SÁNCHEZ LABRADOR, JOSÉ (1716–1798)
Spanish Jesuit, who shortly after becoming a priest moved to Paraguay as a
teacher. In 1760 he abandoned teaching to preach to the Guaicurú, among whom
he lived until the expulsion of the Jesuits from America in 1767. His work, *El
Paraguay Católico*, was not published until 1910–1917, but today it is considered
to be one of the most important sources for the history of the Guaicurú. His work
not only is rich in historical information but also provides detailed ethnographic
and linguistic data on the Guaicurú and their Guaná tributaries.

SCHMIDL, ULRICH (1510–1579)
Bavarian officer, who at the time when Charles V ruled over Spain and Germany,
joined Pedro de Mendoza in his 1534 expedition to the River Plate. He stayed in
America for twenty years, participating in all the early expeditions throughout
Argentina, Paraguay, and Bolivia. The veracity of his *Historia y descubrimiento
de el Río de la Plata y Paraguay*, first published in 1567, has been contested by
some historians on the grounds that he omits important historical details that he
should have known. Others justify these omissions as the result of his particular

perspective as a man of arms. Be that as it may, the information he provides on the Guaicurú and Guaná is confirmed by all subsequent chroniclers.

SERRA, RICARDO FRANCO DE ALMEIDA (1748?–1809)

Brazilian officer commissioned by the imperial government in 1798 to nucleate the Guaicurú and Guaná, who had recently moved from Paraguayan into Brazilian territory. By the time he wrote his *Parecer sobre o aldeamento dos Indios Uaicurús e Guanás* in 1803, Serra had a comprehensive knowledge of regional politics. Following contemporary prejudices, he described the Guaicurú as "inconstant and condescending." But in discussing the difficulties that there would be to nucleate them in villages, he shows a surprising knowledge of Guaicurú cultural practices and social mores and betrays a scarcely concealed admiration for their pride.

SOLÍS DE MERÁS, GONZALO (SIXTEENTH CENTURY)

Spanish clergyman and physicist. He was the brother-in-law of Pedro Menéndez de Avilés, the Spanish conquistador who expelled the French from Florida in 1565, and subjected the native Floridans to the Spanish crown. He accompanied Menéndez de Avilés on the four expeditions the latter made to Florida between 1565 and 1567. His *Memorial* was written in 1567 but was not published until 1893. Like most Spanish chroniclers of his day, he was more interested in reporting the events concerning the Spanish conquistadores than in describing the native populations. However, his lengthy work contains important ethnographic information and is an essential source for the understanding of Calusa regional politics.

STAHL, EURICO (NINETEENTH CENTURY)

Peruvian(?) author who lived in the Ucayali region at the end of the nineteenth century. It is unclear whether he was a local authority or worked for one of the commercial houses of Iquitos that had branches in the region. He was educated and corresponded with members of the National Geographic Society of Lima, in whose bulletin he published his work. Stahl must have spent several years in the region, for he asserts that he learned enough of Conibo language to understand what was being said and to make himself understood. This, he says, opened the door to his attending Conibo ceremonies "never before seen by White men." He is, however, very critical of the "fantastic" stories that nonnatives had told about the Conibo and affirms that all of what he reports is based on what he has personally witnessed. His observations and remarks on Conibo social and cultural life are extremely refined and betray an insider's knowledge seldom equaled by any of his contemporaries, even those with scientific training.

STRADELLI, ERMANNO (1852–1926)

Italian count, lawyer, and self-taught geographer, with interests in ethnography, botany, zoology, and topography. He visited the Vaupés River basin three times, in 1881, 1882, and 1890. His main works, published in the bulletin of the Italian

Geographic Society, show a rare understanding of indigenous societies and practices in the region. Refreshingly, his writings lack the Eurocentric prejudices of his time, are critical of the "civilizing" methods of the military, merchants, and missionaries, and show a great respect for indigenous peoples.

THOUAR, EMILE ARTHUR (1853–1908)

Self-trained French geographer. In 1882 he was commissioned by the French government to search for the remains of the explorer Jules Crevaux, killed by the Toba of the Grand Chaco that same year. Subsequently, he made three other expeditions across the Chaco, commissioned by the Argentinean and Bolivian governments. Thouar asserts that he obtained much of the ethnographic data on the Chiriguaná from missionary Doroteo Giannecchini (see above). But Giannecchini (1996[1898]: 374) warns his readers against adventurers who write about the Chiriguaná after only a few days' stay among them and who, having obtained information from missionaries, proceed to distort it in their publications. This clear allusion to Thouar suggests that, unless verified by other sources, his information must be used with caution.

Bibliography

Abbeville, Claude d'. 1614. *Histoire de la mission des pères capucins en l'isle de Maragnan et terres circonvoisines*. Paris: Impr. de F. Huby.

Adkins, Leslie, and Roy A. Adkins. 1994. *Handbook to Life in Ancient Rome*. New York: Oxford University Press.

AGI. *See* Archivo General de Indias.

Alcántara, Tomás. 1900. Viaje al Ucayali (1807). *Boletín de la Sociedad Geográfica de Lima* 9(4): 442–461; 10(1): 77–92.

Alcaya, Diego Felipe de. 1961. Relación cierta que el Padre Diego Felipe de Alcaya, Cura de Mataca, envió a su excelencia el Señor Marqués de Montes Claros, Visorrey de estos reynos. . . . In Hernando Sanabria Fernández (ed.), *Cronistas Cruceños del Alto Perú Virreinal*, pp. 47–68. Santa Cruz de la Sierra: Universidad Gabriel René Moreno.

Alegría, Ricardo. 1981. Las primeras noticias sobre los indios Caribes. In Manuel Cárdenas Ruiz (ed.), *Crónicas francesas de los indios Caribes*. Compiled, translated, and annotated by Manuel Cárdenas Ruiz. Río Piedras, Puerto Rico: Universidad de Puerto Rico/Centro de Estudios Avanzados de Puerto Rico y el Caribe.

Alès, Catherine. 1981. Les tribus indiennes de l'Ucayali au XVIe siècle. *Bulletin de l'Institut Français d'Etudes Andines* 10(3–4): 87–97.

Alonso de Jesús, Francisco. 1993. Memorial of Fray Francisco Alonso de Jesus on Spanish Florida's Missions and Natives. Translated by John H. Hann. *Americas* 50:85–105.

Alvarez Chanca, Diego. 1978. A letter addressed to the Chapter of Seville by Dr. Chanca, native of that city, and physician to the fleet of Columbus, in his second voyage to the West Indies. In R. H. Major (ed.), *Four Voyages to the New World: Letters and Selected Documents*, pp. 18–68. Gloucester, MA: Peter Smith.

Amich, José. 1975. *Historia de las misiones del convento de Santa Rosa de Ocopa*. Lima: Editorial Milla Batres.

Anderson, Mary M. 1990. *Hidden Power: The Palace Eunuchs of Imperial China*. Buffalo, NY: Prometheus.

Anonymous. 1769. *Voyages et aventures du chevalier de * * *, contenant les voyages de l'auteur dans les isles Antilles Françoises du vent de l'Amérique Septentrionale*. 4 vols. London and Paris: Chez Dessain Junior.

———. 1905. Descripción de las misiones del río Ucayali. In Larrabure y Correa 1905, 14:257–265.

———. 1927. Diccionario cunibo-castellano y castellano-cunibo. In Izaguirre 1922–1929, 13:391–474.

———. 1929. Missio in Provinciam Santae Crucis, 1589. In Alfred Métraux, Un ancien document peu connu sur les Guarayu de la Bolivie orientale: Missio in Provinciam Santae Crucis in Annuae Litterae Societatis Iesu. *Anthropos* 24(5–6): 913–941.

———. 1938. *Vocabulario na lingua brasilica: Manuscrito português-tupí do seculo XVII, coordenado e prefaciado por Plinio Ayrosa.* São Paulo: Departamento de Cultura.

———. 1941. Relación anónima en la que se hace referencia al descubrimiento hecho por Solís del Río de la Plata. In *Documentos históricos y geográficos relativos a la conquista y colonización rioplatense,* 1:65–68. Buenos Aires: Talleres S.A. Casa Jacobo Peuser.

———. 1965. Relación verdadera del asiento de Santa Cruz de la Sierra. In Marcos Jiménez de la Espada (ed.), *Relaciones geográficas de Indias,* Biblioteca de Autores Españoles, 183:397–401. Madrid: Ediciones Atlas.

———. 1988. *Un flibustier français dans la mer des Antilles en 1618–1620.* Clamart: Editions Jean-Pierre Moreau.

Appadurai, Arjun (ed.). 1986. *The Social Life of Things.* Cambridge: Cambridge University Press.

Archivo General de Indias. 1577. Residencia de Pedro Menéndez de Avilés, Adelantado de la provincia de la Florida, por Iñigo Ruiz de Castro, 1577. Escribanía S.15, 154A. Seville.

———. 1735. Carta del Maestre de Campo General, sargento mayor y demás capitanes vivos al General Don Lorenzo del Río y Amézaga, September 1735. Charcas 360, Cuaderno 5, fol. 53r–59v. Seville.

Århem, Kaj. 1981. *Makuna Social Organization: A Study in Descent, Alliance and the Formation of Corporate Groups in the North-Western Amazon.* Stockholm: LiberTryck.

———. 1996. The Cosmic Food Web: Human-Nature Relatedness in the Northwest Amazon. In Philippe Descola and Gísli Pálsson (eds.), *Nature and Society: Anthropological Perspectives,* pp. 185–204. London and New York: Routledge.

Arriaga, Pablo Joseph. 1970. Carta annua del P. Pablo Joseph de Arriaga, por comisión al P. Claudio Aquaviva, Lima, 6 Abril 1594. In Antonio de Egaña (ed.), *Monumenta Peruana,* 5:338–484. Monumenta Historica Societatis Iesu, vol. 102. Rome: Apud "Institutum Historicum Societatis Iesu."

———. 1974. Carta annua del P. Pablo Joseph de Arriaga, por comisión al P. Claudio Aquaviva, Lima, 3 Abril 1596. In Antonio de Egaña (ed.), *Monumenta Peruana,* 6:12–81. Monumenta Historica Societatis Iesu, vol. 110. Rome: Apud "Institutum Historicum Societatis Iesu."

Arteaga, Pedro de. 1961. Relación de todo lo que en el viaje de socorro que el Señor Gobernador Martín de Almendras Holguín vino a dar al cacique

Cuñayuru y sus comarcanos contra el pueblo de Charagua y Tatamiri
y Sebastián Rodríguez y Don Pedro y sus aliados. . . . In Hernando
Sanabria Fernández (ed.), *Cronistas Cruceños del Alto Perú Virreinal*,
pp. 171–178. Santa Cruz de la Sierra: Universidad Gabriel René Moreno.

Arvelo-Jiménez, Nelly, and Hector Biord. 1994. The Impact of Conquest on
Contemporary Indigenous Peoples of the Guiana Shield: The System of
Orinoco Regional Interdependence. In Anna Roosevelt (ed.), *Amazonian
Indians from Prehistory to the Present: Anthropological Perspectives*,
pp. 55–78. Tucson: University of Arizona Press.

Audiencia. 1918–1922a. Carta a S.M. de la Audiencia de Charcas, 30 Octubre
1564. In Levillier 1918–1922, 1:133–144.

———. 1918–1922b. Carta a S.M. de la Audiencia de Charcas, 17 Febrero
1595. In Levillier 1918–1922, 3:220–244.

Azara, Félix de. 1809. *Voyages dans l'Amérique Méridionale*. Edited by C. A.
Walckenaer. 4 vols. Paris: Dentu.

Balée, William. 1992. People of the Fallow: A Historical Ecology of Foraging
in Lowland South America. In Kent Redford and Christine Padoch (eds.),
*Conservation of Neotropical Forests: Working from Traditional Resource
Use*, pp. 35–57. New York: Columbia University Press.

Barco Centenera, Martín del. 1836. La Argentina o la conquista del Río de
la Plata. In Pedro de Angelis (ed.), *Colección de obras y documentos
relativos a la historia antigua y moderna de las provincias del Río de la
Plata*, 2:1–312, i–xxv. Buenos Aires: Imprenta del Estado.

Barrientos, Bartolomé. 1965. Vida y hechos de Pero Menéndez de Aviles,
Caballero de la Hordem de Sanctiago, Adelantado de La Florida. In
Bartolomé Barrientos, *Pedro Menéndez de Avilés, Founder of Florida*,
translated with an introduction by Anthony Kerrigan, pp. 1–152.
Gainesville: University of Florida Press.

Basso, Ellen. 1995. *The Last Cannibals: A South American Oral History*.
Austin: University of Texas Press.

Belaúnde, Luisa Elvira. 2001. *Viviendo bien: Género y fertilidad entre los Airo-
Pai de la amazonía peruana*. Lima: Centro Amazónico de Antropología
y Aplicación Práctica/Banco Central de Reserva del Perú.

———. 2007. The Strength of Thoughts, the Stench of Blood: Amazonian
Hematology and Gender. In Fernando Santos-Granero and George
Mentore (eds.), *No mundo e pelo mundo: Modos de conhecimento
ameríndio*, special issue in honor of Prof. Joanna Overing, *Revista
de Antropología* (Brazil) 49(1): 205–243.

Benjamin, A. J. McR. 1987. The Guyana Arawaks in the 16th and 17th
Centuries. In *Proceedings of the Conference on the Arawaks of Guyana*,
October 14–15, pp. 5–21. Georgetown: University of Guyana.

Benoit, Pierre Jacques. Circa 1858. *Scènes de la vie américaine, description
de la Guyane Hollandaise*. Brussels: Bruylant-Christophe et Comp.

Beraún, Francisco de. 1981a. Carta del Capitán . . . al Gobernador D. Francisco de Elso y Arbizú, 23 Octubre 1686. *Amazonía Peruana* 4(7): 177–178.

———. 1981b. Carta de los buenos sucesos de la entrada a la montaña, relación del Capitán . . . , 23 Octubre 1686. *Amazonía Peruana* 4(7): 178–182.

Biedma, Manuel. 1981. *La conquista franciscana del Alto Ucayali.* Lima: Milla Batres.

Biocca, Ettore. 1965. *Viaggi tra gli Indi Alto Rio Negro-Alto Orinoco.* 3 vols. Rome: Consiglio Nazionale delle Ricerche.

Bodley, John H. 1973. Deferred Exchange among the Campa Indians. *Anthropos* 68:589–596.

———. 1984. Deferred Exchange among the Campa: A Reconsideration. In Peter D. Francis, F. J. Kense, and P. G. Duke (eds.), *Networks of the Past: Regional Interaction in Archaeology*, Proceedings of the 12th Annual Conference of the Archaeological Association of the University of Calgary, pp. 19–28. Alberta.

Boggiani, Guido. 1945. *Os Caduveo.* São Paulo: Livraria Martins Editôra.

Bohannon, Paul. 1963. *Social Anthropology.* New York: Holt, Rinehart and Winston.

Bonte, Pierre. 1998. Esclaves ou cousins: Evolution du statut servile dans la société mauritanienne. In Bernard Schlemmer (ed.), *Terrains et engagements de Claude Meillasoux*, pp. 157–182. Paris: Editions Karthala.

Boomert, Arie. 1986. The Cayo Complex of St. Vincent: Ethnohistorical and Archaeological Aspects of the Island Carib Problem. *Antropológica* 66:3–68.

Bouton, Jacques. 1640. *Relation de l'establissement des François depuis l'an 1635 en l'isle de la Martinique.* Paris: Chez Sebastien Cramoisy.

Braudel, Fernand. 1958. Histoires et sciences sociales: Longue durée. *Annales* 4:716–753.

Breton, Raymond Guillaume. 1665. *Dictionaire caraibe-françois.* Auxerre: Gilles Bouquet.

———. 1666. *Dictionaire françois-caraibe.* Auxerre: Gilles Bouquet.

———. 1978. *Relations de l'Ile de la Guadeloupe.* Basse-Terre: Société d'Histoire de la Guadeloupe.

Brooks, James E. 2002. *Captives and Cousins: Slavery, Kinship and Community in the Southwest Borderlands.* Chapel Hill and London: University of North Carolina Press.

Brown, Michael F. 1993. *Tsewa's Gift: Magic and Meaning in an Amazonian Society.* Washington, DC: Smithsonian Institution Press.

Buenaventura Bestard, Juan. 1906. Carta de . . . acompañada de un mapa é informe de la misiones del río Ucayali . . . 21 Noviembre 1819. In Víctor M. Maúrtua (comp.), *Juicio de límites entre el Perú y Bolivia*, pp. 12: 339–355. Barcelona: Imprenta de Henrich y Comp.

Burnham, Philip. 1980. Raiders and Traders in Adamawa: Slavery as a Regional System. In James L. Watson (ed.), *Asian and African Systems of Slavery*, pp. 41–72. Oxford: Blackwell.

Butt-Colson, Audrey. 1973. Inter-tribal Trade in the Guiana Highlands. *Antropológica* 34:4–70.

———. 2001. Itoto (Kanaima) as Death and Anti-Structure. In Rival and Whitehead 2001, pp. 221–234.

Cabrera Becerra, Gabriel, Carlos E. Franky Calvo, and Dany Mahecha Rubio. 1999. *Los Nʉkak: Nómadas de la amazonia colombiana*. Bogotá: Universidad Nacional de Colombia.

Cañete, Marqués de. 1921–1926. Carta del Marqués de Cañete a S.M., 28 Enero 1560. In Roberto Levillier (ed.), *Gobernantes del Perú: Cartas y papeles*, 1:347–351. Madrid: Sucesores de Rivadeneyra S.A.

Carneiro, Robert L. 1970. A Theory of the Origin of the State. *Science* 196:733–738.

———. 1990. Chiefdom-level warfare as exemplified in Fiji and the Cauca Valley. In Jonathan Haas (ed.), *The Anthropology of Warfare*, pp. 190–211. Cambridge: Cambridge University Press.

———. 1994. War and Peace: Alternating Realities in Human History. In S. P. Reyna and R. E. Downs (eds.), *Studying War: Anthropological Perspectives*, pp. 3–27. Langhorne, PA: Gordon and Breach.

Carneiro da Cunha, Manuela (org.). 2002. *História dos índios do Brasil*. São Paulo: FAPESP/Compañia das Letras/Secretaria Municipal de Cultura.

Carneiro da Cunha, Manuela L., and Eduardo B. Viveiros de Castro. 1985. Vingança e temporalidade: Os Tupinamba. *Journal de la Société des Américanistes* 71:191–208.

Cassá, Roberto. 1992. *Los indios de las Antillas*. Madrid: Editorial MAPFRE.

Castelnau, Francis de. 1850–1859. *Expédition dans les parties centrales de l'Amérique du Sud, de Rio de Janeiro à Lima, et de Lima au Para, exécutée par ordre du gouvernement français pendant les années 1843 à 1847*. 17 vols. Paris: Chez P. Bertrand.

Castro, Licenciado. 1921–1926. Carta del licenciado Castro a S.M., 7 Febrero 1568. In Roberto Levillier (ed.), *Gobernantes del Perú: Cartas y papeles*, 3:297–303. Madrid: Sucesores de Rivadeneyra S.A.

Cepeda, Licenciado. 1918–1922a. Carta del Licenciado Cepeda a S.M., 10 Febrero 1590. In Levillier 1918–1922, 3:1–17.

———. 1918–1922b. Carta a S.M. del Licenciado Cepeda, 28 Marzo 1595. In Levillier 1918–1922, 3:259–281.

Chacon, Richard J., and Ruben G. Mendoza (eds.) 2007. *Latin American Indigenous Warfare and Ritual Violence*. Tucson: University of Arizona Press.

Chagnon, Napoleon. 1968. Yanomamo Social Organization and Warfare. In Morton Fried (ed.), *War: The Anthropology of Armed Conflict and Aggression*. Garden City, NY: Natural History Press.

Chagnon, Napoleon A., and Raymond Hames. 1979. Protein Deficiency and Tribal Warfare in Amazonia. *Science* 203:910–913.

Chaumeil, Jean-Pierre. 1983. *Voir, savoir, pouvoir: Le chamanisme chez les Yagua du Nord-Est péruvien*. Paris: Editions de l'Ecole des Hautes Etudes en Sciences Sociales.

———. 1985. Echange d'énergie: Guerre, identité et reproduction sociale chez les Yagua de l'Amazonie Péruvienne. *Journal de la Société des Américanistes* 71:143–157.

———. 2001. Un viajero sin prisa a mediados del siglo XIX: Laurent Saint-Cricq (Paul Marcoy). Prologue to Paul Marcoy, *Viaje a través de América del Sur: Del Océano Pacífico al Océano Atlántico*, 1:15–45. Lima: IFEA/BCRP/PUCP/CAAAP.

———. 2007. Bones, Flutes, and the Dead: Memory and Funerary Treatments in Amazonia. In Fausto and Heckenberger 2007, 243–283.

Chernela, Janet. 1993. *The Wanano Indians of the Brazilian Northwest Amazon: A Sense of Place*. Austin: University of Texas Press.

———. 1997. Review of Brian Ferguson's Yanomami Warfare: A Political History. *American Ethnologist* 24(1): 227–229.

———. 2001. Piercing Distinctions: Making and Remaking the Social Contract in the North-West Amazon. In Rival and Whitehead 2001, pp. 177–195.

Chevillard, André. 1659. *Les Desseins de son Eminence de Richelieu pour l'Amérique: Ce qui s'y est passé de plus remarquables depuis l'Etablissement des Colonies; Et un ample Traite du Naturel, Religion & Moeurs des Indiens Insulaires & de la Terre Ferme*. Rennes: Chez Jean Durand.

Chiappino, Jean. 1997. Las piedras celestes: Para una nueva forma de intercambio en el ámbito de la salud. In Jean Chiappino and Catherine Alès (eds.), *Del microscopio a la maraca*, pp. 253–272. Caracas: Ex Libris.

Clastres, Pierre. 1998a. Exchange and Power: Philosophy of the Indian Chieftainship. In Clastres 1998e, pp. 27–47.

———. 1998b. Independence and Exogamy. In Clastres 1998e, pp. 49–77.

———. 1998c. Of the One without the Many. In Clastres 1998e, pp. 169–175.

———. 1998d. Of Torture in Primitive Societies. In Clastres 1998e, pp. 177–188.

———. 1998e. *Society against the State*. New York: Zone Books.

Clayton, Lawrence A., Vernon James Knight Jr., and Edward C. Moore (eds.). 1995. *The De Soto Chronicles: The Expedition of Hernando de Soto to North America in 1539–1543*. 2 vols. Tuscaloosa: University of Alabama Press.

Columbus, Christopher. 1991. *The Diario of Christopher Columbus's First Voyage to America, 1492–1493*. Norman and London: University of Oklahoma Press.

Columbus, Ferdinand. 1992. *The Life of the Admiral Christopher Columbus by His Son Ferdinand*. New Brunswick, NJ: Rutgers University Press.

Coma, Guillermo. 1903. The Syllacio-Coma Letter. In John Boyd Thacher, *Christopher Columbus, His Life, His Works, His Remains as Revealed by Original Printed and Manuscript Records*, 2:223–262.

Combès, Isabelle, and Kathleen Lowrey. 2006. Slaves without Masters? Arawakan Dynasties among the Chiriguano (Bolivian Chaco, Sixteenth to Twentieth Centuries). *Ethnohistory* 53(4): 689–714.

Combès, Isabelle, and Thierry Saignes. 1991. *Alter ego: Naissance de l'identité Chiriguano*. Paris: Editions de l'Ecole des Hautes Etudes en Sciences Sociales.

Cominges y Prat, Juan de. 1892. *Obras escogidas de Don Juan de Cominges*. Buenos Aires: Casa Editora de Juan A. Alsina.

Compostela, Diego Ebelino de. 1991. Don Diego Ebelino de Compostela, Bishop of Santiago de Cuba, to the Dean and Chapter of Holy Cathedral Church of Santiago de Cuba, January 2, 1690. In Hann 1991b, 85–91.

Condominas, Georges (ed.). 1998. *Formes extrêmes de dépendance: Contributions à l'étude de l'esclavage en Asie du Sud-est*. Paris: Edition de l'Ecole des Hautes Etudes en Sciences Sociales.

Conklin, Beth A. 2001. Women's Blood, Warriors' Blood, and the Conquest of Vitality in Amazonia. In Thomas A. Gregor and Donald Tuzin (eds.), *Gender in Amazonia and Melanesia: An Exploration of the Comparative Method*, pp. 141–174. Berkeley: University of California Press.

———. 2003. Engendering Warriors: Reproductive Imagery in Enemy-Killer's Rituals. In Paul Valentine and Catherine Julien (eds.), *War and Peace in Aboriginal South America*, special issue, *Antropológica* 99–100:31–43.

Contreras, Francisco de. 1991. Testimony of Friars Relating to the Calusa Mission, February–March 1698. In Hann 1991b, 162–181.

Coppi, Illuminato Giuseppe. 1885. La Provincia delle Amazzoni secondo la relazione del P. . . . missionario nel Brasile. *Bollettino de la Società Geografica Italiana* 22(2): 136–141; 22(3): 193–204.

Cormier, Loretta A. 2003a. Animism, Cannibalism, and Pet-keeping among the Guajá of Eastern Amazonia. *Tipití* 1(1): 81–98.

———. 2003b. *Kinship with Monkeys: The Guajá Foragers of Eastern Amazonia*. New York: Columbia University Press.

Corrado, Alejandro M., and Antonio Comajuncosa. 1990. *El colegio franciscano de Tarija y sus misiones*. 2 vols. Tarija: Editorial Offset Franciscana.

Coudreau, Henri Anatole. 1887. *La France équinoxiale*. 2 vols. Paris: Challamel ainé.

———. 1893. *Chez nos Indiens: Quatre années dans la Guyane Française (1887–1891)*. Paris: Hachette et Cie.

Crocker, Jon Christopher. 1985. *Vital Souls: Bororo Cosmology, Natural Symbolism, and Shamanism*. Tucson: University of Arizona Press.

Crocker, William, and Jean Crocker. 1994. *The Canela: Bonding through Kinship, Ritual and Sex*. Fort Worth: Harcourt Brace College Publishers.

Cúneo, Miguel de. 1928. De Novitatibus Insularii Occeani Heperii Repertata a Don Xpoforo Columbo, Genuensi. In Rómulo Cúneo-Vidal, *Cristóbal Colón, Genovés*, Apéndice, pp. 277–301. Barcelona: Casa Editorial Maucci.

DeBoer, Warren R. 1984. The Machete and the Cross: Conibo Trade in the Late Seventeenth Century. In Peter D. Francis, F. J. Kense, and P. G. Duke (eds.), *Networks of the Past*, Proceedings of the 12th Annual Conference of the Archaeological Association of the University of Calgary, pp. 31–48. Alberta.

———. 1986. Pillage and Production in the Amazon: A View through the Conibo of the Ucayali Basin, Eastern Peru. *World Archaeology* 18(2): 231–246.

Debret, Jean Baptiste. 1993. *O Brasil do Debret*. Rio de Janeiro: Villa Rica Editoras Reunidas Limitada.

De Bry, Theodor. 1590. *Admiranda narratio, fida tamen, de commodis et incolarum ritibus Virginiae*. Francoforti ad Moenum: Wecheli, sumtibus T. de Bry.

———. 1591. *Brevis narratio eorum quae in Floridae Americae provincia Gallis acciderunt, secunda in illam navigatione, duce Renato de Laudoniere*. Francoforti ad Moenum: Typis I. Wecheli, sumtibus vero T. de Bry.

De la Borde, Father. 1886. History of the Origin, Customs, Religion, Wars, and Travels of the Caribs, Savages of the Antilles in America. *Timehri—The Journal of the Royal Agricultural and Commercial Society of British Guiana* 5:224–254.

De las Casas, Bartolomé. 1986. *Historia de las Indias*. Edición, Prólogo, Notas y Cronología de André Saint-Lu. 3 vols. Caracas: Biblioteca Ayacucho.

———. 1992. *Apologética historia sumaria*. 3 vols. Madrid: Alianza Editorial.

Deleuze, Gilles, and Félix Guattari. 1987. *A Thousand Plateaus: Capitalism and Schizophrenia*. Minneapolis and London: University of Minnesota Press.

Descola, Philippe. 1988. La chefferie amérindienne dans l'anthropologie politique. *Revue Française de Science Politique* 38(5): 818–827.

———. 1992. Societies of Nature and the Nature of Society. In Adam Kuper (ed.), *Conceptualizing Society*, pp. 107–126. London and New York: Routledge.

———. 1994. Pourquoi les Indiens d'Amazonie n'ont-ils pas domestiqué le pécari? Généalogie des objets et anthropologie de l'objectivation. In Bruno Latour and Pierre Lemonnier (eds.), *De la préhistoire aux missiles balistiques: L'intelligence sociale des techniques*, pp. 329–344. Paris: Editions La Découverte.

———. 1996. *In the Society of Nature: A Native Ecology in Amazonia*. Cambridge: Cambridge University Press.

Díaz Castañeda, César. 2001. Ligeros apuntes históricos sobre los Indios Cunivos. In Bernardino Izaguirre (ed.), *Historia de las misiones franciscanas y narración de los progresos de la geografía en el Oriente del Perú*, 1:345–362. Lima: Librería Editorial Salesiana.

Díaz de Guzmán, Rui. 1836. Historia Argentina del descubrimiento, población y conquista de las provincias del Río de la Plata. In Pedro de Angelis (ed.), *Colección de obras y documentos relativos a la historia antigua y moderna de las provincias del Río de la Plata*, 1:1–140, i–lxxxvii. Buenos Aires: Imprenta del Estado.

———. 1979a. Relación breve y sumaria que haze el governador don Ruiz Díaz de Guzmán al Real Consejo de Su Majestad, y a su Visorey destos reynos del Piru, y a su Real Audiencia de la Plata, en razón de las crueldades, muertes, y robos que an hecho los Indios Chiriguanas desta provincia, donde al presente está en su conquista y pacificación. In Ruy Díaz de Guzmán, *Relación de la entrada a los Chiriguanos*, pp. 71–80. Santa Cruz de la Sierra: Fundación Cultural «Ramón Darío Gutiérrez.»

———. 1979b. Relación breve y sumaria de las cosas subcedidas en el discurso de la jornada, conquista y población del governador Ruy Diaz de Guzmán. In Ruy Díaz de Guzmán, *Relación de la entrada a los Chiriguanos*, pp. 81–112. Santa Cruz de la Sierra: Fundación Cultural "Ramón Darío Gutiérrez."

Dietrich, Wolf. 1986. *El idioma chiriguano*. Madrid: Instituto de Cooperación Iberoamericana.

Divale, William T., and Marvin Harris. 1976. Population, Warfare, and the Male Supremacist Complex. *American Anthropologist* 78(3): 521–538.

Donald, Leland. 1997. *Aboriginal Slavery on the Northwest Coast of North America*. Berkeley: University of California Press.

Dow, James. 1983. Woman Capture as a Motivation for Warfare. In R. Dyson-Hudson and M. A. Little (eds.), *Rethinking Human Adaptation: Biological and Cultural Models*, pp. 97–115. Boulder, CO: Westview Press.

Drake, Sir Francis. 1992. Early English and French Voyagers. In Hulme and Whitehead 1992, pp. 53–54.

Dreyfus, Simone. 1983–1984. Historical and Political Anthropological Interconnections: The Multilinguistic Indigenous Polity of the "Carib" Islands and Mainland Coast from the 16th to the 18th Century. In Audrey Butt-Colson and H. Dieter Heinen (eds.), Themes in Political Organization: The Caribs and Their Neighbors, special issue, *Antropológica* 59–62:39–55.

Dueñas, Juan. 1924. Carta y diario del P. Fr. . . . misionero del Colegio de Ocopa que manifiesta el importantísimo camino de comunicación desde Manoa al pueblo de Cumbaza del partido de Lamas, Agosto y Septiembre 1792. In Izaguirre 1922–1929, 8:229–256.

Dumont, Jean-Paul. 1976. *Under the Rainbow: Nature and Supernature among the Panare Indians*. Austin: University of Texas Press.

Du Tertre, Jean-Baptiste. 1654. *Histoire Generale des Isles de S. Christophe, de la Guadeloupe, de la Martinique, et autres dans l'Amérique*. Paris: Jacques Langlois.

———. 1667. *Histoire Generale des Antilles Habitées par les François*. Paris: Thomas Jolly.

Edwards, Bryan. 1793. *The History, Civil and Commercial, of the British Colonies in the West Indies*. 2 vols. London: Printed for J. Stockdale.

Elvas, Gentleman from. 1995. True Relation of the Hardships Suffered by Governor Don Hernando de Soto and Certain Portuguese Gentlemen during the Discovery of Florida. In Clayton, Knight, and Moore 1995, 1:19– 219.

Erikson, Philippe. 1986. Altérité, tatouage et anthropophagie chez les Pano: La belliqueuse quête du soi. *Journal de la Société des Américanistes* 72:185– 209.

———. 1993. Une nébuleuse compacte: Le macro-ensemble pano. *L'Homme* 126–128, 33(2–4): 45–58.

———. 2000. The Social Significance of Pet-keeping among Amazonian Indians. In Paul Podberseck and James Serpell (eds.), *Companion Animals and Us*, pp. 7–26. Cambridge: Cambridge University Press.

Escalante Fontaneda, Hernando de. 1575. Memoria de las cosas i costa i Indios de la Florida. Photocopy of a transcript of the original document extant at the archive of Simancas, attested by Muñoz and preserved in the Lenox Library. Washington, DC: Library of Congress.

Evans, Clifford. 1971. Review of Donald W. Lathrap's The Upper Amazon. *American Anthropologist* 73(6): 1414–1416.

Fausto, Carlos. 1999. Of Enemies and Pets: Warfare and Shamanism in Amazonia. *American Ethnologist* 26(4): 933–956.

———. 2001. *Inimigos fiéis: História, guerra e xamanismo na Amazônia*. São Paulo: Editora da Universidade de São Paulo.

Fausto, Carlos, and Michael Heckenberger (eds.). 2007. *Time and Memory in Indigenous Amazonia: Anthropological Perspectives*. Gainesville: University Press of Florida.

Ferguson, R. Brian. 1990. Blood of the Leviathan: Western Contact and Warfare in Amazonia. *American Ethnologist* 17(2): 237–257.

———. 1995. *Yanomami Warfare: A Political History*. Santa Fe, NM: School of American Research Press.

———. 2000. The Causes and Origins of "Primitive Warfare": On Evolved Motivations for War. *Anthropological Quarterly* 73(3): 159–164.

Ferguson, R. Brian, and Neil L. Whitehead. 1992. The Violent Edge of Empire. In R. Brian Ferguson and Neil L. Whitehead (eds.), *War in the Tribal Zone: Expanding States and Indigenous Warfare*, pp. 1–30. Santa Fe, NM: School of American Research Press.

Fernández de Oviedo, Gonzalo. 1851. *Historia general y natural de las Indias, islas y tierra-firme del mar océano*. 4 vols. Madrid: Imprenta de la Real Academia de la Historia.

Ferreira, Alexandre Rodrigues. 1974. *Viagem filosófica pelas capitanias do Grão Pará, Rio Negro, Mato Grosso e Cuiabá*. Rio de Janeiro: Conselho Federal de Cultura.

Finley, Moses I. 1968. Slavery. In *International Encyclopedia of the Social Sciences*, 14:307–313. New York: Macmillan.

Florence, Hercules. 1941. *Viagem fluvial do Tietê ao Amazonas, de 1825 a 1829*. São Paulo: Edições Melhoramentos.

Frank, Erwin. 1994. Los Uni. In Fernando Santos-Granero and Frederica Barclay (eds.), *Guía etnográfica de la alta amazonía*, vol. 2, *Mayoruna, Uni, Yaminahua*, pp. 129–238. Quito: Facultad Latinoamericana de Ciencias Sociales/Instituto Francés de Estudios Andinos.

Frič, Pavel, and Yvonna Fričova (eds.). 1997. *Guido Boggiani: Fotograf (1861–1901)*. Prague: Nakladatelstvi Titanic.

Fry, Carlos. 1907. Diario de los viajes y exploración de los ríos Urubamba, Ucayali, Amazonas, Pachitea y Palcazu, 1888. In Larrabure y Correa 1905, 11:369–589.

Gage, Thomas. 1992. The Jesuit Massacre on Guadeloupe. In Hulme and Whitehead 1992, pp. 83–88.

Garcilaso de la Vega, Inca. 1963. *Comentarios reales de los Incas*. Montevideo: Ministerio de Instrucción Pública y Previsión Social.

———. 1995. La Florida. In Clayton, Knight, and Moore 1995, 2:25–560.

Gardner, Jane F., and Thomas Wiedemann. 1991. *The Roman Household: A Sourcebook*. London: Routledge.

Giacone, Antonio. 1949. *Os Tucanos e outras tribus do rio Uaupés, afluente do Negro-Amazonas*. São Paulo: Imprensa Oficial do Estado São Paulo.

———. 1965. *Gramática, dicionários e fraseología da língua dahceié ou tucano*. Belém: Universidade do Pará.

Giannecchini, Doroteo. 1996. *Historia natural, etnografía, geografía y lingüística del Chaco Boliviano (1898)*. Tarija: Fondo de Inversión Social/ Centro Eclesial de Documentación.

Giannecchini, Doroteo, and Vincenzo Mascio. 1995. *Álbum fotográfico de las misiones franciscanas en la República de Bolivia a cargo de los colegios apostólicos de Tarija y Potosí, 1898*. La Paz and Sucre: Banco Central de Bolivia/Archivo y Biblioteca Nacionales de Bolivia.

Girbal y Barceló, Narciso. 1924a. Diario del viaje que yo Fr. . . . , misionero apostólico del Colegio de Ocopa . . . hice desde el pueblo de Laguna, capital de Mainas, por los famosos ríos Marañón y Ucayali, Año 1790. In Izaguirre 1922–1929, 8:101–184.

———. 1924b. Nuestro viaje al Ucayali y exploración del Pachitea e intento de pasar al Pozuzo por el Mairo por el P. Fr. Narciso Girbal y Barceló. In Izaguirre 1922–1929, 8:299–309.

———. 1964. Prosiguen los viages del padre misionero Fray Narciso Girbal. *Mercurio Peruano* 11: 276–291.

Goggin, John M., and William C. Sturtevant. 1964. The Calusa: A Stratified, Nonagricultural Society (with Notes on Sibling Marriage). In Ward H. Goodenough (ed.), *Explorations in Cultural Anthropology: Essays in Honor of George Peter Murdock*, pp. 179–219. New York: McGraw-Hill.

Goldman, Irving. 1963. *The Cubeo: Indians of the Northwest Amazon*. Urbana: University of Illinois Press.

———. 2004. *Cubeo Hehénewa Religious Thought: Metaphysics of a Northwestern Amazonian People*. New York: Columbia University Press.

Goody, Jack. 1980. Slavery in Time and Space. In James L. Watson (ed.), *Asian and African Systems of Slavery*, pp. 16–42. Oxford: Blackwell.

Gow, Peter. 1989. The Perverse Child: Desire in a Native Amazonian Subsistence Economy. *Man* 24: 299–314.

———. 1991. *Of Mixed Blood: Kinship and History in Peruvian Amazonia*. Oxford: Clarendon Press.

Gross, Daniel R. 1975. Protein Capture and Cultural Development in the Amazon Basin. *American Anthropologist* 77(3): 526–549.

Guyot, Mireille. 1984. Cantos del Hacha de los Bora y Miraña de las selvas colombiana y peruana. *Amazonía Indígena* 4(8): 19–21.

Hajda, Yvonne P. 2005. Slavery in the Greater Lower Columbia Region. *Ethnohistory* 52(3): 563–588.

Halbmayer, Ernst. 2004. "The One Who Feeds Has the Rights": Adoption and Fostering of Kin, Affines and Enemies among the Yupka and Other Carib-Speaking Indians of Lowland South America. In Fiona Bowie (ed.), *Cross-Cultural Approaches to Adoption*, 145–164. London and New York: Routledge.

Hallpike, C. R. 1973. Functionalist Interpretations of Primitive Warfare. *Man* 8(3): 451–470.

Hann, John H. 1991a. Introduction to part 1, Calusa in the Late Seventeenth Century. In Hann 1991b, pp. 3–48.

——— (ed.). 1991b. *Missions to the Calusa*. Gainesville: University Press of Florida.

———. 2003. *Indians of Central and South Florida, 1513–1763*. Gainesville: University Press of Florida.

Harner, Michael J. 1973. *The Jivaro: People of the Sacred Waterfalls*. Garden City, NY: Anchor Press/Doubleday.

———. 1977. The Ecological Basis for Aztec Sacrifice. *American Ethnologist* 4(1): 117–135.

Harris, Marvin. 1974. *Cows, Pigs, Wars and Witches: The Riddles of Culture*. New York: Random House.

———. 1979. The Yanomamö and the Causes of War in Band and Village Societies. In Maxime Margolis and William E. Carter (eds.), *Brazil:*

Anthropological Perspectives, pp. 121–132. New York: Columbia University Press.

———. 1984. Animal Capture and Yanomamö Warfare: Retrospect and New Evidence. *Journal of Anthropological Research* 40(1): 183–201.

Heckenberger, Michael J. 2002. Rethinking the Arawakan Diaspora: Hierarchy, Regionality, and the Amazonian Formative. In Jonathan D. Hill and Fernando Santos-Granero (eds.), *Comparative Arawakan Histories: Rethinking Language Family and Culture Area in Amazonia*, pp. 99–122. Urbana and Chicago: University of Illinois Press.

———. 2003. The Enigma of the Great Cities: Body and State in Amazonia. *Tipití* 1(1): 27–58.

———. 2005. *The Ecology of Power: Culture, Place and Personhood in the Southern Amazon, AD 1000–2000*. New York: Routledge.

Helbig, Jörg. 1994. *Brasilianische Reise 1817–1820: Carl Friedrich Philipp von Martius zum 200*. Munich: Hirmer Verlag München.

Hern, Warren M. 1992. Polygyny and Fertility in a Peruvian Amazon Indian Village. *Population Studies* 46:53–64.

Herndon, William L., and Lardner Gibbon. 1854. *Exploration of the Valley of the Amazon*. 2 vols. Washington, DC: Navy Department.

Herrera y Tordesillas, Antonio de. 1601–1615. *Historia general de los hechos de los castellanos en las Islas i Tierra Firme del Mar Océano*. 9 vols. Madrid: Emplenta Real.

Hill, Jonathan D. (ed.). 1988. *Rethinking History and Myth: Indigenous South American Perspectives on the Past*. Urbana and Chicago: University of Illinois Press.

———. 1993. *Keepers of the Sacred Chants: The Poetics of Ritual Power in an Amazonian Society*. Tucson: University of Arizona Press.

——— (ed.). 1996. *History, Power, and Identity: Ethnogenesis in the Americas, 1492–1992*. Iowa City: University of Iowa Press.

Hill, Jonathan D., and Fernando Santos-Granero (eds.). 2002. *Comparative Arawakan Histories: Rethinking Language Family and Culture Area in Amazonia*. Urbana: University of Illinois Press.

Hirschfeld, Lawrence A., James Howe, and Bruce Levin. 1978. Warfare, Infanticide, and Statistical Inference: A Comment on Divale and Harris. *American Anthropologist* 80(1): 110–115.

Hoff, Berendf J. 1995. Language Contact, War, and Amerindian Historical Tradition: The Special Case of the Island Carib. In Whitehead 1995, pp. 37–60.

Holmberg, Allan R. 1969. *Nomads of the Long Bow: The Siriono of Eastern Bolivia*. Garden City, NY: Natural History Press.

Hornborg, Alf. 2005. Ethnogenesis, Regional Integration, and Ecology in Prehistoric Amazonia: Toward a System Perspective. *Current Anthropology* 46(4): 589–620.

Huerta, Francisco de la. 1983. Relación hecha a nuestro reverendísimo Padre Fray Félix de Como . . . de la entrada y sucesos a las santas conversiones de San Francisco Solano en los gentiles Conibos hecha por el Padre Predicador Fray . . . presidente de dichas santas conversiones, 29 Noviembre 1686. *Amazonía Peruana* 4(8): 113–124.

Hugh-Jones, Christine. 1977. Skin and Soul: The Round and the Straight; Social Time and Social Space in Pira-Paraná Society. *Actes du XLIIe Congrès International des Américanistes* 2:185–204. Paris.

———. 1979. *From the Milk River: Spatial and Temporal Processes in Northwest Amazonia*. Cambridge: Cambridge University Press.

Hugh-Jones, Stephen. 1988. *The Palm and the Pleiades: Initiation and Cosmology in Northwest Amazonia*. Cambridge: Cambridge University Press.

———. 1992. Yesterday's Luxuries, Tomorrow's Necessities: Business and Barter in Northwest Amazonia. In Caroline Humphrey and Stephen Hugh-Jones (eds.), *Barter, Exchange, and Value: An Anthropological Approach*, pp. 42–74. Cambridge: Cambridge University Press.

———. 1993. Clear Descent or Ambiguous Houses? A Re-Examination of Tukanoan Social Organisation. *L'Homme* 126–128, 33(2–4): 95–120.

Hulme, Peter, and Neil L. Whitehead (eds.). 1992. *Wild Majesty: Encounters with Caribs from Columbus to the Present Day; An Anthology*. Oxford: Clarendon Press.

Ingold, Tim. 1998. Totemism, Animism, and the Depiction of Animals. In Marketta Seppälä, Jari-Pekka Vanhala, and Linda Weintraub (eds.), *Animal. Anima. Animus*. Pori: Pori Art Museum.

ISA. *See* Instituto Socioambiental.

Instituto Socioambiental. 2001. Povos indígenas no Brasil. http://www.socioambiental.org/pib/index.html.

Izaguirre, Bernardino (ed.). 1922–1929. *Historia de las misiones franciscanas y narración de los progresos de la geografía en el oriente del Perú, 1619–1921*. 14 vols. Lima: Talleres Gráficos de la Penitenciaría.

Jackson, Jean E. 1983. *The Fish People: Linguistic Exogamy and Tukanoan Identity in the Northwest Amazon*. Cambridge: Cambridge University Press.

———. 1984. Vaupés Marriage Practices. In Kenneth M. Kensinger (ed.), *Marriage Practices in Lowland South America*, pp. 156–179. Urbana and Chicago: University of Illinois Press.

———. 1991. Hostile Encounters between Nukak and Tukanoans: Changing Ethnic Identity in the Vaupés, Colombia. *Journal of Ethnic Studies* 19(2): 17–39.

———. 1999. The Politics of Ethnographic Practice in the Colombian Vaupés. *Identities* 6(2–3): 281–317.

Jolís, José. 1972. *Ensayo sobre la historia natural del Gran Chaco*. Resistencia, Chaco: Universidad Nacional del Nordeste.

Julien, Catherine. 1997. Colonial Perspectives on the Chiriguaná (1528–1574). In María Susana Cipolletti (coordinator), *Resistencia y adaptación nativas en las tierras bajas latinoamericanas*, pp. 17–76. Quito: Abya-Yala.

Karsten, Rafael. 1923. *Blood Revenge, War, and Victory Feasts among the Jíbaro Indians of Eastern Ecuador*. Bureau of American Ethnology, Bulletin 79. Washington, DC: Government Printing Office.

Kelekna, Pita. 1991. El comercio achuara: Contrapeso y complemento para la guerra. In Jeffrey Ehrenreich (ed.), *Antropología política en el Ecuador: Perspectivas desde las culturas indígenas*, pp. 253–294. Quito: Abya-Yala.

———. 1998. War and Theocracy. In Elsa Redmond (ed.), *Chiefdoms and Chieftaincy in the Americas*, pp. 164–168. Gainesville: University Press of Florida.

Klein, Martin. 1998. *Slavery and Colonial Rule in French West Africa*. Cambridge: Cambridge University Press.

Knobloch, Francis J. 1972. The Maku Indians and Racial Separation in the Valley of the Rio Negro. *Mankind Quarterly* 13(2): 100–109.

Koch-Grünberg, Theodor. 1906. Die Makú. *Anthropos* 1(4): 877–899.

———. 1909–1910. *Zwei Jahre unter den Indianern: Reisen in Nordwest-Brasilien 1903–1905*. Stuttgart: Strecker and Schröder.

———. 1995. *Dos años entre los indios: Viajes por el noroeste brasileño, 1903–1905*. 2 vols. Bogotá: Editorial Universidad Nacional.

Kok, R. Pedro. 1925–1926. Quelques notices ethnographiques sur les Indiens du Rio Papuri. *Anthropos* 20(3–4): 624–637; 21(5–6): 921–937.

Kopytoff, Igor. 1982. Slavery. *Annual Review of Anthropology* 11:207–230.

———. 1986. The Cultural Biography of Things: Commoditization as Process. In Arjun Appadurai (ed.), *The Social Life of Things: Commodities in Cultural Perspective*, pp. 64–94. Cambridge: Cambridge University Press.

Kopytoff, Igor, and Suzanne Miers. 1977. African "Slavery" as an Institution of Marginality. In Suzanne Miers and Igor Kopytoff (eds.), *Slavery in Africa: Historical and Anthropological Perspectives*, pp. 3–81. Madison: University of Wisconsin Press.

Labat, Jean-Baptiste. 1724. *Nouveau Voyage aux Isles de l'Amérique contenant l'Histoire Naturelle de ces Pays, l'Origine, les Moeurs, la Religion & le Gouvernement des Habitans anciens & modernes*. 2 vols. The Hague: Pierre Husson, Thomas Johnson, Pierre Gosse, Jean Van Duren, Rutgert Alberts, and Charles le Vier.

Lafone y Quevedo, Samuel Alexander. 1896. *Idioma Mbaya*. Buenos Aires: Imprenta de Pablo E. Coni e Hijos.

Langebaek, Carl Henrik. 1992. *Noticias de caciques muy mayores*. Bogotá: Uniandes/Editorial Universidad de Antioquia.

Larrabure y Correa, Carlos (ed.). 1905. *Colección de leyes, decretos, resoluciones y otros documentos oficiales referentes al Departamento de Loreto*. 18 vols. Lima: Imprenta La Opinión Nacional.

Lathrap, Donald W. 1962. Yarinacocha: Stratigraphic Excavations in the Peruvian Montaña. Ph.D. dissertation, Department of Anthropology, Harvard University.

———. 1970. *The Upper Amazon.* London: Thames and Hudson.

Laudonnière, René. 2001. *Three Voyages.* Tuscaloosa and London: University of Alabama Press.

Leach, Edmund R. 1967. Caste, Class and Slavery: The Taxonomic Problem. In Anthony de Reuck and Julie Knight (eds.), *Caste and Race: Comparative Approaches*, pp. 5–16. London: Churchill.

Le Breton, Adrien. 1998. *The Caribs of St. Vincent: Historic Account of Saint Vincent, the Indian Youromayn, the Island of the Karaybes.* With an Introduction by Fr. Robert Divonne. Kingstown: Model Printery.

León de Santiago, Pedro. 1985. Que les Chiriguanos présentent d'avantageuses dispositions à l'égard de nombreuses autres nations barbares, pour reçevoir l'Evangile. Appendix 2 of Thierry Saignes' Chiriguano, Jésuites et Franciscains: Généalogie du regard missionnaire, pp. 224–231; in Claude Blanckaert (ed.), *Naissance de l'Ethnologie? Anthropologie et missions en Amérique XVIe–XVIIIe siècle*, pp. 195–231. Paris: Editions du Cerf.

Lévi-Strauss, Claude. 1943. Guerre et commerce. *Renaissance* 1(1–2): 122–139.

———. 1974. *Tristes Tropiques.* New York: Atheneum. First published in 1955.

———. 1993. Un autre regard. *L'Homme* 126–128, 33(2–4): 7–10.

———. 1995. *Saudades do Brasil: A Photographic Memoir.* Seattle and London: University of Washington Press.

Levillier, Roberto (ed.). 1918–1922. *Audiencia de Charcas: Correspondencia de presidentes y oidores.* 3 vols. Madrid.

Lévy-Bruhl, Henri. 1931. Théorie de l'esclavage. *Revue Générale de Droit* 55(1): 1–17.

Lewis, Clifford M. 1978. The Calusa. In Jerald Milanich and Samuel Proctor (eds.), *Tacachale: Essays on the Indians of Florida and Southeastern Georgia during the Historic Period.* Gainesville: University Presses of Florida.

Linares, Olga F., Payson D. Sheets, and E. Jane Rosenthal. 1975. Prehistoric Agriculture in Tropical Highlands: Settlement Patterns in Western Panama Reflect Variations in Subsistence Adaptations to the Tropics. *Science* 187:137–145.

Lizárraga, Reginaldo de. 1968. *Descripción breve de toda la tierra del Perú, Tucumán, Río de la Plata y Chile.* Biblioteca de Autores Españoles, 216:1–213. Madrid: Ediciones Atlas.

Loaisa, Cardenal. 1885–1932. Real Cédula del Gobernador Gral. Cardenal Loaisa para la Audiencia y el Obispo de Panamá. Madrid, 15 April 1540. In *Colección de documentos inéditos relativos al descubrimiento, conquista y organización de las antiguas posesiones españolas de ultramar*, 2nd ser., 10:473ff. Madrid: Sucesores de Rivadeneyra.

Londoño Sulkin, Carlos David. 2004. *Muinane: Un proyecto moral a perpetuidad*. Medellín: Editorial Universidad de Antioquia.

López, Feliciano. 1991. Fray Feliciano López to Fray Pedro Taybo, 1697. In Hann 1991b, 158–161.

López, Martín. 1964. Memoria y relación que hizo Martín López de su viaje desde la Margarita hasta el río Curetin, Año de 1550. In Antonio Arellano Moreno (comp.), *Relaciones geográficas de Venezuela*, pp. 43–49. Caracas: Italgráfica.

López de Gómara, Francisco. 1946. *Hispania Victrix: Primera y Segunda Parte de la Historia General de las Indias, con todo el descubrimiento, y cosas notables que han acaecido desde que se ganaron hasta el año 1551*. In Biblioteca de Autores Españoles, 22:155–455. Madrid: Ediciones Atlas.

López de Velasco, Juan. 1991a. Brief Memorials and Notes (1569?). In Hann 1991b, pp. 315–319.

———. 1991b. Juan López de Velasco on the Geography and Customs of Florida, 1575. In Hann 1991b, pp. 308–315.

Lorant, Stefan (ed.). 1965. *The New World: The First Pictures of America, Made by John White and Jacques Le Moyne and Engraved by Theodore de Bry, with Contemporary Narratives of the French Settlements in Florida, 1562–1565, and the English Colonies in Virginia, 1585–1590*. New York: Duell, Sloan and Pearce.

Lothrop, Samuel Kirkland. 1937. Coclé: An Archaeological Study of Central Panama, Part I. *Memoirs of the Peabody Museum of Archaeology and Ethnology*, vol. 7.

Lovejoy, Paul E. 2000. *Transformations in Slavery: A History of Slavery in Africa*. Cambridge: Cambridge University Press.

Lowie, Robert H. 1948. Social and Political Organization of the Tropical Forest and Marginal Tribes. In Julian H. Steward (ed.), *Handbook of South American Indians*, 5:313–350. Washington, DC: Government Printing Office.

Lozano, Pedro. 1733. *Descripción chorographica del terreno, ríos, árboles, y animales de las dilatadísimas provincias del Gran Chaco, Gualabamba; y de los ritos, y costumbres de las innumerables naciones bárbaras, e infieles que le habitan*. Córdoba: Colegio de la Assumpcion.

Luer, George M. 1989. Calusa Canals in Southwestern Florida: Routes of Tribute and Exchange. *Florida Anthropologist* 42(2): 89–130.

MacCreagh, Gordon. 1926. *White Waters and Black*. New York and London: Century Co.

MacLeod, William Christie. 1928. Economic Aspects of Indigenous American Slavery. *American Anthropologist* 30(4): 632–650.

Mader, Elke. 1999. *Metamorfosis del poder: Persona, mito y visión en la sociedad Shuar y Achuar*. Quito: Abya-Yala.

Mader, Elke, and Richard Gippelhauser. 2000. Power and Kinship in Shuar and Achuar Society. In Peter P. Schweitzer (ed.), *Dividends of Kinship:*

Meanings and Uses of Social Relatedness, pp. 61–91. London and New York: Routledge.

Marcoy, Paul. 1869. *Voyage a travers l'Amérique du Sud de l'Océan Pacifique a l'Océan Atlantique*. 2 vols. Paris: Librairie de L. Hachette et Cie.

Maroni, Pablo. 1988. Noticias auténticas del famoso río Marañón y misión apostólica de la Compañía de Jesús en los dilatados bosques de dicho río. In Pablo Maroni et al., *Noticias auténticas del famoso río Marañón*, Monumenta Amazónica B4:89–396. Iquitos: Instituto de Investigaciones Científicas de la Amazonía Peruana/Centro de Estudios Teológicos de la Amazonía.

Marquardt, William H. 1987. The Calusa Social Formation in Protohistoric South Florida. In Thomas C. Patterson and Christine W. Gailey (eds.), *Power Relations and State Formation*, pp. 98–116. Washington, DC: American Anthropological Association.

Marqués, Buenaventura. 1931. Vocabulario de la lengua Cuniba. *Revista Histórica* 9(2–3): 117–195.

Martínez, Diego. 1944. Carta del P. Diego Martínez al P. Juan Sebastián, en que le da cuenta de las nuevas provincias de indios infieles de aquellas partes, 24 Abril 1601. In Francisco Mateos (ed.), *Historia General de la Compañía de Jesús en la Provincia del Perú*, 2:504–507. Madrid: Consejo Superior de Investigaciones Científicas/Instituto Gonzalo Fernández de Oviedo.

Martínez de Irala, Domingo. 1912. Relación de Domingo Martínez de Irala acerca de los descubrimientos que iba haciendo cuando fue navegando Paraguay arriba por orden del gobernador Cabeza de Vaca, desde el 18 de diciembre de 1542. In P. Groussac (ed.), *Anales de la Biblioteca: Publicación de documentos relativos al Río de la Plata*. Buenos Aires: Imprenta y Casa Editora de Coni Hermanos.

Martire d'Anghiera, Pietro. 1966. *The Decades of the Newe Worlde or West India*. Ann Arbor: University Microfilms.

Matienzo, Juan de. 1918–1922. Carta a S.M. del licenciado Matienzo con larga noticia de los indios chiriguanaes, 1564. In Levillier 1918–1922, 1:54–60.

Mauss, Marcel. 1936. Les techniques du corps. *Journal de Psychologie* 32(3–4).

Maybury-Lewis, David. 1974. *Akwẽ-Shavante Society*. New York: Oxford University Press.

McCallum, Cecilia. 2001. *Gender and Sociality in Amazonia: How Real People Are Made*. Oxford and New York: Berg.

McGovern, William Montgomery. 1927. *Jungle Paths and Inca Ruins*. New York and London: Century Co.

McNicoll, Robert E. 1941. The Caloosa Village Tequesta: A Miami of the Sixteenth Century. *Tequesta—The Journal of the Historical Association of Southern Florida* 1(1): 11–20.

Meggers, Betty J. 1971. *Amazonia: Man and Culture in Counterfeit Paradise*. Chicago: Aldine Atherton.

Meillasoux, Claude. 1975. *L'esclavage en Afrique précolonial*. Paris: François Maspero.

———. 1991. *The Anthropology of Slavery: The Womb of Iron and Gold*. Chicago: University of Chicago Press.

Méndez, Francisco. 1969. Carta do Franciscano Frei Francisco Mendes sôbre os costumes dos Indios Mbaiá e Guaná, no Alto-Paraguai. In Jaime Cortesão (comp.), *Do Tratado de Madri à conquista dos sete povos (1750–1802)*. Rio de Janeiro: Biblioteca Nacional.

Mendoza, Diego de. 1976. *Chrónica de la Provincia de San Antonio de los Charcas del Orden de Nuestro Seraphico Padre San Francisco en las Indias Occidentales y Reyno del Perú*. La Paz: Editorial Casa Municipal de la Cultura «Franz Tamayo.»

Menéndez de Avilés, Pedro. 1991. Pedro Menéndez de Avilés to the King, October 20, 1566. In Hann 1991b, 302–303.

Menget, Patrick. 1985. Jalons pour une étude comparative. *Journal de la Société des Américanistes* 71: 131–141.

———. 1988. Notes sur l'adoption chez les Txicão du Brésil Central. *Anthropologie et Sociétés* 12(2): 63–72.

———. 1996. De l'usage des trophées en Amérique du Sud: Esquisse d'une comparaison entre les pratiques nivaclé (Paraguay) et mundurucú (Brésil). *Systèmes de Pensée en Afrique Noire* 14:127–143.

Mentore, George. 2004. The Glorious Tyranny of Silence and the Resonance of Shamanic Breath. In Neil L. Whitehead and Robin M. Wright (eds.), *In Darkness and Secrecy: Witchcraft and Sorcery in Native South America*, pp. 132–156. Durham: Duke University Press.

Métraux, Alfred. 1927. Migrations historiques des Tupi-Guaraní. *Journal de la Société des Américanistes* 19:1–45.

———. 1930. Etudes sur la civilisation des Indiens Chiriguano. *Revista del Instituto de Etnología de la Universidad Nacional de Tucumán* 1(3): 295–493.

———. 1946. Ethnography of the Chaco. In Julian H. Steward (ed.), *Handbook of South American Indians*, 1:197–370. Washington, DC: Government Printing Office.

Milanich, Jerald T. 1998. *Florida Indians and the Invasion from Europe*. Gainesville: University Press of Florida.

Minges, Patrick N. 2003. *Slavery in the Cherokee Nation: The Keetoowah Society and the Defining of a People*. New York: Routledge.

Mingo de la Concepción, Manuel. 1981. *Historia de las misiones franciscanas de Tarija entre chiriguanos*. 2 vols. Tarija: Universidad Boliviana «Juan Misael Caracho.»

Mitchell, Donald. 1984. Predatory Warfare, Social Status, and the North Pacific Slave Trade. *Ethnology* 23(1): 39–48.

Mocquet, John. 1696. *Travels and Voyages into Africa, Asia, and America, the East and West-Indies; Syria, Jerusalem, and the Holy-Land*. London:

Printed for William Newton, Bookseller, in Little Britain; and Joseph Shelton; and William Chandler, Booksellers, at the Peacock in the Poultry.

Monaco, Joseph María, and Joseph Javier Alaña. 1991. Report on the Indians of Southern Florida and its Keys . . . 1760. In Hann 1991b, 418–431.

Mondragón, Héctor. 1999. La familia lingüística Tukano-Makú. http://www.gratisweb.com/nukakwa/FMaku.htm.

Morey, Robert V., Jr., and John P. Marwitt. 1975. Ecology, Economy, and Warfare in Lowland South America. In Martin A. Nettleship, R. Dalegivens, and Anderson Nettleship (eds.), *War: Its Causes and Correlates*, pp. 439–450. The Hague and Paris: Mouton Publishers.

Morin, Françoise. 1998. Los Shipibo-Conibo. In Fernando Santos-Granero and Frederica Barclay (eds.), *Guía etnográfica de la alta amazonía*, vol. 3, *Cashinahua, Amahuaca, Shipibo-Conibo*, pp. 275–435. Quito: Smithsonian Tropical Research Institute/Instituto Francés de Estudios Andinos/Abya-Yala.

Morton, John. 1984. Women as Values, Signs and Power: Aspects of the Politics of Ritual among the Waiwai. *Antropológica* 59–62:223–261.

Moser, Brian, and Donald Tayler. 1963. Tribes of the Pirá-paraná. *Geographical Journal* 129:437–448.

Murphy, Robert. 1957. Intergroup Hostility and Social Cohesion. *American Anthropologist* 52:317–330.

Murphy, Yolanda, and Robert F. Murphy. 1985. *Women of the Forest*. New York: Columbia University Press.

Myers, Thomas. 1988. El efecto de las pestes sobre las poblaciones de la amazonía alta. *Amazonía Peruana* 8(15): 61–81.

———. 1990. *Sarayacu: Ethnohistorical and Archaeological Investigations of a Nineteenth-Century Franciscan Mission in the Peruvian Montaña*. Lincoln: University of Nebraska Press.

Navarrete, Luisa de. 1992. Proceedings and Testimony Taken in the Island of Puerto Rico Concerning the Injuries and Wrongs Done by the Indian Caribes of the Island of Dominica. In Hulme and Whitehead 1992, pp. 39–44.

Newcomb, W. W. 1950. A Re-examination of the Causes of Plains Warfare. *American Anthropologist* 61:317–58.

Nimuendajú, Curt. 1950. Reconhecimento dos rios Içana, Ayarí e Uaupés: Relatório apresentado ao Serviço de Proteção aos Indios do Amazonas e Acre, 1927. *Journal de la Société des Américanistes* 39:125–182.

Nino, Bernardino de. 1912. *Etnografía chiriguana*. La Paz: Tipografía Comercial de Ismael Argote.

Noronha, José Monteiro de. 1862. *Roteiro da viagem da cidade do Pará, até as ultimas colonias do sertão da provincia*. Pará: Typographia de Santos e Irmãos.

Norton, Helen H. 1978. The Male Supremacist Complex: Discovery or Invention? *American Anthropologist* 80(3): 665–667.

Núñez Cabeza de Vaca, Alvar. 1585. Comentarios de Alvar Núñez Cabeza de Vaca, adelantado y gobernador de la provincia del Río de la Plata. In Alvar Núñez Cabeza de Vaca, *La relación y comentarios del gobernador . . . de lo acaecido en las dos jornadas que hizo a las Indias*, pp. lvii–clxiiii. Valladolid: Francisco Fernández de Córdova.

Oberg, Kalervo. 1949. *The Terena and the Caduveo of Southern Mato Grosso, Brazil*. Washington, DC: Government Printing Office.

Ordinaire, Olivier. 1887. Les sauvages du Pérou. *Revue d'Ethnographie* 6:265–322.

Overing, Joanna. 1975. *The Piaroa: A People of the Orinoco Basin; A Study in Kinship and Marriage*. Oxford: Clarendon Press.

———. 1976. Comments. In Joanna Overing Kaplan (ed.), Social Time and Social Space in Lowland South American Societies. *Actes du XLIIe Congrès des Américanistes* 2:387–394. Paris.

———. 1984. Dualisms as an Expression of Difference and Danger: Marriage Exchange and Reciprocity among the Piaroa of Venezuela. In Kenneth M. Kensinger (ed.), *Marriage Practices in Lowland South America*, pp. 127–155. Urbana and Chicago: University of Illinois Press.

———. 1986. Images of Cannibalism, Death and Domination in a "Non-Violent" Society. *Journal de la Société des Américanistes* 72:133–156.

———. 1999. Elogio do cotidiano: A confiança e a arte da vida social em uma comunidade amazônica. *Mana* 5(1): 81–107.

Pané, Fray Ramón. 1999. *An Account of the Antiquities of the Indians*. Durham and London: Duke University Press.

Patterson, Orlando. 1982. *Slavery and Social Death: A Comparative Study*. Cambridge, MA: Harvard University Press.

Pelleprat, Pierre. 1655. *Relation des missions des PP. de la Compagnie de Jesus dans les Isles & dans la terre ferme de l'Amérique Méridionale*. Paris: Sebastien Cramoisy and Gabriel Cramoisy.

Perdue, Theda. 1993. *Slavery and the Evolution of Cherokee Society, 1540–1866*. Knoxville: University of Tennessee Press.

Pershits, Abraham I. 1979. Tribute Relations. In S. Lee Seaton and Henry J. M. Claessen (eds.), *Political Anthropology: The State of the Art*, pp. 149–156. New York: Mouton.

Pineda Camacho, Roberto. 1985. *Historia oral y proceso esclavista en el Caquetá*. Bogotá: Canal Ramírez-Antares.

Polo de Ondegardo, Juan. 1991. Relation du Licencié Polo au vice-roi Toledo sur les moeurs des Chiriguano et comment leur faire la guerre. In Isabelle Combès and Thierry Saignes, *Alter ego: Naissance de l'identité Chiriguano*, pp. 135–142. Paris: Editions de l'Ecole des Hautes Etudes en Sciences Sociales.

Porcallo de Figueroa, Vasco. 1522. Testimonio de interrogatorio a Vasco Porcallo de Figueroa. Santiago de Cuba, 28 February 1522. Manuscript,

9/4838, 585, fols. 274–274v. Real Academia de la Historia de España, Madrid.

Prado, Francisco Rodrigues do. 1839. *Historia dos Indios Cavalleiros ou da nação Guaycurú*. *Revista do Instituto Historico e Geographico do Brazil* 1(1): 25–57.

Provins, Père Pacifique de. 1939. *Le voyage de Perse et brève relation du voyage des îles de l'Amérique*. Assisi: Collegio S. Lorenzo da Brindisi dei Minori Cappuccini.

Radin, Paul. 1946. *Indians of South America*. Garden City, NY: Doubleday and Co.

RAH. *See* Real Academia de la Historia de España.

Raimondi, Antonio. 1905. Informe sobre la provincia litoral de Loreto por. . . . In Larrabure y Correa 1905, 7:118–278.

Ramírez de Quiñones, Pedro. 1918–1922a. Carta a S.M. del Licenciado Pedro Ramírez de Quiñones, 6 Mayo 1575. In Levillier 1918–1922, 1:319–330.

———. 1918–1922b. Parecer del Licenciado Pedro Ramírez de Quiñones . . . 18 Mayo 1573. In Levillier 1918–1922, 1:280–288.

Ramos, Alcida Rita, Peter Silverwood-Cope, and Ana Gita de Oliveira. 1980. Patrões e clientes: Relações intertribais no alto Rio Negro. In Alcida Rita Ramos (comp.), *Hierarquia e simbiose: Relações intertribais no Brasil*, pp. 135–182. São Paulo: Editora Hucitec.

Real Academia de la Historia de España. 1549. Relación de La Florida para el señor Visorrey de la Nueva España, la cual trajo Fray Gregorio de Beteta, 19 de julio de 1549. RAH 9/4847, fols. 99–109v. Madrid.

Reichel-Dolmatoff, Gerardo. 1971. *Amazonian Cosmos: The Sexual and Religious Symbolism of the Tukano Indians*. Chicago: University of Chicago Press.

———. 1996. *Yuruparí: Studies of an Amazonian Foundation Myth*. Cambridge, MA: Harvard University Press.

Reid, Howard. 1979. Some Aspects of Movement, Growth and Change among the Hupdu Maku Indians of Brazil. Ph.D. dissertation, University of Cambridge.

Renard-Casevitz, France-Marie. 1988. Introducción. In Olivier Ordinaire, *Del Pacífico al Atlántico y otros escritos*. Monumenta Amazónica D1. Iquitos: Centro de Estudios Teológicos de la Amazonía/Instituto Francés de Estudios Andinos.

Renard-Casevitz, France-Marie, Thierry Saignes, and Anne-Christine Taylor. 1986. *L'Inca, l'espagnol et les sauvages: Rapports entre les sociétés amazoniennes et andines du XVe au XVIIe siècle*. Paris: Editions Recherche sur les Civilisations.

Ribeiro, Darcy. 1970. *Os índios e a civilização: A integração das populações indígenas no Brasil moderno*. Rio de Janeiro: Editora Civilização Brasileira.

Riester, Bárbara, Jürgen Riester, Bárbara Schuchard, and Brigitte Simon. 1979. Los Chiriguano. *Suplemento Antropológico* (Asunción) 14(1–2): 259–304.

Rival, Laura. 2002. *Trekking through History: The Huaorani of Amazonian Ecuador.* New York: Columbia University Press.

Rival, Laura M., and Neil L. Whitehead (eds.). 2001. *Beyond the Visible and Material: The Amerindianization of Society in the Work of Peter Rivière.* Oxford: Oxford University Press.

Rivière, Peter. 1969. *Marriage among the Trio: A Principle of Social Organisation.* Oxford: Clarendon Press.

———. 1984. *Individual and Society in Guiana: A Comparative Study of Amerindian Social Organisation.* Cambridge: Cambridge University Press.

———. 1993. The Amerindianization of Descent and Affinity. *L'Homme* 126–128, 33(2–4): 507–516.

———. 1997. Carib Soul Matters—since Fock. *Journal of the Anthropological Society of Oxford* 28(2): 139–148.

Rochefort, Charles de. 1658. *Histoire naturelle et morale des Îles Antilles de l'Amérique.* Rotterdam: Chez Arnout Leers.

———. 1666. *The History of the Caribby-Islands.* London: Printed by J .M. for Thomas Dring and John Starkey.

Roe, Peter G. 1982. *The Cosmic Zygote: Cosmology in the Amazon Basin.* New Brunswick, NJ: Rutgers University Press.

Rogel, Juan. 1991a. Father Juan Rogel to Father Didacus Avellaneda, November 1566 to January 1567. In Hann 1991b, 278–285.

———. 1991b. Father Juan Rogel to Father Jerónimo Ruiz del Portillo, April 25, 1568. In Hann 1991b, 230–278.

Romans, Bernard. 1775. *A Concise Natural History of East and West Florida.* New York: printed for the author.

Roosevelt, Anna C. 1993. The Rise and Fall of the Amazon Chiefdoms. *L'Homme* 126–128, 33(2–4): 255–283.

———. 1994. Amazonian Anthropology: Strategy for a New Synthesis. In Anna C. Roosevelt (ed.), *Amazonian Indians from Prehistory to the Present: Anthropological Perspectives*, pp. 1–29. Tucson: University of Arizona Press.

Ross, Eric, and Jane Bennet Ross. 1980. Amazon Warfare. *Science* 207:592.

Ross, Jane Bennett. 1988. A Balance of Deaths: Revenge Feuding among the Achuara Jivaro of the Northwest Peruvian Amazon. Ph.D. dissertation, Columbia University.

Rouse, Irving. 1951. *A Survey of Indian River Archeology, Florida.* New Haven: Yale University Press.

Ruby, Robert H., and John A. Brown. 1993. *Indian Slavery in the Pacific Northwest.* Spokane, WA: Arthur H. Clark.

Ruiz de Montoya, Antonio. 1876. *Conquista espiritual hecha por los religiosos de la Compañía de Jesús, en las provincias del Paraguay, Paraná, Uruguay, y Tape.* Madrid: Imprenta del Reyno.

Sabaté, Luis. 1877. *Viaje de los padres misioneros del Convento del Cuzco a las tribus salvajes de los Campas, Piros, Cunibos y Sipibos en el año de 1874.* Lima: Tipografía de «La Sociedad.»

Sahlins, Marshall. 2005. Preface to Outside Gods: History Making in the Pacific. Special issue, *Ethnohistory* 52(1): 3–6.

Sala, Gabriel. 1897. *Apuntes de viaje: Exploración de los ríos Pichis, Pachitea y Alto Ucayali y de la región del Gran Pajonal.* Lima: Imprenta «La Industria.»

Salomon, Frank, and Stuart B. Schwartz (eds.). 1999. *The Cambridge History of the Native Peoples of the Americas.* Cambridge: Cambridge University Press.

Samanez y Ocampo, José B. 1980. *Exploración de los ríos peruanos, Apurímac, Eni, Tambo, Ucayali y Urubamba, hecho por . . . en 1883 y 1884.* Lima: SESATOR.

Samaniego, Diego de. 1944. Relación del P. Diego de Samaniego, con muchas noticias sobre misiones hechas a los Chiriguanos, Itatines y Chiquitos. In Francisco Mateos (ed.), *Historia General de la Compañía de Jesús en la Provincia del Perú,* 2:471–496. Madrid: Consejo Superior de Investigaciones Científicas/Instituto Gonzalo Fernández de Oviedo.

Sampaio, Francisco Xavier Ribeiro de. 1985a. Apêndice ao diário da viagem que em visita, e correição das povoações da Capitania de S. José do Rio Negro. In Francisco Xavier Ribeiro de Sampaio, *As viagens do Ouvidor Sampaio (1774–1775),* pp. 121–173. Manaus: Editora Umberto Calderaro.

———. 1985b. Diário da viagem que em visita, e correição das povoações da Capitania de S. José do Rio Negro. In Francisco Xavier Ribeiro de Sampaio, *As viagens do Ouvidor Sampaio (1774–1775),* pp. 13–119. Manaus: Editora Umberto Calderaro.

Sanabria Fernández, Hernando. 1949. *Los Chanés: Apuntes para el estudio de una incipiente cultura aborigen prehispánica en el Oriente Boliviano.* Santa Cruz de la Sierra: Editorial Santa Cruz.

Sánchez Labrador, José. 1910–1917. *El Paraguay Católico.* 3 vols. Buenos Aires: Imprenta de Coni Hermanos.

Sandi, Luis. 1905. Exploración del Ucayali por el teniente de marina . . . , 1865. In Larrabure y Correa 1905, 2:252–266.

San Miguel, Andrés. 2001. *An Early Florida Adventure.* Translated by John H. Hann; foreword by James J. Miller. Gainesville: University Press of Florida.

Santos-Granero, Fernando. 1991. *The Power of Love: The Moral Use of Knowledge amongst the Amuesha of Central Peru.* London: Athlone Press.

———. 1992. *Etnohistoria de la alta amazonía, siglos XV al XVIII.* Quito: Abya-Yala/CEDIME/MLAL.

———. 1995. ¿Historias étnicas o historias interétnicas? Lecciones del pasado Amuesha (Selva Central, Perú). In Guido Barona and Francisco Zuluaga (eds.), *Memorias del I Seminario Internacional de Etnohistoria del Norte de Ecuador y Sur de Colombia*, pp. 351–371. Santiago de Cali, Colombia: Universidad del Valle/Universidad del Cauca.

———. 2002a. The Arawakan Matrix: Ethos, Language, and History in Native South America. In Jonathan D. Hill and Fernando Santos-Granero (eds.), *Comparative Arawakan Histories: Rethinking Language Family and Culture Area in Amazonia*, pp. 25-50. Urbana: University of Illinois Press.

———. 2002b. St. Christopher in the Amazon: Child Sorcery, Colonialism, and Violence among the Southern Arawak. *Ethnohistory* 49(3): 507–543.

———. 2004. The Enemy Within: Child Sorcery, Revolution and the Evils of Modernization in Eastern Peru. In Neil L. Whitehead and Robin M. Wright (eds.), *In Darkness and Secrecy: Witchcraft and Sorcery in Native South America*, pp. 272–305. Durham: Duke University Press.

———. 2007. Of Fear and Friendship: Amazonian Sociality beyond Kinship and Affinity. *Journal of the Royal Anthropological Institute* 13(1): 1–18.

Santos-Granero, Fernando, and Frederica Barclay. 1998. Introducción. In Fernando Santos-Granero and Frederica Barclay (eds.), *Guía etnográfica de la alta amazonía*, vol. 3, *Cashinahua, Amahuaca, Shipibo-Conibo*, pp. xv–xxxii. Quito: Smithsonian Tropical Research Institute/Instituto Francés de Estudios Andinos/Abya-Yala.

———. 2000. *Tamed Frontiers. Economy, Society, and Civil Rights in Upper Amazonia*. Boulder, CO: Westview Press.

Schell, Rolfe F. 1968. *1,000 Years on Mound Key*. Fort Myers Beach, FL: Island Press.

Schindler, Helmut. 1983. *Die Reiterstämme des Gran Chaco*. Berlin: Dietrich Reimer Verlag.

Schmidl, Ulrich. 1599. *Vera historia, Admirandae Cuiusdam navigationis, quam Huldericus Schmidel, Straubingensis, ab anno 1534*. Noribergae: Impensis Levini Hulsij.

———. 1749. Historia y descubrimiento de el Río de la Plata y Paraguay. In Andrés González de Barcia (ed.), *Historiadores primitivos de las Indias Occidentales*, vol. 3. Madrid.

Schwerin, Karl H. 2003. Carib Warfare and Slaving. In Paul Valentine and Catherine Julien (eds.), War and Peace in Aboriginal South America. Special issue, *Antropológica* 99–100:45–72.

Seeger, Anthony, Roberto da Matta, and Eduardo Viveiros de Castro. 1979. A construção da pessoa nas sociedades indígenas brasileiras. *Boletim do Museu Nacional*, n.s., 28:2–19.

Serra, Ricardo Franco de Almeida. 1845. Parecer sobre o aldeamento dos Indios Uaicurús e Guanás, com a descripção dos seus usos, religião, estabilidade, e costumes. *Revista do Instituto Historico e Geographico Brasileiro* 7(26): 204–212.

————. 1850. Continuação do parecer sobre os índios Uaicurus e Guanás. *Revista do Instituto Historico e Geographico Brasileiro*, 2nd ser., 6(19): 348–395.

SIL. *See* Summer Institute of Linguistics.

Silva, Alcionilio Brüzzi Alves da. 1962. *A civilização indigena do Uaupés*. São Paulo: Missão Salesiana do Rio Negro.

Silverwood-Cope, Peter. 1990. *Os Makú: Povo caçador do noroeste da Amazônia*. Brasília: Editora Universidade de Brasília.

Solís de Merás, Gonzalo. 1990. Memorial que hizo el Doctor Gonzalo Solís de Merás, de todas las jornadas y sucesos del Adelantado Pedro Menéndez de Avilés. . . . In José M. Gómez-Tabanera (ed.), *Pedro Menéndez de Avilés y la conquista de la Florida (1565)*, pp. 1–243. Oviedo: Imprenta Gofer.

Sotomayor, José Antonio. 1905. Relación de los infieles del Ucayali, el Marañón y el Amazonas, 1899. In Larrabure y Correa 1905, 14:353–360.

Souza, André Fernandes de. 1848. Noticias geographicas da Capitania do Rio Negro no grande Rio Amazonas. *Revista Trimestral de Historia e Geographia* 12(4): 411–504.

Sparrey, Francis. 1625. The description of the Ile of Trinidad, the rich Countrie of Guiana, and the mightie River of Orenoco, written by. . . . In Samuel Purchas (ed.), *Purchas, his Pilgrimages*, vol. 4, book 6, chap. 11, pp. 1247–1250. London: printed by William Stansby for Henrie Fetherstone.

Sponsel, Leslie E. 1983. Yanomama Warfare, Protein Capture, and Cultural Ecology: A Critical Analysis of the Arguments of the Opponents. *Interciencia* 8(4): 204–210.

Spruce, Richard. 1908. *Notes of a Botanist on the Amazon and Andes*. 2 vols. London: Macmillan and Co.

Stahl, Eurico G. 1928. La tribu de los Cunibos en la región de los lagos del Ucayali. *Boletín de la Sociedad Geográfica de Lima* 45(2): 139–166.

Stearman, Allyn M. 1989. *Yuquí: Forest Nomads in a Changing World*. New York: Holt, Rinehart, and Winston.

Steward, Julian H., and Louis C. Faron. 1959. *Native Peoples of South America*. New York: McGraw-Hill.

Stiglich, Germán. 1905. La región peruana de los bosques, 1904. In Larrabure y Correa 1905, 15:308–495.

Stirling, James. 1969. *Letters from the Slave States*. New York: Negro Universities Press.

Stradelli, Ermanno. 1890. L'Uaupés e gli Uaupés. *Bolletino della Società Geografica Italiana* 3(5): 425–453.

Strathern, Marilyn. 1999. *Property, Substance and Effect: Anthropological Essays on Persons and Things*. London and New Brunswick, NJ: Athlone Press.

Suárez de Figueroa, Lorenzo. 1965. Relación de la ciudad de Santa Cruz de la Sierra, 1586. In Marcos Jiménez de la Espada (ed.), *Relaciones*

geográficas de Indias, Biblioteca de Autores Españoles, 183:402–406.
Madrid: Ediciones Atlas.

Sued-Badillo, Jalil. 1995. The Island Caribs: New Approaches to the Question of Ethnicity in the Early Colonial Caribbean. In Whitehead 1995, pp 61–90.

Summer Institute of Linguistics. 2004. Ethnologue: Languages of the World. http://www.ethnologue.com.

Surrallés, Alexandre. 2000. La passion génératrice: Prédation, échange et redoublement de mariage candoshi. L'Homme 154–155:123–144.

———. 2007. Los Candoshi. In Fernando Santos-Granero and Frederica Barclay (eds.), Guía etnográfica de la alta amazonía, vol. 6, Achuar, Candoshi. Lima: Smithsonian Tropical Research Institute/Instituto Francés de Estudios Andinos.

Susnik, Branislava. 1968. Chiriguanos: Dimensiones etnosociales. Vol. 1. Asunción: Museo Etnográfico Andrés Barbero.

———. 1971. El indio colonial del Paraguay: El Chaqueño; Guaycurúes y Chanés-Arawak. Vol. 3. Asunción: Museo Etnográfico Andrés Barbero.

Swanton, John R. 1922. Early History of the Creek Indians and Their Neighbors. Bureau of American Ethnology Bulletin 73. Washington, DC: Government Printing Office.

———. 1946. The Indians of the Southeastern United States. Bureau of American Ethnology Bulletin 137. Washington, DC: Government Printing Office.

Taunay, Alfredo de Escragnolle de. 1931. Entre os nossos indios: Chanés, Terenas, Kinikinaus, Guanás, Laianas, Guatós, Guaycurús, Caingangs. São Paulo: Companhia Melhoramentos de São Paulo.

Taussig, Michael. 1999. Defacement: Public Secrecy and the Labor of the Negative. Stanford: Stanford University Press.

Taylor, Anne Christine. 1985. L'art de la réduction: La guerre et les mécanismes de la différenciation tribale dans la culture Jivaro. Journal de la Société des Américanistes 71:159–173.

———. 1993. Remembering to Forget: Identity, Mourning, and Memory among the Jivaro. Man 28(4): 653–678.

———. 1994. Les bons ennemis et les mauvais parents: Le traitement symbolique de l'alliance dans les rituels de chasse aux têtes des Shuar (Jivaro) de l'Equateur. In Elisabeth Copet-Rougier and Françoise Héritier-Augé (eds.), Les complexités de l'alliance (economie, politique et fondements symboliques de l'alliance), pp. 73–105. Paris: Archives Contemporaines.

———. 1999. The Western Margins of Amazonia from the Early Sixteenth to the Early Nineteenth Century. In Salomon and Schwartz 1999, vol. 3, part 2, pp. 204–256.

———. 2000. Le sexe de la proie: Représentations jivaro du lien de parenté. L'Homme 154–155:309–334.

———. 2001. Wives, Pets, and Affines: Marriage among the Jíbaro. In Rival and Whitehead 2001, pp. 45–56.

Taylor, Charles Edwin. 1888. *Leaflets from the Danish West Indies: Descriptive of the Social, Political, and Commercial Condition of these Islands.* London: William Dawson and Sons.

Techo, Nicolás del. 1897. *Historia de la Provincia del Paraguay de la Compañía de Jesús.* 5 vols. Madrid: A. de Uribe y Cia.

Terribilini, Mario, and Michel Terribilini. 1961. Resultats d'une enquête faite chez les Maku (Brésil). *Bulletin Annuel Musée e Institut d'Ethnographie de la Ville de Genève* 4(4): 39.

Testart, Alain. 1998. L'esclavage comme institution. *L'Homme* 145:31–69.

Tessmann, Günter. 1928. *Menschen ohne Gott.* Stuttgart: Verlag von Strecker und Schröder.

Thouar, Emile Arthur. 1884. A la recherche des restes de la mission Crevaux. *Le Tour du Monde* 2:209–272.

———. 1991. *A travers le Gran Chaco: Chez les Indiens coupeurs de têtes, 1883–1887.* Paris: Phébus.

Tournon, Jacques. 2002. *La merma mágica: Vida e historia de los Shipibo-Conibo del Ucayali.* Lima: Centro Amazónico de Antropología y Aplicación Práctica.

Tovar y Montalvo, Jerónimo. 1918–1922. Carta a S.M. del Dr. D. Jerónimo Tovar y Montalvo, fiscal de la Audiencia de Charcas, 20 Febrero 1595. In Levillier 1918–1922, 3:247–258.

Turner, Terence S. 1979. The Gê and Bororo Societies as Dialectical Systems: A General Model. In David Maybury-Lewis (ed.), *Dialectical Societies: The Gê and Bororo of Central Brazil*, pp. 147–178. Cambridge, MA: Harvard University Press.

———. 1995. Social Body and Embodied Subject: Bodiliness, Subjectivity, and Sociality among the Kayapo. *Cultural Anthropology* 10(2): 143–170.

Unánue, Hipólito. 1924. Expedición del P. Fr. Narciso Girbal de Sarayacu (Sarayaquillo) a los lagos de Azuaya (Cruz Muyuna) y Sanaya (Tipisca). In Izaguirre 1922–1929, 8:267–297.

Unger, Elke. 1972. Resumen etnográfico del Vocabulario Eyiguayegi-Mbayá del P. José Sánchez Labrador. In Branislava Susnik (ed.), *Familia Guaycurú*, vol. 3, part 6. Asunción: Museo Etnográfico Andrés Barbero.

Uriarte, Luis M. 2007. Los Achuar. In Fernando Santos-Granero and Frederica Barclay (eds.), *Guía etnográfica de la alta amazonía*, vol. 6, *Achuar, Candoshi*, pp. 1–241. Lima: Smithsonian Tropical Research Institute/ Instituto Francés de Estudios Andinos.

Valentine, Paul, and Catherine Julien (eds.). 2003. War and Peace in Aboriginal South America. Special issue, *Antropológica* 99–100.

Van Berkel, Adriaan. 1695. *Amerikaansche Voyagien, Behelzende een Reis na Rio de Berbice Gelegen op het vaste land van Guiana*. Amsterdam: Johan ten Hoorn.

Van Velthem, Lúcia Hussak. 2003. *O belo é a fera: A estética da produção e da predação entre os Wayana*. Lisbon: Assírio and Alvim.

Vaughan, James H. 1979. Makafur: A Limbic Institution of the Margi. In Suzanne Miers and Igor Kopytoff (eds.), *Slavery in Africa: Historical and Anthropological Perspectives*, pp. 85–102. Madison: University of Wisconsin Press.

Vayda, Andrew P. 1961. Expansion and Warfare among Swidden Agriculturalists. *American Anthropologist* 63(2, part 1): 346–358.

Vidal, Silvia, and Alberta Zucchi. 1996. Impacto de la colonización hispanolusitana en las organizaciones sociopolíticas y económicas de los Maipures-Arawakos del Alto Orinoco-Río Negro, siglos XVII–XVIII. *América Negra* 11:107–129.

Viedma, Francisco de. 1970. Descripción geográfica y estadística de la provincia de Santa Cruz de la Sierra. In Pedro de Angelis (ed.), *Colección de obras y documentos relativos a la historia antigua y moderna de las provincias del Río de la Plata*, 6:519–794. Buenos Aires: Talleres Gráficos Garamond S.C.A.

Vilaça, Aparecida. 1992. *Comendo como gente: Formas do canibalismo Wari'*. Rio de Janeiro: Editora Universidade Federal do Rio de Janeiro.

———. 2002. Making Kin Out of Others in Amazonia. *Journal of the Royal Anthropological Institute* 8:347–365.

Villasante-de Beauvais, Mariella (ed.). 2000. *Groupes serviles au Sahara: Approche comparative à partir du cas des arabophones de Mauritanie*. Paris: CNRS Editions.

Viveiros de Castro, Eduardo. 1979. A fabricação do corpo na sociedade xinguana. *Boletim do Museu Nacional* 32:40–49.

———. 1992. *From the Enemy's Point of View: Humanity and Divinity in an Amazonian Society*. Chicago and London: University of Chicago Press.

———. 1993. Alguns aspectos da afinidade no dravidianato amazônico. In Eduardo Viveiros de Castro and Manuela Carneiro da Cunha (ed.), *Amazônia: Etnologia e história indígena*, pp. 149–210. São Paulo: Núcleo de História Indígena e do Indigenismo da USP, FAPESP.

———. 1996. Images of Nature and Society in Amazonian Ethnology. *Annual Review of Anthropology* 25:179–200.

———. 2001. GUT Feelings about Amazonia: Potential Affinity and the Construction of Sociality. In Rival and Whitehead 2001, pp. 19–44.

———. 2004. Exchanging Perspectives: The Transformation of Objects into Subjects in Amerindian Ontologies. *Common Knowledge* 10(3): 463–484.

Wagley, Charles, and Eduardo Galvão. 1949. *The Tenetehara Indians of Brazil: A Culture in Transition*. New York: Columbia University Press.

Wallace, Alfred R. 1853. *A Narrative of the Travels on the Amazon and Rio Negro, with an Account of the Native Tribes, and Observations of the Climate, Geology, and Natural History of the Amazon Valley*. London: Reeve and Co.

Watson, James L. 1980. Introduction: Slavery as an Institution; Open and Closed Systems. In James L. Watson (ed.), *Asian and African Systems of Slavery*, pp. 1–15. Oxford: Blackwell.

Wertheman, Arturo. 1905. Exploración de los ríos Perené, Tambo y Ucayali por el ingeniero . . . , 1877. In Larrabure y Correa 1905, 3:174–204.

Wheeler, Ryan J. 2000. *Treasure of the Calusa: The Johnson/Willcox Collection from Mound Key, Florida*. Monographs in Florida Archaeology. Tallahassee: Rose Printing.

Whiffen, Thomas W. 1915. *The North-West Amazon: Notes of Some Months Spent among Cannibal Tribes*. London: Constable and Co.

Whitehead, Neil L. 1988. *Lords of the Tiger Spirit: A History of the Caribs in Colonial Venezuela and Guyana, 1498–1820*. Dordrecht and Providence: Foris Publications.

———. 1990. Carib Ethnic Soldiering in Venezuela, the Guianas, and the Antilles, 1492–1820. *Ethnohistory* 37(4): 357–385.

———. 1992. Tribes Make States and States Make Tribes: Warfare and the Creation of Colonial Tribes and States in Northeastern South America. In R. Brian Ferguson and Neil L. Whitehead (eds.), *War in the Tribal Zone: Expanding State and Indigenous Warfare*, pp. 127–150. Santa Fe, NM: School of American Research.

———. 1993. Recent Research on the Native History of Amazonia and Guayana. *L'Homme* 126–128, 33(2–4): 495–506.

——— (ed.). 1995. *Wolves from the Sea*. Leiden: KITLV Press.

———. 1999. Native Peoples Confront Colonial Regimes in Northeastern South America (c. 1500–1900). In Salomon and Schwartz 1999, vol. 3, part 2, 382–442.

———. 2002. Arawak Linguistic and Cultural Identity through Time: Contact, Colonialism, and Creolization. In Jonathan D. Hill and Fernando Santos-Granero (eds.), *Comparative Arawakan Histories: Rethinking Language Family and Culture Area in Amazonia*, pp. 51–73. Urbana and Chicago: University of Illinois Press.

——— (ed.). 2003a. *Histories and Historicities in Amazonia*. Lincoln and London: University of Nebraska Press.

———. 2003b. Introduction. In Whitehead 2003a, pp. vii–xx.

———. Forthcoming. Indigenous Slavery in South America, 1492–1820. In David Eltis and Stanley L. Engerman (eds.), *The Cambridge World History of Slavery*. Cambridge: Cambridge University Press.

Widmer, Randolph J. 1988. *The Evolution of the Calusa, A Nonagricultural Chiefdom on the Southwest of Florida*. Tuscaloosa and London: University of Alabama Press.

Wilbert, Johannes. 1993. *Mystic Endowment: Religious Ethnography of the Warao Indians.* Cambridge, MA: Harvard University Center for the Study of World Religions.

Wilbert, Johannes, and Karin Simoneau (eds.). 1989. *Folk Literature of the Caduveo Indians.* Los Angeles: UCLA Latin American Center Publications.

Wilson, H. Clyde. 1958. Regarding the Causes of Mundurucú Warfare. *American Anthropologist* 60(6): 1193–1196.

Wilson, Samuel M. 1990. *Hispaniola: Caribbean Chiefdoms in the Age of Columbus.* Tuscaloosa and London: University of Alabama Press.

Wright, Robin M. 1998. *Cosmos, Self, and History in Baniwa Religion: For Those Unborn.* Austin: University of Texas Press.

———. 2002. História indígena do Noroeste da Amazônia: Hipótesis, questões e perspectivas. In Manuela Carneiro da Cunha (org.), *História dos Indios no Brasil*, pp. 253–266. São Paulo: FAPESP/Compañía das Letras/Secretaria Municipal de Cultura.

Index